AF805771

Contributions to Public Administration and Public Policy

The series Contributions to Public Administration and Public Policy contains publications in all areas of public administration and public policy, such as governance, public finance, public management, organization theory, institutional theory, administrative theory and practice, ethics and others. Publications are primarily monographs and multiple author works containing new research results, but conference and congress reports are also considered. The series covers both theoretical and empirical aspects and is addressed to researchers and policy makers.

Tharun Dolla • Boeing Laishram
Ganesh Devkar
Editors

Revisiting Public-Private Partnerships

Lessons from COVID-19

Springer

Editors
Tharun Dolla
Department of Civil Engineering
Indian Institute of Technology Bombay
Mumbai, Maharashtra, India

Boeing Laishram
Department of Civil Engineering
Indian Institute of Technology Guwahati
Guwahati, Assam, India

Ganesh Devkar
Faculty of Technology
CEPT University
Ahmedabad, Gujarat, India

ISSN 2731-9385 ISSN 2731-9393 (electronic)
Contributions to Public Administration and Public Policy
ISBN 978-3-031-37014-4 ISBN 978-3-031-37015-1 (eBook)
https://doi.org/10.1007/978-3-031-37015-1

© The Editor(s) (if applicable) and The Author(s), under exclusive license to Springer Nature Switzerland AG 2023
This work is subject to copyright. All rights are solely and exclusively licensed by the Publisher, whether the whole or part of the material is concerned, specifically the rights of translation, reprinting, reuse of illustrations, recitation, broadcasting, reproduction on microfilms or in any other physical way, and transmission or information storage and retrieval, electronic adaptation, computer software, or by similar or dissimilar methodology now known or hereafter developed.
The use of general descriptive names, registered names, trademarks, service marks, etc. in this publication does not imply, even in the absence of a specific statement, that such names are exempt from the relevant protective laws and regulations and therefore free for general use.
The publisher, the authors, and the editors are safe to assume that the advice and information in this book are believed to be true and accurate at the date of publication. Neither the publisher nor the authors or the editors give a warranty, expressed or implied, with respect to the material contained herein or for any errors or omissions that may have been made. The publisher remains neutral with regard to jurisdictional claims in published maps and institutional affiliations.

This Springer imprint is published by the registered company Springer Nature Switzerland AG
The registered company address is: Gewerbestrasse 11, 6330 Cham, Switzerland

Paper in this product is recyclable.

Foreword 1

The study of public-private partnership (PPP) is the study of how governments can best combine with the private (or not for profit) sector to produce long-term assets and services of public value. It has long been acknowledged as resulting in a hybrid governance arrangement, and the general notion has been hugely popular around the world. In the field of infrastructure provision, the early PPP 'hype' has waned in countries such as the UK, but it has also simultaneously increased in others. At the same time, though, infrastructure PPP practice remains an enigma. Despite its popularity, we do not fully understand it. Despite its potential, its efficiency remains hotly contested. And despite its ubiquity, governments often remain wary of PPP project advocates in the same way as many were wary of advocates for its policy cousin, privatisation.

So, how might one begin thinking through this PPP phenomenon?

In terms of PPP outcomes, there has been much already said over decades, and there is now an extensive PPP discourse. Outcomes appear to have ranged at the one extreme from impressive and well-delivered engineering marvels of sublime beauty and functionality, to expensive failures involving poorly delivered projects and weak governance. In retrospect, perhaps we ought not be too surprised by this. These outcomes probably just mirror the range of outcomes we might have expected from either the public sector or the private sector when acting alone. So how do we ensure that PPP arrangements get the best of both sectors rather than outcomes which are no better than 'business as usual', or in the worst case scenario, outcomes which are the worst of both sectors? A good question, and one certainly deserving continued research priority.

There is little doubt that at its broadest conception, the promise of public-private partnership – getting the best of both sectors – remains both alluring and relevant. In many ways, this has always been a central challenge for governments. There have long been many forms of PPP, and this breadth has seen the evolution of a global PPP language nowadays and a shared desire for improved government operations. But the breadth of alternative arrangements possible in infrastructure PPPs makes inter-country analysis and learning tricky. Moreover, the fact is that even when an identical contractual and governance arrangement is apparently adopted in two countries, their meanings can be quite different because people behave differently under the unique cultural and social paths we have taken through history. Thus, on a global stage, we may see the assumption of a black letter law rigid long-term contract in one jurisdiction existing uneasily alongside the reality of a softer grey, flexible guide to a partnering relationship in another jurisdiction. To the engineer or public policy and administration analyst, this inability to assume we can keep one variable constant whilst analysing the others is troubling, because generalities become almost impossible to make! But to the sociologist or political scientist, this is the richness of real life which multi-disciplinarity reveals.

Fortunately for us, PPP research has today clearly become a multidisciplinary endeavour, with an impressive body of scholarship. Our PPP research is further dependent on careful theorizing as to the likely effects of new arrangements. But theories of PPP are unfortunately not always so helpful, because these hybrid ideas are drawn from diverse theoretical orientations in order to acclaim partnership effectiveness and its value.

Luckily, such research design, methodological and theoretical challenges have not dampened the enthusiasm of PPP scholars around the world. It is terrific to see this new book which 'revisits' PPPs and aims to learn lessons from our experience of a contemporary issue, the effects of the global COVID 19 outbreak. Experiences from a dozen countries have been included with chapters written by both practitioners and academics. Importantly, too, contributions come from several disciplinary lenses as well as those responsible for the delivery of public infrastructure. I take my hat off to all courageous researchers who tackle such issues. I am also glad that researchers in this volume have not been dissuaded in their efforts by the added complexity of how PPPs fit into the context of transition countries. As this volume attests, we still care deeply about PPPs and we seek lessons from experience.

It is always interesting and informative to contemplate the questions at the centre of research efforts. The effects of COVID19 on our PPP delivery experience and how disruptions caused by the outbreak have been managed are clearly central concerns of this volume. But such questions cannot be answered in isolation from the context of inquiries into traditional matters of operationalising risk bearing, how to best regulate PPPs and the overall merit and worth of the PPP policy approach. Moreover, whilst COVID 19 will no doubt have affected PPP delivery in quite dramatic ways, the extent to which these dynamics are new or are simply issues of risk or governance long present in PPP arrangements and magnified through the COVID19 outbreak deserves to be addressed. In other words, discerning what is really new here and what this implies for the future of PPPs is a significant intellectual challenge on its own. This volume tackles such questions head-on.

I am sure that this volume will add significant insights and lessons from experience to the existing PPP knowledge base. And we will all benefit when the next pandemic, or will it be some other discontinuity such as a major military outbreak, inevitably occurs. Such thoughts are scary, but they can quickly become the basis of a new reality check, with lessons learned through careful research transforming overnight into tomorrow's necessary practices.

What does all this mean? What it means is that this published volume is indeed a timely and significant book on an important topic.

Monash University
Melbourne, VIC, Australia

Graeme A. Hodge,

Foreword 2

Public Private Partnerships (PPPs) have become increasingly accepted as a way of providing for public infrastructure and services globally. While many forms of PPPs have existed even over the last couple of centuries, formalisation of it both for policy making and execution have happened more since the last four decades. Academic study of it has started happening after such formalisation, and concepts and frameworks are evolving.

During 2020, a new virus called the Corona Virus affected the world, resulting in what the World Health Organisation termed as the Covid-19 pandemic. It held sway for a little over two years, requiring efforts for social distancing through high impact measures like mass lockdowns, travel bans, work from home, etc. across the globe for containment. While no cure really evolved, vaccines came in to mitigate the health consequences of the virus. The pandemic effectively reduced activities, kept people at home, changed formats of work and engagement, and brought in new paradigms which people stated calling the 'new normal'.

The effect of Covid-19 is being studied in various domains. This edited book is an attempt to study the impact of Covid-19 on PPPs. I must congratulate the editors for exploring this domain, since it will bring out lessons for the 'new normal' and of course for dealing with similar situations in the future.

The book brings in experiences from 11 countries, both developed and developing, over 13 chapters. There is one chapter which does a literature review of 100 systematically selected papers. Twenty-four authors have contributed to the chapters.

The coverage of the book reflects that most PPPs are in the economic (hard) infrastructure sector. And within that, the transportation sector (roads, metros, airports, ports, etc.). PPPs are also moving into social sectors like hospitals.

In the context of Covid and PPPs, the policy discourse has raised many questions.

- What law governs the functioning of PPPs?
  - If they are mandated to perform and face relative losses, who pays?
  - If they are mandated to close, and face relative losses, who pays?
  - If they continue their own volition, and face relative losses, who pays?

- Even if 'force majeure' is provided for and invoked, is the context 'wicked' enough that resolution for different stakeholders including the 'authority' and/or the Government proves very difficult and thus best left to 'status quo', in a humane manner?
- If compensation is due, how much to the PPP players? Monetary or concession period modification?
- Depending on the final beneficiaries who were affected, are there distinctions to be made among the PPPs?
- Should compensation be one time or in a continuing manner linked to some metrics?
- How should online mode be leveraged for various PPP processes including tendering and bidding?
- Should this be an opportunity to rewrite contracts? Including for preparation for future pandemics?
- What would be the role of regulators and judiciary?

Contracts and contract renegotiation came into focus. Interestingly, there are differences. Developed countries like Australia and France seem to have been open to renegotiation, unlike India, where matters have been addressed by extending contract periods. The response is presumably a result of how contracts were written in the first place. These bring out lessons for contracts, in terms of what kind of flexibility to provide, and based on what triggers.

My own studies of select transport literature beyond this book and observing the response of the transport sector show that transport demand fell substantially during Covid, and with a greater impact on public passenger transportation, especially due to lockdowns and work from home. Freight transportation came back to normal, within a few months, as soon as a sense of control through protocols were brought in. Post Covid, a sense of needing to reconnect has increased passenger demand, but more around events and holidays. Some literature results are that the long-term equilibrium on public passenger transportation will settle to a marginally reduced trip rate, due to partial work from home and/or increased substitution of video conferences for certain activities. During Covid, the organised sector (like Indian Railways) could respond quickly by bringing back human resource supply and focussing on freight movement (average freight train speeds went up from 25 kmph to 45 kmph, due to very little passenger services) and executing repairs and maintenance which were held up from earlier due to there being continuous traffic during normal times.

The word 'resilience' has gained prominence over 'sustainability', since there is need for supply chains and infrastructure to be able to survive pandemics and other significant 'force majeure' events. Some of the chapters bring out this point.

In my view, there are eight key pillars of success of PPPs in infrastructure: (i) project structuring, (ii) project evaluation (including risks); (iii) sourcing of funds; (iv) tendering and bidding; (v) contracts and agreements; (vi) project management; (vii) post project issues; and (viii) regulation and dispute resolution.

In my opinion, the serious policy discourse on aftermath of Covid-19 and PPPs have not begun in India and the reading of chapters of this book indicates a similar trend in other parts of the World as well. The initial discussion related to PPPs in India was confined to the conundrum of whether to give compensation or not. Keeping this discussion aside, if the Covid-19 warrants a specific focused discourse or not, this pandemic made it very evident that there is a need to improve underlying fabric of PPP comprising of policy, institutional, contractual, and relational frameworks, for making PPPs more resilient. These improvements are to be done on an urgent basis rather than waiting for another wave of disruptions in the future. For example, trigger can be defined in the contract which would actuate necessary compensation and reward mechanism. Although, these improvements would make PPPs more responsive, there are still possibilities that some scenarios cannot be anticipated. Hence, going forward, there is a need for all PPP stakeholders to devise a much more humane approach to deal with disruptions.

Overall, many chapters indicate that the impact of Covid not only provided reflections for how contracts and underlying frameworks for PPPs can be improved for resilience but also gave ideas for strengthening them even during normal times.

Distinguished Visiting Faculty, National Rail and Transportation Institute, Professor (Emeritus), Gujarat Maritime University, Former Director Indian Institute of Management, Bangalore, India

G. Raghuram

Contents

About the Editors

Tharun Dolla, PhD is an active researcher in the areas of public-private partnerships and infrastructure delivery models, Construction 4.0, infrastructure sustainability, governance, smart cities, among others. He worked on various research assignments and projects funded by agencies such as Arun Jaitley National Institute of Financial Management (Ministry of Finance), Human Settlement Management Institute (HUDCO), New Delhi, Project Management Institute, and Erasmus+ of the European Union. He has published more than forty research articles in book chapters, journals, and conferences of international repute. He is the recipient of the "Highly Commended Paper Award" at CIB's World Building Congress (WBC 2022), Melbourne, Australia. He is currently a member of working commissions of Collaborating for Innovation in the Built environment (CIB), Canada, on the "W122 Public Private Partnership" Commission, "W113 Law and Dispute Resolution," and "W092 Procurement Systems."

Ganesh Devkar, PhD is a senior associate professor at the Faculty of Technology at the CEPT University, Ahmedabad, India. He holds a Doctorate in Construction Management from Indian Institute of Technology Madras (IIT Madras). His doctoral work focuses on competencies in urban local bodies for implementing water, sanitation, and solid waste management public private partnership (PPP) projects in India. During his doctoral research work, he was involved in research projects for Tamil Nadu Urban Development Fund; Ministry of Urban Development; and Institute of Water Policy, National University of Singapore. Ganesh teaches construction quality and safety management, project appraisal, lean construction, and public private partnerships. He has been researching in the area of public private partnerships, lean construction, and megaprojects. He has participated in four systematic reviews focusing on delivery of infrastructure like water supply, sanitation, hygiene, telecom, electricity, and transport. He received the "Young Research Scholar Award" from Project Management Institute, India, in 2014.

Boeing Laishram, PhD is a professor in Department of Civil Engineering and is also the head of School of Business at IIT, Guwahati. His research focuses on public-private partnerships, building information modelling, procurement frameworks such as unsolicited proposals and partnering, sustainability assessment, and construction quality assurance. He has wide professional experience varying from construction industry to investment banking. After the completion of PhD, he has worked in an investment bank engaged in appraisal and structuring of project finance deals for infrastructure projects in India. Prof Laishram has been associated with several governmental organizations and have rendered his expertise in several fields such as quality assurance, project performance monitoring, bid advisory, cost auditing, procurement process assessment, and infrastructure cost appraisal.

About the Contributors

Manik Ahmed got his BS in Civil Engineering from Bangladesh University Engineering and Technology (BUET) in 1999. He had his MS from in 2017 and a PhD in 2021 in Civil Engineering from Virginia Tech, Blacksburg, USA. He has been engaged in construction engineering and management, project delivery, and public-private partnerships for 17 years.

Güzin Akyildiz Alçura, PhD , specializes in transportation systems planning, travel behaviour, transit service quality, railway and highway systems, and urban transportation systems. She has various studies presented at conferences and published in journals. In addition to giving lectures at undergraduate and postgraduate level, she takes part in various research projects as a researcher and coordinator.

R. Aravindan Mukkai is a research scholar at IIT Madras. His area of research is Public Private Partnerships. Earlier, he has worked for over 35 years in the field of projects and project finance, in developer organizations as well as consultancies. He has worked at senior positions in leading infrastructure organizations in PPP projects in sectors like roads, airports, ports and water. He was involved in feasibility studies, bidding, and implementation of these projects.

Matthias P. Beck, PhD (MIT), MUP March (Kansas), FRSA, is a professor of Management at Cork University Business School, University College Cork. He joined UCC in 2017. Prior to coming to UCC, he held professorial posts in public sector management at Queen, Äôs University Belfast and the University of York in England, and a position as professor of Risk Management at Glasgow Caledonian University. He has a keen interest in risk and health services research and is NIHR journals library editor with the National Institute of Health Research, the main research funding and dissemination body of the UK National Health Service. His research interests include risk and risk management, health management, public-private partnership, and public sector management

Nuzia Carbonara is Associate Professor of Strategic Management and Organization at the Politecnico di Bari and Coodinator of the Management Engineering Bachelor's Programme. Her current research interests include corporate strategies and organization, innovation management in public procurement, public private partnerships, and the effect of digital transformation on organizations and business models. Her work on these topics has been published in premier academic journals.

Ganesh Devkar, PhD is a senior associate professor at the Faculty of Technology at the CEPT University, Ahmedabad, India. He holds a Doctorate in Construction Management from Indian Institute of Technology Madras (IIT Madras). His doctoral work focuses on competencies in urban local bodies for implementing water, sanitation, and solid waste management public-private partnership (PPP) projects in India. During his doctoral research work, he was involved in research projects for Tamil Nadu Urban Development Fund; Ministry of Urban Development; and Institute of Water Policy, National University of Singapore.

Tharun Dolla, PhD current research interests include public-private partnerships and infrastructure delivery models, Construction 4.0, infrastructure sustainability, governance, and smart cities. He worked on various research assignments and projects funded by agencies such as the Human Settlement Management Institute, HUDCO, New Delhi, Project Management Institute, and Erasmus+ of the European Union. He has published more than forty research articles in book chapters, journals, and conferences of international repute. He is the recipient of the "Highly Commended Paper Award" at CIB's World Building Congress (WBC 2022), Melbourne, Australia. He is currently a member of working commissions of Collaborating for Innovation in the Built environment (CIB), Canada, on the "W122 Public Private Partnership" Commission, "W113 Law and Dispute Resolution," and "W092 Procurement Systems."

Alexander Eisenkopf is a professor of Economic and Transport Policy at Zeppelin University in Friedrichshafen. His main research areas are Transport Economics and Policy and the interactions between transport and the environment. He focuses on all modes of transportation and their impact on transport markets.

Michael J. Garvin, PhD , is a professor in the Via Department of Civil and Environmental Engineering and Coordinator of the Vecellio Construction Engineering and Management Program at Virginia Tech. He has over thirty years of experience as a professor of civil engineering, consultant, practicing civil engineer, and army officer. Mike has authored over 140 technical papers and reports, and he is a member of the National Academy of Construction.

Asli Pelin Gurgun research interests include risk management, project management, decision making, sustainable structures, public-private partnerships, and technology use in construction industry. She serves on several committees and collaborated with colleagues from various academic and professional institutes in Turkey, USA, and some European countries, and published several studies in peer-reviewed journals, conferences and book chapters; and is a reviewer for several of them.

Mustafa Gursoy studying mostly on transportation planning and transportation economics. He holds his PhD from Yildiz Technical University (YTU) in 2003, and currently employed as an associate professor in YTU Civil Engineering Department. He served at Istanbul Metropolitan Municipality as the director of the Transportation Department between 2019 and 2020. He also served as the director of Transportation Research Center of YTU for 13 years (from 2007 to 2020).

Sajani Jayasuriya is a lecturer at RMIT University, Melbourne, Australia. She received a BSc (Hons.) first-class degree in Quantity Surveying from the University of Moratuwa, Sri Lanka. Following a career as a quantity surveyor, she developed an interest in pursuing a doctoral degree. She completed her doctoral degree from RMIT University. She developed a stakeholder management framework for addressing the stakeholder management-related issues in public-private partnerships projects. She is currently a member of the CIB W122 Working Commission on Public-Private Partnerships.

Andreas Knorr holds the chair of Economics: Economic Policy and Transport Policy at the German University of Administrative Sciences in Speyer. He has published numerous articles in the field of transport economics, European economic integration and competition policy. In 2009, he was appointed a member of the Board of Academic Advisers to Germany, Äôs Federal Minister of Digital and Transport.

Kerim Koc is a research assistant and PhD candidate at Yildiz Technical University, Department of Civil Engineering. His research interests cover a variety of subjects including construction management, occupational health and safety, risk management, green building, machine learning applications, construction contracts, and PPP projects.

Nakhon Kokkaew is an associate professor at the Department of Civil Engineering of Chulalongkorn University in Thailand. He received his PhD from Columbia University in New York in 2010. His research interest includes risk analysis and management in PPP infrastructure, and real options for infrastructure risk management. He publishes regularly in scholarly journals such as *Journal of Infrastructure Systems*, *Construction Management and Economics*, and *KSCE Journal of Civil Engineering*. Prof. Nakhon Kokkaew serves as a consultant conducting the study of infrastructure development for Thai public agencies such as the Department of Highways.

Boeing Laishram, PhD is a professor in Department of Civil Engineering and is also the head of School of Business at IIT Guwahati. His research focuses on public-private partnerships, building information modelling, procurement frameworks such as unsolicited proposals and partnering, sustainability assessment, and construction quality assurance. He has wide professional experience varying from construction industry to investment banking. After the completion of PhD, he has worked in an investment bank engaged in appraisal and structuring of project finance deals for infrastructure projects in India. Prof Laishram has been associated with several governmental organisations and have rendered his expertise in several fields such as quality assurance, project performance monitoring, bid advisory, cost auditing, procurement process assessment, and infrastructure cost appraisal.

Chunlu Liu, PhD is a professor in construction management in School of Architecture and Built Environment, Deakin University, Australia. He has published over 230 peer-reviewed research articles. His research interests are mathematical modelling and numerical simulation in construction management and economics. He has supervised over 30 PhD candidates in emerging research themes in construction and its relations. Currently, he is a member of the Thesis Examination Committee at Deakin University.

Shijing Liu is currently the associate head of discipline of construction management at the School of Management Science and Engineering. She is skilled in the teaching of construction management of international projects. She is also experienced in the research of the innovative application of public-private partnerships in aged care facilities.

Anthony Mills has qualifications, skills, and industry experience in construction management. He currently holds the Deakin University Chair of Construction Management. Anthony is an experienced senior academic leader who advisors the construction industry on governance and quality policies and management practices. He is the former head of School, and now holds senior roles on the University Academic Board. Anthony is a past president of the Australian Institute of Quantity Surveyors. He is also the vice chair of the international umbrella association covering the Asian region. He is a leading researcher and educator in his field.

Yuji Nemoto is a professor and director of Toyo University Public-Private Partnership (PPP) Research Center, Toyo University Graduate School of Economics, Japan. His research areas include public-private partnership, infrastructure, regional revitalization. He concurrently holds the post of Deputy Chairman of the Cabinet Office PPP Promotion Committee. He is a member of PFI Promotion Committee, Cabinet Office of the Japanese Government.

Pascale Accaoui Lorfing, PhD research focuses on international contracts and investment contracts. She co-edited a book with Dr. Yulia Levashova on Balancing the Protection of Foreign Investors and States' Responses in the (Post) Pandemic World, Kluwer (2022), and published a book on The Renegotiation of the International Contract, Bruylant (2011). She co-leads the investment chronicle of the International Business Law Journal. She is member of several working groups including the Working Group on International Contracts (Groupe de Travail sur les Contrats Internationaux), the Society of Comparative Legislation (Société de législation comparée), and the International Law Association (French branch).

Roshani Palliyaguru is a senior lecturer attached to the Department of Quantity Surveying, University of Vocational Technology, Sri Lanka. Currently She is serving as the head of the department. She has a first class in the BSc (Honours) Degree in Quantity Surveying awarded by the University of Moratuwa, Sri Lanka, and a PhD from the School of the Built Environment, University of Salford, United Kingdom. Her research interests are resilience building and regenerative development in the built environment, governance in public-private partnerships, collaboration in BIM-based construction, procurement modelling in construction, life cycle costing in the built environment, and climate mitigation and adaptation in the built environment.

Kumar V. Pratap is currently Senior Economic Adviser, Government of India, and former Joint Secretary (Infrastructure Policy and Finance), Ministry of Finance. He was Member Secretary of the Task Force that prepared India's first National Infrastructure Pipeline, led the Indian delegation at the G20 Infrastructure Working Group meetings, and was on the Board of Directors of several companies. He has written a book "PPPs in Infrastructure: Managing the Challenges" [Springer (Singapore), 2018] and was a visiting professor at the Indian School of Business from 2013 to 2017. He has an MBA from IIM, Lucknow (1987) and a PhD from the University of Maryland, College Park, USA (2011). Views are personal.

Thillai Rajan is a professor in the Department of Management Studies and Centre for Research on Start-ups and Risk Financing (CREST) at the Indian Institute of Technology Madras. He works in the area of Infrastructure Finance and Public Private Partnerships.

Rahel M. Schomaker (born 1977) holds a Doctoral degree from Muenster University and a Habilitation from Speyer University. She is a professor for economics and public administration at WSB University and Carinthia University of Applied Sciences, an adjunct professor at the German University of Administrative Sciences, and a senior fellow at the German Research Institute for Public Administration. Her research focuses on PPP, administrative change, crisis governance, migration, and trust.

Gail Sheppard is an Assistant Professor of Accounting at Maynooth University School of Business. Her research is multidisciplinary, focusing on public resource management and encompassing Public-Private Partnership (PPP) in Ireland and Covid-19 management. Her PPP research examines the performance of PPPs specifically stakeholder interactions, policy transparency, value for money and the sustainability of the policy.

Pauline Teo is a lecturer of Construction Management in the School of Property, Construction and Project Management at RMIT University, Australia. She holds a PhD in Construction Economics from Queensland University of Technology and a Masters in Project Management and Bachelor (Hons) in Building from National University of Singapore. Her research interests are in the area of public-private partnership, project cost overrun, strategic procurement methods, and construction safety and quality.

Nicola Thounaojam is a PhD candidate in the Department of Civil Engineering at Indian Institute of Technology Guwahati, India. She holds a master's in Construction Engineering and Management from CEPT University, Ahmedabad. Her research interests include megaprojects, sustainable development, PPPs, and institutional theory. She is a member of the American Society of Civil Engineers.

Andreas Wibowo, Dr.-Ing. habil. is a senior lecturer in construction management at the Department of Civil Engineering and the chair of the Center of Excellence in Urban Infrastructure Development of Parahyangan Catholic University in Indonesia. He worked as a research professor for the Indonesian Ministry of Public Works and Housing. Among his areas of expertise are public-private partnerships, risk management, financial engineering, project finance, construction procurement, construction project planning and management, and construction economics.

Rebecca Yang is a scholar of building, construction, and social practice who undertakes pure and applied research that can provide innovative solutions to the industry by integrating theories with cutting-edge technologies. Her current research focuses on the application of innovative techniques in the construction industry to improve productivity. Rebecca has contributed to building and construction research in the areas of construction technology uptake, stakeholder alignment, green building development, and social context visualisation.

List of Abbreviations

AAI	Airports Authority of India
ACI	Airports Council International
ADB	Asian Development Bank
AERA	Airports Economic Regulatory Authority
AP	Availability Payment
ARL	Airport Rail Link
B2B	Business-to-Business
BEM	Bangkok Expressway and Metro Public Company Limited
BLT	Build Lease Transfer
BMA	Bangkok Metropolitan Authority
BMDV	Bundesanstalt für Straßenwesen – Federal Ministry of Transport and Digital Infrastructure (Germany)
BOO	Build Own Operate
BOOT	Build Operate Own Transfer
BOT	Build-Operate-Transfer
BOT	Build-Operate-Transfer
BROT	Build-Rehabilitate-Operate-Transfer
BTO	Build-Transfer-Operate
BTS	Bangkok Mass Transit System
BTSC	Bangkok Transit System Corporation Limited
BTSG	Bangkok Transit System Group Public Company Limited
BTSGIF	BTS Rail Mass Transit Growth Infrastructure Fund
CA	Contracting Agency
CAG	Comptroller and Auditor General (India)
COD	Commercial Operation Date
COVID-19	Coronavirus disease caused by SARS-CoV-2 virus
DBFOT	Design-Build-Finance-Operate-Transfer
DIAL	Delhi International Airport Limited
DLA	Directorate of Legal Affairs
DMT	Don Muang Tollway Project
EMDEs	Emerging Markets and Developing Economies

EoDB	Ease of Doing Business
EPC	Engineering-Procurement-Construction
EU	European Union
FAR	Federal Acquisition Regulation
FHWA	Federal Highway Administration
GCA	Government Contracting Agency
GDP	Gross Domestic Product
GoI	Government of India
GoI	Government of Indonesia
GR	Government Regulation
IDR	Indonesian Rupiah
IFF	Infrastructure Fund
IGIA	Indira Gandhi International Airport
IIGF	Indonesian Infrastructure Guarantee Fund
IMF	International Monetary Fund
InvIT	Investment Trust Fund
lps	liters per second
MCA	Model Concession Agreement
MIAL	Mumbai International Airport Limited
MLD	Million Litres per Day
MoA	Memorandum of Agreement
MPPA	Million Passengers Per Annum
MRT	Mass Rapid Transit
MRTA	Mass Rapid Transit Authority of Thailand
MSMEs	Ministry of Micro, Small and Medium Enterprises
NBFC	Non-Banking Financial Company
NDFA	National Development Finance Agency (Ireland)
NEPA	National. Environmental Policy Act
NHAI	National Highway Authority of India
NIP	National Infrastructure Pipeline
NPA	Non Performing Assets
NPHET	National Public Health Emergency Team
NPV	Net Present Value
NRW	Non-Revenue Water
NTMA	National Treasury Management Agency
O&M	Operation and Maintenance
OHS	Occupational Health and Safety
OM	Operation and Maintenance
OMDA	Operation, Management and Development Agreement
OPW	Office of Public Works
PBC	Performance Based Contract
PBC	Performance-based Contract
PDAM	Perusahaan Daerah Air Minum
PFI	Private Finance Initiative
PISU	Private Investment in State Undertaking

PJT	Perum Jasa Tirta II
PPA	Power Purchase Agreement
PPP	Public-Private Partnership
PPPAC	Public-Private Partnership Appraisal Committee
PPSU	Private Participation in State Undertaking Act
PPTA	Public-Private Transportation Action
PR	Presidential Regulation
PSC	Public Sector Comparator
PWH	Public Works and Housing
RDS	Real Demand Survey
RE	Renewable Energy
RFP	Request for Proposal
RFQ	Request for Qualification
RIL	Reliance Industries Limited
RTM	Right-to-Match
SE	Stakeholder Engagement
SECI	Solar Energy Corporation of India
SEP	Special Experimental Proiects
SES	Second Stage Expressway System
SM	Stakeholder Management
SPV	Special Purpose Vehicle
SRT	State Railway of Thailand
STP	Sewage Treatment Plant
TIFIA	Transportation Infrastructure Finance and Investment Act
TOR	Transfer of Rights
TOT	Toll-Operate-Transfer
USD	United States Dollar
USP	Unsolicited Proposals
VDOT	The Virginia Department of Transportation
VfM	Value for Money
VHBA	Victorian Health Building Authority

List of Figures

List of Tables

Introduction

Tharun Dolla, Ganesh Devkar, and Boeing Laishram

State of the Knowledge Concerning Resilience

Crises

COVID-19 is an unprecedented pandemic of modern times that has affected the social and economic fabric of countries across the globe. The quality and quantum of infrastructure has been playing a game-changer role in the times of this pandemic, especially the transport, information technology, and health infrastructure. Although it is believed that infrastructure projects are designed to weather the economic, social, and political storms that will be experienced across the project life cycle, however, the reality is different owing to the bounded rationality of human beings. In the past, infrastructure delivery models have been hit by various unprecedented events. Two major events, such as the great Asian Financial Crisis in 1997 and Global Financial Crisis in 2008, have also affected infrastructure delivery models. It is reported that use of PPPs (private finance initiative) declined after the financial crisis (Booth 2018). But little is known about the lessons learned due to a lack of timely works capturing the repercussions on various infrastructure delivery models. Few investigations exist that focus, more importantly, on the inherent ‘fault

T. Dolla (✉)
Department of Civil Engineering, Indian Institute of Technology Bombay, Mumbai, Maharashtra, India

G. Devkar
Faculty of Technology, CEPT University, Ahmedabad, Gujarat, India

B. Laishram
Department of Civil Engineering, Indian Institute of Technology Guwahati, Guwahati, Assam, India

© The Author(s), under exclusive license to Springer Nature Switzerland AG 2023

T. Dolla et al. (eds.), *Revisiting Public-Private Partnerships*,
Contributions to Public Administration and Public Policy,
https://doi.org/10.1007/978-3-031-37015-1_1

lines' in the contract governance mechanisms, which get exposed when the project faces these unprecedented scenarios (Williams et al., 2017).

Functioning of PPPs

PPPs function on a tight set of business principles and social goals. The private sector participating in infrastructure development acts out of its commercial goals, while the public sector drives its agenda with value for money and social value creation goals. PPPs have always operated on partnership principles considering the overall advantages of this approach, which include better efficiency with the private sector and a lack of competency with the public sector. The institutional framework, laws, and regulations assure rightful and smooth operations. Based on these assumptions, the private sector apportions the risk while bidding. The different expectations of various stakeholders – construction of the assets according to schedule, the expected returns on the debt and equity, timely payment to the contractors, subcontractors, and the operators, the availability of the facilities to the user against direct or indirect payments – strongly influence the project finance business model of the PPPs, and in turn, the profit-making capacity of the concessionaire.

Impact of Crises on PPPs

Public–private partnerships (PPP) are being adopted as one of the most prominent and widely used infrastructure delivery models across the world. The PPP model has encountered shocks owing to these events such as global financial crisis and severely affected the pipeline of PPP projects. It can be argued that the learnings from these events helped in crafting better and more well-paced financing structures and governance mechanisms. However, the scale of disruption caused by Covid-19 is altogether different or rather novel, disruptive, and critical (Morgeson et al., 2015). At the same time, normalcy is a distant expectation, and the majority of the agencies placed at least a two-to three-year period of after-effects of Covid-19. Governments across the world are facing economic downturns on account of Covid-19. In response to this situation, governments of countries such as the United Kingdom, Australia, and India have declared infrastructure stimulus programmes for creating employment opportunities and kick-starting the economy, using the PPP model as a key element of these programmes. Hence, this moment in the history of humankind, as well as global infrastructure space, provides an opportunity to reinvigorate the PPP model.

PPPs are regarded as one of the most contentious project delivery models in recent decades, even after having robust economic analyses and contractual foundations (Sherratt et al., 2020). Yet, it is still regarded to be the only solution to have a project – 'it is either PFI or no funding' (Ball and King, 2006; Henjewele et al.,

2011). Thus, the role of PPP in infrastructure development still remains dominant, particularly in developing countries for a myriad of reasons. Perhaps the debates of social value and cost escalations are prevalent in other project models, even in megaprojects, for instance (Gil & Fu, 2022).

Covid-19 disrupted the usual behaviour and performance of PPP contracts. The lockdown and restrictions of movement have altered the business-as-usual scenario and resulted in hindrance/blockage of imports of raw materials and machinery, labour non-availability, surcharges in prices, and costs of extra health and safety measures. These have exacerbated the complexities in the delivery model and almost acted as the government expropriating the free-market principles and assuming the functions performed by the private sector. The uncertainty encountered in these scenarios triggers claims, which, if not settled on time, will result in a dispute awaiting a resolution either through arbitration or in a court of law. This runs counter to the synergy of partnership and business principles on which the PPP is grounded. As a result, theoretical and policy-level challenges emerge in developing and operating these partnerships. In particular, attention needs to be given to the global economic patterns and changing social, economic, and financial structures across the globe.

PPPs are connected to crisis and resilience in at least two different ways:

1. The effect of unprecedented events such as the Covid-19 pandemic, as an example, on the performance of PPPs from temporal and perpetual perspectives.
2. The mechanisms needed to further improve the resilience of PPPs to deal with situations such as a pandemic.

Resilience in PPPs

Resilience is one of the important parameters of PPP contracts. In infrastructure projects, resilience can be taken as actions that sustain and thrive the operations in spite of the disrupting conditions (Naderpajouh et al., 2020). PPPs, though temporary special-purpose vehicles, are often found to encounter disruptions. While the industry was expecting a recession during early 2020, a sudden and unexpected pandemic, i.e. Covid-19, has caused turmoil in their businesses. As a result, budgets are expected to be stressed further (ENR, 2020), and privately delivered public infrastructure projects that are in operation, construction, or projects that are in the pipeline must adapt to the prevailing conditions. Bold and appropriate measures are expected from governments as well as the private sector to continue business transactions while aiming to sustain growth (Casady & Baxter, 2020).

Why This Book?

Reinvigorating the PPP Model

Reinvigorating the PPP model will involve a two-step process, and this process will be the focus of this book. Firstly, the book seeks to assess the degree to which PPP infrastructure projects are affected by the pandemic, i.e. Covid-19. While doing so, it unearths the short-term and long-term measures undertaken by governments to tide over these disruption-related effects. Secondly, it focuses on improving the state-of-the-art knowledge by suggesting future directions to be taken by governments, practitioners, and researchers in order to create resilience in infrastructure projects when using PPP mode as the delivery model. In this context, more importantly, the effects of the pandemic on the performance of PPPs are still unknown, and this begs special attention. In particular, it collates and generates theory related to the influence of pandemic kind of disruption on PPP's performance by taking all major PPP economies for the inquiry. This book highlights the specificity of pandemics while unearthing the PPP as an infrastructure delivery model. In doing so, the book appreciates that the Covid-19 pandemic should not be generalised to other unprecedented events, and it necessitates special attention and investigation in the context of performance measurement of PPP projects.

Aims and Objectives

Many studies were initiated after the call to reinvigorate the mid-range effect and ground the theoretical underpinning after the extraordinary events. But understanding and analysing the infrastructure delivery context with particular reference to PPP, the popular mode of procurement for infrastructure across the nations, remains poorly developed. The main aim of this book is to provide a systematic review, assessment, and research directions on pertinent issues of governance of PPPs. It also assesses the need to reorganise PPPs to build endurance to the hidden fractures in stressful situations such as the pandemics, thereby presenting a new and better resilient approach to PPP structuring. In particular, the resilience of governance models of PPPs, when viewed from their overall performance and the lessons learned from the adverse effects of the pandemic, is the prime focus of the edited book. This book uncovers the solutions being adopted in those projects that can facilitate resilience in future comparable situations such as the Covid-19. Lessons from these projects enable effective decision-making in the context of governance and assist in improving or sustaining the performance of PPP infrastructure projects. The body of knowledge generated through this volume augments the current theory of PPP development, builds resilience into contracts, and addresses the fault lines in the current governance strategies.

Each chapter is either an empirical (using qualitative, quantitative, or mixed research methods) or analytical discourse by taking a specific case study grounded in the context of a country. Some of the contributors focussed on only one case study to support deeper analysis. This book initiates developing emergent theory of PPP on affects of transient occurrences such as Covid 19 and paves the way for future development. With the help of lessons learned and through the way of stimulating further research, PPPs can emerge as stronger and more resilient infrastructure delivery models.

Readers

One of the hallmarks of this book is the geographical coverage. The disruption faced by PPP projects in different parts of the world, as shown in Fig. 1, has been narrated and amalgamated as individual chapters in this book. We hope that the book will be valuable for the students undertaking graduate courses in the area of construction management, infrastructure management, and public management. Along with this, researchers working in the area of PPPs will also find this book interesting in understanding global practices in PPPs and charting out new research trajectories.

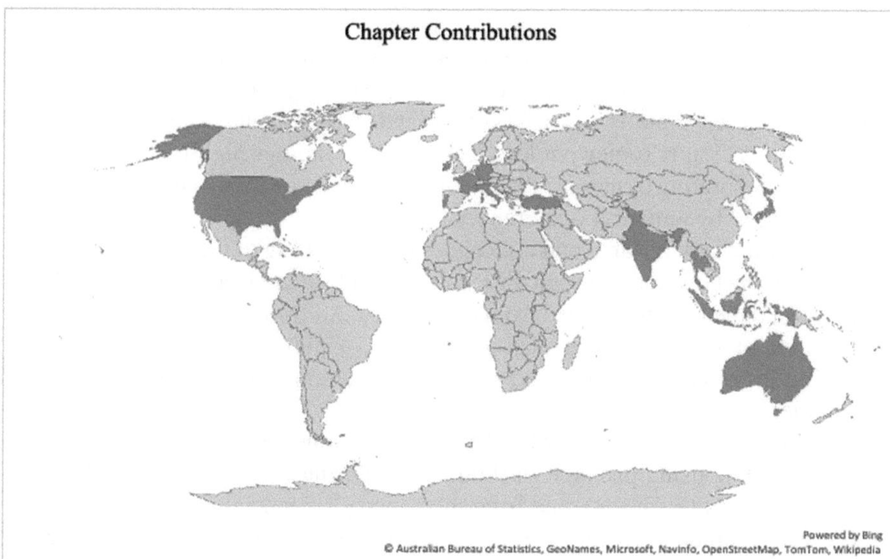

Fig. 1 Map of chapter contributions

There is a growing body of PPP professionals, which includes government officials, infrastructure consultants, and development sector officials, that are at the forefront of putting in place much-needed infrastructure within the paradigm of cost, quality, time, and so on. This book will become a knowledge source for understanding best practices adopted to make PPP projects resilient and craft novel shock-absorbing governance mechanisms to deal with disruptions such as Covid-19.

Parts of the Book

The rest of the book is organised into five parts as mentioned below.

Part I: PPP Review, Policy and Administration

The first part is PPP review, policy, and administration. It deals with understanding the PPP body of knowledge and the lessons for public administration and highlights the learning curve of PPPs both in terms of learning from the past and vision for future PPPs.

The focus of the next chapter by Nicola and Tharun in the first part which is PPP review, policy and administration was on systematically reviewing PPP from resilience perspective to comprehend the patterns, topics, and ideas that had been investigated so far. The authors show that the resilience concept occurs sparingly in PPPs. The most focused topic is risk assessment and management, whereas concession period optimisation is somewhat less focused. The findings highlighted the significance of incorporating dynamic adjustment mechanisms within contracts to adapt to changes caused by temporal occurrences.

In the third chapter, Rahel and colleagues use the setting of German road projects to demonstrate how the German PPP models had already been modified due to readiness and the lessons learned from prior crises. Additionally, they emphasise the significance of the function and accountability of public sector organisations in enhancing information sharing and management amongst distinct institutions and stakeholders.

In the fourth chapter, Sheppard and Matthias demonstrate how Ireland's management of social housing package PPP initiatives during the Covid-19 outbreak was aided by previous lessons learned from the country's financial crisis.

The fifth chapter by Carbonara, in the context of Italy, provides an overview of the state of PPPs in Italy as well as a vision for strategic PPPs as a tool to address the current social, digital, environmental, and economic challenges, not just to increase the pool of public funds but primarily to swiftly implement new investments and services. The author has specifically claimed that PPPs are both an excellent recovery tool and a post-covid recovery tool.

Part II: PPP Financing and Contractual Governance

Moving onto Part II, it is about PPP financing and contractual governance. It deals with aspects related to revenues, relief measures, relational governance, and sustaining the success of PPPs through various governance mechanisms.

In the sixth chapter, Pratap illustrates how upholding the contract's integrity would give time to deal with momentary brief impediments when crises arise by using the context of Indian projects, notably airport constructions. This is significant since the need for remedial measures from numerous stakeholders has intensified during Covid 19 in India.

Seven Indian road projects are used as examples in the seventh chapter by Aravindan and Thillai, and the research suggests that revenues might return to pre-pandemic levels within a year. The authors also demonstrated that the IRB Infrastructure Investment Trust Fund (IRB InvIT is IRB Infrastructure Developers Ltd. - the first infrastructure investment trust in India) was able to service its debts without going into default as a result of the relief measures.

According to the eighth chapter by Garvin and Ahmed, which focuses on US Highways, the combination of clear contractual provisions, established counterparty relationships, and shared interests prevented claims due to Covid-19 pandemic, highlighting the necessity of effective complementarity between contractual and relational governance in PPPs.

In the ninth chapter, Nemoto looks at a mixed-use development project in Japan and demonstrates how compactification and clear risk sharing between the public and private sectors, along with an effective PPP agent who helped unify the concept, have contributed to the PPP projects' ongoing success despite the disruptions brought on by Covid-19.

Part III: Risk Management

The third part is about Risk management in PPPs. In this part, readers can find chapters related to issues and challenges of PPP procurement while proposing innovative financing measures that can effectively manage the risks and build resilience into the PPP model. The tenth chapter by Andreas highlights the flaws in PPP procurement that were exacerbated by the epidemic and focuses on water delivery projects in Indonesia. The Covid-19 epidemic has brought to the fore the problems and difficulties associated with the danger that have been simmering for years. The ability of municipal water utilities to off-take water, end-user rates, the interaction between upstream and downstream, value for money, and coordination among important stakeholders are a few of these factors.

The eleventh chapter by Kokkaew, which is based on Thailand's urban transportation system, advocates the use of financing and risk management tools that appear to be cutting-edge, such as an infrastructure fund (IFF), which transfers market risks such as demand and revenue uncertainty to retail and institutional investors as a way to strengthen the PPP model.

Gurgun and colleagues examine highway projects in Turkey in the twelfth chapter, demonstrating how Covid-19 risks were better managed in a large-scale project procured using a BOT model than with more conventional models by taking proactive steps to address the pandemic effects on the project site. The results showed that at the very beginning of the epidemic, the project participants immediately adjusted to its requirements. This is due to the fact that in the case study, as opposed to projects obtained through regular delivery methods, stronger procedures were employed, especially in relation to the site access and exit.

Part IV: PPP Stakeholder Management

The fourth part is about PPP stakeholder management. This part explicates PPP's effective engagement of stakeholders in PPPs. The thirteenth chapter by Sajani Jayasuriya, Pauline Teo, Roshani Palliyaguru and Rebecca Yang illustrates the need for stakeholder management strategies to embrace communications flexibility for effective consultation while implementing PPPs. This chapter uses a PPP health care project in Australia. Flexibility is essential for productive engagement with user groups, such as physicians. As a result, this chapter recommends hybrid engagement strategies and suggests adding online components to the systems.

Part V: Renegotiation

The fifth part is about renegotiation, and the contributions were in the areas of principles of renegotiation and on the factors that can be considered to enable renegotiation. Shijing Liu, Anthony Mills and Chunlu Liu took the case of PPP rental retirement villages in Australia to focus on renegotiation. They evaluated the effects of Covid-19 on the project and determined that the main implications were an increase in running expenses and a loss of money owing to a decrease in occupancy rate. This may eventually lead to renegotiation.

In fifteenth chapter, Lorfing then focuses on renegotiation at a new level while using the backdrop of France. By using the French context, the author has emphasised the effects of Covid-19 on contracts, the major concerns, the difficulties encountered in contract renegotiations, and the efforts needed to enhance contract renegotiations. The author concentrated on policies that have generally affected contracts. The writers discuss three topics: administrative law, the specificity of the law, the contrast between the legal theories that apply when there is a change in the circumstances, imprévision, and force majeure.

In the last chapter, the editors conclude the discussion and provide recommendations for both theory and practice. We believe that the contributions in this collection will excite, stimulate, and be applicable to both theory and practice as we continue to tackle the difficulties brought on by a crisis such as Covid-19.

--
The Editors

References

Ball, R., & King, D. (2006). The private finance initiative in local government. *Economic Affairs, John Wiley & Sons, Ltd, 26(1), 36–40.* https://doi.org/10.1111/j.1468-0270.2006.00610.x

Booth, L. (2018). Goodbye PFI. House of Commons Library, UK Parliament. Retrieved August 2, 2021 (https://commonslibrary.parliament.uk/goodbye-pfi/).

Casady, C. B., & Baxter, D. (2020). Pandemics, public-private partnerships (PPPs), and force majeure-COVID-19 expectations and implications. *Construction Management and Economics, 38*(12), 1077–1085. Routledge.

ENR. (2020). COVID-19 intensifies infrastructure funding problem, ASCE says. *Engineering News Record.* Available at: www.enr.com/articles/49611-covid-19-intensifies-infrastructure-funding-problem-asce-says. Accessed 10 July 2020.

Gil, N., & Fu, Y. (2022). Megaproject performance, value creation, and value distribution: An organizational governance perspective. *Academy of Management Discoveries, 8*(2), 224–251.

Henjewele, C., Sun, M., & Fewings, P. (2011). Critical parameters influencing value for money variations in PFI projects in the healthcare and transport sectors. *Construction Management and Economics, 29(8), 825–839.* https://doi.org/10.1080/01446193.2011.592204

Morgeson, F. P., Mitchell, T. R., & Liu, D. (2015). Event system theory: An event-oriented approach to the organisational sciences. *Academy of Management Review, 40*(4), 515–537.

Naderpajouh, N., Matinheikki, J., Keeys, L. A., Aldrich, D. P., & Linkov, I. (2020). Resilience and projects: An interdisciplinary crossroad. *Project Leadership and Society, 1*(June), 100001. Elsevier Ltd.

Sherratt, F., Sherratt, S., & Ivory, C. (2020). Challenging complacency in construction management research: The case of PPPs. *Construction Management and Economics, 38*(12), 1086–1100. Routledge.

Williams, T. A., Gruber, D. A., Sutcliffe, K. M., Shepherd, D. A., & Zhao, E. Y. (2017). Organisational response to adversity: Fusing crisis management and resilience research streams. *Academy of Management Annals, 11*(2), 733–769.

Part I
PPP Review, Policy and Administration

Resilience in Public Private Partnerships: A Systematic Literature Review

Nicola Thounaojam and Tharun Dolla

Introduction

PPP contracts are often criticised for their extremely long-duration agreements and may not benefit governments if underlying conditions or assumptions change significantly over time. Notably, the idea of selecting the best contractor, designer, or consultant once and for all might not only be slightly rigid despite the unpredictable and varying circumstances but the opportunities for maximising each of the numerous occasions in refinancing, refurbishment, and entry and exit of owners may be prematurely closed or their impacts blunted with the signing of such a long-term contract. Therefore, given that PPP projects, especially transport projects, face many changing circumstances, more flexibility may be desirable. There is a need to reinforce and design PPP contractual provisions that account for the long-term implications of massive, sudden, and unprecedented impacts from future shocks (Baxter & Casady, 2020). Effective and responsive governance is needed to secure order, especially in times of crisis. In addition, resilient and sustainable considerations in PPP contracts are needed in light of the current COVID-19 crisis.

N. Thounaojam
Infrastructure Engineering and Management Division, Department of Civil Engineering, Indian Institute of Technology, Guwahati, Assam, India

T. Dolla (✉)
Department of Civil Engineering, Indian Institute of Technology Bombay, Mumbai, Maharashtra, India

Department of Civil Engineering, GITAM Deemed to be University, Visakhapatnam, India
e-mail: tdolla@gitam.edu

© The Author(s), under exclusive license to Springer Nature Switzerland AG 2023
T. Dolla et al. (eds.), *Revisiting Public-Private Partnerships*,
Contributions to Public Administration and Public Policy,
https://doi.org/10.1007/978-3-031-37015-1_2

Definitions of Crisis and Resilience

The term "crisis" has evolved to reflect an "all-encompassing" phrase for multidimensional "unexpected situation" that is sparked by a variety of triggers, such as investor fraud, pandemics, and natural catastrophes, and disrupts operations of a country, a society, or a corporation, or several countries that causes dismay or an emergency and a financial threat (Kim & Woo, 2021; Anand et al., 2022). The disturbance and unfavourable shocks from the financial crisis of 2008 affected PPPs around the world, abandoning and delaying the execution of projects, primarily those that were in the planning stages, through both financial and technical channels such as upward pressure on interest rates, decrease in the availability of credit, effects of the economic slowdown on revenue cash flows, and unforeseen exchange rate movements (Burger et al., 2013). The financial crisis was so severe, which negatively influenced the cost and availability of funding, that some significant PPPs for financing market segments, such as the monoline bond market, had to shut down to new transactions (Etienne, 2013). The COVID-19 pandemic triggered an economic crisis just 10 years after the economic shock of the 2008 global financial crisis. Such a crisis is a challenge for the government as public revenue declines due to rising unemployment, fall in household income, and shrinkage in the economy. PPPs are referred to as "one of the most contentious project delivery mechanisms to have been mobilised in recent decades" (Sherratt et al., 2020). The importance becomes exacerbated when crisis conditions are added to it, bringing much more uncertainty and complexity brought on by lengthy contractual periods (Ortega et al., 2016). Strong demand and affordable finance availability are essential for the success of PPP markets. Therefore, the viability of PPP systems could be threatened by any crisis that affects demand, the cost of finance, or the availability of it.

In line with the above issue, there is an urgent need to integrate resilience, agility, and flexibility in the PPP procurement process. A lack of resilience and adaptability to unexpected events undermine the security of PPPs. Resilience means "an overall ability to recover from disruptions caused by infrequent and damaging events" (Hasan et al., 2021). This term is derived from the Latin word "resilio," which is composed of "re"– "for again" and "salire"– "to spring, jump", which deciphers to "bounce back" (Gay & Sinha, 2013). More precisely, it is the "ability to thrive on change and adapt to change and develop new approaches" (Kumaraswamy et al., 2015). The concept of resilience is beginning to attract much attention for employment in the built environment and PPP research. To recover from the disruptions of the global financial crisis in 2008, Burger et al. (2013) and Etienne (2013) highlighted the need for readjustments of the financing structure and schemes of PPP arrangements to increase the role of bilateral and multilateral financial institutions and inclusion of "trip switch" clauses by providing an automatic exit strategy that ensures the temporary nature of government support.

Moreover, the long contract period of PPP arrangements generates greater risks and demands lock-in effects, thereby reducing the overall flexibility and resilience of the arrangement (Nizkorodov, 2021). Therefore, the PPP project risks becoming obsolete if the contract does not include provisions for updating technology, project deliverables, and partner rules and responsibilities. Furthermore, risks and other factors that are neither clearly "documentable" nor "demonstrable" can be addressed in more flexible and feasible contractual clauses if they are accepted by both parties, which creates a certain level of resilience (Kumaraswamy et al., 2015). Hasan et al. (2021) also called attention to re-examining the existing force majeure clauses and finding "collaborative and innovative solutions" between the two parties to incorporate sustainability and resilience measures.

The Aim of the Chapter

The coronavirus outbreak has necessitated significant adjustments in the contractual arrangement of PPPs, starting with the necessity for research. As a result, scholars have highlighted numerous resilient and innovative alterations that would endure crises or shocks in the future. There have been major changes made to the way contracts are written, how debt and equity resources are procured, how financial closure is attained, and how renegotiations are done as a result of such a worldwide crisis, and these changes are still being researched today (Castelblanco et al., 2022). Improving the resiliency of the PPP arrangements is paramount. However, there is a lack of comprehensive examination of current PPP literature and pinpointing the essential elements that make PPP contracts more resilient to deploy in crises, including the economic downturns, bankruptcy, contract termination, or outbreaks. Therefore, this chapter aims to systematically review existing research on PPPs and resilience to identify the key elements critical for strengthening resilience in PPP arrangements in times of crisis.

Research Methodology

To facilitate a clear and in-depth illustration of PPP resilience-related research, a systematic literature review was conducted using the three-step procedure proposed by Chelliah et al. (2021).

The first step concerns the selection of databases and the identification of the right keywords. Two powerful search engines, "Scopus" and "Web of Science", were selected to identify journals that have published PPP resilience-related articles. Based on the building blocks, "PPP," "crisis," and "resilience," and using their synonyms, the following search syntax was adopted under the "title/abstract/keyword" field (Fig. 1):

[Title-Abs-Key ("uncertain*" OR "cris*s" OR "shock" OR "stress" OR "disaster" OR "disrupt*" OR "catastroph*" OR "failure" OR "recess*" OR "force majeure" OR "covid 19" OR "bankrupt*" OR "pandemic" OR "war" OR "recall" OR

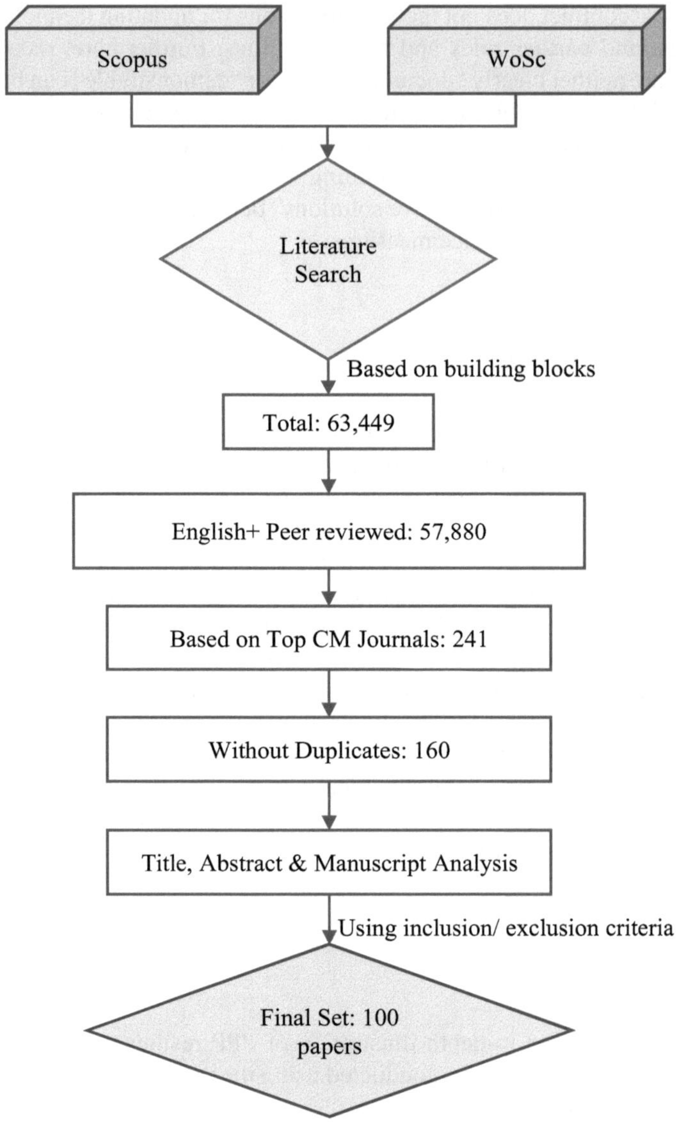

Fig. 1 Research paper selection process

"strike" OR "massacre" OR "terroris*" OR "scandal*" OR "turbulen*" OR "resilien*" OR "flexib*" OR "adaptab*") AND ("PPP" OR "Public-Private Partnership" OR "Private Finance Initiatives" OR "PFI" OR "Build Operate Transfer" OR "BOT" OR "Transfer Operate Transfer" OR "TOT" OR "Build Operate Own Transfer" OR "BOOT")]

The second step is conducting a review that includes filtering of the papers based on journals and filtering criteria. Drawing upon the search results with respect to English and peer-reviewed journals, the papers were further filtered based on 12 top-tier construction journals, namely, IEEE Transaction on Engineering Management (IEEE-TEM), Automation in Construction (AC), International Journal of Project Management (IJPM), Project Management Journal (PMJ), Journal of Construction Engineering and Management (JCEM-Construction), Construction Management and Economics (CME), Journal of Management in Engineering (JME), Engineering, Construction and Architectural Management (ECAM), Journal of Civil Engineering and Management (JCEM-Civil), Habitat International (HI), International Journal of Construction Management (IJCM), and KSCE Journal of Civil Engineering (KSCE-JCE), which were extracted for further analysis. Several reviews on PPP published earlier have also conducted systematic reviews based on this list of journals (Ke et al., 2009; Zhang et al., 2016a, 2020), which were selected as the target journals based on the ranking of construction management journals by (Chau, 1997). In addition, duplicates were identified and removed resulting in 160 papers. After reading through the titles and abstracts, papers not pertaining to PPP and resilience were excluded. In addition, the full manuscripts were carefully read, and articles were further analysed to select papers most relevant to the subject and excluded papers with insufficient information related to PPP and resilience, leaving a final set of 100 research papers.

The final step pertains to analysing and reporting the review. To analyse and assess the trends in the research articles, a data extraction form in Excel was made using pertinent data from the final collected publications. The information incorporated in the form included the title, author, year, journal, abstract, sector details, and country where the study was conducted. The recovered articles were further analysed in terms of annual research publications, methodological classification, top journals, geographical and sector-wise distributions, in addition to the basic classification, which aims to identify the research coverage, foci, and topics. The findings will be shown utilising visualisation tools, including charts, graphs, and tables, in addition to using narrative tactics and descriptive statistics of the data to aid in their interpretation.

Findings

Publications per Year Graph

The study conducted chronological analysis to identify the temporal distribution of articles. The temporal classification of papers shows a growing academic interest in this domain. Figure 2 shows a trend that there is increasing attention in PPP resilience research from three papers found in 1997 to 12 papers found in 2021. Studies on PPP resilience reached a relative balance after 2014, with the annual number of

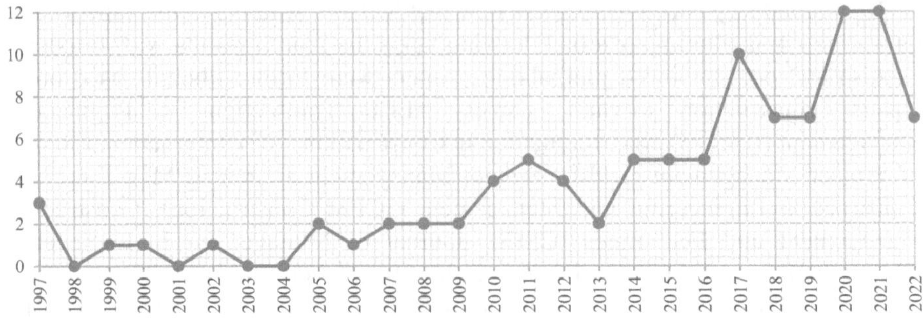

Fig. 2 Annual publication

Fig. 3 Word cloud analysis for author keyword

publications fluctuating between 5 and 12. In the initial years, only a few studies were published. A maximum of 67 papers were published between 2015 and 2022. Of those, 12 papers were published each during 2020 and 2021.

Top Keywords

Word cloud analysis was conducted from a pool of 490 author keywords and 1469 indexed keywords drawn from 100 papers. Word clouds or tag clouds are graphical representations of word frequency that give greater prominence to words that appear more frequently in a source (Riggs & Hu, 2013). Figures 3 and 4 illustrate the results of word cloud analysis. It is observed that "real option", "Monte Carlo simulation", "concession period", "risk", "BOT", "failure", "uncertainty", and "renegotiation" are most highlighted in their keywords.

Fig. 4 Word cloud analysis for Indexed keyword

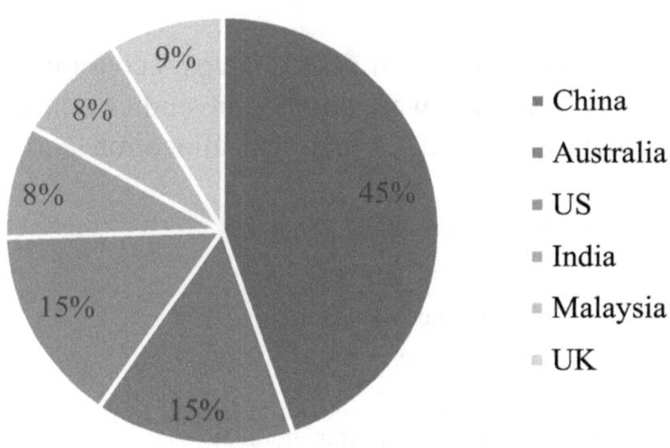

Fig. 5 Geographical distribution of the selected studies

Geographical Graph

Top Five Countries

The geographical distribution analysis from this systematic review revealed that the studies are dispersed globally, including on the continents of America, Asia, Africa, Australia, and Europe. The geographical distribution revealed that most of the research studies was from China (21), Australia (7), the USA (7), India (4), the UK (4), and Malaysia (4). These are shown in Fig. 5.

Top Five Journals

For journals, Journal of Construction Engineering and Management (22 papers), Journal of Management in Engineering (19 papers), Construction Management and Economics (19 papers), and Engineering, Construction and Architectural Management (17 papers) have the highest frequency of papers. These journals are shown in Table 1.

Top Three Sectors as per Focus

The review of sector-wise distribution found that 64 papers appeared from the transportation sector, including road, transport (in general), metro and high-speed rail, tunnel, airport, bridge, and port. Some of the other top sectors include water (13) and energy (7). The highest contributions appeared in the road sector (36 papers), followed by water (13 papers). These are shown in Fig. 6.

Top Five Frequent Theories

Theories such as real options theory, transaction cost economics, and the resource-based view gained popularity and were adopted in studies related to minimum revenue guarantee (Ashuri et al., 2012) and risk allocation and management (Jin,

Table 1 Top five journals of PPPs and resilience studies

Journal	No. of papers
Journal of Construction Engineering and Management	22
Construction Management and Economics	19
Journal of Management in Engineering	19
Engineering, Construction and Architectural Management	17
International Journal of Project Management	8

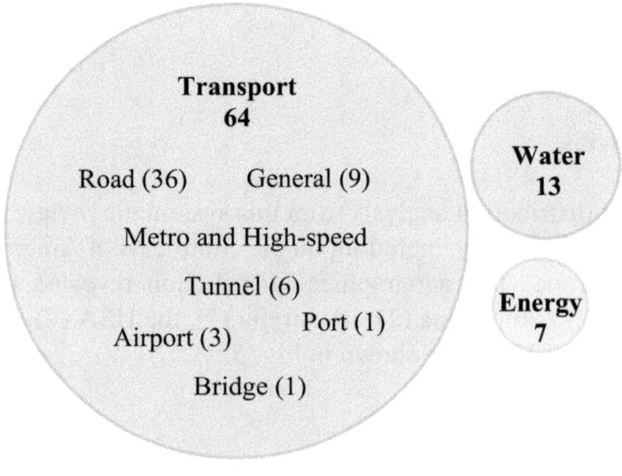

Fig. 6 Sectorial distribution of the selection studies

2010), respectively. The use of real options theory can be seen growing and is considered by many scholars as an effective tool to be incorporated in PPP projects, especially in renegotiation (Xiong & Zhang, 2016), asset pricing and valuation (Liu et al., 2017), and concession period optimisation (Lv et al., 2015). This review also witnessed the growth of other theories, such as game theory/bargaining game theory, to frame risks associated with PPP projects, to model decision-making strategies for renegotiating costs in times of financial difficulties or early termination, and to model the process of determining the optimal values for the concession period and government guarantee when renegotiation occurs (Khallaf et al., 2018; Bayat et al., 2020; Jin et al., 2020; Sharafi et al., 2021). System theory is also adopted to capture factors affecting demand by incorporating a range of interrelated and dynamic factors such as demographic and economic conditions (Alasad & Motawa, 2015). These theories are shown in Table 2.

Table 2 Major theories used in PPPs and resilience studies

Theory	Representative studies	Percentage	Basic constructs of the theory
Real Option Theory	(Cheah & Liu, 2006; Ashuri et al., 2012; Cruz & Marques, 2013; Carbonara et al., 2014b; Huang & Pi, 2014; Lv et al., 2015; Xiong & Zhang, 2016; Attarzadeh et al., 2017; Liu et al., 2017; Buyukyoran & Gundes, 2018; Chen et al., 2018; Sun et al., 2019; Swanson & Sakhrani, 2020; Tavakoli & Hosseini Nourzad, 2020; Guo et al., 2021)	15%	It is derived from the traditional option pricing theory, which tries to value financial options. It helps to determine the alternative actions for the uncertain future, when to apply these actions, and the prices of choosing these actions
Transaction Cost Economics (TCE)	(Jin & Doloi, 2008; Jin, 2010; Jin & Zhang, 2011; Nguyen & Garvin, 2019; Demirel et al., 2022)	5%	It implies that economic institutions adapt their governance structures to achieve the lowest possible transaction costs and maximise profits
Game Theory/ Bargaining Game Theory	(Chen et al., 2012; Xiong & Zhang, 2016; Khallaf et al., 2018; Bayat et al., 2020; Jin et al., 2020; Tavakoli & Hosseini Nourzad, 2020; Sharafi et al., 2021)	7%	It is the mathematical study of situations of conflicts of interest. It explores the dynamics of interactions between actors and explains under what conditions the actors could achieve long-term win-win cooperation through short-term conflict
Resource-Based View (RBV)	(Jin & Doloi, 2008; Jin, 2010; Jin & Zhang, 2011)	3%	It explains competitive heterogeneity based on the premise that close competitors differ in their capabilities and resources in important and durable ways
Systems Theory	(Alasad & Motawa, 2015; Loosemore & Cheung, 2015)	2%	It is the philosophical underpinning of systems thinking. It seeks to understand how subsystems of people, processes, and technologies interact

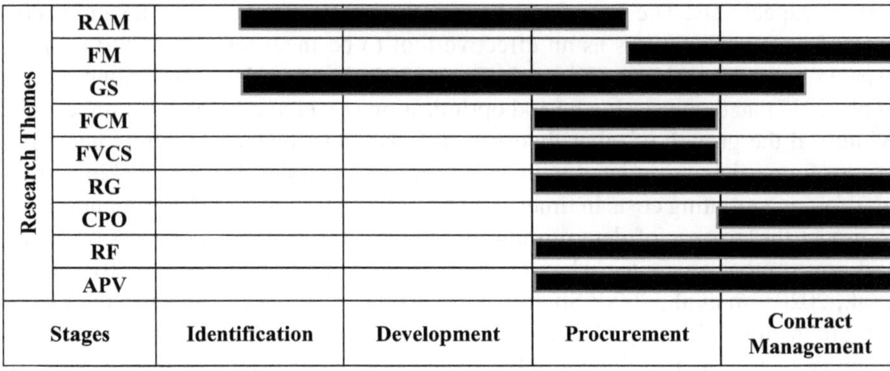

Fig. 7 Major themes related to PPPs and resilience

Research Themes Analysis Tabulation with Percentages

Through content analysis, the review revealed nine key themes: failure drivers and mechanisms; revenue guarantee options; renegotiation framework; concession period optimisation; governance strategies; flexible contract mechanisms; financial viability and capital structure; risk allocation and management; and asset pricing/valuation mechanism (Fig. 7, Table 3).

Discussion and Conclusions

This study identifies the research trends and themes in the domain of PPP and resilience, based on a systematic literature review of 100 publications between 1997 and 2022 from top-tier construction journals. The temporal classification of papers shows a growing academic interest in this domain. The literature review reveals nine distinct research themes: failure drivers and mechanisms; revenue guarantee options; renegotiation framework; concession period optimisation; governance strategies; flexible contract mechanisms; financial viability and capital structure; risk allocation and management; and asset pricing/valuation mechanism. Although many concepts and models have been developed and adopted in line with how to address uncertainty in PPP, the findings reveal that the use of resilience concept is still discreet in theory. The findings revealed the importance of establishing dynamic adjustment mechanisms in the contracts to respond to changes in demand and other project uncertainties. There is a need to rethink PPPs by consciously moving away from rigid contracts to flexibility. Without the right capacity and decision-making knowledge on how resilience is defined, by which variables it is determined, and how it can be tested, maintained, and enhanced over time, PPP projects will find themselves unprepared for the effects of catastrophic occurrences such as the COVID-19 pandemic.

Table 3 Major themes, focus and representative studiesrelated to PPPs and resilience

Themes	Focus	Representative studies	Number of papers
Risk allocation and management (RAM)	Optimum assessment and fair allocation of risks to attain a win-win situation for all parties. Need for ex-post risk management in addition to ex-ante risk management	Songer et al. (1997), Jin and Doloi (2008), Jin (2010), Kokkaew and Wipulanusat (2014), Alasad and Motawa (2015), Loosemore and Cheung (2015), Nguyen et al. (2018), Nguyen and Garvin (2019), Zhang et al. (2021)	19
Failure mechanisms (FM)	Failure drivers associated with both public and private parties. Failures related to poor traffic demand, poor governance, regional economic situations, economic crisis in a country and sociopolitical factors	Trangkanont and Charoenngam (2014), Song et al. (2018), Zhang and Tariq (2020), Tariq and Zhang (2021b), Tariq and Zhang (2021a), Wang and Tiong (2022)	16
Governance strategies (GS)	Proper governance mechanisms to deal with such uncertainties and to avoid bankruptcy	Chen and Messner (2005), Vassallo et al. (2012), Nguyen and Garvin (2019), Delhi and Mahalingam (2020), Devkar et al. (2020), Dewulf and Garvin (2020), Demirel et al. (2022)	14
Flexible contract mechanisms (FCM)	Dynamic adjustable contract mechanism to respond to changes in demand, avoid ex-post renegotiations and to boost the resilience of PPPs against uncertainty	Jie (2009), Chen et al. (2012), Cruz and Marques (2013), Demirel et al. (2017)	14
Financial viability and capital structure (FVCS)	Existing financial analysis methods need improvement using new financial engineering techniques. Evaluating the impact of the government debt guarantee and the developer negotiation option on the financial viability from the perspectives of different project stakeholders when the project is under construction, bankruptcy, and economic risks	Zhang (2005), Jeong et al. (2016), Feng et al. (2017), Wang and Jin (2019), Hou and Wang (2022)	13
Revenue guarantee (RG)	An appropriate combination of minimum revenue guarantees and traffic revenue cap or determining a fair lower limit and an upper cap for operational revenues to mitigate and manage the revenue risk in PPP projects, thus regulating multiple uncertainties and risks embedded in future traffic demands of PPP projects	Shan et al. (2010), Carbonara et al. (2014b), Attarzadeh et al. (2017), Chen et al. (2018), Bae et al. (2019)	12

(continued)

Table 2 (continued)

Themes	Focus	Representative studies	Number of papers
Renegotiation framework (RF)	Contractual adjustment mechanism to minimise the consequences of adverse sudden financial fluctuations and operational costs of an unforeseen event, and enhance the value for money of the project	Xiong and Zhang (2016), Jin et al. (2020), Chen et al. (2022), Feng et al. (2022)	11
Concession period optimisation (CPO)	Determining the length of concession in PPP projects and propose many ways to decide the optimum period, considering the imprecise and uncertain nature of different factors affecting concession period	Ng et al. (2007a), Carbonara et al. (2014a), Zhang et al. (2016b), Guo et al. (2021)	10
Asset pricing/ valuation mechanisms (APV)	Real-option-based valuation approach for the valuation of multistage Bot projects using sequential compound call options	Huang and Pi (2009), Liu et al. (2017)	5

References

Alasad, R., & Motawa, I. (2015). Dynamic demand risk assessment for toll road projects. *Construction Management and Economics, 33*(10), 799–817.

Anand, A., Buhagiar, K., Kozachenko, E., & Parameswar, N. (2022). Exploring the role of knowledge management in contexts of crisis: A synthesis and way forward. *International Journal of Organizational Analysis*. ahead-of-print (ahead-of-print).

Ashuri, B., Kashani, H., Molenaar, K. R., Lee, S., & Lu, J. (2012). Risk-neutral pricing approach for evaluating BOT highway projects with government minimum revenue guarantee options. *Journal of Construction Engineering and Management, 138*(4), 545–557.

Attarzadeh, M., Chua, D. K. H., Beer, M., & Abbott, E. L. S. (2017). Options-based negotiation management of PPP–BOT infrastructure projects. *Construction Management and Economics, 35*(11–12), 676–692.

Bae, D. S., Damnjanoic, I., & Kang, D. H. (2019). PPP renegotiation framework based on equivalent NPV constraint in the case of BOT project: Incheon airport highway, South Korea. *KSCE Journal of Civil Engineering, 23*(4), 1473–1483.

Baxter, D., & Casady, C. B. (2020). A coronavirus (COVID-19) triage framework for (sub)National Public–Private Partnership (PPP) programs. *Sustainability, 12*(13), 5253.

Bayat, M., Khanzadi, M., & Nasirzadeh, F. (2020). Bargaining game model to determine concessionary items in build-operate-transfer contracts. *Journal of Construction Engineering and Management, 146*(2), 04019109.

Burger, P., Tyson, J., Karpowicz, I., & Coelho, M. (2013). Weathering the financial crisis: Public–private partnerships and the government response. In P. De Vries & E. B. Yehoue (Eds.), *The Routledge companion to public-private partnerships* (pp. 325–347). Routledge.

Buyukyoran, F., & Gundes, S. (2018). Optimized real options-based approach for government guarantees in PPP toll road projects. *Construction Management and Economics, 36*(4), 203–216.

Carbonara, N., Costantino, N., & Pellegrino, R. (2014a). Concession period for PPPs: A win–win model for a fair risk sharing. *International Journal of Project Management, 32*(7), 1223–1232.

Carbonara, N., Costantino, N., & Pellegrino, R. (2014b). Revenue guarantee in public-private partnerships: A fair risk allocation model. *Construction Management and Economics, 32*(4), 403–415.

Castelblanco, G., Guevara, J., & Salazar, J. (2022). Remedies to the PPP crisis in the Covid-19 pandemic: Lessons from the 2008 global financial crisis. *Journal of Management in Engineering, 38*(3), 04022017.

Chau, W. K. (1997). The ranking of construction management journals. *Construction Management and Economics, 15*(4), 387–398.

Cheah, C. Y. J., & Liu, J. (2006). Valuing governmental support in infrastructure projects as real options using Monte Carlo simulation. *Construction Management and Economics, 24*(5), 545–554.

Chelliah, V., Thounaojam, N., Devkar, G., & Laishram, B. (2021). Evaluation of systematic literature reviews in built environment research: What are we doing and how can we improve? In E. Manu & J. Akotia (Eds.), *Secondary research methods in the built environment*. Routledge.

Chen, C., & Messner, J. I. (2005). An investigation of Chinese BOT projects in water supply: A comparative perspective. *Construction Management and Economics, 23*(9), 913–925.

Chen, T. C., Lin, Y. C., & Wang, L. C. (2012). The analysis of BOT strategies based on game theory - case study on Taiwan's high speed railway project. *Journal of Civil Engineering and Management, 18*(5), 662–674.

Chen, Q., Shen, G., Xue, F., & Xia, B. (2018). Real options model of toll-adjustment mechanism in concession contracts of toll road projects. *Journal of Management in Engineering, 34*(1), 04017040.

Chen, C., Lv, L., Wang, Z., & Qiao, R. (2022). Bargaining optimization model for risk renegotiation with fairness concerns in infrastructure PPP projects. *Engineering, Construction and Architectural Management*. ahead-of-print (ahead-of-print).

Cruz, C. O., & Marques, R. C. (2013). Flexible contracts to cope with uncertainty in public-private partnerships. *International Journal of Project Management, 31*(3), 473–483.

Delhi, V. S. K., & Mahalingam, A. (2020). Relating institutions and governance strategies to project outcomes: Study on public-private partnerships in infrastructure projects in India. *Journal of Management in Engineering, 36*(6), 04020076.

Demirel, H. Ç., Leendertse, W., Volker, L., & Hertogh, M. (2017). Flexibility in PPP contracts–dealing with potential change in the pre-contract phase of a construction project. *Construction Management and Economics, 35*(4), 196–206.

Demirel, H. C., Leendertse, W., & Volker, L. (2022). Mechanisms for protecting returns on private investments in public infrastructure projects. *International Journal of Project Management, 40*(3), 155–166.

Devkar, G., Palliyaguru, R., & Oyegoke, A. S. (2020). The effects of institutional frameworks on implementation of PPP projects: A comparative perspective in Australia and India. *International Journal of Construction Management, 20*(6), 720–736.

Dewulf, G., & Garvin, M. J. (2020). Responsive governance in PPP projects to manage uncertainty. *Construction Management and Economics, 38*(4), 383–397.

Etienne, B. Y. (2013). Financial and sovereign debt crises and PPP market structure. In *The Routledge companion to public–private partnerships*. Routledge.

Feng, K., Xiong, W., Wang, S., Wu, C., & Xue, Y. (2017). Optimizing an equity capital structure model for public-private partnership projects involved with public funds. *Journal of Construction Engineering and Management, 143*(9), 04017067.

Feng, X., Cao, J., Wu, G., & Duan, K. (2022). A critical review of studies on renegotiation within the public-private partnerships (PPPs) scheme. *Engineering, Construction and Architectural Management*. ahead-of-print (ahead-of-print).

Gay, L. F., & Sinha, S. K. (2013). Resilience of civil infrastructure systems: Literature review for improved asset management. *International Journal of Critical Infrastructures, 9*(4), 330–350.

Guo, K., Zhang, L., & Wang, T. (2021). Concession period optimisation in complex projects under uncertainty: A public–private partnership perspective. *Construction Management and Economics, 39*(2), 156–172.

Hasan, S., Elwakil, E., & Hegab, M. (2021). Opportunities for infrastructure PPP projects in time of COVID-19 - as a resilience strategy. In *2021 IEEE conference on Technologies for Sustainability (SusTech)* (pp. 1–5).

Hou, W., & Wang, L. (2022). Research on the refinancing capital structure of highway PPP projects based on dynamic capital demand. *Engineering, Construction and Architectural Management, 29*(5), 2047–2072.

Huang, Y. L., & Pi, C. C. (2009). Valuation of multi-stage BOT projects involving dedicated asset investments: A sequential compound option approach. *Construction Management and Economics, 27*(7), 653–666.

Huang, Y. L., & Pi, C. C. (2014). Real-option valuation of build-operate-transfer infrastructure projects under performance bonding. *Journal of Construction Engineering and Management, 140*(5), 04013068.

Jeong, J., Ji, C., Hong, T., & Park, H. S. (2016). Model for evaluating the financial viability of the BOT project for highway service areas in South Korea. *Journal of Management in Engineering, 32*(2), 04015036.

Jie, L. I. (2009). Dynamic contract conditions for built operation transfer (bot) projects in China. *International Journal of Construction Management, 9*(2), 55–64.

Jin, X. H. (2010). Determinants of efficient risk allocation in privately financed public infrastructure projects in Australia. *Journal of Construction Engineering and Management, 136*(2), 138–150.

Jin, X. H., & Doloi, H. (2008). Interpreting risk allocation mechanism in public–private partnership projects: An empirical study in a transaction cost economics perspective. *Construction Management and Economics, 26*(7), 707–721.

Jin, X.-H., & Zhang, G. (2011). Modelling optimal risk allocation in PPP projects using artificial neural networks. *International Journal of Project Management, 29*(5), 591–603.

Jin, H., Liu, S., Liu, C., & Udawatta, N. (2019). Optimizing the concession period of PPP projects for fair allocation of financial risk. *Engineering, Construction and Architectural Management, 26*(10), 2347–2363.

Jin, H., Liu, S., Li, J., & Liu, C. (2020). A game-theoretic approach to developing a concession renegotiation framework for user-pays PPPs. *International Journal of Construction Management, 20*(6), 642–652.

Ke, Y., Wang, S., Chan, A. P., & Cheung, E. (2009). Research trend of public-private partnership in construction journals. *Journal of Construction Engineering and Management, 135*(10), 1076–1086.

Khallaf, R., Naderpajouh, N., & Hastak, M. (2018). Modeling three-party interactional risks in the governance of public-private partnerships. *Journal of Management in Engineering, 34*(6), 04018040.

Kim, S., & Woo, H. (2021). Global fashion retailers' responses to external and internal crises during the COVID-19 pandemic. *Fashion and Textiles, 8*(1), 32.

Kokkaew, N., & Wipulanusat, W. (2014). Completion delay risk management: A dynamic risk insurance approach. *KSCE Journal of Civil Engineering, 18*(6), 1599–1608.

Kumaraswamy, M., Zou, W., & Zhang, J. (2015). Reinforcing relationships for resilience – By embedding end-user 'people' in public–private partnerships. *Civil Engineering and Environmental Systems, 32*(1–2), 119–129.

Liu, J., Gao, R., & Cheah, C. Y. J. (2017). Pricing mechanism of early termination of PPP projects based on real option theory. *Journal of Management in Engineering, 33*(6), 04017035.

Loosemore, M., & Cheung, E. (2015). Implementing systems thinking to manage risk in public private partnership projects. *International Journal of Project Management, 33*(6), 1325–1334.

Lv, J., Ye, G., Liu, W., Shen, L., & Wang, H. (2015). Alternative model for determining the optimal concession period in managing BOT transportation projects. *Journal of Management in Engineering, 31*(4), 04014066.

Ng, S. T., Xie, J., Cheung, Y. K., & Jefferies, M. (2007a). A simulation model for optimizing the concession period of public–private partnerships schemes. *International Journal of Project Management, 25*(8), 791–798.

Nguyen, D. A., & Garvin, M. J. (2019). Life-cycle contract management strategies in US highway public-private partnerships: Public control or concessionaire empowerment? *Journal of Management in Engineering, 35*(4), 04019011.

Nguyen, D. A., Garvin, M. J., & Gonzalez, E. E. (2018). Risk allocation in U.S. public-private partnership highway project contracts. *Journal of Construction Engineering and Management, 144*(5), 04018017.

Nizkorodov, E. (2021). Evaluating risk allocation and project impacts of sustainability-oriented water public–private partnerships in Southern California: A comparative case analysis. *World Development, 140*, 105232.

Ortega, A., De Los Angeles Baeza, M., & Vassallo, J. M. (2016). Contractual PPPs for transport infrastructure in Spain: Lessons from the economic recession. *Transport Reviews, 36*(2), 187–206.

Riggs, R. J., & Hu, S. J. (2013). Disassembly liaison graphs inspired by word clouds. *Procedia CIRP, 7*, 521–526.

Shan, L., Garvin, M. J., & Kumar, R. (2010). Collar options to manage revenue risks in real toll public-private partnership transportation projects. *Construction Management and Economics, 28*(10), 1057–1069.

Sharafi, A., Amalnick, M. S., & Taleizadeh, A. A. (2021). Outcome of financial conflicts in the operation phase of public-private partnership contracts. *Journal of Construction Engineering and Management, 147*(6), 04021047.

Sherratt, F., Sherratt, S., & Ivory, C. (2020). Challenging complacency in construction management research: The case of PPPs. *Construction Management and Economics, 38*(12), 1086–1100.

Song, J., Hu, Y., & Feng, Z. (2018). Factors influencing early termination of PPP projects in China. *Journal of Management in Engineering, 34*(1), 05017008.

Songer, A. D., Diekmann, J., & Pecsok, R. S. (1997). Risk analysis for revenue dependent infrastructure projects. *Construction Management and Economics, 15*(4), 377–382.

Sun, H., Wang, Y., & Meng, J. (2019). A trading and pricing method of expansion options for BOT freeway projects in China. *Engineering, Construction and Architectural Management, 26*(7), 1406–1423.

Swanson, R., & Sakhrani, V. (2020). Appropriating the value of flexibility in PPP megaproject design. *Journal of Management in Engineering, 36*(5), 05020010.

Tariq, S., & Zhang, X. (2021a). Critical analysis of the private sector roles in water PPP failures. *Journal of Construction Engineering and Management, 147*(4), 04021015.

Tariq, S., & Zhang, X. (2021b). Socioeconomic, macroeconomic, and sociopolitical issues in water PPP failures. *Journal of Management in Engineering, 37*(5), 04021047.

Tavakoli, N., & Hosseini Nourzad, S. H. (2020). Win-win pricing method for BOT projects using a simulation-based evolutionary optimization. *Construction Management and Economics, 38*(2), 157–171.

Trangkanont, S., & Charoenngam, C. (2014). Critical failure factors of public-private partnership low-cost housing program in Thailand. *Engineering, Construction and Architectural Management, 21*(4), 421–443.

Vassallo, J. M., Ortega, A., & Baeza, M. D. L. Á. (2012). Impact of the economic recession on toll highway concessions in Spain. *Journal of Management in Engineering, 28*(4), 398–406.

Wang, Y., & Jin, X. (2019). Determine the optimal capital structure of BOT projects using interval numbers with Tianjin Binhai New District Metro Z4 line in China as an example. *Engineering, Construction and Architectural Management, 26*(7), 1348–1366.

Wang, Y., & Tiong, R. L. K. (2022). Public-private partnership contract failure prediction using example-dependent cost-sensitive models. *Journal of Management in Engineering, 38*(1), 04021079.

Xiong, W., & Zhang, X. (2016). The real option value of renegotiation in public–private partnerships. *Journal of Construction Engineering and Management, 142*(8), 04016021.

Zhang, X. (2005). Financial viability analysis and capital structure optimization in privatized public infrastructure projects. *Journal of Construction Engineering and Management, 131*(6), 656–668.

Zhang, X., & Tariq, S. (2020). Failure mechanisms in international water PPP projects: A public sector perspective. *Journal of Construction Engineering and Management, 146*(6), 04020055.

Zhang, S., Chan, A. P. C., Feng, Y., Duan, H., & Ke, Y. (2016a). Critical review on PPP research – A search from the Chinese and International Journals. *International Journal of Project Management, 34*(4), 597–612.

Zhang, X., Bao, H., Wang, H., & Skitmore, M. (2016b). A model for determining the optimal project life span and concession period of BOT projects. *International Journal of Project Management, 34*(3), 523–532.

Zhang, Y.-C., Luo, W.-Z., Shan, M., Pan, D.-W., & Mu, W.-J. (2020). Systematic analysis of PPP research in construction journals: From 2009 to 2019. *Engineering, Construction and Architectural Management, 27*(10), 3309–3339.

Zhang, S., Li, J., Li, Y., & Zhang, X. (2021). Revenue risk allocation mechanism in public-private partnership projects: Swing option approach. *Journal of Construction Engineering and Management, 147*(1), 04020153.

Federal Road Infrastructure PPP in Germany: The Impact of COVID-19 and Lessons Learned

Rahel M. Schomaker, Andreas Knorr, and Alexander Eisenkopf

Introduction

Road infrastructure PPP do not have a long tradition in Germany due to longstanding legal restrictions of private sector involvement. This changed in 2003 when Germany's first road infrastructure PPP project ever – the *Warnowquerung*, a tunnel project near Rostock and integral part of *Bundesstraße* (federal highway) B105 – opened for traffic in September 2003. It was realized according to the so-called *F model* PPP type which is exclusively dedicated to bridge, tunnel, and mountain pass projects. In addition, with the original *A model* PPP and the more recent *V model* PPP, two distinct PPP variants were specifically developed for extensions of existing federal road infrastructures (both motorways and interstate highways).[1]

[1]While road infrastructure PPP were also implemented at lower levels of government, they are essentially confined to ring roads or bypasses around small to medium-sized municipalities. Typically, local construction companies act as concessionaires and are in charge of pre-financing and building these infrastructures. Immediately after completion, ownership is routinely transferred to the respective local or state government, while maintenance services throughout the con-

R. M. Schomaker (✉)
Carinthia University of Applied Sciences, Villach, Austria

WSB University, Dąbrowa Górnicza, Poland

A. Knorr
German University of Administrative Sciences, Speyer, Germany
e-mail: knorr@uni-speyer.de

A. Eisenkopf (✉)
Zeppelin University, Friedrichshafen, Germany
e-mail: alexander.eisenkopf@zu.de

© The Author(s), under exclusive license to Springer Nature Switzerland AG 2023
T. Dolla et al. (eds.), *Revisiting Public-Private Partnerships*,
Contributions to Public Administration and Public Policy,
https://doi.org/10.1007/978-3-031-37015-1_3

This specific area was selected for our country study for two reasons. First, as the EU's largest economy and resulting from its central local within the EU, Germany is also its most important origin, destination and transit country, in particular for the transport of goods by road (and rail). In fact, the country is at the crossroads of most of the continent's major road haulage corridors, i.e. those connecting Northern Europe/Scandinavia with Southern and Southwestern Europe, as well as those linking Central Europe with Western Europe.

Second, transport services, as superior goods, display an income elasticity of demand $\varepsilon > 1$ (the only exception applies to local public transit with $\varepsilon < 1$ as it is substituted for passenger cars and, in agglomerations, bicycles at higher income levels) (Paulley et al., 2004; Fouquet, 2012). This means that demand increases or decreases at a higher rate than the growth rate of GDP and is therefore characterized by a comparatively higher volatility. Accordingly, the economic impact of the pandemic on road infrastructure PPP was particularly harsh compared to other sectors of the German economy where PPP exist. Thus, analysing this case for public–private partnerships (PPP) has become more compelling, also as an integral element of a large-scale reform package to massively improve the resilience of public service delivery to citizens and companies alike.[2]

This section proceeds as follows: After a brief overview of the COVID-19 situation in Germany and the governmental responses to the threat, we will first delineate the general framework for PPP in Germany. We will then analyse and discuss the specifics of road infrastructure PPP and their variants, which fall in the exclusive legislative and administrative competence of the Federal government. Next we will address the impact of COVID-19 on the economic viability of the respective PPP variants regarding the implications in theory and practice before our analysis will conclude with a wrap-up of the lesson learned.

COVID-19 in Germany

Home to a population of 82 million and a high-income country and ranked at an eminent sixth position in the United Nations' Human Development Index (United Nations, 2020), Germany is not among the worst affected countries, either in its

tract period remain the responsibility of the construction firm. After the ownership transfer, the government owner repays, in monthly instalments, the loan plus interest and the maintenance fee to the construction company. Due to the lack of public data on their usage, the lack of an operations component in the contracts, the small number and scale of these projects and the different legal framework for state and municipal road infrastructure planning and funding, we will not discuss them further in this chapter.

[2] Being beyond the scope of this article and hence not to be further discussed here, this reform package should include a fundamental redesign of the hitherto existing multilevel system of legal and political governance of Germany to streamline the often utterly complex and frequently dysfunctional political decision-making process as well as administrative procedures within and among Germany's sixteen states (*Länder*). It should also include the comprehensive digitization of administrative processes, both internally and at all government–citizen interfaces.

geographic or its socioeconomic peer group. This notwithstanding, the country was heavily burdened by the pandemic. A recent study by the *German Economic Institute* (Institut der deutschen Wirtschaft, 2022) estimated the accumulated loss of value added since the outbreak of COVID-19 until the end of 2021 at €350bn compared to a non-pandemic scenario based on an extrapolation of previous growth trends. Private consumption was down €270bn. Ongoing supply chain disruptions continue to stymie the economic recovery as vital inputs for key industries, in particular car manufacturers, remain either in short supply or are subject to massive delays in delivery (Bardt & Grömling, 2021).

Part of the ongoing economic contraction can be ascribed to the comprehensive public health measures which were adopted by Germany's Federal government in cooperation with the government of the 16 German states (*Länder*) and frequently modified at different stages of the pandemic with much of the single measure being carried out at the local level (Schomaker & Bauer, 2020a). The measures taken were not too dissimilar from most other EU member states or the G20 countries and included mask mandates, stay-at-home restrictions, repeated lockdowns of shops, hotels, restaurants, bars, cultural, and educational facilities for several months on end, temporary border closures for leisure travel and strict self-isolation requirements for positively tested persons. However, and remarkably so for swimming against the current global trend (with the exception of Austria and Italy) of relaxing or phasing out the above-mentioned measures, Germany had been continuously retightening them throughout the winter season. As reflected in the authoritative Oxford COVID-19 Government Response Tracker,[3] at the time of writing, Germany had assumed a global pole position in terms of stringency.[4]

As for the public health impact of the COVID-19 pandemic, the number of new cases per week (i.e. the number of new positive tests) per one million inhabitants displays a clear pattern of seasonality, but no clear-cut correlations exist between the number of new cases, the number of new deaths, and the stringency of the government response measures, or the number of new cases and the progress of the vaccination campaign (Fig. 1).[5]

[3] The stringency index reflects, in nine components, restrictions of the lockdown type such as, inter alia, school closures, the cancellation of public gatherings and public event, and domestic and international travel bans. For detailed information on the index, current numbers and the underlying methodology see Petherick et al. (2021) and University of Oxford (2022).

[4] This is partly due to the substantial strengthening of measures directed at the unvaccinated part of the population which remains stuck at around 28%. In terms of the stringency of restrictions concerning international travel, to date the most restrictive measures by a wide margin were adopted by Asian countries such as China, Hongkong, and Japan that have effectively shut their borders for international visitors. For example, Hongkong International Airport's passenger numbers dropped from 71.5 million in 2019 to a mere 1.35 million in 2021, which is roughly the figure handled in 1967 (Bloomberg, 2022).

[5] In Germany, the first vaccinations were applied in late December 2020 to the age bracket of those of 80 years or older. At the end of January 2022, the vaccination rate had reached 72.9% ("basic immunization"), while 48.3% of the population had already received a third shot ("booster shot") (Robert-Koch-Institut, 2022).

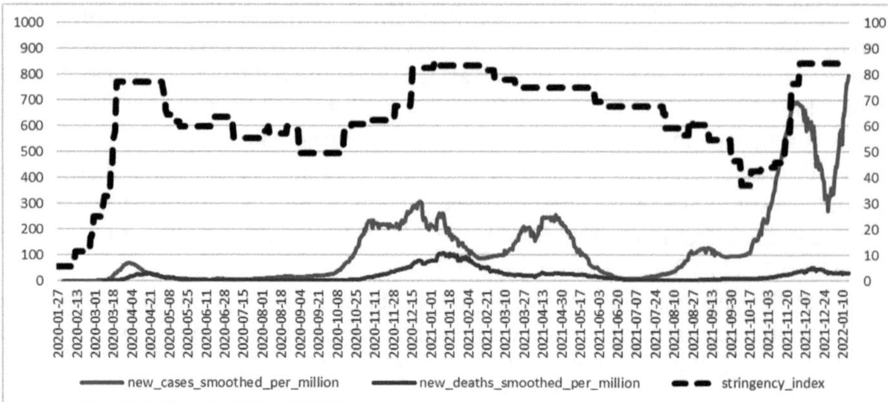

Source: Masser (2022), data from Our World in Data (2022)

Fig. 1 New daily cases, new daily deaths, and the stringency of governmental anti-COVID-19 measures. (Source: Masser (2022), data from Our World in Data (2022))

Nonetheless, given the high standards of the overall health system in Germany and particularly with a view on the quality of – public and private – hospitals as well as the high number of intensive care units, the German health system was able to manage the increased demand due to the pandemic, even if the health administration that was in duty to register and track infections was overburdened in some regional entities.

Moreover, policy measures were implemented to mitigate the social and economic effects of the crisis, including immediate emergency aid for social infrastructure and short-term financial support for enterprises, start-up entrepreneurs, and employees. In detail, short-time compensation was provided, direct financial transfers, and tax deferrals were provided. In addition, long-term measures such as fiscal rescue packages, investment in crucial social infrastructures, and plans for strengthening national investment in public health, including the production of protective equipment or vaccines and medicine, were induced not only on the national level but also on the EU level (Schomaker & Bauer, 2020a).[6]

[6] Being beyond the scope of this article and hence not to be further discussed here, this reform package should include a fundamental redesign of the hitherto existing multilevel system of legal and political governance of Germany to streamline the often utterly complex and frequently dysfunctional political decision-making process as well as administrative procedures within and among Germany's 16 states (*Länder*). It should also include the comprehensive digitization of administrative processes, both internally and at all government–citizen interfaces.

Road Infrastructure Provision in Germany and the Role of PPP

Backgrounder

Based on the model of a 'social market economy', the Federal Republic of Germany does not only boast a comprehensive welfare state. Also, infrastructure provision was traditionally considered to be a key function of government, with tax revenues – as opposed to user charges – the principal source of funding. However, this historical arrangement no longer holds, for two reasons. First, Germany has experienced a steady decline in the modernity level of key transport infrastructures, in particular roads and bridges, over at least the last two decades before 2016, as net investment was consistently lower than depreciations (Bundesministerium für Verkehr und digitale Infrastruktur, 2021, p. 42f.). This trend was reversed only recently due to the extra revenues generated by the truck toll as these are partly earmarked by law for road infrastructure funding, and the additional investment from PPP concessionaires. Second, a as founding member of the EU, Germany's legal and regulatory framework for infrastructure funding and provision is also bound by the respective provisions in the EU's *Acquis communautaire*, i.e. EU law.

Germany is no unitary state but a highly decentralized political entity. In short, the country is organized into three layers of government: the federal level, the 16 states (*Länder*), and the 12,312 local municipalities, 2077 of which are cities. Only in a few fields have policy competences been exclusively assigned to a specific branch of government. By contrast, it is estimated that around 70% of all legislation must be jointly passed by the *Bundestag* – the German parliament – and the *Bundesrat* (the Federal Council which represents the *Länder*); transport infrastructure policy is a case in point (Institut für Mobilitätsforschung, 2007).

According to article 90 (1) of the German Constitution, the Federal government must remain the only legal owner of all Federal trunk roads, i.e. of motorways (*Autobahnen*) and federal highways (*Bundesstraßen*). However, their administration – including the competence for planning and completion – rests with the respective state governments by proxy. Moreover, the Länder exert substantial influence during the entire planning process concerning Federal road projects (and any other Federal transport infrastructures as well). Formally, the responsibility for transport infrastructure planning at the Federal level resides with the *Bundesministerium für Digitales und Verkehr* (*BMDV*; Federal Ministry of Transport and Digital Infrastructure). The *Autobahn GmbH des Bundes*, a law entity in the form of a limited liability company, is responsible for the administration of motorways and can decide, given the Federal government's consent, to apply PPP structures for motorway projects (Bonhage & Roberts, 2021).

Since the 1970s, the *Bundesverkehrswegeplan* (Federal Transport Infrastructure Plan) has provided a ranking of all Federal transport infrastructure projects, based on a thorough cost-benefit analysis (complemented by an environmental impact assessment and an assessment of potential regional development effects); it has been updated at irregular intervals and on average less than once in a decade. As a rule of thumb, only projects with an expected benefit-cost ratio greater than three will be realized. In addition, until very recently, all road infrastructure projects in Germany have been financed out of general and, though to a much lesser degree, transport-specific tax revenues (i.e. the vehicle tax and the gasoline tax). However, the *Fernstraßenbauprivatfinanzierungsgesetz* – the Private Financing of Highway Construction Act – of 1994 created the legal prerequisites for levying tolls for road infrastructure use under certain circumstances. In its wake, starting 1 January 2005, an electronic toll system for all trucks with a gross vehicle weight over 7.5 tons was introduced which travel on any *Autobahn* or *Bundesstraße*. Furthermore, the law also created the legal prerequisites for the toll-based *F model* PPP variant.

The Politics and Laws Behind Road Infrastructure PPP in Germany

While PPP are a rather common investment model in most industrialized countries, especially in the Anglo-Saxon world, Germany remains a clear 'latecomer' and 'underperformer' by international standards (Deutsches Institut für Urbanistik, 2005); a report by the *European Courts of Auditors* (2018, p. 14) revealed that Germany ranks only fourth in the EU behind France, Spain, and Portugal; former EU member Great Britain remains, by a very wide margin, the leader in PPP realization in Europe. According to the report, only 14 large-scale PPP projects have so far been implemented in Germany, most of them in federal road infrastructure – compared to over one thousand in the UK – while their combined value was estimated at around 17 billion Euro (UK: > €160 bn).[7] This is despite the early establishment of a national PPP unit in 2005, at the federal level, the *ÖPP Deutschland AG* (PPP Germany Corp.), a state-owned enterprise. In 2017, after massive criticism of the strong involvement of private consultancies and construction companies as potential beneficiaries of PPP (taz, 2012), it was converted into the *PD – Berater der öffentlichen Hand GmbH* (Partnership Germany – Consultant of the Public Sector Ltd). While the former was only active as a consultancy in PPP projects, the purpose of the latter was substantially extended at the instigation of the Federal government. Since 2017, it has offered consulting services exclusively to public clients at all levels of government for the planning and implementing of PPP projects. Additionally, and below the federal level, almost every German state has established public 'PPP task force' or 'PPP unit' which are actively involved in the conception, implementation, and management of state-level PPP, e.g. via consultancy in the tendering process or during the implementation stage (Schomaker & Bauer, 2020).

[7] According to a central database, a total of 239 PPP is currently in operation in Germany now, most of which are small-scale and implemented at the municipal levels, e.g. public schools, local swimming pools, and administration buildings which are not considered in EU statistics. A further 27 PPP are currently in the tendering process (https://www.ppp-projektdatenbank.de/index.php?id=9)

Politically, four principal considerations stood behind the attempt to promote private sector participation in road infrastructure funding and provision in Germany (Beckers et al., 2006):

- The unabated rise of road haulage demand, combined with increasing shortages of available public funding, especially due to the enormous fiscal burden of German reunification in 1990 (and later the financial crisis from 2008), with the resulting increase in infrastructure bottlenecks and/or the continuous degradation of road quality standards.
- The wish to overcome a fundamental flaw in the traditional tax-based provision of road infrastructure: the lack of market-based scarcity signals to guide investment decisions.
- The expected increase in efficiency due to private sector involvement.
- The ideologically motivated will to reduce the size and scope of the public sector, e.g. in the course of the introduction of the 'new public management' paradigm.

So far, however, the economic benefits of PPP expected ex ante (Grimsey & Lewis, 2004; Picot & Kamp, 2007) have rarely ever materialized in a real-world setting in Germany. This is particularly true for road transport infrastructure PPP as the *German Court of Auditors* has found in several reports (Bundesrechnungshof, 2009, 2013). This mismatch is essentially owed to the (negligent or intentional) omission of the frequently greater transactions costs of PPP compared to the conventional procurement method and/or the welfare losses which have resulted from opportunistic behaviour on both sides (Schomaker & Bauer, 2020; Ryan & Menzes, 2015; Mühlenkamp, 2016).

PPP in Practice: The Case of Federal Road Infrastructures

Road infrastructure PPP in Germany come in three variants, which will be discussed separately below. Each serves a specific purpose, so private investors cannot choose among them. In addition, legal approval procedures and funding mechanism differ.

F Model PPP

F model PPP were designed to implement PPP in special infrastructures, i.e. bridges, tunnels, and mountain passes. Toll-based and essentially a variant of a standard BOT-model, they boast the following features (Gawel, 2005, p. 175):

- Eligible projects are pre-selected in unison by the Federal government (represented by the *Verkehrsinfrastrukturfinanzierungsgesellschaft* (Transport Infrastructure Financing Agency)) and the respective state government according to a feasibility study. Here, the business case of every proposed *F model* is

appraised beforehand by comparing the estimated project costs with the assumed revenue streams as a function of different toll levels and structures. In case of a positive assessment, its result also provides the basis for the calculation of the federal knock-on financing of up to 20% of the construction costs and the future toll level.
- A concession may be granted either during or after the formal planning approval procedure. The former is based on a 'beauty contest' (the so-called 'ideas competition') which offers potential concessionaire opportunity to influence the final technical design of the project. Under option two – the so-called conventional planning approach – the concession is not awarded until after the approval procedure's conclusion, depriving the concessionaire of any (legal) influence over the technical aspects of the project.
- Formally, the PPP contract is signed between the private party and the respective regional government (or the local authority). It obliges the designated concessionaire to build or expand the road infrastructure in question, to maintain and operate it over a period of up to 30 years, and to transfer it back to the public sector in a pre-defined condition afterwards.
- The administration of *F model* PPP is the responsibility of the *Länder* government or the municipality where it is located (subject to a formal managerial prerogative of the Federal government).
- Most importantly, the toll – which accrues directly to the concessionaire – must be approved beforehand by the respective *Länder* government. This means that under an *F model* PPP, the traffic volume risk is borne by the concessionaire alone.

The original plan of the Federal Ministry of Transport was to realize up to 32 F model PPP; by 2005, the list had shrunk to a mere ten, of which eventually only two – both of them tunnels – were realized (Gawel, 2005): *Warnowquerung* (*Warnow* river crossing) near *Rostock* opened in September 2003 and *Herrentunnel* – a *Trave* river crossing – in *Lübeck* in August 2005. Of the other proposed *F model* PPP from the shortlist, one – *Strelasundquerung*, a 4 km suspension bridge to link the island of *Rügen*, one of Germany's most popular seaside resorts on the *Baltic Sea*, with the mainland – failed to attract any interest from the private sector.[8] Finally, a fourth *F model* project, *Hochmoselquerung* – a steel box beam bridge across the *Moselle* river near the cities *Bernkastel* and *Wittlich* – was put on hold during the prequalification stages when a local court declared the planning approval procedure null and void on environmental law grounds. Meanwhile, both projects were conventionally realized.

From the official opening in 2003 until today, *Warnowquerung's* commercial performance was way below the French–Australian–German concessionaires'

[8] The state government of *Mecklenburg-Western Pomerania* had demanded that *Rügendamm* – the old link between the mainland and the island of *Rügen* – should remain open for traffic at no charge after the completion of the new (parallel) tolled suspension bridge. Unsurprisingly, all potential private investors decided to opt out of the bidding process under these circumstances.

expectations as traffic figures continue to trail the forecast demand of 40,000 daily crossings substantially. The consortium's estimate was primarily based on the daily transit traffic of 60,000 vehicles through Rostock for which the tunnel would provide a short-cut of 15 km (Brantsch, 2005, p. 15). They had calculated that to recoup their investment during the concession period (based on the approved toll structure at that time), on average 20,000 cars would have to use the tunnel daily (Hamburger Abendblatt, 2003, p. 6.). Even today, the average figure of daily usage is only 17,000 cars (Lübeck + Ostholstein Wochenspiegel, 2022). The most important forecasting error was the far too optimistic demand estimate with respect to the number of commercial goods trucks that would use the tunnel (Hamburger Abendblatt, 2004). Confronted with the consortium's threat of bankruptcy, the city of *Rostock* agreed to renegotiate the concession. In 2006, it was prolonged from the original 30–50 years until 2053, when the tunnel will be transferred to the Federal government (Verkehrsinfrastrukturfinanzierungsgesellschaft mbh, 2017a). In addition, the consortium secured a rebalanced and more diversified toll structure to boost revenues. The commercial problems of the *Warnowquerung* F model PPP did not come unexpected, however, as the tunnel was not classified as a priority project in the Bundesverkehrswegeplan due to an insufficient expected benefit-cost ratio of only 2.2, which made it ineligible for conventional realization (Beckers, 2005, p. 161).

Herrentunnel in the city of *Lübeck* was the designated replacement of a dilapidated bascule bridge which formed an integral part of federal highways *B75* and *B10*; it was used by 38,000 vehicles per day on average before the tunnel opened for traffic in August 2005. The concessionaire, an All-German consortium, was also selected by means of an 'ideas competition'. Commercially, *Herrentunnel* suffered a similar shortfall of actual usage compared to initial estimates as *Warnowquerung*. During the first 3 years of operation, no more 20,000 vehicles were counted on average on a daily basis (Schleswig-Holsteinischer Zeitungsverlag, 2009). By 2016, daily ridership figures had plummeted to less than 17,000 since an unexpectedly high number of motorists continue to prefer a toll-free detour of 5 km to the speedier but charged-for passage via the tunnel (Schleswig-Holsteinischer Zeitungsverlag, 2016). In an attempt to improve revenues and earnings, the concessionaires were repeatedly allowed to raise the toll six times so far. Moreover, during renegotiations of the concession, the consortium was able to extract from the city of Lübeck the option of a 10-year extension until 2045 in case the average daily numbers of vehicle between 2015 and 2025 would be less than 22,000 (Schleswig-Holsteiner Zeitungsverlag, 2019).

A Model PPP and *V Model* PPP

As was briefly discussed above, the *A model* PPP variant was developed to extend typically from four to six lanes and/or to maintain heavily travelled congested sections of select *Autobahnen* (motorways). Originally designed as a pilot scheme for a total of four PPP projects which were announced from 2005, it was replaced in 2009 by *V model* PPP. The transition reflected the commercial fallout in the wake of the global financial and economic crisis which had led to a tangible, though temporary traffic reduction which, in turn, put substantial stress on the balance sheets of some *A model* concessionaires. Critically redesigned over the *A model* in terms of risk-sharing, the *V model* is currently the only PPP model – and hence the only alternative to the conventional approach – for federal road infrastructure extension projects.

Based on a standard BOT model, *A model* PPP displayed the following characteristics:

- Initially, the Federal government assessed whether an *Autobahn* extension project might be fit for *A Model* implementation.
- Next, a private concessionaire was selected through a process of collective bidding.
- The concession period was set at 30 years.
- The concessionaire was not permitted to levy road users a toll. Instead, the concessionaire would receive a fixed percentage of the toll revenues which had been charged to trucks using the concessionaire's section of the *Autobahn*. So, just as in *F model* PPP, the concessionaire must bear the truck traffic volume risk in full (while passenger and freight vehicles are subject to the toll in *F model* PPP which also accrues exclusively to the concessionaire).
- In some cases, the Federal government provided limited initial public funding.

The *A model* was implemented in four pilot projects ('first batch PPP') with a total construction value of €1.1bn over 230 km (Bundesministerium für Digitales und Verkehr, 2013, where detailed data sheets for each project are available):

- *Autobahn A8*, section *Augsburg – Munich* (52 km of operation and maintenance, of which 37 km of extension).
- *Autobahn A4*, section from the state border of *Hessen* and *Thuringia – Gotha* (44 km of operation and maintenance, of which 25 km of extension).
- *Autobahn A5*, section *Malsch – Offenburg* (72 km of extension, of which 60 km of operation and maintenance).
- *Autobahn A1*, section *Bremen– Hamburg* (60 km of operation and maintenance, of which 41 km of extension).

At least two of the four pilot projects have turned out to be substantial commercial failures: As was repeatedly leaked to the press, the *Autobahn A1*'s concessionaires sought to renegotiate their concession from 2009 (in vain), a moratorium with their private investors in 2012 and, in the same year, €124 m in compensation from the Federal government, citing unexpectedly low traffic volumes after the 2008 global financial and economic crisis (Telepolis, 2017). Eventually, in 2018, the consortium sued the Federal government for €778 m in compensation, arguing that the basis of the transaction had ceased to exist due to the lower than anticipated traffic volume. However, the court and the appeals courts dismissed the case (Legal Tribune Online, 2019). Also, the concessionaire of the *Autobahn A8 A model* PPP took legal action in a minor case unrelated to traffic volume risk against the Federal government in September 2017 after a failed mediation attempt. It sought compensation for alleged 'extra' costs of €35 m (down from a €65 m claim during the mediation), arguing that the respective works were not covered by the concession agreement. In early 2018, the court of first instance dismissed the case as unfounded. No appeal was lodged (JUVE, 2018).

Economically, there are two competing explanations for the financial difficulties experienced, or claimed, by the two aforementioned *A model* concessionaires. First, they may reflect 'winner's curse', resulting from an overly optimistic ex ante assessment of the respective business case which proved unsustainable during the unexpected economic downturn following the 2008 global financial and economic crisis. Alternatively, the combination of a 30-year concession and specific, irreversible investment in road infrastructure may have incentivized concessionaires to attempt a hold-up scenario. Interestingly, the Federal government's strong signalling (by accepting the legal challenge) that it would not consent to any ex post renegotiations, let alone bailouts, is in striking contrast to the willingness of local governments to surrender to the ex post request of two *F model* concessionaires. As Table 1 below shows, the drop of traffic volumes – measured in recorded mileage – after the beginning of the economic crisis of 2008, was rather short-lived; by 2010, traffic, for the average of all German (truck and *F model* PPP) toll roads, had almost rebounded to pre-crisis level Bundesamt für Güterverkehr (2011), Verkehrsinfrastrukturinanzierungsgesellschaft mbh VIFG (2017b). The short duration of reduced traffic volumes is likely to have convinced the Federal government to demonstrate a 'no deal' attitude towards concessionaires so as to not to establish a precedent vis-à-vis *A model* concessionaires for future economic downturns with the corresponding decline of traffic (and toll) volumes.

This notwithstanding, in order to preserve the financial attractiveness to concessionaires of additional federal road infrastructure PPP, the Federal government reacted to the A model concessionaires' (real or pretended) concerns by fundamentally altering key rules of the PPP game when, in 2009, a second batch of PPP

Table 1 Percentage mileage change over 2008, all German toll roads

Month	2009 vs 2008	2010 vs 2008
January	−18.51%	−3.89%
February	−18.56%	1.36%
March	−5.83%	10.25%
April	−19.95%	5.32%
May	−14.83%	6.61%
June	−14.03%	10.82%
July	−12.24%	3.19%
August	−10.01%	9.54%
September	−9.93%	5.03%
October	−9.59%	2.71%
November	−3.63%	8.67%
December	−0.39%	7.07%

Source: Bundesamt für Güterverkehr (2022)

projects covering another 450 km was launched. With one exception,[9] all new projects were not based on the original, but on a substantially revised *A model*: the so-called *V model* (Bundesministerium für Digitales und Verkehr, 2016, where detailed data sheets for each project are available):

- *Autobahn A8*, section *Ulm/Elchingen – Augsburg West* (58 km of operation and maintenance, of which 41 km of extension).
- *Autobahn A9*, section from the state border of *Bavaria* and *Thuringia – Lederhose* (44 km of operation and maintenance, 25 km of extension).
- *Autobahn A7*, section from the state border of *Hamburg* and *Schleswig-Holstein – Bordesholm* (65 km of extension, of which 59.8 km of operation and maintenance).
- *Autobahn A94*, section *Forstinning – Marktl* (71 km of operation and maintenance, of which 41 km of new construction).

Two more *V model* PPP projects were close to completion at the time of writing: *Autobahn A6* section *Wiesloch/Rauenberg – Weinsberg* (47.2 km) is scheduled to be completed by June 2022, while *Autobahn A7* section *Göttingen – Bockenem* (60 km) will be fully operational from March 2022. Finally, another three *V model* PPP are undergoing the planning and approval stages.[10]

Essentially, in stark contrast to *F model* PPP and *A model* PPP, *V model PPP* completely reverse the allocation of traffic volume risk which is now exclusively borne by the Federal government. The concessionaires obtain a so-called availability remuneration, which is calculated on the basis of the quality and accessibility of the specific *Autobahn* stretch from a road user perspective; a bonus–malus component was added to reward or punish any deviation from the pre-agreed availability indicators.

Eventually, in April 2015, the Federal Ministry of Transport announced a "new generation" of PPP projects, which, when completed, will cover around 670 km. For the first time, in addition to *Autobahnen*, stretches of federal highways (*Bundesstraßen*) are also included. Moreover, concessionaires are permitted to attract capital from institutional private investors such as pension funds and insurance companies (Bundesministerium für Digitales und Verkehr, 2017). Except for three *Autobahn* projects, where construction has begun,[11] seven additional "new generation" *V model* PPP are still in early stages of the planning and approval

[9] *Autobahn A8*, section *Ulm/Elchingen – Augsburg West* is an *A model* PPP with a slightly higher share of truck toll revenues guaranteed to the concessionaire.

[10] *Autobahn A1/Autobahn A30*, sections *Münster/Nord – Lotte/Osnabrück – AS Rheine* (91 km, of which 37 km of extension); *Autobahn A61*, section from the state border of *Rhineland-Palatinate* and *Baden Württemberg – Frankenthal* (57 km, of which 31 km of extension); *Autobahn A44*, section *Diemelstadt – Kassel-Süd* (routing not yet fully defined).

[11] The final deals for two of the "new generation" PPP were closed shortly after the outbreak of the COVID-19 pandemic. *Autobahn A3* (Biebelried – Fürth/Erlangen), to be completed by 2025, comprises 76 km of operation and maintenance, including 71 km of a four to six-lane extension. With a construction volume of €1.5bn, it is the largest German PPP project in the transport sector to date. *Autobahn A49* (Ohmtal – Fritzlar), also due for completion in 2025, comprises 62 km of operation and maintenance, including 31 km of new construction (section Schwalmstadt – Ohmtal) (VIFG, 2020).

process. Investment costs are currently being projected at around seven billion Euros. If implemented as designed, private investors will play a substantially larger role in project funding and project management. While this may be economically beneficial in terms of cost savings with respect to project management, comparatively higher funding costs of the private sector will likely remain a potential downside.

Analysis

While two of the four pilot projects of the *A model* have demonstrated to be a commercial failure, and *F model* projects were not realized anymore within the last years, this is rooted in a lack of private interest or their commercial implications, not the COVID-19 pandemic. All *V model* PPP projects have so far proven their commercial viability due to the full transfer of any traffic volume risk to the Federal government. This judgement holds also at the time of writing, the beginning of 2022, after the COVID-19 pandemic has been ongoing for 2 years. For any outsider to the behind-the-scenes discussions and negotiations, it must remain a matter of speculation by how much the resulting guarantee of a steady stream of revenues has increased the attractiveness of federal road infrastructure PPP for private investors.

What is known, however, is that even during the ongoing COVID-19 crisis, during whose early months road traffic volumes – measured in recorded mileage – declined massively (Table 2), only to rebound from mid-2021, no V model PPP concessionaire reported financial dire straits of any kind.

What is more, the planning and approval procedure of the outstanding "new generation" PPP projects remain fully on track, even if there were single reports that the talks took somewhat longer than in normal times due to the absence of face-to-face meetings. So far, no single case of time- or cost-overruns due to the COVID-19 pandemic has been reported, either officially or unofficially.

This is even more surprising against the backdrop of the general vulnerability, *in principle*, of the PPP concept in times of deep economic crises when unanticipated commercial risks for which no contractual arrangement was made beforehand hit, and as in other European countries, PPP were severely affected (EIB, 2021). Consequently, the European Union provided some additional flexibility to the affected administrations by assuring that an increased financial burden on the public administration due to support for the private partner does not violate the 'Maastricht criteria'. Nonetheless, this instrument was hardly used in Germany, also adjustments of the overall public support for PPP are missing.

Table 2 Percentage mileage change over 2019, all German toll roads

Month	2020 vs 2019	2021 vs 2019
January	−1.71%	−7.54%
February	−0.01%	−2.54%
March	0.63%	11.12%
April	−13.68%	16.84%
May	−14.33%	10.75%
June	2.99%	11.03%
July	−2.83%	−0.07%
August	−3.87%	4.37%
September	4.04%	0.07%
October	0.90%	−2.47%
November	3.21%	2.92%
December	11.64%	2.71%

Source: Bundesamt für Güterverkehr (2022)

Discussion

The main characteristics of the PPP variants which were launched in Germany over the last 30 years for federal road infrastructure PPP are summarized in Table 3 below.

Germany's road infrastructure PPP were not significantly harmed by the economic impact of COVID-19. Moreover, there is very little evidence that PPP in other sectors were severely affected, neither via delays in financial closure or project implementation, nor by complaints or legal proceedings emerging from the exceptional situation. In particular, regarding road infrastructure, this surely does not come out of the blue, but is to some extent a result of a continuous learning process since they were first introduced. The transition from the original *A model* to the *V model* – which effectively relieved concessionaires from any financial risk due to unexpected revenue volatility – is a case in point.

The authors interpret this transition as a lesson learned by the Federal government from the 2008 economic and financial crisis which exposed the weakness, in principle, of the original risk-sharing arrangements in *A model* PPP – although, compared to the COVID-19 ongoing situation, the dimension and duration of the decline in traffic volume and revenues were potentially much less perilous to the concessionaires' economic survival; interestingly, and for reasons unbeknownst to the authors, the Federal government did not explicitly offer *A model* concessionaires the option to 'update' their concessions accordingly or any financial compensation for their evident traffic volume risk. However, from the established fact that a government's principal advantage as a party to any PPP is its ability to obtain funding from the capital markets at lower costs than any of its private sector partners due to its (usually) superior rating, it follows that *V model* PPP offer no meaningful economic gains over the conventional procurement alternative that they replaced.

Table 3 Key features of PPP variants in federal road infrastructures

Characteristic/PPP variant	F model	A model	V model
Launch year	1994	2005	2009 and 2015 ('new generation' projects)
Eligible road infrastructures	Bridges, tunnels, mountain passes, multilane federal interstate highways	Federal motorways	Federal motorways, federal interstate highways ('new generation' projects)
Concessionaires' tasks	Construction (incl. planning), operation, maintenance, co-funding	Road expansion (incl. planning), operation, maintenance, co-funding	Road expansion (incl. planning), operation, maintenance, co-funding
Concessionaires' revenues	Toll (regulated by local authorities)	Percentage share of truck toll levied on respective road section	CPI-based availability payments (paid by Federal government), incl. bonus–malus provisions
Allocation of traffic volume risk	Concessionaire	Concessionaire	Federal government
Standard contract duration	30 years	30 years	20–30 years
Number of projects	2	4	9 + 10 'new generation' projects

Source: Own representation

Finally, as regards the *F model*, as the first variant to be rolled out for road infrastructure PPP in Germany, the authors are inclined towards a similarly ambivalent overall assessment. While it is obvious that the novelty of a toll-based infrastructure was met with some psychological resistance from potential users – which may explain part of the initial financial troubles of the concessionaires, if the winner's curse hypothesis holds. However, concessionaires were successful in securing meaningful extensions of their concessions (or an option therefor) in the aftermath of the 2008 crisis. As a result, they also were equipped with a safety net similar to, though arguably less potent, than the *V model* concessionaires when COVID-19 struck. Hence, as for the *F model*'s aptitude as an alternative to a convention procurement solution, our conclusions are no different to the *V model*, however.

Key Inferences for Theory and Practice

The economic fallout from pandemic has demonstrated, in a historically unprecedented manner, the necessity to invest into the resilience of PPP. Not only is it the rigour to develop new approaches to contractual flexibility, especially with respect to risk-sharing arrangements in the occurrence of force majeure or even 'black swan' events. However, this is running counter to the traditional argument that long-term contracts should provide for 'stable' arrangements. This means that all contracts of all PPP projects, which may be subject to out of the ordinary volatility of key performance variables and risk, ought to include an emergency clause to clarify beforehand how unforeseen, and unforeseeable, exogenous shocks and their impact on the PPP will be dealt with.

Cleary, this also means that both (prospective) partners also need to develop an enlightened mindset: 'Where PPPs are attempting to solve "wicked problems," their success criteria cannot sensibly be restricted to the efficiency with which they produce their out-puts or even how well each partner is able to improve its performance against its own objectives – although both of these remain important. It is essential that these partnerships are prepared to take responsibility for achieving improvements in those "wicked problems" which gave rise to their formation' (Bovaird, 2004, p. 209). Thus, education and trainings for public servants may in future include specific modules for PPP. Moreover, the existing PPP units in Germany could play a crucial role in helping to prepare German administrative units on all federal levels for the specific challenges related to PPP in the time of crisis, implying a respective capacity of the PPP units for this additional task.

Furthermore, the findings as discussed provide leeway for further research on how the public administration, in particular in a federal multilevel system, can strengthen knowledge management and information exchange between single entities and stakeholders, and the role of PPP units as potential gatekeeper within this system. Moreover, as in the course of the COVID-19 pandemic, the case for public–private partnerships (PPP) has become more compelling, e.g. in the health sector, in social services, but also, e.g. the insurance sector, a further analysis of the resilience of different types of PPP against the backdrop of crises of different kind may be insightful. This should be done carefully considering the respective risk distribution in single PPP models, estimating scenarios – e.g. using Monte Carlo simulation models – for different forms of economic constrictions.

Conclusion

While the ongoing COVID-19 pandemic demonstrates the vulnerability of the PPP concept in times of deep economic crises, when financial resources are at stake and unanticipated commercial risks for which no contractual arrangement was made beforehand occur, the impact on the different forms of PPP in the German road infrastructure was not as strong as expected. Due to preparedness and learning effects from former crises, PPP models were already adjusted. Also other PPP sectors were not significantly affected, so that large-scale governance adjustments or policy responses were not necessary. Thus, even if the German PPP environment was not substantially affected by the COVID-19 pandemic, it is unclear in how far the adaptations made beforehand that now partly realize may influence the attractiveness of PPP for the public sector in the future.

Being particular complex in a federal system, learning from crises is somewhat related to a necessary precondition for successful PPPs,, increased openness - this just started in Germany,as in 2020 the Federal Ministry of Transport and Digital Infrastructure for the first time published ongoing PPP contracts related to the construction of federal motorways (Bonhage & Roberts, 2021).

References

Bardt, H., & Grömling, M. (2021). Anhaltende Produktionslücken durch Vorleistungsengpässe. *Wirtschaftsdienst, 102*(2) https://www.wirtschaftsdienst.eu/inhalt/jahr/2022/heft/2/beitrag/anhaltende-produktionsluecken-durch-vorleistungsengpaesse.html. Last accessed 28 Jan 2022.

Beckers, T. (2005). Die Realisierung von Projekten nach dem PPP-Ansatz bei Bundesfernstraßen. Ökonomische Grundlagen und eine Analyse des F Modells, des A Models sowie des Funktionsbauvertrags. Ph.D. thesis, Technical University of Berlin. https://depositonce.tu-berlin.de/handle/11303/1548. Last accessed 28 Jan 2022.

Beckers, T., Hirschhausen, C.v., & Plaat, J. P. (2006). Reformbedarf bei den Bundesfernstraßen und das Potential des PPP-Ansatzes, Technical University Berlin. Center for Network Industries & Infrastructure (CNI) Working Paper 2006–03, Berlin. https://www.wip.tu-berlin.de/fileadmin/fg280/forschung/working_paper/cni/cni-wp_2006-03-beckers_hirschhausen_klatt_2006-reformbedarf_bei_den_bundesfernstrassen_und_das_potential_des_ppp-ansatzes.pdf. Last accessed 28 Jan 2022.

Bloomberg. (2022). *Hong Kong airport passenger volumes lowest since 1967: Chart.* https://www.bloomberg.com/news/articles/2022-01-26/hong-kong-airport-passenger-volumes-lowest-since-1967-chart. Last accessed 28 Jan 2022.

Bonhage, J., & Roberts, M. (2021). The public-private partnership law review: Germany. *The Law Reviews.* https://thelawreviews.co.uk/title/the-public-private-partnership-law-review/germany. Last accessed 28 Jan 2022.

Bovaird, T. (2004). Public–private partnerships: From contested concepts to prevalent practice. *International Review of Administrative Sciences, 70*(2), 199–215.

Brantsch, A. (2005). Treffsicherheit von Verkehrs- und Erlösprognosen für bemautete Verkehrswege und -anlagen. Master Thesis, University of Applied Sciences Heilbronn, Germany. https://www.world-of-digitals.com/de/arthur-brantsch-verkehrs-und-erlosprognosen-fur-bemautete-verkehrswege-und-anlagen-ebook-pdf. Last accessed 28 Jan 2022.

Bundesamt für Güterverkehr. (2011). Mautstatistik. https://www.bag.bund.de/DE/Service/OpenData/Mautstatistik/mautstatistik_node.html. Last accessed 28 Jan 2022.

Bundesamt für Güterverkehr. (2022). Mautstatistik. https://www.bag.bund.de/DE/Service/OpenData/Mautstatistik/mautstatistik_node.html. Last accessed 28 Jan 2022.

Bundesministerium für Digitales und Verkehr. (2013). ÖPP-Projekte der 1. Staffel (A-Modell), Berlin. https://www.bmvi.de/SharedDocs/DE/Artikel/StB/oepp-projekte-1-staffel-a-modell.html. Last accessed 28 Jan 2022.

Bundesministerium für Digitales und Verkehr. (2016). ÖPP-Projekte der 2. Staffel, Berlin. https://www.bmvi.de/SharedDocs/DE/Artikel/StB/oepp-projekte-der-2-staffel.html. Last accessed 28 Jan 2022.

Bundesministerium für Digitales und Verkehr. (2017). „Neue Generation" von ÖPP-Projekten, Berlin. https://www.bmvi.de/SharedDocs/DE/Artikel/StB/oepp-projekte-der-neuen-generation-liste.html. Last accessed 28 Jan 2022.

Bundesministerium für Verkehr und digitale Infrastruktur. (2021). Verkehr in Zahlen 2021/2022, Vol. 50, Berlin. https://www.bmvi.de/SharedDocs/DE/Artikel/G/verkehr-in-zahlen.html. Last accessed 28 Jan 2022.

Bundesrechnungshof. (2009). Gutachten des Bundesbeauftragten für Wirtschaftlichkeit in der Verwaltung zu Öffentlich Privaten Partnerschaften (ÖPP) im Bundesfernstraßenbau, Bonn. https://www.bundesrechnungshof.de/de/veroeffentlichungen/produkte/gutachten-berichte-bwv/berichte/sammlung/2009-bwv-gutachten-oeffentlich-private-partnerschaften-oepp-im-bundesfernstrassenbau-1. Last accessed 28 Jan 2022.

Bundesrechnungshof. (2013). Gutachten des Bundesbeauftragten für Wirtschaftlichkeit in der Verwaltung zu Wirtschaftlichkeitsuntersuchungen bei Öffentlich Privaten Partnerschaften (ÖPP) im Bundesfernstraßenbau v. 24.09.2013, Gz. V 3–2013–0144, Bonn. https://www.bundesrechnungshof.de/de/veroeffentlichungen/produkte/gutachten-berichte-bwv/berichte/sammlung/2013-bwv-gutachten-wirtschaftlichkeitsuntersuchungen-bei-oeffentlich-privaten-partnerschaften-oepp-im-bundesfernstrassenbau. Last accessed 28 Jan 2022.

Deutsches Institut für Urbanistik. (2005). Public Private Partnership Projekte. Eine aktuelle Bestandsaufnahme in Bund, Ländern und Kommunen, Berlin. https://repository.difu.de/jspui/bitstream/difu/135461/1/DF9767.pdf. Last accessed 28 Jan 2022.

European Court of Auditors. (2018). Public Private Partnerships in the EU: Widespread shortcomings and limited benefits. Special report 18–09, Luxembourg. https://www.eca.europa.eu/Lists/ECADocuments/SR18_09/SR_PPP_EN.pdf. Last accessed 28 Jan 2022.

European Investment Bank EIB. (2021). Interview with Julia Kennedy at the European PPP Expertise Centre in the European Investment Bank. https://www.eib.org/en/stories/coronavirus-impact-public-private-partnerships. Last accessed 28 Jan 2022.

Fouquet, R. (2012). Trends in income and price elasticities of transport demand (1850–2010). *Energy Policy, 50*(22), 62–71. https://doi.org/10.1016/j.enpol.2012.03.001

Gawel, E. (2005). Private Finanzierung von Fernstraßen – Erfahrungen und Probleme. *Wirtschaftsdienst, 85*, 173–181.

Grimsey, D., & Lewis, M. (2004). *Public private partnerships. The world-wide revolution in infrastructure provision and finance, Cheltenham and Northampton*. Edward Elgar Publishing.

Hamburger Abendblatt. (2003). Privattunnel-Premiere: Erst zahlen, dann fahren, September 3rd, 2003, p. 6. https://www.abendblatt.de/archive/2003/pdf/20030903.pdf/HAHA20030903lf006.pdf. Last accessed 28 Jan 2022.

Hamburger Abendblatt. (2004). Autofahrer meiden den ersten Privattunnel, March 11th, 2004, p. 7. https://www.abendblatt.de/archive/2004/pdf/20040311.pdf/HAHA20040311lf007.pdf. Last accessed 28 Jan 2022.

Institut der deutschen Wirtschaft. (2022). Ökonomische Verluste nach zwei Jahren Corona-Pandemie. IW-Kurzbericht Nr. 3/2022, Cologne. https://www.iwkoeln.de/fileadmin/user_upload/Studien/Kurzberichte/PDF/2022/IW-Kurzbericht_2022-Oekonomische-Kosten-nach-Corona.pdf. Last accessed 28 Jan 2022.

Institut für Mobilitätsforschung. (2007). Verkehrsinfrastruktur-Benchmarking Europa. Verkehrsinfrastrukturausstattung und verkehrspolitische Rahmenbedingungen in ausgewählten europäischen Staaten, Berlin. https://www.ifmo.de/files/publications_content/2007/ifmo_2007_Verkehrsinfrastruktur_Benchmarking_Europa_de.pdf. Last accessed 28 Jan 2022.

JUVE. (2018). Kostenrisiko im ÖPP-Vertrag. Leinemann scheitert mit erster Klage gegen den Bund, February 16th, 2018. https://www.juve.de/verfahren/kostenrisiko-im-oepp-vertrag-leinemann-scheitert-mit-erster-klage-gegen-den-bund/. Last accessed 28 Jan 2022.

Legal Tribune Online. (2019). OLG Celle zum Autobahnausbau. Kein Millionennachschlag für A1 mobil, November 26th, 2019. https://www.lto.de/recht/kanzleien-unternehmen/k/olg-celle-13u127-18-a1-mobil-bund-muss-keine-hoehere-verguetung-zahlen/. Last accessed 28 Jan 2022.

Lübeck + Ostholstein Wochenspiegel. (2022). Herrentunnel Lübeck: Mauterhöhung soll zum 1. März kommen, January 26th, 2022. https://www.wochenspiegel-online.de/index.php/2022/01/26/herrentunnel-luebeck-mauterhoehung-soll-zum-1-maerz-kommen/. Last accessed 28 Jan 2022.

Masser, K. (2022). Länder Stringency Index, p. 14. https://www.uni-speyer.de/fileadmin/Lehrstuehle/Knorr/5_11_Laender_Stringency_Index_Vaccinations.pdf. Last accessed 28 Jan 2022.

Mühlenkamp, H. (2016). Wirtschaftlichkeitsuntersuchungen bei ÖPP – Zwischen methodischer Konsistenz und interessengeleiteter Ergebnisgestaltung. In H. Mühlenkamp (Ed.), *Öffentlich-Private Partnerschaften – Potentiale und Probleme* (pp. 60–85). Baden-Baden.

Our World in Data. (2022). Covid-19 Dataset, San Francisco. https://github.com/owid/covid-19-data. Last accessed 28 Jan 2022.

Paulley, N., Balcombe, R., Mackett, R., Titheridge, H., Preston, J., Wardman, M., Shires, J., & Whitee, P. (2004). The demand for public transport: The effects of fares, quality of service, income and car ownership. *Transport Policy, 13*(4), 295–306. https://doi.org/10.1016/j.tranpol.2005.12.004

Petherick, A., Kira, B., Cameron-Blake, E., Tatlow, H., Hallas, L., Hale, T., Phillips, T., Zhang, Y., Webster, S., Anania, J., Ellen, L., Majumdar, S., Goldszmidt, R., Boby, T., Angrist, N., Luciano, M., Nagesh, R., & Wood, A. (2021). Variation in government responses to COVID-19, University of Oxford. Blavatnik School of Government Working Paper BSG-WP-2020/032. Version 12.0, July 2021, Oxford. https://www.bsg.ox.ac.uk/sites/default/files/2021-06/BSG-WP-2020-032-v12_0.pdf. Last accessed 28 Jan 2022.

Picot, G., & Kamp, S. (2007). Nachtrag: Public Private Partnerships – Allheilmittel oder Risikofaktor für die Finanzkrisen der öffentlichen Hand. *ifo-Schnelldienst, 60*(1), 3–7. https://www.ifo.de/publikationen/2007/zeitschrift-einzelheft/ifo-schnelldienst-012007

Robert-Koch-Institut. (2022). Wöchentlicher Lagebericht des RKI zur Coronavirus-Krankheit-2019 (COVID-19). 20.01.2022, Berlin. https://www.rki.de/DE/Content/InfAZ/N/Neuartiges_Coronavirus/Situationsberichte/Wochenbericht/Wochenbericht_2022-01-20.pdf?__blob=publicationFile. Last accessed 28 Jan 2022.

Ryan, M., & Menzes, F. (2015). Public-private partnerships for transport infrastructure: Some efficiency risks. *New Zealand Economic Papers, 49*(3), 276–295. https://doi.org/10.1080/00779954.2014.955625

Schleswig-Holsteiner Zeitungsverlag. (2019). Herrentunnel rund zehn Prozent teurer, February 25th, 2019. https://www.shz.de/regionales/luebeck/herrentunnel-rund-zehn-prozent-teurer-id22794147.html. Last accessed 28 Jan 2022.

Schleswig-Holsteinischer Zeitungsverlag. (2009). Lübeck. Der Maut-Tunnel rechnet sich nicht, May 22nd, 2009. https://www.shz.de/regionales/schleswig-holstein/panorama/der-maut-tunnel-rechnet-sich-nicht-id1027696.html. Last accessed 28 Jan 2022.

Schleswig-Holsteinischer Zeitungsverlag. (2016). Lübeck. Jahrhundertflop: Warum kaum jemand den Lübecker Herrentunnel nutzt, May 21st, 2016. https://www.shz.de/regionales/schleswig-holstein/jahrhundertflop-warum-kaum-jemand-den-luebecker-herrentunnel-nutzt-id13759836.html. Last accessed 28 Jan 2022.

Schomaker, R. M., & Bauer, C. (2020). Trust and transaction costs in public-private-partnerships – Theoretical reflections and empirical findings. *Public Money & Management.* https://doi.org/10.1080/09540962.2020.1801882

Schomaker, R. M., & Bauer, M. W. (2020a). Mild hit, flexible response—How local administrations in Austria and Germany confronted the (first wave of the) Covid-19 pandemic. In P. Joyce, F. Maron, & P. S. Reddy (Eds.), *IIAS special report the COVID-19 pandemic: Early lessons for public governance*.

taz. (2012). Öffentlich-Private Partnerschaften: Satzungsgemäßes Schmarotzertum, December 12th, 2012. https://taz.de/ffentlich-Private-Partnerschaften/!5101792/. Last accessed 28 Jan 2022.

Telepolis. (2017). A1 Mobil: PPP birgt auch für Unternehmen Risiken, September 5th, 2017. https://www.heise.de/tp/features/A1-Mobil-PPP-birgt-auch-fuer-Unternehmen-Risiken-3822436.html. Last accessed 28 Jan 2022.

United Nations. (2020). Human Development Report 2020, New York et al. http://hdr.undp.org/sites/default/files/hdr2020.pdf. Last accessed 28 Jan 2022.

University of Oxford. (2022). Covid-19 government response tracker. https://www.bsg.ox.ac.uk/research/research-projects/covid-19-government-response-tracker. Last accessed 28 Jan 2022.

Verkehrsinfrastrukturfinanzierungsgesellschaft mbh VIFG. (2017a). Projektsteckbrief F-Modell Warnowtunnel, Berlin. https://www.vifg.de/_downloads/kompetenzen/f-modell/2008-12_Projektsteckbrief_F-Modell_Warnowtunnel.pdf. Last accessed 28 Jan 2022.
Verkehrsinfrastrukturfinanzierungsgesellschaft mbh VIFG. (2017b). Projektsteckbrief F-Modell Herrentunnel, Berlin. https://www.vifg.de/_downloads/kompetenzen/f-modell/2008-12_Projektsteckbrief_F-Modell_Herrentunnel.pdf?m=1564558762&. Last accessed 28 Jan 2022.
Verkehrsinfrastrukturfinanzierungsgesellschaft mbh VIFG. (2020). Infrastrukturfinanzierung und PPP Finanzmarkbericht 2020. https://www.vifg.de/_downloads/service/infrastrukturfinanzierung-und-ppp/Finanzmarkbericht_2020-10-22.pdf. Last accessed 28 Jan 2022.

The Impact of Covid-19 on PPP in Ireland

Gail Sheppard and Matthias Beck

Introduction

The island of Ireland is situated to the west of the European land mass. Historically part of the UK, the south of the island gained independence in the early part of the twentieth century. The island is now divided into the Republic of Ireland (henceforth known as Ireland) and Northern Ireland, which is part of the United Kingdom. Ireland is a member state of the EU and has a population of approximately 4.9 million people. The predominant economic activity in Ireland was agriculture, but this has now evolved into agribusiness and high-tech, pharma and financial services. During the late 1990s and early 2000s, Ireland benefited from the 'Celtic Tiger' dynamic and experienced a period of rapid economic growth with a growth in technology manufacturing, the service sector and a boom in the housing and property market (Kitchin et al., 2012). The global financial crises had a significant impact on the Irish economy, and in December 2010, the Irish government signed a memorandum of understanding with the European Investment Bank, EU and IMF, the so-called Troika, to support the Irish economy (Sheppard, 2016).

Public Private Partnership [PPP] in Ireland was introduced in 1998, driven by the Minister for Finance McCreevy who was intent on embracing UK-style new public management approaches (Sheppard & Beck, 2018). PPP development in Ireland was backed by advisory bodies and consultants who saw it as a way to bring efficiency gains into the public sector while addressing the infrastructure deficit of the 1980s and early 1990s (NESC, 1999). The first Irish PPP projects were in the

G. Sheppard (✉)
School of Business, North Campus, Maynooth University, Maynooth, Co, Kildare, Ireland
e-mail: gail.sheppard@mu.ie

M. Beck
Cork University Business School, University College Cork, Cork, Ireland

© The Author(s), under exclusive license to Springer Nature Switzerland AG 2023

T. Dolla et al. (eds.), *Revisiting Public-Private Partnerships*,
Contributions to Public Administration and Public Policy,
https://doi.org/10.1007/978-3-031-37015-1_4

education and roads sectors. During the global financial crisis, the PPP programme in Ireland accelerated. At the time, PPP was seen as a way to boost the economy, create construction industry jobs and keep capital off the balance sheet (Sheppard, 2019). Construction in education, justice and primary care became the predominant areas of PPP activity.

The Irish government initially looked to the UK Treasury Task Force for advice on implementing PPP. This led to the establishment in Ireland in January 1999 of a central PPP unit in the Department of Finance to oversee the PPP process. Smaller units were established at this time in the Departments of the Environment and Local Government, Education and Science and Public Enterprise (Connolly & Wall, 2009). A central PPP unit now resides in the Expenditure Policy and Reporting Division in the Department of Public Expenditure and Reform. The unit also hosts a high-level Steering Committee which oversees progress on PPP projects. This unit publishes guidance to facilitate the PPP process and published new Guidelines for the use of Public Private Partnerships in December 2019.[1]

Today the National Development Finance Agency [NDFA] acts as central PPP procurement body for Ireland. It was created under the National Development Finance Agency Act 2002 to offer financial advice to State authorities under the umbrella of the National Treasury Management Agency [NTMA].[2] The final decision on whether to proceed with a PPP project resides with the minister responsible for the area for which the PPP is procured (Sheppard, 2019). The NDFA was originally tasked with raising funds for government infrastructure projects. The role of the NDFA was expanded in 2007 when it established a Centre for Excellence in PPP procurement to conduct value for money calculations for PPP projects and to assist in PPP procurement and delivery. In 2012, this role was further developed to provide management services for PPPs.

The NDFA defines a PPP as 'an arrangement between a public sector contracting authority and a private sector PPP company … which provides public works and/or services in exchange for a monthly unitary charge commencing when construction of the building is complete … the duration of the services element of a PPP is usually 25 years'.[3] The NDFA oversees 'availability'-type PPPs where the PPP company designs, builds, finances and maintains public buildings on sites provided by the State. Payment of the monthly unitary charge depends on the buildings meeting the defined availability criteria and the PPP company providing the associated services.

Ireland is described as a county which has successfully implemented PPP (UNECE, 2008). A large part of this is due to the development of institutional supports for PPP (Sheppard & Beck, 2018) which incorporate a strong legal and regulatory framework. This was put in place for PPP procurement and is supported by

[1] Central Unit | Public Private Partnership (ppp.gov.ie)

[2] About the NDFA - National Development Finance Agency National Development Finance Agency

[3] Frequently Asked Questions - National Development Finance Agency National Development Finance Agency (ndfa.ie)

regularly updated and amended legislation (Sheppard, 2019). A dispute resolution procedure is carried out by an independent arbitrator, and in the event of this process failing, redress to the courts is the next stage (Sheppard, 2019). Research on PPP in Ireland has found that the procurement process is generally 'rules-based', but that flexibility can be applied (Sheppard, 2019). In 2016, BAM took a High Court action against the NTMA/NDFA over the awarding of the Grangegorman contract, a large-scale tertiary education project. The winning bidder, Eriugena, violated the procurement rules by submitting its tender after the specified time. The High Court ruled in favour of the NTMA/NDFA, allowing the procuring body to have discretion to accept tender documents after the deadline. This protection of both parties in the event of a project delay or cancellation is important in the context of Covid-19 when construction was halted and delayed in lockdowns.

This chapter explores the impact the Covid-19 pandemic has had on PPP in Ireland. We examine whether past lessons from the financial crisis in Ireland have impacted on the handling of PPP during the Covid-19 crisis, and we explore whether the country is now proactively supporting PPP as a means of reducing the economic impact of the pandemic, as has been advocated by Baxter and Casady (2020).

PPP Project Portfolio in Ireland

Prior to the financial crisis, there was a continuous flow of PPP projects in Ireland. However, during the financial crisis, 24 projects were put on hold or cancelled. These included a third level education bundle, a prison, refurbishment of the National Concert Hall, a new theatre, a metro project in Dublin, Office of Public Works decentralised offices and a national plan for radiation oncology. This resulted in bidders losing substantial sums of money and was followed by very little PPP activity from 2008 to 2012. Following on from the Troika bailout, a pipeline of PPP was announced in 2012, a second phase in 2014 and a third phase in 2015 (Department of Public Expenditure and Reform, 2015). A summary of PPP projects to date is provided in Table 1:

Methodology

This study follows Merriam's (1998) case study approach in that we examine the impact of Covid-19 on PPP in Ireland, as a distinct phenomenon. Specifically, we focus on two distinct periods in time. These are the 'first lockdown' period, which refers to measures introduced from March 2020 to May 2020, and the 'second lockdown' period, which refers to measures introduced from January 2021 to May 2021. Merriam's (1998) approach to designing a case study includes use of qualitative data, which is the method of data collection in this case study. Specifically, we use speeches of politicians and leaders, social housing status reports from a government

Table 1 Summary of PPP projects

Transport	Education	Office of Public Works OPW)	Justice	Health	Social Housing
N4 Kilcock/ Kinnegad (contract signed 2003)	Pilot Schools Bundle (contract signed 2001)	Convention Centre (contract signed 2007)	Criminal Courts of Justice Building (contract signed 2007)	Primary Care (financial close May 2016)	Social Housing Bundle 1[a] (completed)
M1 Dundalk Western Bypass (contract signed 2004)	National Maritime College (contract signed 2003)		Courts Bundle (contract awarded December 2015)	HSE Community Nursing Units (PIN notice issued August 2019; Tender Phase Oct 2021)	Social Housing Bundle 2 (contract awarded 2019)
N8 Rathcormac-Fermoy (contract signed 2004)	Cork School of Music (contract signed 2005)				Social Housing Bundle 3 (OJEU notice anticipated Q3 2021)
N25Waterford City Bypass (contract signed 2006)	Schools Bundle 1 (contract signed 2009)				
Limerick Tunnel (contract signed 2006)	Schools Bundle 2 (contract signed 2010)				
M3 Clonee/ Kells (contract signed 2007)	Schools Bundle 3 (contract signed 2012)				
M7 Portlaoise/ Cullahill (contract signed 2007)	Schools Bundle 4 (contract awarded 2014)				
N6 Galway to East Ballinsaloe (contract signed 2007)	Schools Bundle 5 (financial close July 2016)				

(continued)

Table 1 (continued)

Transport	Education	Office of Public Works OPW)	Justice	Health	Social Housing
M50 Upgrade (contract signed 2007)	Grangegorman (construction to begin late 2017 – completed in the East Quad Dec 2020 and Central Quad March 2021)				
N11 Arklow/ Rathnew & N7 Newlands Cross (financial close 2013)	Higher Education PPP Bundle 1 (three candidates shortlisted August 2020)				
N17/18 Gort to Tuam (financial close April 2014)	Higher Education PPP Bundle 2 (four candidates shortlisted June 2021)				
M6 & M9 Motorway Service Stations (Preferred tenderer awarded May 2015)					
M11 Gorey to Enniscorty (financial close October 2015)					
N25 New Ross Bypass (financial close January 2016)					

Source: Sectors & Projects – National Development Finance Agency National Development Finance Agency (ndfa.ie) and Comptroller and Auditor General, Annual Report 2008 and 2011. [Accessed: 13 May 2022]

[a]gov.ie - Social Housing Construction Projects Status Report Q2 2021 (www.gov.ie)

website (www.gov.ie), material from government department websites and the parliament (www.oireachtas.ie). We also utilise data on current and past projects found on the NDFA website (www.ndfa.ie), the academic literature sources and the media.

Analysis

Ireland has been praised by the World Health Organization for its handling of the Covid-19 crisis.[4] The country took steps early in March 2020 to protect its health-care system and its citizens from the ensuing pandemic. Table 2 shows a timeline relating to measures introduced by the Irish government in March 2020. This time-line constitutes what we will refer to as the 'first lockdown'.

Initial confusion over the working from home rule was clarified by then Prime Minister, Leo Varadkar on 24 March 2020[5]:

> The requirement that workers work from home, unless attendance is absolutely essential, is not to be read as meaning that factories or construction sites have to shut. The authorities are available to work with employers and unions on how to make physical distancing effective
>
> (Leo Varadkar, 24 March 2020)

However, the situation moved very quickly and on 27 March 2020,[6] the stay-at-home rule was introduced allowing

> … travel to and from work, or for purposes of work, only where the work is an essential health, social care or other essential service and cannot be done from home
>
> (Leo Varadkar, 27 March 2020)

Essential services relating to construction and development[7] included essential work relating to the construction and development at Technological University Dublin Campus, Grangegorman, which is a PPP. Construction on this project began in late 2017 and continued during the first lockdown. The East Quad was opened in

Table 2 Measures introduced in March 2020

Date	Measures introduced
12 March 2020	Schools, colleges and childcare facilities closed. Mass gatherings banned and employees instructed to work from home where possible.
17 March 2020	All public gatherings cancelled, pubs and bars closed.
24 March 2020	Leisure centres, hairdressers, non-essential retail outlets, playgrounds, sporting events and places of worship closed.
27 March 2020	Stay-at-home rule introduced and further non-essential shops closed

[4] https://www.oireachtas.ie/en/debates/debate/seanad/2020-07-24/10/

[5] gov.ie - Speech of the Taoiseach, Leo Varadkar TD, Post Cabinet Statement, Tuesday 24 March 2020 (www.gov.ie)

[6] gov.ie - Speech of the Taoiseach Leo Varadkar TD, Government Buildings, 27 March 2020 (www.gov.ie)

[7] gov.ie - View the list of essential services at Level 5 (www.gov.ie)

December 2020 and the Central Quad opened in March 2021,[8] during the second lockdown. The definition of 'essential services' in March 2020 also related to 'educational facilities at primary and post-primary level, including school building projects, which will provide additional capacity for students or involve essential maintenance or refurbishment works in support of the continued provision of education'. There were no PPPs in these project areas at this time.

The only other construction-active PPPs at the time of the first lockdown were Social Housing developments (see Table 1). €300 million was committed in the 2015 Budget to providing 1500 new social housing homes using an 'availability-based PPP model'. The private partner designs, builds, finances and maintains the social housing units and receives a unitary payment over the 25 years of the contract. These social housing units were divided into three bundles.[9] These social housing projects were deemed not to be essential and were shut down during the first wave of Covid-19 in March 2020.[10] Construction on Social Housing resumed in May 2020. The closure of Social Housing PPP construction sites during the first lockdown led to many projects being delayed. However, the number of homes delivered in 2020 was maximised due to 'all stakeholders working tirelessly' (Social Housing Construction Update March 2021) and all of Social Housing Bundle 1 (see Table 3), apart from the Ayrfield site, was completed in 2020.

The Covid-19 situation in Ireland deteriorated at the end of 2020, and on 8 January 2021, a second lockdown was introduced. During the second lockdown, it was decided that 'a very limited amount of essential sites and a small number of designated social housing construction projects which are due for completion within a 6–8 week period would continue during this time' (Minister Darragh O'Brien,

Table 3 Social Housing Bundle 1

Social Housing Bundle 1	Status
Ayrfield, Malahide Road	Completed Q2 2021
Corkagh Grange	Completed Q4 2020
Scribblestown, Finglas	Completed Q4 2020
Dunleer, Co Louth	Completed Q2 2020
Convent Lands, Wicklow Town (phase 1)	Completed Q2 2020
Convent Lands, Wicklow Town (phase 2)	Completed Q3 2020
Craddockstown, Naas (phase 1)	Completed Q2 2020
Craddockstown, Naas (phase 2)	Completed Q3 2020

Source: Social Housing Construction Projects, Status Report Q2 2021, Department of Housing, Local Government and Heritage, 22 September 2021

[8] TU Dublin Campus at Grangegorman - National Development Finance Agency National Development Finance Agency (ndfa.ie)

[9] 211015 Social Housing Construction project update March 2021.pdf

[10] Social housing construction needs to resume quickly, says builder (irishtimes.com)

TD).[11] During this second lockdown, the Ayrfield project (Table 3) from Social Housing Bundle 1 was completed in Q2 2021.

Table 4 shows the status of Social Housing Bundle 2 at September 2021.

We can see that The Walk, The Miles (Phase 1), Slievekeale (Phase 1), Ballyburke (Phase 1), Shannon East (Phase 1), Poundhill (Phase 1) and Oakwood (Phase 1) were all completed during Q2 2021. This suggests that these PPPs continued to be worked on during the second lockdown as they met the criteria outlined by Minister O'Brien, which stated that social housing construction projects due for competition within 6–8 weeks should continue during the second lockdown. This was agreed at the Cabinet level by the Irish government. All residential construction projects recommenced from 12 April 2021 and all construction was allowed to go ahead from 4 May 2021.[12]

Risk Management: The Risk Management and Defaults During COVID-19 Outbreak

Ireland minimised legal risks associated with PPP completion or non-completion by allowing a large share of ongoing PPP projects that were in the construction phase to continue. At the same time, stringent guidance on pandemic-related safety

Table 4 Social Housing Bundle 2

Social Housing Bundle 2	Status
The Walk, Roscommon Town, Co Roscommon	Completed Q2 2021
The Miles, Clonakilty, Co Cork (Phase 1)	Completed Q2 2021
The Miles, Clonakilty, Co Cork (Phase 2)	On Site Q4 2019
Slievekeale, Waterford City (Phase 1)	Completed Q2 2021
Slievekeale, Waterford City (Phase 2)	On Site Q4 2021
Ballyburke, Galway City (Phase 1)	Completed Q2 2021
Ballyburke, Galway City (Phase 2)	On Site Q4 2019
Shannon East, Co Clare (Phase 1)	Completed Q2 2021
Shannon East, Co Clare (Phase 2)	On Site Q4 2019
Poundhill, Skibbereen, Co Cork (Phase 1)	Completed Q2 2021
Poundhill, Skibbereen, Co Cork (Phase 2)	On Site Q4 2019
Oakwood, Macroom, Co Cork (Phase 1)	Completed Q2 2021
Oakwood, Macroom, Co Cork (Phase 2)	On Site Q4 2019
Nancy's Lane, Clane, Co Kildare	On Site Q4 2019

Source: Social Housing Construction Projects, Status Report Q2 2021, Department of Housing, Local Government and Heritage, 22 September 2021

[11] gov.ie - Minister O'Brien confirms shutdown in construction activity (www.gov.ie)

[12] gov.ie - Minister of State Burke facilitates prompt commencement of construction work in accordance with lifting of Covid restrictions (www.gov.ie)

measures such as social distancing was provided. Moreover, this approach was made politically palatable through the emphasis by the government on socially beneficial projects in the areas of education and social housing, which were widely supported by the population in general. During peak periods of the pandemic, some work was nonetheless suspended, but work on these projects was restarted as soon as the country's National Public Health Emergency Team [NPHET] thought this advisable.

This approach, where government policy was sensitive to commercial interests and social needs, but closely followed the advice of its expert pandemic advisory team, was characteristic of Irish policy since the pandemic began. NPHET as a national body itself has been and continues to be well-staffed, with more than 30 staff members from diverse backgrounds who draw on areas of expertise in public health, health administration, expertise in infectious diseases, modelling, health communication, law and healthcare regulation.[13]

The prioritisation of NPHET's advice in government policy together with the broad composition of NPHET itself also created public trust in the government's handling of the pandemic, with comparably few anti-lockdown protests by European standards as well as widespread compliance with vaccination measures and government recommendations on mask wearing and social distancing.

Overall, this situation also seems to have been helped by the country's traditionally consensualist political culture, where governments are frequently coalitions involving several parties and extremist parties are notably absent. Hofstede (2001) ranks Ireland among more collectivist countries with a score of 70, similar to Sweden (71) and Finland (63). These scores contrast with the high scores for individualism in the USA (91) and the United Kingdom (89). There is a possibility that consensualist sociopolitical systems such as Ireland and some of the Scandinavian countries mentioned by Hofstede perform better when it comes to crisis management. This advantage potentially affects a number of aspects of crisis management, including the speed at which policy measures are agreed and passed by parliament, the level of comprehensiveness or generosity of these measures and potentially the creativity with which existing policies such as PPP are adapted to function under crisis conditions (see also Becker, 2001).

What is particularly remarkable in this context is that the Irish government not only has actively engaged in policy measures that allowed work on PPP projects to continue at the planned pace but also has focused these activities on what is considered widely as the most pressing social issue the country faces, namely, the provision of affordable housing. By focusing PPP activity during the crisis on an activity that adds to the legitimacy of PPP, this will have contributed to the broad acceptance of the scheme as a policy measure.

Like other European countries, Ireland's government has been generous with financial support aimed at compensating private industries for losses resulting from

[13] https://www.gov.ie/en/publication/de1c30-national-public-health-emergency-team-nphet-for-covid-19-governance-/

the pandemic. This has benefited among others the construction industry, which has seen no bankruptcies or closures following the onset of the pandemic. It seems apparent that the careful handling of these subsidies builds on experiences the country had during and after the global financial crisis, which highlighted the need for macroeconomic stabilisation and cross-party collaboration. It is unclear, however, whether current levels of financial support could be maintained if the pandemic were to intensify further and/or continue over an extensive additional time period.

References

Baxter, D., & Casady, C. B. (2020). Proactive and strategic healthcare public-private partnerships (PPPs) in the coronavirus (COVID-19) epoch. *Sustainability, 12*(12), 5097.

Becker, U. (2001). 'Miracle' by consensus? Consensualism and dominance in Dutch employment development. *Economic and Industrial Democracy, 22*(4), 453–483.

Connolly, C., & Wall, T. (2009). *Public private partnerships in Ireland benefits, problems and critical success factors*. The Institute of Chartered Accountants in Ireland.

Department of Public Expenditure and Reform. (2015). *Building on recover: Infrastructure and capital investment 2016–2021*. Available at: 171045a52627428eb387a2ccff21db84.pdf (assets.gov.ie). Accessed 23 Dec 2021.

Hofstede, G. (2001). *Culture's consequences: Comparing values, behaviors, institutions and organizations across nations*. Sage Publications.

Kitchin, R., O'Callaghan, C., Boyle, M., Gleeson, J., & Keaveney, K. (2012). Placing neoliberalism: The rise and fall of Ireland's Celtic Tiger. *Environment and Planning A, 44*(6), 1302–1326.

Merriam, S. B. (1998). *Qualitative research and case study applications in education. Revised and expanded from " Case Study Research in Education"*. Jossey-Bass Publishers.

NESC (National Economic and Social Council). (1999). *Opportunities, challenges and capacities for choice.*

Sheppard, G. (2016). Public private partnerships in the Republic of Ireland. In A. Akintoye, M. Beck, & M. Kumaraswamy (Eds.), *Public-private partnerships-a global review* (pp. 180–194). Routledge.

Sheppard, G., & Beck, M. (2018). The evolution of public–private partnership in Ireland: A sustainable pathway? *International Review of Administrative Sciences, 84*(3), 579–595.

Sheppard, G. (2019). *The sustainability of public–private partnership in Ireland* (Doctoral Dissertation University College Cork).

UNECE. (2008). *Guidebook on promoting good governance*. United Nations.

Part II
PPP Financing and Contractual Governance

Public–Private Partnerships to Face the Challenges of Covid-19 in Italy

Nunzia Carbonara

Introduction

In Italy, Public–Private Partnerships (PPPs) have become regulated by the Code of Public Contracts (article 3 [15-ter]) in 2008, following the development of the partnership market in the early 2000s. In recent years, though, Italian legislation has been amended several times in order to encourage the involvement of private capital in the realization of public works under PPP arrangements, given the country's significant efforts to keep its accounts under control and the scarcity of public resources available for investment. In this context, the Italian public infrastructure market has undergone a great transformation, new models for public procurement have emerged, characterized by an ever-greater involvement of the private sector, not only in the design and construction phases but also in the management and financing phases.

The growing interest in PPP operations is confirmed by the data on the incidence of this new market on the total public works market provided by the National Observatory on Public–Private Partnership, which has grown both in terms of value and in terms of number of tenders. From the analysis of data, it emerges that the impact of PPP on public works in Italy has gone from a percentage of less than 1%, with 331 tenders for the amount of 1.4 billion euros in 2002, to a percentage of 9.2% in 2018, with 3806 tenders for the amount of 9.4 billion euros. For the seventeen years from 2002 to 2018, there are over 35,000 proceedings in place, i.e., tenders awarded and tenders in progress, for a total amount of over 95 billion euros (Fig. 1).

The evolution of the PPP market in Italy can been divided into four phases:

N. Carbonara (✉)
Politecnico di Bari, Bari, Italy
e-mail: nunzia.carbonara@poliba.it

© The Author(s), under exclusive license to Springer Nature Switzerland AG 2023

T. Dolla et al. (eds.), *Revisiting Public-Private Partnerships*,
Contributions to Public Administration and Public Policy,
https://doi.org/10.1007/978-3-031-37015-1_5

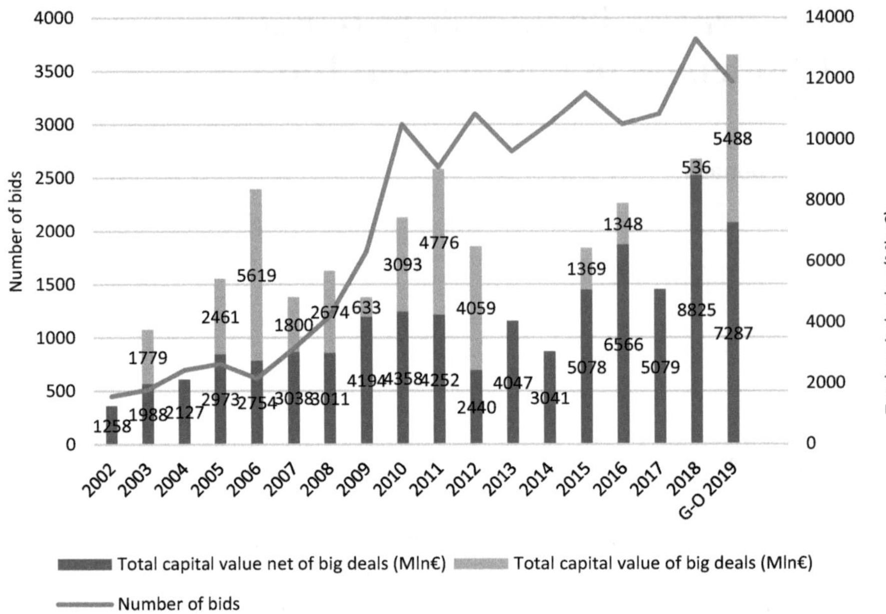

Fig. 1 PPP market in Italy: Number and value of PPP bids in the period 2002–2019. (Source: infopp.it)

- 2002–2007: start of legislation
- 2008–2011: regulatory settlement
- 2012–2016: financial settlement
- 2017–2020: consolidation

Each phase corresponds to the "evolutionary cycles" of the legislation aimed at making "the most appropriate tool to interpret the needs of the markets, to ensure regulatory compliance or to enable the use of new contractual tools and/or new procedures."

During the four phases, an increase in the number of tenders was recorded – with an annual trend strongly influenced by large projects – which reached, in 2018, the value of approximately 9.4 billion euros (8.8 billion net of big deals[1]), determined by the presence of an exceptional number of major works and services worth more than 50 million euros (33 tenders worth over 10 billion, against an annual average of 13 tenders worth 3.9 billion in the entire period 2002–2016) (Table 1).

Overall, between 2002 and 2011, the incidence of PPP grew fairly linearly compared to the entire public works market: it went from 0.9% in 2002 to 16.7% in 2011 in terms of number of calls, and from 6% to 35.8% in terms of amounts in the tender.

[1] Calls for tenders with amounts exceeding 500 million euros.

Table 1 PPP market in Italy, number and value of bids and incidence of PPP on public works (2002–2018)

	PPP bids		Incidence of PPP on public works (%)	
Years	Number	Value (Mln €)	Number	Value (Mln €)
2002	330	1.258	0.9%	5.3%
2003	514	3.767	1.5%	11.5%
2004	801	2.127	2.6%	6.6%
2005	959	5.434	3.2%	17.0%
2006	765	8.373	2.9%	28.2%
2007	949	4.838	3.7%	17.2%
2008	1.290	5.685	5.3%	18.5%
2009	1.853	4.827	10.0%	18.8%
2010	2.966	7.451	16.1%	27.0%
2011	2.760	9.028	16.6%	33.8%
2012	3.017	6.499	9.1%	30.7%
2013	2.840	4.047	20.3%	23.3%
2014	3.029	3.041	17.4%	11.3%
2015	3.254	6.447	17.5%	22.6%
2016	3.050	7.914	18.2%	40.8%
2017	3.217	5.079	17.4%	20.9%
2018	3.806	9.361	16.3%	29.4%
2002–2018	**35.400**	**95.176**	**9.20%**	**20.70%**

Source: Public Works Observatory and infoppp.it

The two-year period 2012–2013 was characterized by a sharp decline in the value of PPP bids. This trend indicates that the financial crisis has increased the difficulties in finding financial resources, especially for large-value transactions.

In 2014, the incidence of PPP on public works was 17.4% in terms of PPP projects that had been called for tenders (a significant share of the total public infrastructure market) and 11.3% in terms of value (the lowest share low over the last ten years). In 2015, there was a recovery, both for the number of calls (17.5%) and for the number of tenders (22.6%), percentages that in 2016 increased further, reaching respectively 18.2% and 40.8% of the public works market.

Since 2017, with the growth of traditional execution-only contracts, driven by the new regulatory provisions, the incidence of PPP has been reduced. In 2017, the registered percentages were similar to those in 2015. In 2018, the incidence of PPP on public works was 16.3% in terms of number of bids and 29.4% in terms of amount. In 2019, PPP contracts grew by only 3.5% (from 3131 to 3241).

As for the awarded PPP projects, from January 2002 to December 2018, a total number of 9387 projects had been awarded, with a value of almost €75 billion (79% of the total amount of bids equaling over €95 billion).

Tables 2 and 3 show the segmentation of the PPP market in Italy with respect to the types of PPP that, according to the Italian juridical framework, can be

Table 2 PPP market by types: number and value of awarded PPP projects (2002–2018)

	Total 2002–2018		Annual average 2002–2018	
Types of PPP	Number	Value (Mln€)	Number	Value (Mln€)
Work concessions	2680	47.733	158	2808
Service concessions	6156	21,123	362	1243
Other PPP	551	6287	32	370
Total	**9387**	**75,143**	**552**	**4420**

Source: Public Works Observatory and infoppp.it

Table 3 PPP market by types: number and value of PPP under bidding (2002–2018)

	Total 2002–2018		Annual average 2002–2018	
	Number	Value (Mln€)	Number	Value (Mln€)
PPP	**33,400**	**95,176**	**2082**	**5599**
Work concessions	6124	50,427	360	2966
Service concessions	25,662	37,086	1510	2182
Other PPP	3614	7662	213	451
Other public procurement forms[a]	**349,701**	**363,712**	**20,571**	**21,395**
Total	**385,101**	**458,888**	**22,653**	**26,993**

Source: Public Works Observatory and infoppp.it
[a]It includes: execution-only contracts, integrated contracts, general contractor, and mixed works and services contracts without private capital

distinguished into three main categories: (1) public works concessions, (2) service concessions, and (3) other PPP forms.

According to the Italian Code of Public Contracts, the public work concessions can be awarded following two procedures:

- Work concession under public initiative (Art. 144 of the Code), whereby the Public Administration (PA) invites tenders to a restricted/open procedure on the basis of a preliminary draft, a business plan and a concession contract. The PA evaluates the received tenders following the criterion of the most economically advantageous tender.
- Work concession under private initiative/Project financing (Art. 153 of the Code), whereby the project is designed and presented by a promoter on the basis of a Prior Information Notice (PIN) by the PA. Following the selection of the best proposal, the PA puts the promoter proposals out to tender and identifies the Concessionaire.

Service concessions are contracts of the same nature of public service contracts, except in that the provision of services consists either solely of the right to exploit the service or the right plus payment.

In the third residual category, other PPP forms, we consider the Institutional PPP, where public–private companies aim at providing public services. In this category, there are several PPP schemes, each governed by specific statutory provisions.

Table 2 reports the number and value of the PPP projects awarded over the period 2002–2018, Table 3 reports the number and value of the PPP projects that have been called for tenders in the same period.

Driving the PPP are mainly public works concession contracts and services concessions. The latter are more numerous – with 25,662 calls for tenders throughout the period 2002–2018, which account for 72% of the PPP market. Public works concessions are less numerous (18% of the total PPP), but of greater value with about €50 billion representing the 53% of total value of PPP projects (Table 3).

Between 2002 and 2016, the National Observatory on Public Private Partnership surveyed 1578 PPP contracts with project finance (5.5% of the total PPP procedures) and the total value of the market, i.e., the total capital value of the PPP projects under bidding, stands at around €31.6 billion (35.5% of the value of the entire PPP market, equal to around €89 billion).

A variegated world that ranges from the few large national competitions for strategic works and infrastructures to the myriad of mostly local competitions of relatively modest amount, but which has an enormous impact on the lives of citizens as they concern sports facilities, schools, cemeteries, etc. In fact, it is recorded that only 1% of PPP tenders individually exceed the value of €50 million, which, however, represent 67% of the total economic value. This means that 99% of the tenders capitalize the remaining 33% of the value of the PPP market, which (also) poses a problem of quality of the procedures whose cost, of course, must be accounted in the economic investment framework.

Public administrations and managers of networks, infrastructures and public services make use of project finance to create and manage works and services in various market sectors. In particular, over the period 2002–2018, social and public housing and sports facilities are the sectors with a relevant number of PPP projects, whereas transport, energy, and telecommunications are sectors with less numerous projects but with higher amounts.

Table 4 reports the number and value of PPP projects classified by sector. The sectors with a relevant number of PPP projects include sporting facilities and social and public construction, with 15,323 tenders for an average amount of about €1 million, which represent 43% of the tenders and 11% of the amounts (around €10.3 billion). On the other hand, the energy and telecommunications and transport sectors, with a total amount of approximately €48.7 billion related to 5763 tenders with an average amount of €14.5 million, are entitled to 51% of the value of the PPP market. If we consider the value net of big deals, the importance of the energy and telecommunications network sector emerges, which, over the entire period considered, has a 34% share of the market. In particular, the main PPP projects in these sectors are gas distribution, public lighting, production and distribution of renewable energy, energy requalification, systems and networks for telecommunications. Looking at the last years, social and public housing and sports facilities still stand out in terms of the number of tenders, with 1906 total competitions (about 50% of the total). Regarding the amount, the energy and telecommunications sectors prevail, with over €4.6 billion (49% of the total).

Table 4 PPP market by sector 2002–2018

Sector	Number of PPP bids (%)	Value (%)	Value net of big deals (%)	Number of awarded PPP (%)	Value (%)	Value net of big deals (%)
Social and Public construction	21%	7%	10%	17%	6%	10%
Urban regeneration	2%	3%	4%	2%	3%	4%
Health	3%	9%	13%	4%	9%	15%
Schooling	3%	2%	3%	5%	2%	3%
Cemetery	4%	3%	4%	7%	3%	5%
Sporting facilities	22%	4%	6%	17%	4%	6%
Leisure	5%	1%	1%	3%	0,5%	1%
Parking	5%	3%	4%	7%	3%	5%
Urban development	15%	2%	2%	12%	1%	2%
Energy and telecommunication	13%	26%	34%	18%	20%	28%
Environment	1%	13%	10%	2%	14%	12%
Transport	3%	25%	4%	2%	33%	5%
Seaport and harbor	2%	3%	5%	2%	3%	5%
Others	0.3%	0.1%	0.0%	0.3%	0.1%	0.0%

Source: infoppp.it

The analysis of PPP adoption in Italy shows that its use is widely spread. Data on the PPP market show:

- A strong dynamism in terms of a high number of bids, this also as a consequence of the fact that PPP is often the only way that the public administrations have to develop public infrastructures.
- A gap between the growth of the potential market (number of tenders) and the growth of the real market (number of awards), which does not increase at the same rate, although the share of interrupted proceedings (9%) is far lower than that recorded in 2002, which presented mortality values of the initiatives of about 27%.
- Low values of the projects in tender, the total average amount of 3.4 billion in the period 2002–2018 and 76% of the calls refer to 2% of the value of the potential market of the PPP, which reflect the pulverization of the contracting authorities and the average size of public procurement in Italy.
- High concentration of the market for investments of greater value: in the case of healthcare, 35% of the players contribute 80% of the invested capital.

Context of the Inquiry

The Covid-19 pandemic is undoubtedly an unprecedented global crisis that has overwhelmed national systems all over the world, leading them to procure emergency healthcare services and equipment and to implement strategies to counter the spread of the virus. This challenge, albeit with many difficulties, has been faced mostly with great speed and efficiency, thanks to the institutions and organizations around the world that, since the Coronavirus was first reported at the end of 2019, have started hundreds of research studies on diagnosis, prevention, and treatment strategies, all fundamental to allow the entire global community to return to normal. In addition, it was necessary to implement additional strategies enabling to meet the ever-increasing demand, especially in the healthcare systems.

The previous shocks (2008–2009 and 2011–2012) had already dramatically highlighted the fragility of the Italian economy. Economic growth rates and productivity levels that have been lower than those of other major European nations for years, a ratio of public debt to GDP among the highest in the OECD area, the poor efficiency and effectiveness of the public administrative machinery, a significant underground economy (12% of GDP) with significant tax evasion (over 110 billion euros per year), a high level of gender, social, and territorial inequalities. To these weaknesses, which have contributed to the low resilience of the Italian economy in response to past economic shocks, is added the squeeze on public investment. In Italy, between 2008 and 2016, public investments fell by 27% for about 13 billion euros and private investments for almost 58 billion euros, while representing, with a total value of about 260 billion per year, 86% of the total value of investments and only 2.1% of the total public expenditure is intended for investments.[2]

The Covid-19 outbreak arrived in this already very critical scenario, so much so that a severe recession could be expected.

On the other hand, the great amount of resources made available by the European Union represents a great opportunity for the recovery, for addressing existing weaknesses, strengthening the resilience of the socioeconomic system, and favoring its evolution toward greater economic, social, environmental, and institutional sustainability.

In Italy, for the period 2021–2026, the Next Generation EU plan, called National Plan for Recovery and Resilience (PNRR), finances 248 billion euros, to which are added 13 billion euros from React EU, thus arriving at a total funding of over 260 billion euros, destined to activate a real transformation of the country, based on six areas' intervention. About 70 billion are earmarked for the ecological transition and plans to develop a sustainable economy also from an environmental point of view. For the digital transition, which means, for example, ultra-broadband across the country, 50 billion are earmarked. To infrastructures for mobility and sustainable mobility, i.e., not only high speed but also the upgrading of regional lines, are allocated 31.46 billion euros. More than 4 billion of euro will be allocated for education

[2] Bank of Italy (2019), The Public investments, Annual Report.

and research.[3] The funding provided for both inclusion and cohesion and for health is also significant, the first aimed at bridging social gaps, including those of gender and facilitating access to the world of work, the second for the strengthening of local health and the digitization of the healthcare system.

For the implementation of the PNRR, it will be necessary to rely both on massive public investments, but also on the contribution of private individuals, in financial terms, skills and planning. In such a context, PPP is regaining interest, in order to respond to current social, digital, environmental, and economic challenges and seize opportunities offered by the PNRR, not just to increase the pool of public money but mainly to quickly implement new investments and services.

In the next few years, it will be necessary to resort to all forms of Public–Private Partnership, as essential tools for building a modern future and with adequate infrastructures to support the growth and development of the country. Partnerships between public and private will be necessary and functional to the digitization of the Public Administration (PA), more efficient management of health, physical, and intangible infrastructures, education, public services, transport as well as functional to greater protection of the environment.

In particular, for social care infrastructures, it will be possible to resort to PPPs for the financing of services and technologies to support initiatives such as smart health and/or assisted living, which allow remote monitoring of patients and consequently limit the overload of infrastructures.

Brief Description Context of the Case

The PPP Initiatives to Face the Covid-19 Pandemic

During the first wave of the Covid-19 pandemic, when Italy, like many other countries across the world, was scrambling to find enough masks and ventilators, Italian public and private organizations showed an extraordinary ability to forge new collaborations. In the academic glossary, these partnerships have been referred to as "hastily generated," i.e., created in a hurry and without preconceptions, with the sole objective of giving an immediate response to the looming health crisis.

Exscalate4Cov (E4C) is one of the larger PPP projects developed in Italy to face the pandemic, started in 2020 and closed on September 2021, with a total cost of about 3 billion euros. E4C is a public–private partnership backed by the European Commission's H2020 program, aimed at fighting the coronavirus by combining the best supercomputing resources and artificial intelligence with state-of-the-art experimental facilities up through clinical validation. The project is coordinated by one of the leading Italian biopharmaceutical companies, the Dompè Farmaceutici, and involves more than 18 private and public institutions and research centers. On the

[3] Ministry of Economic Development (MISE).

public side, the key stakeholders involved are Politecnico di Milan, University of Milan, University of Naples, University of Cagliari, CINECA – Interuniversity Consortium, Swiss Institute of Bioinformatics, and the National Institute of Nuclear Physics (INFN). At the core of the project is the use of a supercomputing system (Exscalate – Exascale Smart Platform Against Pathogens) to evaluate more than three million molecules per second and thanks to which it is possible to identify the safest drugs and promising to cure the disease and the molecules capable of inhibiting the pathogenesis of the virus to counteract future infections.[4]

The emblematic examples of public–private collaboration to tackle the Covid-19 pandemic are undoubtedly those for vaccine research and development. However, the partnerships between public and private in the Covid-19 era did not only concern the development of the medical value chain (drugs, products, and medical devices) but were also activated to accelerate technological innovation in support of contact tracing solutions, to develop new techniques for the production of filter masks intended for the population, and to define standards for filter mask certification. In some Italian regions, the public sector has played a key role in promoting partnerships between public universities and research centers and local textile companies that intended to convert their production lines to meet the demand for healthcare devices.

On almost the entire national territory, forms of partnership between public and private have been activated to deal with the hospital emergency due to the number of hospitalizations of Covid patients. Covid beds and Covid wards have been activated in various accredited private hospitals to expand the hospital offer, defining ad hoc rates for the remuneration of Covid admissions.

The Relevance of PPP as a Post-Covid-19 Recovery Tool

The law 11 September 2020, n. 120, which converted into law the D.L. 76/2020, known as the "Simplifications" Decree, intervenes in various ways to encourage the construction of public works and relaunch infrastructure investments in order to overcome the economic difficulties in which our country finds itself, strongly aggravated by the Covid-19 emergency, enhancing the public–private alliance for the realization of investments in favor of the community and citizens.

The changes to the code of public contracts introduced by the law expand the role of the private lender for the construction of public works or public utility works: in this sense, Article 8, (paragraph 5, lett. D), allows the submission of proposals under the PPP regime also in relation to interventions already included in the approved planning acts. To the private sector, therefore, is given the opportunity to request the initiation of the so-called project finance procedure also in relation to interventions already included in the approved planning documents, which makes

[4] https://cordis.europa.eu/project/id/101003551/results/it

the role of private finance decisive for the activation of public projects that, especially in the immediate future, they risk being blocked, either by the inertia of the administration, or by the current unavailability of many of the public resources announced, destined to arrive at a later time.[5]

In addition, the law converting the "Simplification" Decree gives the private sector the opportunity to act as a real promoter and activator of the public initiative, or to present its own proposals for the assignment of works and services for which the PA has already planned the acquisition, so as to allow collaboration between the public and private sectors as well as in the implementation and investment management phase, also in the conception and programming phase.

The law re-proposes the true meaning of the PPP, that is, the enhancement and attraction of the competences of the private sector. In fact, in order to ensure the best feasibility of the projects and remedy the potential inertia of the administration, it grants the promoter the right to propose also alternative projects, improved and refined with respect to those already included in the programming tools. In particular, the legislation expands the range of action of a procedure and does so substantially at no cost, due to the fact that the private prepares all the documentation relating to the implementation of an infrastructure investment, from design to finance to construction and subsequent functional and economic management of the work, and can also intervene to improve and refine the intervention hypotheses already envisaged. All this, without in any way compromising the role of the public administration, which has the final word in terms of acceptance or rejection of the intervention.

The expansion is linked not only to the possibility of overcoming situations of inertia but also to favoring the implementation of interventions in relation to which the public interest has already been acquired, if anything, by improving them in the perspective pursued by institutional investors, for example, by making them more compatible on the environmental plan or technologically more advanced in view of the greater effectiveness of the (public) service that the infrastructure will have to render.

The regulatory change also reviews the nature of energy efficiency contracts (Energy Performance Contract – EPC), recognizing them as PPP contracts, and the methods of remuneration of the economic operator under such contracts.

The EPC is a contractual case introduced by Directive 2012/27/EU, implemented in the Italia legal framework with the Legislative Decree n. 102/2014, to promote energy efficiency. In particular, the EPC, according to the definition given in Article 2 of Legislative Decree no. 102/2014 is a "contractual agreement between the beneficiary and the supplier of an energy efficiency improvement measure, verified and monitored during the entire duration of the contract, where investments (works, supplies or services) are provided as part of the measure according to the level of

[5] Until the introduction of these changes, in fact, the rule provided that economic operators could submit to the contracting authorities proposals for the construction of public works or public utility works based on the use of all types of PPP contracts, but only in relation to projects not included in the Government programming plan.

energy efficiency improvement established contractually or other agreed energy performance criteria, such as financial savings." The main object of the contract is, therefore, the achievement of an "energy efficiency improvement measure" established by the parties, also in terms of financial savings, which at the same time constitutes the parameter according to which the investments made by the private entity (of any nature: works – supplies or services). The EPC is the contractual model through which Energy Service Companies (ESCo) typically operate, specialized entities able to offer their customers, beneficiaries of energy efficiency and saving services, the following services: energy diagnosis and energy audit; feasibility study of energy efficiency improvement interventions; planning of interventions; procurement of financial resources; implementation of the intervention; management of upgraded systems; financing through third parties. In practice, several EPC contractual models have been developed, so that it can take on different connotations and contents based on the specific regulation of the relationship between the parties.

The new provision on EPC specifies that "the operating revenues of the economic operator can be determined and paid according to the level of energy efficiency improvement or other contractually established energy performance criteria, as long as they can be quantified in relation to consumption; the energy efficiency improvement measure, calculated in accordance with the standards on certifying the energy performance of buildings and other energy-intensive infrastructures, must be made available to the granting administration by the economic operator and must be verified and monitored during the "entire duration of the contract, also making use of specific IT platforms used for the collection, organization, management, processing, evaluation and monitoring of energy consumption." With the proposed change, it is established that operating revenues can be determined and paid according to the level of energy efficiency improvement, or they can be commensurate with other energy performance criteria, defined contractually, as long as they are clearly quantifiable. In essence, it seems that the law is concerned with ensuring that, in the context of PPP operations qualified as EPCs, the correct allocation of contractual risks is ensured, establishing that the remuneration of the private partner must be dependent on the results actually achieved and the services rendered.

Finally, the new law amends Article 151 of the Public Contracts Code containing "Sponsorships and special forms of partnership" in the field of cultural heritage. The latter provided that to ensure the use of the national cultural heritage and promote scientific research applied to protection, the Ministry of Cultural Heritage and Activities and Tourism could activate "special forms of partnership with public bodies and organizations and with private entities, aimed at allowing the recovery, restoration, scheduled maintenance, management, opening to public use and enhancement of immovable cultural assets, through simplified procedures for identifying the private partner."

The amendment provides that not only the competent Ministry but also the State, the regions, and the territorial administrations can, in partnership with private (but also public) subjects, can activate these special forms of PPP, in order to activate forms of protection of the cultural heritage spread throughout the national territory, including small towns and villages, and to expand the forms of use and enhancement of the cultural and landscape heritage. The intervention is of considerable importance for the relaunch of the cultural heritage sector as it expands the number of public entities authorized to implement PPP initiatives in the sector through simplified procedures for the choice of the private partner as well as innovative and experimental forms of partnership between the public and private.

The PPP for Innovation

The Ministry of Economic Development (MISE), the Ministry of University and Research (MUR), and the Ministry for Technological Innovation and Digitization (MID) have signed a memorandum of understanding in order to promote the use of PPP for innovation, understood as essential tools for increasing the competitive capacity of companies and considered a strategic lever for modernizing the infrastructures and services of the Public Administration, as well as increasing investments in public research. The Parties have initiated this collaboration by also entrusting AgID (Agency for Digital Italy) with the task of promoting and implementing innovative procurement, with the aim of achieving the following objectives within the next few years:

- Stimulate and support the creation of an industry and a market for innovative solutions encouraged by public demand, also supporting research and development (R&D) and experimentation activities, as well as access to the market for companies in the area.
- Implement the structural transformation of digital infrastructures and public administration services, promoting collaboration between the public and private sectors to generate and disseminate innovation.
- Improving the quality of life of citizens and businesses, encouraging the introduction of innovative solutions and emerging technologies to respond to those simplification needs manifested in daily contact with the public sector.

The first program launched as a result of this partnership is Smarter Italy, born with the Decree of the Ministry of Economic Development of January 31, 2019 and which became operational with the agreement between the MISE and the AgID in order to implement innovative public demand calls.

The Smarter Italy strategic program provides for the definition and launch of innovative tenders. It aims to accelerate the growth of the country and meet the needs expressed by communities, cities, and villages, starting with four areas of intervention:

- Smart mobility to allow people in urban areas to move in a faster, more agile, and sustainable way thanks to the use of technology and innovation.
- The enhancement of cultural heritage for the economic and touristic enhancement of areas of historical and artistic importance.

- Social and people's well-being (well-being) to improve the psycho–physical health of people.
- Protection of the environment for the improvement of the environmental situation in all its aspects.

Recently, two other mega digital projects to be developed in PPP have been announced as part of the Next Generation plan: (1) the national cloud and (2) the national telemedicine platform.

Discussion

The ongoing Covid-19 pandemic has especially revealed the vulnerability of the Italian healthcare system and, at the same time, has highlighted its importance in society. Since the start, the pandemic crisis brought into light several weaknesses of the healthcare delivery services, including inappropriate coordination between facilities and suppliers, inaccessibility of facilities, interruption or cancellation of medical services, and inadequate staff, insufficiency of equipment and spaces on hospital sites. In particular, the healthcare organizations are probably the most heavily affected because of unprecedented strain due to the substantial increase in demand for their services and the flow of patients seeking a cure (Ghobadian et al., 2022). Moreover, their ability to effectively provide timely and good quality treatment to existing and new patients affected by a disaster is often badly compromised (Donelli et al., 2022). Healthcare facilities, as centers of medical services, play a critical role in the continuation of the recovery of the cure (Tippong et al., 2022).

Current events have proven that formal partnerships between the public and private sectors that harmonize the efforts of multiple stakeholders (at international, national, and subnational levels) partnerships between the public and private sectors are critically needed. PPP projects will then be able to support sustainable and resilient healthcare systems that can combat pandemics and other health crises. The use of PPPs will make it possible to respond to multiple objectives, satisfy different needs, and overcome certain constraints (Abuzaineh et al., 2018):

- Build new structures or modernize existing ones.
- Overcome the public budget constraints that limit public spending.
- Improve the managerial competences of hospitals or the quality of the health service.
- Improve supplies and supply chains.
- Offer additional services (specializations, etc.) or increase the service capacity.

Up to now, in Italy, healthcare PPP projects have been mainly "infrastructure-oriented," that is, aimed at the construction, renovation, or maintenance of existing structures, and the offer of non-health services.

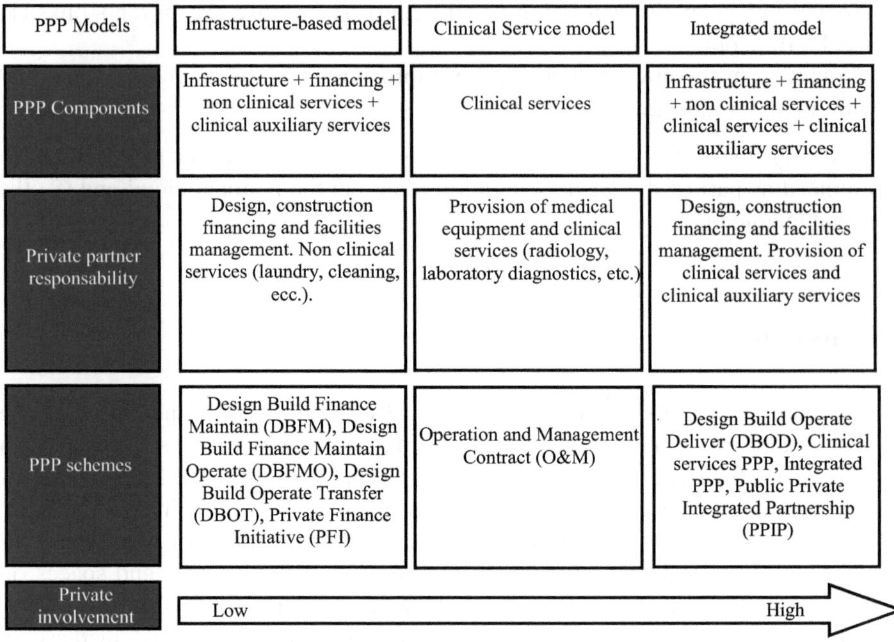

Fig. 2 Healthcare PPP models. (Adapted from Abuzaineh et al., 2018)

In the future, it will be appropriate to develop "clinical service-oriented" PPP projects or, better still, "integrated" PPP projects, which concern both infrastructure and clinical services (Sekhri et al., 2011).

These PPP models (Fig. 2) will allow to increase the variety of services offered, improve the quality and accessibility of the services offered, as well as allow to increase the service capacity of existing structures, build health infrastructures in generally shorter times, access to private capital and competences.

Conclusion

Confronting the huge need to quickly spend the Next Generation budget, Italian public authorities seem to have successfully overcome their fears and skepticism toward PPP, which, before the pandemic, hindered the development of partnership models. However, such a vibrant pro-collaborative mood may bring impending doom if Italian authorities are unable to use PPP strategically. Indeed, a PPP is not just an alternative procurement route or a way to outsource big bundled contracts to the market, as has been intended so far across the world, but should be conceived as an approach to achieve more challenging results, thanks to a system of incentives for the market to generate innovation, change, and public value, as co-shared bold goals.

These are realistically the truly challenging goals beyond Next Gen and the European structural and investments funds, which Italy is one of the main beneficiaries of. To realize a strategic approach to PPP, rather than a contingent one (i.e., to quickly spend the EU budget and deliver the projects negotiated with the EU Commission), it is salient to re-invest in public management and public sector leaders after a decade dominated by severe spending reviews and a return to bureaucracy and formalism. It requires public managers with vast knowledge of societal needs, vision, leadership, and project management skills, able to face the responsibility dictated by urgency and risks inherent in social innovation and value creation, capable of interacting with the market and acting as sophisticated buyers, i.e., challenging the market to identify and experiment new, sustainable, and measurable collaboration paths, according to the motto "horses for courses." This is at least a priority when the PPP is applied not just to hard infrastructure development but especially to public service innovation. Only in this way will it be possible to create widespread legitimacy, trust, and capacity (Casady et al., 2020), which are critical to make PPP a future-proof approach. Public private collaborations will be given true longevity only if authorities, not only in Italy, are able to use PPP/concession contracts strategically, based on renewed collaboration and alignment with the private sector, beyond mere short-term goals, as either quick spending or macroeconomic arguments. The success of PPP depends also on a renewed approach in private management, whose challenge is to better understand public sector priorities and how to truly generate public value. To do this, it will be salient to promote and sustain an osmosis between public and private managers to support a co-evolution toward a public-value management. In many countries, and not only in Italy, the tendency is to underestimate the capabilities of public managers, which do exist and can contribute to make the private sector more responsive and ready to a new approach to PPP.

References

Abuzaineh, N., Brashers, E., Foong, S., Feachem, R., & Da Rita, P. (2018). "*PPPs in healthcare: Models, lessons and trends for the future*". Healthcare public-private partnership series, No. 4. San Francisco: The Global Health Group, Institute for Global Health Sciences, University of California, San Francisco and PwC. Produced in the United States of America. First Edition, January.

Bank of Italy (2019), Annual Report, Rome.

Casady, C. B., Eriksson, K., Levitt, R. E., & Scott, W. R. (2020). (re)defining public-private partnerships (PPPs) in the new public governance (NPG) paradigm: An institutional maturity perspective. *Public Management Review, 22*(2), 161–183.

Donelli, C. C., Fanelli, S., Zangrandi, A., & Elefanti, M. (2022). Disruptive crisis management: Lessons from managing a hospital during the COVID-19 pandemic. *Management Decision, 60*(13), 66–91. https://doi.org/10.1108/MD-02-2021-0279

Edler, J., & Georghiou, L. (2007). Public Procurement and Innovation - esurrecting the demand side. *Research Policy, 36*(7), 949–963. https://doi.org/10.1016/j.respol.2007.03.003

Ghobadian, A., Han, T., Zhang, X., O'Regan, N., Troise, C., Bresciani, S., & Narayanan, V. (2022). COVID-19 pandemic: The interplay between firm disruption and managerial attention focus. *British Journal of Management, 33*(1), 390–409. https://doi.org/10.1111/1467-8551.12556

Roehrich, J. K., Lewis, M., & George, G. (2014). Are Public Private Partnerships a healthy option? A systematic literature review. *Social Science & Medicine, 113*, 110.

Sekhri, N., Feachem, R., & Ni, A. (2011). Public–private integrated partnerships demonstrate the potential to improve health care access, quality, and efficiency. *Health Affairs, 30*(8), 1498–1507.

Tippong, D., Petrovic, S., & Akbari, V. (2022). A review of applications of operational research in healthcare coordination in disaster management. *European Journal of Operational Research, 301*(1), 1–17.

PPP Procurement and Governance in India: Lessons from COVID-19 and Way Forward

Kumar V. Pratap

Introduction

COVID-19 is a black swan event (Forbes, 2020) with major impact on economies, and people's lives and livelihoods. The IMF estimated the global growth rate to be (−) 3.3% in 2020 (IMF, 2021a). The distress was disproportionately higher for women, youth, and lower educational attainment individuals (IMF, 2021a). Close to 95 million more people worldwide are estimated to have fallen below the threshold of extreme poverty in 2020 (India's numbers account for nearly 60% of the global increase in poverty [India Today, 2021]) compared with pre-pandemic projections (IMF, 2021a). The potential economic impact of the pandemic on Asia and the Pacific range from $1.7 trillion to $2.5 trillion, across different containment scenarios (ADB, 2021).

With the disruption in global supply chains, demand slowdown in transport infrastructure industries and increased uncertainty across economies, risk perception reached high levels, with commensurate impact on infrastructure investments. As per the Private Participation in Infrastructure database of the World Bank (ppi.worldbank.org), private sector investment in 2020 (US$45.7 billion in 252 projects[1]) dropped by an unprecedented 52% compared to 2019 (World Bank, 2021)

[1] This data is only for developing countries. As per the Infrastructure Monitor, 2021 of the Global Infrastructure Hub, all countries, including High-Income Countries (HICs), saw USD156 billion invested in infrastructure projects by private investors in 2020, representing 0.2% of global GDP and was little affected by the pandemic for HICs, while private investment in middle and low income countries declined significantly. The Infrastructure Monitor adds that HICs attract around three-quarters of all private investment in infrastructure projects. To put this in perspective, high-income countries represent around 60% of global GDP.

K. V. Pratap (✉)
Government of India, New Delhi, India

© The Author(s), under exclusive license to Springer Nature Switzerland AG 2023

T. Dolla et al. (eds.), *Revisiting Public-Private Partnerships*,
Contributions to Public Administration and Public Policy,
https://doi.org/10.1007/978-3-031-37015-1_6

(see Fig. 1). Private investment commitments have not fallen to these levels since 2004, when investment totalled US$31.3 billion. Nevertheless, despite the pandemic, investments in the second half of 2020 (H2) increased by 15% from the first half of the year (H1).

India saw a more pronounced COVID-19 impact with a growth rate of (−) 6.6% in Financial Year (April–March) 2020–21. This was the worst ever performance in independent India till date (there have been only four years of negative GDP growth in Independent India [excluding 2020–21]: 1957–58 [−0.5%], 1965–66 [−2.7%], 1972–73 [−0.5%]), and 1979–80 (−5.1%)] (Economic Survey, 2019–20). The negative growth rate in 2020–21 came at a time when the country's economy was already doing poorly with economic growth of barely 4% in 2019–20, which implied that the economy's capacity to cope with a one-in-a-century pandemic was low (Acharya, 2021).

The first COVID wave in 2020 was followed by a more ferocious second COVID wave in 2021. However, as the country had learnt somewhat to deal with the pandemic (local lockdowns compared to national lockdown in the first wave) and the second wave being of a shorter duration compared to the first, combined with the low base GDP of 2020–21, the GDP growth rate recovered in Financial Year 2021–22 to 8.7%. Nonetheless, the GDP growth in the last two financial years brings the GDP to slightly more than the GDP in 2019–20, effectively wiping out the economic achievements of the last two years because of COVID-19.

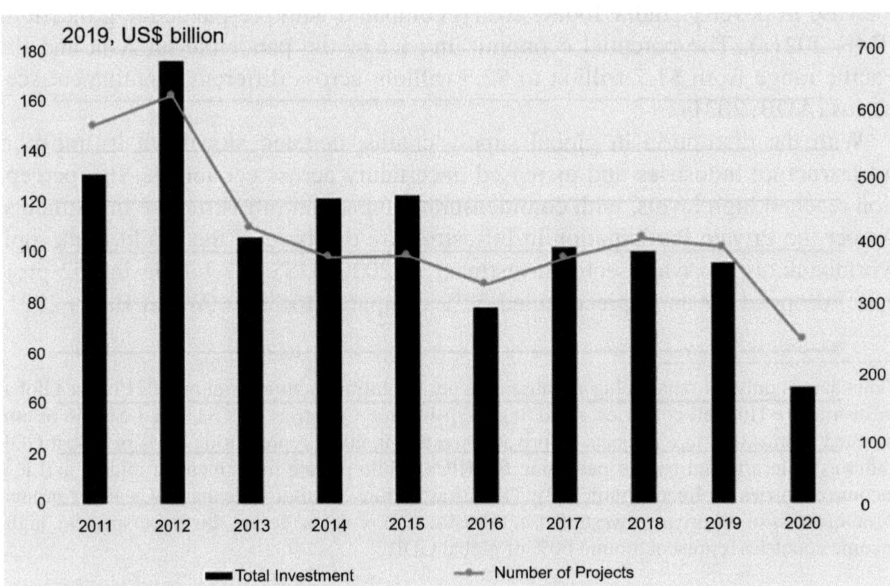

Source: World Bank. 2021. *Private Participation in Infrastructure 2020 Annual Report*

Fig. 1 Private investment in infrastructure projects in EMDEs (emerging markets and developing economies), 2011–2020

There was a comparatively lighter third wave in January–February 2022. Three shocks in the space of two years in India, is estimated to have resulted in total COVID-19 infections of 43 million accounting for 525,000 deaths [Government of India (MyGov), 2022].

The rest of the paper is planned as follows: In section "The Context", we try to assess the impact of COVID-19 on Indian infrastructure, which is among the world leaders in private participation in infrastructure. In section "Case Study: Delhi International Airport Limited", we delve deeper, with a case study on a major Public–Private Partnership (PPP) project (Delhi International Airport Limited, DIAL) that was adversely impacted by COVID-19 to understand the options in dealing with the issue so that it is fair to all stakeholders. In sections "Analysis" and "Discussion", we analyse and discuss the issue, while in sections "Key Inferences for Theory" and "Key Inferences for Practice", we derive inferences for theory and practice. This will show the way for more resilient PPPs in the future. Section "Conclusion" concludes.

The Context

Impact of COVID-19 on the Scale of PPP Procurement in India

As per the Private Participation in Infrastructure (PPI) database of the World Bank (ppi.worldbank.org), India is second in the developing world both by the number of Public–Private Partnership (PPP) projects as well as the associated investments (Table 1).

Table 1 Top 10 countries by Private Participation in Infrastructure in the developing world (1990–2021)[a]

Rank	Country	Investments ($ billion)	Number of projects
1	Brazil	446	1074
2	India	281	1128
3	China	250	1933
4	Turkey	147	254
5	Mexico	96	360
6	Russian Federation	82	383
7	Indonesia	67	142
8	Argentina	59	252
9	Philippines	58	170
10	Malaysia	54	126

Source: Private Participation in Infrastructure database of the World Bank (ppi.worldbank.org) (viewed on 10 April 2022)
[a]Ranked by Investment

Table 2 PPP projects in India (1990–2021), by sector

Sector	Number of projects	Investment ($ billion)
Energy	468	155
ICT	25	3
Transport	563	120
Water & Sewerage	72	3
Total	1128	281

Source: Private Participation in Infrastructure database of the World Bank (ppi.worldbank.org) (viewed on 10 April 2022)

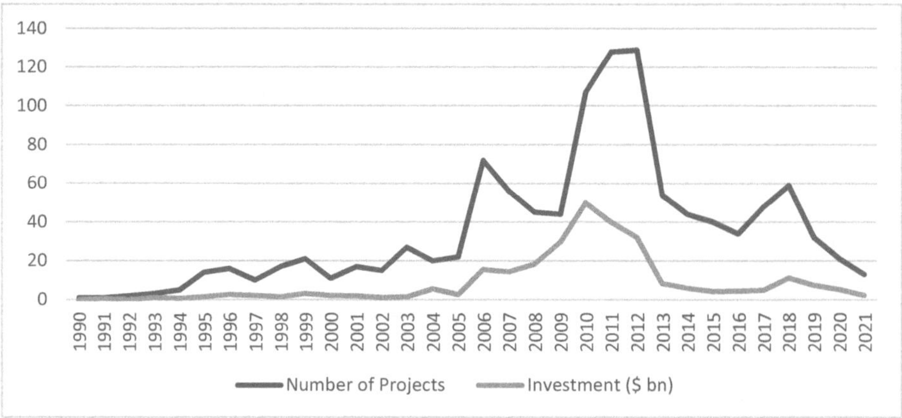

Source: Private Participation database of the World Bank (ppi.worldbank.org) (viewed on 3 April 2022)

Fig. 2 India – number of PPP projects and investment ($ bn) (by year)

As can be seen from Table 1, India has 1128 Public–Private Partnership (PPP) projects accounting for an investment of $281 billion. The sectoral break-up of PPP infrastructure projects and investment in India may be seen in Table 2.

In India, most number of projects have come up in the transport sector (563 projects) (and within transport, in the road sub-sector, 494 projects). Most private investment has flown into the energy sector (mainly electricity generation) at $155 billion. The sector where there is large infrastructure deficit and could gain immensely from private investment is the water and sewerage sector.

The year-wise break-up of Indian PPP projects (1128 PPP projects with associated investments of $281 bn between 1990 and 2021) is shown in Fig. 2 below.

As is apparent from Fig. 2, there has been a pronounced slowdown in PPP procurement in India in the last two COVID-afflicted years. On an average, India contracted 35 PPP projects accounting for an investment of $8.77 bn per year (averaged over 32 years from 1990 to 2021). However, the number of PPP projects contracted in 2020 and 2021 are 21 and 13, respectively, with the investments dwindling to $5.25 bn and $2.16 bn, respectively. The numbers show that what India has achieved in the last two COVID-afflicted years in terms of number of PPP projects and the associated investments are still below the average achievements of a single year for the country. The reasons could be the private sector becoming more risk averse and their outlook changing to conserving cash from making investments in the extremely risky COVID period. Contact-intensive sectors like aviation (airports and airlines) and hospitality (hotels, restaurants, and tourism) were disproportionately impacted.

COVID-19's Impact on India's PPP Market

Following a strict national lockdown imposed from 24 March to early June 2020, the COVID pandemic slowed down the infrastructure programme of the country, both from the demand and the supply side. Passenger traffic on roads, railways, and by air was locked down, and in the power sector, there was a major demand slow down (about 28% less than business-as-usual) with most industrial and commercial activity locked up. This had left airports and travel terminals largely underutilized, which denied these projects their usual source of air-side revenue (such as gate and landing fees) and land-side revenue (such as retail). Conversely, there was increased uptake and traffic for telecommunications infrastructure, as well as personal modes of transport. Health infrastructure also experienced increased demand.

On the supply side, supply chains and construction labour force were dislocated because of the pandemic. The net result was that India suffered a (−) 23.8% GDP growth rate in the period April–June (Q1) 2020, the largest decline among the G20 countries. But, the economy recovered progressively in later quarters (July–Sept [Q2] 2020 [−] 6.6%; Oct–Dec 2020 [Q3] [+] 0.7%; Jan–March [Q4] 2021 [+]2.5%), with the overall real GDP growth being (−) 6.6% in Financial Year 2020–21 (National Stock Exchange, 2022).

With the above economic environment, the PPP market was adversely impacted (see Fig. 2). Risk aversion became a dominant depressant to economic recovery for enterprises, workers, and consumers. Contact intensive sectors like aviation (airlines and airports), travel (roads, railways), and hospitality (restaurants, hotels, tourism) and many other service sectors suffered disproportionately.

User fee-based infrastructure and PPP projects suffered from demand slowdown, which has a direct impact on the revenues and therefore the financial viability of these projects (it is estimated that NHAI incurred toll revenue loss of Rs. 3513 crore [USD 468 mn at the average exchange rate of $1 = Rs. 75] in 2020–21 due to COVID-related restrictions [Business Standard, 2021]). Availability-based projects (BOT annuity road projects, for example) did not have immediate adverse financial impact, but stretched public sector finances in an environment in which they were already strained because of high priority demands of the pandemic.

There are implications of the pandemic on the National Infrastructure Pipeline (NIP) too. The government, in a major pro-active initiative, drew up the NIP with an ambitious plan to invest Rs.111 lakh crore (about USD1.5 trillion) on infrastructure in the six-year period up to FY2025, roughly planning to double the annual infrastructure investment compared to what has been achieved in recent years. As per estimates in the NIP Task Force Report (the author was Member Secretary of the NIP Task Force), about 79% of the required investment would come from the Central and the State governments and the associated Public Sector Undertakings, and this would be constrained given the state of the Indian public finances and the higher priority demands of the pandemic. Strong government expenditure was a key driver of economic growth in the years before and during COVID. Government consumption went up by an annual rate of 9% between 2014 and 2019. This resulted in a significant expansion in borrowing and the pandemic further pushed up the fiscal deficit (9.2% of GDP in 2020–21 [with the combined federal and state fiscal deficit being an unprecedented over 12.8% in that year] and 6.7% of GDP in 2021–22). Since the public debt has increased to about 90% of GDP from 74% in FY2020 (global debt has jumped to $226 trn in 2020, including debt of governments, households, and non-financial corporations, which is $27 trn above 2019 and the largest ever on record [IMF, 2021b]), the government's ability to support growth with higher expenditure would remain limited.

This would adversely impact the implementation of the NIP unless the slack is picked up by the private sector, which is unlikely in the Financial Years 2021 and 2022. But, since NIP is a six-year infrastructure investment plan, the FY 2021 and 2022 slack may be bridged in the later years given the infrastructure investment green shoots that have appeared recently (see Box 1) (Pratap, 2022).

Box 1 Infrastructure investment green shoots

Even as infrastructure investment slowed down due to COVID-19, there is anecdotal evidence that some important deals happened. The noteworthy transactions after-COVID (post-March 2020) were:

- Adani Green Energy bagged the world's largest solar tender to construct 8 GW photovoltaic power plant and 2 GW solar cell and module manufacturing capacity at a total envisaged investment of $6 billion (June 2020). It also signed the world's largest green Power Purchase Agreement with Solar Energy Corporation of India (SECI) to supply 4667 MW of green power (December 2021).
- IRB Infrastructure achieved financial closure of Mumbai–Pune Expressway in a major brownfield asset monetization initiative at the state level for a total consideration of Rs 8262 crore (June 2020).
- Spanish Solarpack Corporation won the bid at Rs 2.36 per unit for 300 MW of solar power (lowest solar bid in India till then) in a SECI tender (June 2020). In subsequent tenders, the price of solar power has gone down to Rs.1.99 per unit (US 2.7 cents).
- Acquisition by Reliance of Norway-based REC Solar Holdings (100% stake for $771 mn), a well-established global player in solar cells, panel, and polysilicon manufacturing, and Sterling & Wilson Solar (40% stake for $379 mn), a strong player for EPC and O&M services in the RE sector (October 2021). Reliance, subsequently, raised a $736 mn green loan to finance its largest overseas purchase, REC Solar Holdings, joining the

Box 1 (continued)

growing list of Indian companies embracing sustainable finance to fund environment-friendly projects (Times of India, 2021). Reliance has been investing in new energy assets like Germany's NexWafe, Denmark's Stiesdal, USA's Ambri, and UK-based sodium–ion battery technology provider Faradion (for £100 million).

- The most noteworthy transaction was raising of Rs 152,057 crore (USD 20.3 bn) by Reliance by selling just under a third of the stake of RIL in Jio Platforms (April–July 2020).
- The Adani Group has bagged the contract to build India's longest expressway project – the Rs.17,000 crore (USD 2.3 bn) and 594 km long Meerut–Prayagraj e-way – in Uttar Pradesh (December 2021). This would be a six-lane access-controlled expressway built on PPP (DBFOT) mode with a concession period of 30 years.
- CDPQ, a Canadian pension fund, has bought 40% stake in Odisha toll road (67 km long Shree Jagannath Expressway) for Rs.2100 crore (USD 280 mn) (December 2021).
- Ola Electric has raised over $200 million from Tekne Private Ventures, Alpine Opportunity Fund, Edelweiss, and others, valuing the Electric Vehicle maker at $5 bn (January 2022).
- Blackrock Real Assets and Mubadala Investment Company will put Rs.4000 crore (USD 533 mn) into Tata Power's renewable energy business for an 11% stake (April 2022).

The total value of these transactions is about ₹ 2.5 trn (US$ 33.3 bn), which has been achieved in the extremely difficult COVID times. What is noteworthy about these transactions is the diversity of sectors – roads, telecom, solar, and renewable energy – in which investment has come, which demonstrates the overall attraction of Indian infrastructure to investors; in addition to brownfield assets, investment also in greenfield projects with high construction risk; transactions at both the federal and the state level; funding predominantly from foreign investment, implying internalization of currency risk inherent in infrastructure investments, which in turn shows that foreign investors are betting on a stable Indian economy over the longer term; and the large size of projects. All this augurs well for future infrastructure resource mobilization (Pratap, 2020a).

The Major Issues That Have Emerged Due to COVID-19

In the wake of COVID-19, there have been demands for relief packages (from airlines, airports, power, etc.) amidst severe fiscal constraints. In addition, there were demands for deferring revenue share due to the Government and deferring required capital investments.

Delhi International Airport Limited (DIAL) has invoked *force majeure* clause to suspend revenue share (45.99%) with Airports Authority of India (AAI) during FY2021. DIAL has also sought other reliefs, including "cash support …to sustain operations" (dealt at length later in this chapter). In addition, DIAL has pushed back its expansion plan of Terminal 1 (T1) by a year because of COVID-19.

Mumbai International Airport Limited (MIAL) had got a reprieve from Delhi High Court in December 2020, as it had restrained AAI from collecting 38.7% revenue share from MIAL. It has also restrained AAI from transferring funds from the escrow account to itself. The relief was to be in place till an arbitral tribunal decides on the issue. MIAL has also deferred capital expenditure of Rs.3000 crore (US$ 400 mn).

COVID-19 would also increase the risk of PPP project failures and the Government should not be aiming at rehabilitating all distressed firms. Commercial discipline and the "freedom to fail" are a big part of the rationale for turning to the private sector, and some project failures should therefore be expected, since some projects or concessionaires will underperform. Rather than going in for repeated renegotiations to sweeten the deal for the private sector, allowing some PPP projects to be cancelled (or allowing them to fail) is probably the only way to elicit more realistic bidding from the private sector. While the importance of infrastructure investment in economic recoveries is well documented, the government would be well-advised not to save zombies, as trying to save each and every distressed firm would be extremely inefficient expenditure in these fiscally trying times (Pratap, 2020b).

Response to COVID-19 by the Government for Protecting Operational PPP Projects as Well as PPP Project Pipeline

Government of India, Ministry of Finance has held that COVID-19 would be considered a *force majeure* event, which implies that the remedies provided in the *force majeure* clauses of the Concession Agreement can be invoked.

As per Model Concession Agreement (MCA) of the road sector, the remedy for a force majeure event (non-political event) is extending the concession period; however, this does not address immediate liquidity issues for which the country's central bank, Reserve Bank of India (RBI) allowed moratorium on debt payments for 6 months. Also, the deadline for the fulfilment of contractual obligations of all government projects, including PPPs, which were due for completion on or after February 2020, was increased by up to 6 months in view of the COVID-19 pandemic.

For protecting liquidity of firms, in the Road sector, the Government took a number of additional measures: allowed direct payment to approved sub-contractors through escrow account; allowed release of retention money in proportion of the work already executed by the companies; no reduction against bills raised by contractor; reduction of performance security from 5–10% of contract value to 3%; extension of concession period for concessionaire in case of reduction in user fee collections in Build-Operate-Transfer (BOT)/Toll-Operate-Transfer (TOT) models; and waiver of penalty in case of delay in submission of performance security.

Then there are "Change in Law" clauses in the Concession Agreement, which could be invoked, because of the Ministry of Home Affairs orders imposing nationwide lockdown. The relief provided in the MCA is to restore concessionaires to the same position in Net Present Value (NPV) terms, as they would have been in, if this Change in Law had not occurred, which would be of significant financial help. In addition, moratorium of one year on the initiation of insolvency (as per Insolvency and Bankruptcy Code, IBC) proceedings has been provided.

The degree to which the aforementioned avenues may provide relief would have to be evaluated in accordance with the provisions of the operative contract (Concession Agreement).

Case Study: Delhi International Airport Limited

Project Details

The Indian aviation sector, as a major component of the Indian growth story, was sailing smoothly before being buffeted by the COVID wave in 2020. The number of airports in the country had risen from 74 in 2014 to 140 by 2021, and is further set to reach 220 by 2025. To match the growth in infrastructure, the aircraft fleet is also likely to grow from 710 today, by 110–120 every year, as well as expand the share of wide-bodied aircraft for greater long-haul connectivity.

Delhi International Airport Limited (DIAL) is one of the 140 airports in the country. It is the Special Purpose Vehicle (SPV) for the Indira Gandhi International Airport at New Delhi and is the crown jewel of the Indian aviation story. It is a Transport sector project, with Airport as the sub-sector and segment being Runway and Terminal. It is a brownfield project with the concession type being Build-Rehabilitate-Operate-Transfer (BROT). The original contract period is 30 years, with the option of extending the contract period by another 30 years, provided certain conditions are met.

The contract award method was competitive bidding (5 bids were received). The bidding parameter was revenue share with the public entity, AAI, and the winning bid provided for 45.99% revenue share. The financial closure of DIAL happened in 2006. While DIAL is the SPV, the winning bidder was a consortium led by GMR Infrastructure Limited, including Fraport of Frankfurt, Germany, and others. GMR Infrastructure Limited is part of the GMR Group, one of India's fastest growing infrastructure companies with interests in airports, energy, highways, and urban infrastructure, and with a presence in several countries beyond India, including Turkey, South Africa, Indonesia, and Singapore. It had been partnering with the Government in the popular Public–Private Partnership (PPP) model that the Indian government had adopted since the late 1990s. GMR has also built the iconic Rajiv Gandhi International Airport at Shamshabad near Hyderabad.

The modernized international airport in Delhi was opened for traffic in 2010 just in time for the 2010 Commonwealth Games. It became South Asia's largest hub, which handled about 36 mn passengers in 2011–12 and 69.23 mn in 2018–19. Its Terminal 3 was completed within the time for the Commonwealth Games. In the years 2012 and 2013, the DIAL was consistently ranked the second-best airport in the world in the 25–40 million-passenger category by the Airports Council International (ACI). More recently, DIAL was rated the Best Airport in over 40 million passengers per annum (MPPA) category in Asia Pacific region by ACI in the Airport Service Quality (ASQ) Programme 2019 rankings. DIAL has also been adjudged the "best airport in India and South Asia" in the 2022 Skytrax World Airport Awards.

Besides upgrading the existing terminals, DIAL commissioned a new runway 11–29 in September 2008. It also commissioned the new domestic departure terminal – 1D (T1D) in February 2009. In March 2010, DIAL has completed the construction of integrated passenger terminal (Terminal 3) marking the completion of the first phase of development. Terminal 3 is the largest single terminal in India and fifth largest in the world. IGIA is India's only Airport with three operational runways. With this, IGIA is now capable of handling 62 MPPA. The airport infrastructure will be enhanced further based on passenger demand and market needs. Terminals and runway capacity will be added in a modular manner to form a "U" shaped complex with an ultimate design capacity of 100 million passengers per annum.

DIAL is the first Carbon Neutral Airport in the Asia Pacific Region, under Airport Carbon Accreditation Program of ACI. Delhi Airport has installed 7.84 MW solar power plant in the airside area, and is the first airport in the country to have such a facility. The airport also has a very robust energy efficiency programme in place and is the first airport globally to have ISO 50001 certified Energy Management System. For water management, significant initiatives have been undertaken including 16.6 MLD Zero Discharge Sewage Treatment Plant (STP), more than 300 rainwater harvesting structures and water efficient fixtures in the Terminals (DIAL, 2022).

Overview of Planning, Procurement, Construction and Operation Activities

On 31 January 2006, a consortium led by GMR Infrastructure Limited won the contract to modernize the international airport at India's capital, New Delhi. This came about slightly over two and a half years from the approval of the proposal for modernization (via PPP) of the Delhi airport by the AAI.

The AAI signed an Operation, Management and Development Agreement (OMDA) with the Special Purpose Vehicle created by the winning bidder, Delhi International Airport Limited (DIAL) on 4 April 2006, as a state promoter with 26% equity holding, and the private sector consortia holding the balance 74%. On 3 May 2006, AAI handed over IGI Airport, Delhi to DIAL on "as is where is" basis and granted DIAL the exclusive right to undertake the functions of its operations, maintenance, development, design, construction, modernization, finance, and management.

But this journey of privatization and modernization of the Delhi airport was neither smooth nor free from controversy. The projected costs ballooned to nearly four times from Rs. 3297 crore (US$ 440 mn) at the time of bidding to an eventual Rs. 12,857 crore (USD 1.7 bn) as per DIAL. This increase in cost, in turn, was initially thought to be funded through a rights issue which ran into difficulty owing to AAI's inability to subscribe to it. The final recourse, therefore, was to the markedly unpopular levy of Development Fees. While all these steps were taken with the knowledge and approval of Airport Economic Regulatory Authority (AERA) and relevant government agencies, that was not enough to avoid subsequent controversies and acrimonies.

Of the controversies surrounding the project, two main sets of issues were the most important and visible – one surrounding the process of awarding of the contract, highlighted by a court case alleging unfairness on the part of the Government in awarding the contract to the GMR-led group by a competing group led by Reliance Infra. The second controversy was one that stemmed from the Indian Comptroller and Auditor General's (CAG) audit report in 2012 for DIAL for the period 2006–11 pointing out several ways in which the Government appeared to have undersold the airport operations to DIAL at significant opportunity loss to the exchequer. The court case got dismissed and the debate around the CAG allegations ultimately subsided. However, the issues raised by the much-publicized CAG report indicated the nature of conflict and misunderstanding that large and iconic PPPs can generate in emerging market environments (Pratap & Chakravarti, 2018).

DIAL saw significant losses in 2010–11 and 2011–12 before turning into profits in 2012–13. Thereafter, it made profits for the next five years. In more recent years, its profitability was very limited (see Fig. 3). In 2020–21, the losses increased (Rs (−) 188 crore, USD 25 mn)] owing to less revenue generation due to COVID-19.

A look at Fig. 3 reveals that Revenues and the PAT curves mirror each other and in recent times, DIAL's financial position has deteriorated. So, the ability of the company to withstand the challenges of COVID-19 was considerably attenuated. The total passengers handled at DIAL came down sharply from 69.23 mn in 2018–19 to 67.30 mn in 2019–20 (3% decrease from previous year), and further to 22.58 mn in 2020–21 (66% decrease from the previous year, mainly due to COVID-19). In fact, in absolute terms, over the last 11 years, DIAL has made a total net profit of only Rs. 30 crore (US$ 4 mn). Table 3 shows the timeline of the DIAL project.

Analysis

The private airports in the country have demanded a relief package from the government on account of low traffic because of the COVID pandemic ("cash support …to sustain operations"). This was expected, given the severe hit to airport financials as

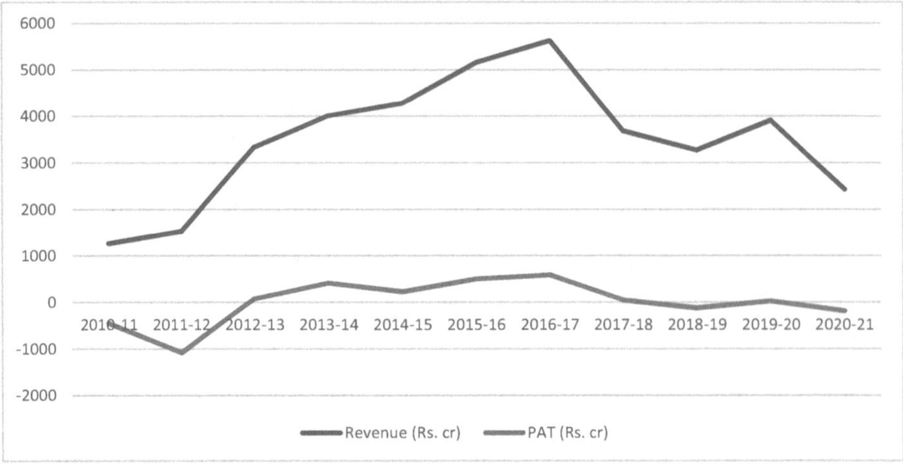

Source: Profit and Loss Statements of DIAL, 2011-21

Fig. 3 DIAL performance – revenues and profit after tax (PAT)

Table 3 Timeline of Delhi International Airport Limited (DIAL)

31 January 2006	Delhi Airport awarded to consortium of GMR-Fraport whose SPV was DIAL
4 April 2006	Airports Authority of India (AAI) signs Operation, Management and Development Agreement (OMDA) with DIAL
3 May 2006	AAI hands over Delhi Airport to DIAL on "as is where is" basis and grants DIAL the exclusive right to undertake the functions of its operations, maintenance, development, design, construction, modernization, finance, and management
2008	Airport Economic Regulatory Authority (AERA) established to regulate the economic aspects of airports
2010	DIAL completes the construction of integrated passenger terminal (Terminal 3) marking the completion of the first phase of development. Terminal 3 is the largest single terminal in India and fifth largest in the world. Modernized Delhi Airport opened to traffic
2019	DIAL was rated the Best Airport in over 40 million passengers per annum (MPPA) category in Asia Pacific region by ACI in the Airport Service Quality (ASQ) Programme rankings
2020–21	DIAL's losses increased to Rs. (−) 188 crore (USD 25 mn) owing to massive decrease in the number of passengers (22.58 mn, 66% decrease from the previous year) and consequently less revenue generation, mainly due to COVID-19
2021	DIAL demands a relief package from the government on account of low traffic because of the COVID pandemic ("cash support …to sustain operations")

contact-intensive sectors like aviation (airports and airlines) and hospitality (hotels and restaurants) have borne the brunt of the COVID-19 pandemic.

DIAL Concession Agreement: Operation, Management and Development Agreement

India relies on the written and signed (by both the public and the private parties) concession agreements for contract management and other aspects of governance of Public–Private Partnerships. There are five key areas of PPP contract design included in the concession agreement – performance requirements (defining the required quality and quantity of assets/services, and monitoring and enforcement mechanisms, including penalties); payment mechanisms (defining how the private party will be paid, through user charges, government payments based on usage or availability, or a combination, including incentives and penalties); adjustment mechanisms (building in contract mechanisms for handling changes, such as extraordinary review of tariffs, or changing service requirements); dispute resolution procedures (defining institutional mechanism for dealing with contractual disputes – conciliation, arbitration, adjudication); and termination provisions (defining the contract term, handover provisions, and circumstances and implications of early termination).

Therefore, the way to deal with this demand of airports, in general, and DIAL, in particular, is to follow the Concession Agreement. The private sector has entered into an agreement with the government entity (in this case, AAI) that defines the risk and the returns of the private sector. The agreement, in the case of DIAL, is called the Operation, Management and Development Agreement (OMDA), which has *force majeure* provisions (chapter 16 of OMDA) that deal with events or circumstances that "materially and adversely affects the performance" of the parties, "are beyond the reasonable control" of the parties, the parties "could not have prevented or reasonably overcome with the exercise of Good Industry Practice or reasonable skill and care," and do not result from the negligence or misconduct of parties or the failure of the parties to perform their obligations. As per the OMDA, the events that merit invocation of *force majeure* include an "epidemic." The WHO declared COVID a Public Health Emergency of International Concern on 30 January 2020, and a pandemic on 11 March 2020. Therefore, the COVID pandemic falls within the ambit of "epidemic," which can cause the invocation of *force majeure* clauses in the OMDA.

The OMDA also describes the relief (suspend performance of an obligation by the contracting party), including termination of the contract for reasons of *force majeure*. Nowhere is it written in the *force majeure* clauses that the government will provide "cash support ...to sustain operations." The government has already taken a number of measures to ameliorate the impact of COVID on infrastructure projects – it has accepted that COVID-19 would be considered a *force majeure* event. To

Table 4 COVID-19 relief as provided in the OMDA (concession contract) signed between the AAI and DIAL

What is *force majeure*?	Events or circumstances that "materially and adversely affects the performance" of the parties, "are beyond the reasonable control" of the parties, the parties "could not have prevented or reasonably overcome with the exercise of Good Industry Practice or reasonable skill and care," and do not result from the negligence or misconduct of parties or the failure of the parties to perform their obligations
Does COVID-19 qualify to be a force majeure event?	As per the OMDA, the events that merit invocation of *force majeure* include an "epidemic." The WHO declared COVID a pandemic on 11 March 2020. Therefore, the COVID pandemic falls within the ambit of "epidemic," which can cause the invocation of *force majeure* clauses in the OMDA
What is the relief provided for *force majeure* in the OMDA?	Relief provided in the OMDA for a *force majeure* event is to suspend performance of an obligation by the contracting party (say, revenue share by the SPV with the public entity), including termination of the contract

address immediate liquidity concerns, the RBI has allowed moratorium on debt payments for six months. The above analysis is summarized in Table 4 below.

In fact, DIAL, on the basis of an estimated loss in FY2021, against a profit in FY2020, has invoked *force majeure* to suspend revenue share (45.99%) with AAI during FY21. DIAL has also moved Delhi High Court to recover Rs. 399.20 crore (USD53.2 mn) it has paid to AAI in FY2021 on the lines of Mumbai International Airport Limited (MIAL). In a major relief to MIAL, the Delhi High Court restrained AAI from collecting 38.7% revenue share from MIAL in December 2020. It has also restrained AAI from transferring funds from the escrow account to itself.

DIAL wrote to the Union Civil Aviation ministry in December 2020, saying it anticipates a loss of Rs. 3538 crore from April 2020 to March 2024. It informed the government of suffering a cash loss of Rs 419 crore in April–September 2020 (H1) and projected a loss of Rs. 939 crore in the COVID-ravaged FY 2020–21. The airport, which saw 67.30 mn passenger usage in FY 2019–20 falling to 22.58 mn in FY 2020–21, has projected that losses like these will continue till FY 2024: "*Viability gap support of Rs 3,538 crore will be required for third control period (till FY 2024) to maintain operations, service levels, safety and security of the airport... the (declining) traffic scenario has taken a toll on DIAL's financial position and put forth a challenge for sustainable operations. ... In case, AERA does not consider our request of viability gap, DIAL will end up in serious cash flow deficit situation finding itself difficult to continue the airport operations*" (Business Today, 2021).

Discussion

Enforcing contracts and ensuring sanctity of contracts should be a major thrust area of the Government. India has one of the highest infrastructure deficits in the world. To bridge the infrastructure deficit and to attract private investment into infrastructure, India is trying to improve its position in the World Bank's Ease of Doing

Business (EoDB) rankings. Enforcing Contracts is one of the ten parameters considered for the rankings. India ranks 63 among 190 countries in the current rankings, but the country's rank in "enforcing contracts" at 163 out of 190 countries is the worst among all parameters (World Bank's Ease of Doing Business rankings, 2020). Given that COVID-19 is covered under the ambit of epidemic, which qualifies DIAL to invoke *force majeure* clauses of the OMDA, it would stand to reason to provide it the relief provided in the Concession Agreement. This would also uphold the sanctity of the contract (OMDA).

The Government likely did not agree to DIAL's request for "cash support…to sustain operations," which was the right thing to do, as the decrease in demand for air travel was temporary. In March 2022, DIAL became the third busiest airport in the world (as per data released by UK-based global travel data provider company, OAG) with the decline in COVID cases and rising demand for air travel. In March 2020, DIAL held the 20th rank.

So, knee-jerk reactions should be avoided. Had the Government agreed to provide the relief that was sought, it would have made contracts more fragile (with adverse impact on EoDB) and would have made India a less desirable destination for Foreign Direct Investment.

Any move to provide relief beyond what is provided in the OMDA would also amount to privatizing profits and socializing losses. It would give rise to moral hazard, as no matter how reckless companies are in good times, there is always the government (and taxpayers) to bail them out during the bad. Such companies fail to build resilience in good times that could help them weather the inevitable downturns that come. Some justify such demands as a mechanism to prevent systemic failure and further damage to the economy. In reality, this is lemon socialism, a political and economic system where profits are strictly the property of shareholders, and catastrophic losses are an externality to society (World Economic Forum, 2020).

Any relief beyond what is provided in the concession agreement also sets a bad precedent. India is second in the developing world both by the number of PPP projects and the associated investments as per the World Bank's Private Participation in Infrastructure database (ppi.worldbank.org). India currently has 1128 PPP projects, amounting to an investment of $281 billion. The successful implementation of PPP projects across sectors in India also means that there would be unending demands from other sectors (roads, metro, ports, telecom, power, etc.) once a precedent has been established by giving COVID relief beyond the concession agreement to the airport sector. Finally, the capacity of the Government to provide any such relief is severely attenuated with an unprecedented federal fiscal deficit of 9.2% in FY21 (Pratap, 2021).

Key Inferences for Theory

It is true that all eventualities cannot be foreseen and included in the contract. So, concession contracts, by their very nature, are incomplete. Renegotiations, if any, should happen only on account of incompleteness of the contract. If remedy is provided in the contract (say in *force majeure* clauses in the OMDA with DIAL), one should proceed accordingly. If remedy is not provided in the contract, objective should be to bring the parties to the same level in Net Present Value terms, as they would have been without the unforeseen event. Relief should be limited to this objective and designed accordingly.

The Indian policy and regulatory framework does not provide for easy renegotiations, which is how it should be. Allowing for easy renegotiations would mean doing away with sanctity of contracts and as we have already seen, enforcing contracts is one of the ten parameters considered for determining Ease of Doing Business rankings and India ranks the worst (163) on this parameter. So, it serves the country well if the policy and regulatory framework does not provide for easy renegotiations.

As we have seen, India is second in the developing world, both by the number of PPP projects as well as the associated investments. One of the most important reasons for the Indian success story is standardization of contracts. Accordingly, clauses relating to *force majeure* find mention in the Concession Agreement, which also provide the remedy for such events.

Key Inferences for Practice

One of the things to realize is that Concession Contracts for PPPs are long-term and some glitches would occur along the way. Rather than have knee-jerk reactions like "cash support …to sustain operations," following the contract will allow time for these temporary setbacks to work themselves out. In March–April 2022, there has been an upsurge in demand in the airports, airlines, travel, and the hospitality sector and profitability in these sectors is much improved. Two Indian airlines registered profits in the January–March 2022 quarter, and two new airlines are gearing up to emerge in the Indian skies.

Given these positive developments, care has to be taken that COVID-19 does not turn out to be another occasion for opportunistic behaviour. It is widely felt that the Indian Government's action to deal with the fallout of COVID-19 was swift and prevented large scale disruptions.

Conclusion

Concession Contracts for PPPs are long-term and some glitches would occur on the way. Rather than have knee-jerk reactions like "cash support …to sustain operations," which are in the nature of contract renegotiations because they go beyond what is provided in the contract, upholding sanctity of the contract will allow time for these temporary setbacks to work themselves out. In March–April 2022, there has been an upsurge in demand across sectors, including the badly bruised aviation and hospitality sectors, and profitability in these sectors is much improved.

Care has to be taken that COVID-19 does not become another occasion for opportunistic behaviour in the form of demands, effectively, for renegotiation of contracts. Renegotiations are bad in principle and practice and would hurt the Ease of Doing Business. Therefore, upholding sanctity of contracts should be an important part of the strategy to deal with unforeseen events like COVID-19.

The Public–Private Partnership regime has been painstakingly built over the years to place India in the top league of countries on this metric. Efforts should be made to think long-term to build on what has already been achieved, rather than squander the achievements for short-term expediency.

References

Acharya, S. (2021). *An Economist at Home and Abroad – A personal journey*. Harper Collins.

ADB. (2021). *An updated assessment of the economic impact of COVID-19.*

Business Standard. (2021, August 6). *NHAI incurred revenue loss of around Rs 3,512 cr in FY21: Gadkari*. https://www.business-standard.com/article/economy-policy/nhai-incurred-revenue-loss-of-around-rs-3-512-cr-in-fy21-gadkari-121080500806_1.html

Business Today. (2021). DIAL CEO's note to the federal Civil Aviation Secretary in December 2020 as widely reported in the media (e.g.). https://www.businesstoday.in/latest/economy-politics/story/flying-out-of-delhi-to-be-costlier-from-feb-heres-why-283295-2021-01-02

DIAL. (2022). Airport website https://www.newdelhiairport.in/corporate/our-company

Forbes. (2020). *COVID19 is a black swan.* https://www.forbes.com/sites/forbesbooksauthors/2020/03/19/covid-19-is-a-black-swan/?sh=79fc33127b4b

Government of India. (2022). *MyGov Covid-19 website* (https://www.mygov.in/covid-19) (viewed on 19 June 2022).

Government of India, Ministry of Finance. (2020). *Economic Survey 2019–20.*

India Today. (2021, August 23). *Distress Signals.*

International Monetary Fund. (2021a, April). *World Economic Outlook.*

International Monetary Fund. (2021b). *Fiscal Monitor Report.*

National Stock Exchange. (2022, June 1). *NSE Macro Review.*

Pratap, K. V. (2020a). *A new normal in infrastructure - Barring the onset of second COVID wave, the worst is behind us*. The Financial Express.

Pratap, K. V. (2020b). *Public-Private Partnership (PPP) project failures: Don't put zombies on life-support.* The Financial Express (https://www.financialexpress.com/opinion/public-private-partnership-ppp-project-failures-dont-put-zombies-on-life-support/2146855/).

Pratap, K. V. (2021, June 7). *Don't give in to airports' COVID-relief demand.* Financial Express. https://www.financialexpress.com/opinion/dont-give-in-to-airports-COVID-relief-demand/2266191/

Pratap, K. V. (2022). *Infrastructure Financing in India – Trends, challenges and the way forward.* Oxford University Press (forthcoming).

Pratap, K. V., & Chakravarti, R. (2018, January). *Public private partnerships in infrastructure: Managing the challenges*. Springer Science and Business Media Singapore Pte Ltd. http://www.springer.com/la/book/9789811033544

Times of India. (2021, December 7). *RIL makes green finance debut with $736 mn loan.*

World Bank. (2021). Private participation in infrastructure 2020 Annual Report.

World Bank. Private Participation in Infrastructure database. ppi.worldbank.org

World Bank's Ease of Doing Business rankings. (2020). https://www.doingbusiness.org/content/dam/doingBusiness/country/i/india/IND-LITE.pdf

World Economic Forum. (2020). *Why bailing out companies doesn't help people recover from economic shocks of COVID-19.* https://www.weforum.org/agenda/2020/10/governments-stop-bailing-out-companies-readjust-incentives-and-support-people/

Covid-19 Impact on the Highway Sector PPPs in India – Government Support and Implications on Financial Agreements

Mukkai R. Aravindan and A. Thillai Rajan

Introduction

The coronavirus pandemic of 2020–2022 affected the global economy significantly. India was no exception. In this chapter, we will review how the PPP businesses, specifically the road projects, in India fared – in what ways were they affected and how did they come out of the disruption. We will also see whether the relief measures offered by various government bodies played a part in the revival. Were the Public Private Partnership (PPP) companies, or Special Purpose Vehicles (SPVs) as they are called, able to meet their financial obligations or did they default on their loan repayment commitments? These are some questions we intend to answer in this chapter. This chapter is organized in seven sections. The first section talks about the background to this study – history and maturity of the PPP model in India. We formulate the research objectives and the methodology in the second section. The third section covers the scale of the pandemic in India. It also briefly talks about the relief measures and response by the government agencies. In the fourth section, an illustrative case from the roads PPP sector is taken up for detailed study and analysis. Findings from focus interviews conducted with senior executives in the banking system have been described in the fifth section. The implications and learnings from this study are discussed in the sixth section, which is followed by conclusions in the final section.

M. R. Aravindan (✉) · A. Thillai Rajan
Indian Institute of Technology, Madras, Chennai, India

© The Author(s), under exclusive license to Springer Nature Switzerland AG 2023

T. Dolla et al. (eds.), *Revisiting Public-Private Partnerships*,
Contributions to Public Administration and Public Policy,
https://doi.org/10.1007/978-3-031-37015-1_7

Overview of India's Tryst with the PPP Model

India is the seventh largest country in the world in terms of area and the largest in terms of population with about 1.40 billion inhabitants. In 2022, India's economy became the fifth largest by nominal GDP (US$ 3.18 trillion) and the third largest (US$ 10.22 trillion), behind only China and the USA, by purchasing power parity. Among the developing countries, India has been in the forefront of implementing Public Private Partnership (PPP) projects. Since 1990, more than US$ 333 billion have been invested in PPP projects in India, with two sectors – energy and roads – grabbing a lion's share of these investments (Department of Economic Affairs, 2019; Bloomberg, 2022).

India's tryst with the PPP model goes a long way back. The earliest known PPP project in India was the Great Indian Peninsular Railway (presently Central Railway), which was built, owned and operated by a private company incorporated in the UK in 1845 and started operations in 1853 when the first line opened between Mumbai, modern India's financial capital (previously named Bombay), and Thane (a suburb of Mumbai). A minimum dividend of 5 percent was guaranteed to the company by the East India Company, which was ruling most of India at that time. However, PPP projects took off in India only in the 1990s and 2000s with a number of Independent Power Plants and Roads being set up in this mode. Of the total US$ 333 billion invested in PPP projects in India since the 1990s, US$ 110 billion has been invested in the Energy sector and US$ 72 billion in the roads sector in PPP projects (Department of Economic Affairs, 2019).

Public sector procurement process in India for PPP projects had evolved since the 1990s and had gained significant maturity in the next two decades. The process varied from sector to sector, though there was an underlying thread unifying the processes. PPP formats have been used for national as well as state (provincial government) projects. Projects to be implemented through the PPP route were proposed by the respective ministry and approved by a centralized committee, the Public Private Partnership Appraisal Committee (PPPAC). Certain sectors such as roads and ports had a well-defined system with model RFQ (Request for Qualification), model RFP (Request for Proposal) and model concession agreement in place. For the power sector, a model Power Purchase Agreement was available. Apart from the implementing authorities, there were also regulatory authorities in some sectors. Power sector (Generation, Transmission and Distribution) came under the regulation of the Central Electricity Authority as well as the state level power regulators. For roads, though, the Government-owned National Highway Authority of India (NHAI) was both a project developer and a regulator.

World-Bank (2020) had, in a benchmarking study for infrastructure projects, assessed countries and regions on various parameters with respect to implementation of infrastructure projects under PPP and the traditional route. Tables 1 and 2 depict the results of this benchmarking study with respect to India.

Table 1 India PPP implementation score comparison with peers and leaders (scores out of 100)

Stage of PPP	India	Global mean	Income group mean	Regional mean (South Asia)	USA	China	Australia	UK
Preparation	60	44	40	45	61	54	87	82
Procurement	67	63	56	59	63	80	71	77
Contract Management	85	63	63	63	58	81	87	85

Table 2 India project implementation scores: PPP versus traditional (scores out of 100)

Stage of Project	India PPP	India Traditional Public Sector Infra Project
Preparation	60	74
Procurement	67	76
Contract Management	85	87

It can be seen that India was far ahead of the global and regional averages. It also compared well with developed countries like the UK and Australia in terms of Contract Management and was better than USA in procurement and contract management. However, there was room for improvement in "preparation" and "procurement" stages for India's PPP projects in order to bring them up to the standards set by Australia and the UK. As can be seen from the scores, contract management was well developed in India. This also included dispute resolution mechanisms. Typically, all the concession agreements had the "arbitration" clause, thereby enabling the aggrieved party to initiate arbitration proceedings rather than the lengthy judicial process. We have extensive experience of working with PPP concessionaires, and have seen in practice that the rancour caused by disputes was generally not carried forward to the next project, even though the concessionaire and the public authority were the same.

From the above, it is evident that (a) India has had one of the largest quantum of investments under the PPP route and (b) that the PPP model has been accepted well in India. While India was one of the countries that bore the brunt of Covid-19, it had used lockdowns and vaccination as strategies to handle the pandemic.

Previous Studies and Motivation

In a study commissioned by the World Bank, Jamieson et al. (2021) had described the challenges facing PPP infrastructure projects due to the increased risk on account of the pandemic and the inability of the private partner to absorb such risks. The note described key operational challenges and advised governments across the world on Covid-19 response and mitigation policies for business disruptions in PPP projects. Thaker and Athar (2022) concluded, after studying 16 concession agreements in transport sector PPPs covering roads, airports, metro rail and ports, that force majeure criteria need to be open-ended to account for unforeseen events like the pandemic. They also recommend that financial relief be offered to PPP projects under such force majeure events apart from mere extension of concession period. Castelblanco et al. (2022), after analysing literature on PPP-related areas, found that drivers of PPP research shifted during times of crisis like the COVID-19 pandemic. In normal times, economic and performance aspects of the private sector-managed projects are studied, whereas during crisis times, risk management ability and public institutional factors came to the fore. There have been no specific studies carried out on the effect of Covid-19 pandemic on PPP projects in India. Castelblanco et al. (2022)'s findings, therefore, reinforces our resolve to study how institutional relief measures offered by various arms of the public sector helped PPP projects in India to manage the risk and overcome the debilitating effects of the pandemic.

In this chapter, we shall see how the Covid-19 pandemic affected the PPP projects in India. We shall also study whether the government, including the regulatory and public authorities, rose to the occasion to provide much needed relief to PPP projects. We shall also see how this relief was useful for certain sectors to help them tide over the crisis. A case from the Road Sector has been chosen for detailed study.

Research Objectives and Methodology

Research Objectives

The COVID-19 pandemic had thrown up many challenges affecting life and livelihood. However, in this chapter, we shall restrict ourselves to find the answers to the following questions:

1. Were the PPP projects in India affected due to the pandemic? If so, how fast did they recover to pre-pandemic levels?
2. Did the government agencies provide support to the PPP projects? Was this support helpful?
3. What was the effect of the pandemic on the financial agreements and project finance?

Methodology

One of the largest sectors for PPPs in India has been the highway sector. Other major sectors were electricity generation, including renewable energy and airports. We focus mainly on the highway sector in this study. For this, we select a group of operating PPP projects and compare the trends in their quarterly gross toll revenue. In order to study the effect of the pandemic on the road project finances, we select a period such that it covers the time before the onset of the pandemic, during the pandemic and at the end of the pandemic. The trends indicate the effect of the pandemic on the road sector PPP projects as well as the time taken to recover from these effects. We also compile a list of government support schemes and measures that were announced and implemented during the pandemic. We estimate the monetary benefit that accrued to the PPP projects due to these measures. We also ascertain whether financial agreements and loan agreements were breached for the projects studied.

We shall also study whether the highways sector PPPs fared better or worse as compared to the rest of the economy. To generalize our findings, we also validate our results through macroeconomic indicators.

For the other sectors, such as renewable energy, we base our research on focus interviews with three senior executives – one representing a private sector bank and two from a non-banking financial company (NBFC). These organizations are involved in lending to PPP projects in the highway, airports and renewable energy sectors. The interviews helped us gain insight into how the sectors were affected. The executives interviewed were (a) the managing director of the NBFC, (b) the head (credit) of the NBFC and (c) the head (credit) of the private sector bank.

Data Sources

For the quarterly toll revenue trends of highway projects, we select the projects covered under an Investment Trust Fund (InvIT). As the units of this InvIT are listed, the performance of the constituent road projects were publicly available through quarterly publication of results. For government support measures, we rely on publicly announced circulars issued by the Reserve Bank of India (RBI) and the NHAI. For macroeconomic data, we rely on RBI database and Ministry of Petroleum database.

Covid-19 – Effect and Response

Covid Incidence

India was one of the countries in the world seriously affected by the COVID-19 pandemic. As per data obtained from www.worldometers.com, which tracks the progress of the pandemic on a daily basis, India had recorded the second highest number of total cases till 04 September 2022. These are shown in Table 3 (Worldometers, 2022).

As can be seen from the above data, though India had a high incidence of Covid-19, it fared better than the world as well as the USA in terms of recovery rates. The pandemic progressed in India in three waves – in mid-2020, mid-2021 and early 2022, as can be seen from Fig. 1 (Worldometers, 2022).

Timelines – Covid Spread and Government Relief Measures

The timeline of the pandemic in India, including the government's response to tackle it, is given in Table 4.

Table 3 Comparison of Covid-19 onslaught between India, the USA and the entire world (as on 4 Sep 2022)

Country	Total cases (in millions)	Total Recovered (in millions)	Total Deaths (in millions)	Recovery Rate %	Death Rate %
World	609.9	586.4	6.5	96.15	1.07
USA	96.6	92.4	1.07	95.65	1.11
India	44.4	43.9	0.53	98.87	1.19

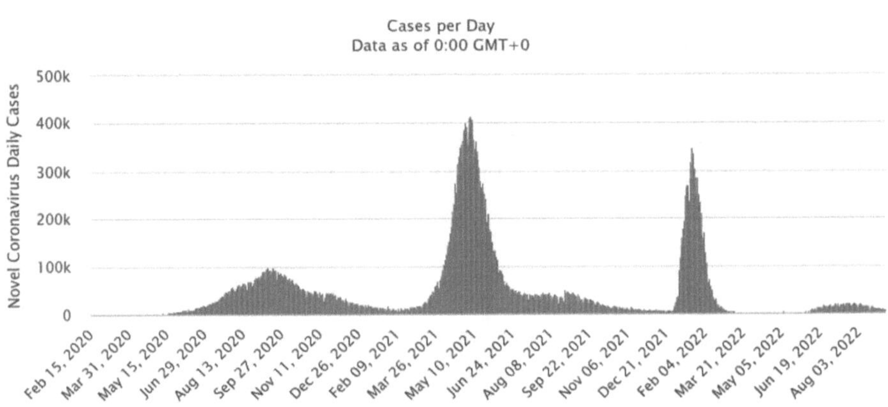

Fig. 1 Covid-19 spread in waves over time in India

Table 4 Timeline of key events during the COVID-19 pandemic in India

Date	Description
Jan 30, 2020	First Covid-19 case in the country
Mar 15, 2020	100th case
Mar 25–Jun 7, 2020	Complete lockdown
Jun 8, 2020	Phased reopening of economic activities
Mar 27 and May 23, 2020	Reserve Bank provides relief package in terms of moratorium on interest and principal repayment as well as reduction in bank rates
May 13–16, 2020	Government of India announces Covid relief package – sops for MSMEs, free food grains for the poor, agri-infra projects and social infra projects totalling a total of ₹10 trillion ($133 billion)[a]
Aug 2020 to Jan 2021	Successful trials of vaccines (vaccination starts in Jan 2021)
April–May 2021	Second wave, causing severe disease and maximum deaths
Jan 2022	Third wave, mild disease
Apr 2022	Withdrawal of all Covid restrictions, including lockdowns

[a]Taking exchange rate of $1 = ₹75. This is followed uniformly in this chapter

The national government, the state governments, regulatory agencies and municipal corporations did their bit to contain and mitigate the effects of the pandemic. In this study, we shall restrict ourselves to the support provided for industry, including operating PPP projects. The Reserve Bank reduced the benchmark rates, thereby making credit cheaper. The Bank also announced moratorium on interest and principal repayment for a period of six months from March to August 2020. The finance ministry offered sops worth ₹5940 billion ($79 billion) for the Medium Small and Micro Enterprises (MSMEs) in the form of collateral free automatic loans, 100 percent credit guarantee cover, ₹200 billion ($2.7 billion) subordinate loan and ₹500 billion ($6.7 billion) equity infusion in stressed MSMEs.

An Illustrative Case: Seven Operating Road Sector Projects of IRB InvIT Fund – Data and Analysis

Selection of the Case and Description of the Project

In order to study the effect of the pandemic on PPP projects, we first select the "Roads" sector for our study, as it was one of the largest PPP sectors in India. To study the effect of the pandemic, we needed to collect data that is pre-pandemic, during the pandemic and at the end of the pandemic. Hence, our selection of the case study was based on the following three conditions:

- Sufficient track record before the onset of the pandemic in India in March 2020
- Operations during and after the pandemic
- Publicly available data

Based on these criteria, we zeroed in on the IRB InvIT Fund, an Infrastructure Investment Trust Fund which managed and operated seven toll road projects (constituted as Special Purpose Vehicles – SPVs) spread across southern, western and northern India.

The fund was listed on the key stock exchanges in India, the National Stock Exchange and the Bombay Stock Exchange. All the roads under the fund's management were operating toll roads with a history of toll collection. Being listed, the annual reports and quarterly reports were available in public domain.

To understand how an infrastructure investment trust functions, one must study the interrelationships between the constituent parts of the fund, which we term as the "structure." The structure of a typical InvIT Fund is depicted in Fig. 2. It can be seen from the structure that the roads which were originally developed and operated by the sponsor are transferred to the fund. They are again managed by the sponsor. All the seven road SPVs in our study subject – IRB InvIT Fund – were operating under BOT (Build/Operate/Transfer) concession agreements with the NHAI and had a track record of toll collection. Major details of the road projects and their concession period are given in Table 5 (IRB InvIT Fund, 2021). Figure 3 shows the geographic extent covered by the roads. It can be seen that the projects covered had a wide geographical spread and thus our analysis can be considered representative of the industry trends.

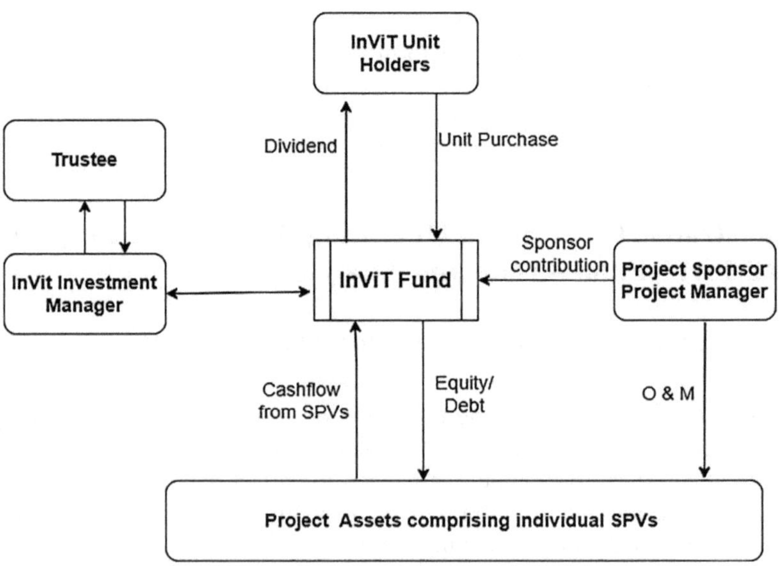

Fig. 2 Structure of a typical InvIT Fund

Table 5 Major parameters of roads managed by IRB InvIT Fund

S. No.	Project name	State	Length (km)	Lane km	Project cost ($ million)	Conc. period years	Toll started	End of concession period
1	Surat–Dahisar	Gujarat/ Maharashtra	239	1434	337	12	Feb 2009	Jan 2022[a]
2	Tumkur–Chitradurga	Karnataka	114	684	152	26	Jun 2011	Jun 2037
3	Bharuch–Surat	Gujarat	65	390	187	15	Sep 2009	Jan 2022[b]
4	Jaipur–Deoli	Rajasthan	149	595	237	25	Sep 2013	Sep 2037
5	Omalur–Salem–Namakkal	Tamil Nadu	69	275	41	20	Aug 2009	Aug 2026
6	Talegaon–Amravati	Maharashtra	67	267	119	22	Apr 2013	Jan 2037
7	Pathankot–Amritsar	Punjab	102	410	193	20	Nov 2014	Jan 2035

[a]extended to May 2022
[b]extended to March 2022

Fig. 3 Geographic spread of IRB InvIT's SPVs

From the above, it can be seen that two of the roads, Surat–Dahisar and Bharuch–Surat, were almost at the end of the respective concession periods. The sponsor was planning to add more roads to the Investment Trust to offset this. The first three roads were of six lanes and the balance roads were of four lanes each.

Effect of the Pandemic on the Selected SPVs

The government imposed a lockdown on 25 March 2020 for a period of 21 days, which was continuously extended till 8 June 2020, when the economy was partially opened up. The transport sector was badly affected due to the lockdown. Toll roads were also adversely affected. As most industries were under lockdown, industrial production reduced, thereby affecting movement of cargo – both raw material and finished goods. Passenger traffic was also reduced substantially as the populace put off non-essential travel. The result was much lower collection of toll fees, the main revenue source for the PPP road projects. By comparing the quarterly revenue of these roads over a period of time, covering both the pre-pandemic, the pandemic and the recovery phases, we will be able to appreciate the effect that the pandemic had on the PPP toll road business. Table 6 gives details of the quarterly gross toll revenue of the seven roads individually (IRB InvIT Fund, 2020).

We plot the quarter-wise trends of the gross revenues of the seven roads managed by the Investment trust individually and these are shown in Fig. 4a. For a better comparison of the contours of the projects, a stacked chart of the same data is drawn and shown in Fig. 4b. This is a cumulative chart with the bottom-most line depicting quarterly revenue of Surat–Dahisar road and the toll revenue of each successive road project gets added as we progress to the top. The dip in revenues due to the pandemic can be clearly seen in all the roads, especially in the stacked chart. Lockdowns induced by the first wave of the pandemic in FY21Q1 (and the second wave in FY22Q1) caused the revenue dips.

From Fig. 4a, b, we can see that the pandemic uniformly affected all the road projects. There was a major dip in gross toll revenue in FY21Q1. Thereafter, once the lockdown restrictions were eased gradually, the traffic and revenue picked up and crossed the pre-pandemic level by March 2021, before the second wave induced another dip in FY22Q1 quarter. As the lockdowns imposed by the government during the second wave was localized and less severe than that in the first wave, the dip observed in toll revenues during the second wave was also less.

From Fig. 4a, we can see that the contours of the quarterly revenues were almost identical for all the projects except for the Pathankot–Amritsar project. Therefore, we can infer that the underlying cause for the dips in FY21Q1 and FY22Q1 were the same, namely, loss of traffic due to the pandemic. For the Pathankot–Amritsar stretch, the contour is similar till recovery after the first wave. However, the road traffic went to zero from November 2021 onwards for more than a year. This was

Table 6 Quarter-wise gross BOT toll revenues ($ million)

Description	FY20Q1	FY20Q2	FY20Q3	FY20Q4	FY21Q1	FY21Q2	FY21Q3	FY21Q4	FY22Q1	FY22Q2	FY22Q3
Surat–Dahisar	24	22	25	24	11	21	27	28	22	26	29
Tumkur–Chitradurga	8.4	7.8	8.1	7.6	4.6	7.8	9.3	9.4	6.8	9.1	9.4
Bharuch–Surat	8.0	7.7	8.7	8.5	4.3	7.8	9.6	9.8	7.8	10	11
Jaipur–Deoli	3.5	3.1	3.5	3.3	2.3	3.4	4.0	4.0	3.0	3.8	4.3
Omulur–Namakkal	3.4	3.3	3.5	3.3	1.9	3.0	3.8	4.1	2.8	3.9	4.4
Talegaon–Amravati	2.5	2.3	2.5	2.4	1.4	2.4	2.9	2.9	2.3	2.7	2.7
Pathankot–Amritsar	4.5	3.8	4.4	3.8	2.2	3.7	0.2	0.0	0.0	0.0	0.7

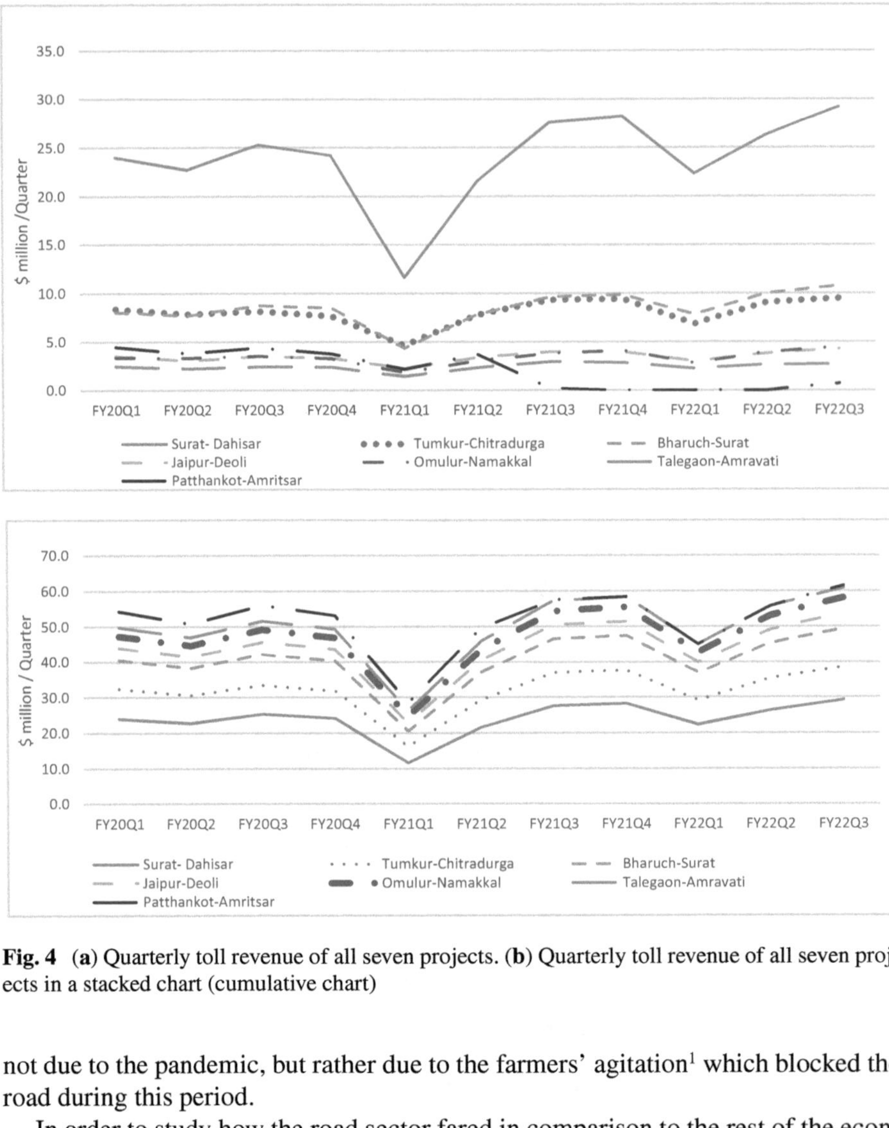

Fig. 4 (**a**) Quarterly toll revenue of all seven projects. (**b**) Quarterly toll revenue of all seven projects in a stacked chart (cumulative chart)

not due to the pandemic, but rather due to the farmers' agitation[1] which blocked the road during this period.

In order to study how the road sector fared in comparison to the rest of the economy, we collected data on quarterly GDP at constant prices from the Reserve Bank of India (RBI) database and compared it with the sum of the gross BOT toll revenues for all the projects, except the Pathankot–Amritsar Project. We have excluded the Pathankot–Amritsar road from gross revenues as its traffic was adversely

[1]Agitation by farmers against new farm laws enacted to change market access for agricultural products. Several roads accessing Delhi were blocked by the agitators for almost one year. Punjab province in India, where Pathankot–Amritsar stretch is located, was significantly affected.

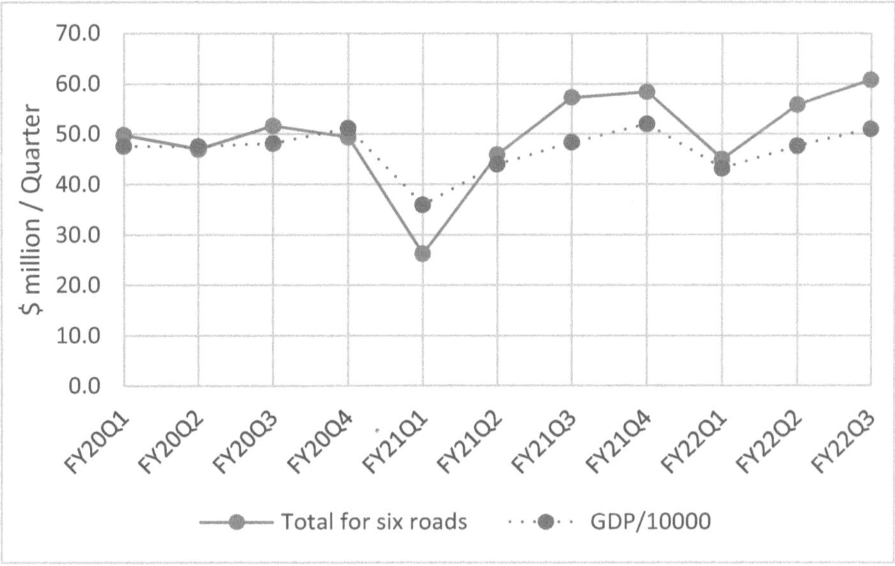

Fig. 5 GDP and Toll Revenue Trends ($ million)

affected not only by the pandemic but by other extraneous factors like the farmers' agitation.

In order to plot the GDP and the total revenue from the road projects on the same graph, we scale down GDP by a factor of 10,000. The value of GDP/10000 and the total revenue from the six roads are plotted in Fig. 5.

It is visually evident that during the two waves of the pandemic, i.e. FY21Q1 and FY22Q1, there was a marked dip in the toll revenue numbers as well as the GDP. However, the effect was more severe for the roads sector. Similarly, recovery was also sharper for the roads sector. Intuitively, we feel that there must be a correlation between the fall in GDP and the fall in Toll revenues. GDP represents the economic activity in the country; and lower economic activity during the quarter may result in lower passenger and cargo traffic resulting in lower toll revenue. A correlation test revealed that there is 88 percent correlation between toll revenue of the roads and GDP. However, GDP also accounts for other sectors which may have performed better than the roads sector. These may include essential services, agriculture, health, information technology services, etc. Thus, the effect of the lockdowns were less severe on the GDP than on the roads sector.

Another point of comparison can be the stock markets. If we look at IRB InvIT's unit price traded in the National Stock Exchange (NSE), we see that the market is also closely following the same trends. We see that by April 2021, the unit price has recovered to the pre-pandemic levels (see Fig. 6). Also, the second wave of the pandemic has not had any significant effect on the unit price. The first and second waves of Covid are marked on the graph.

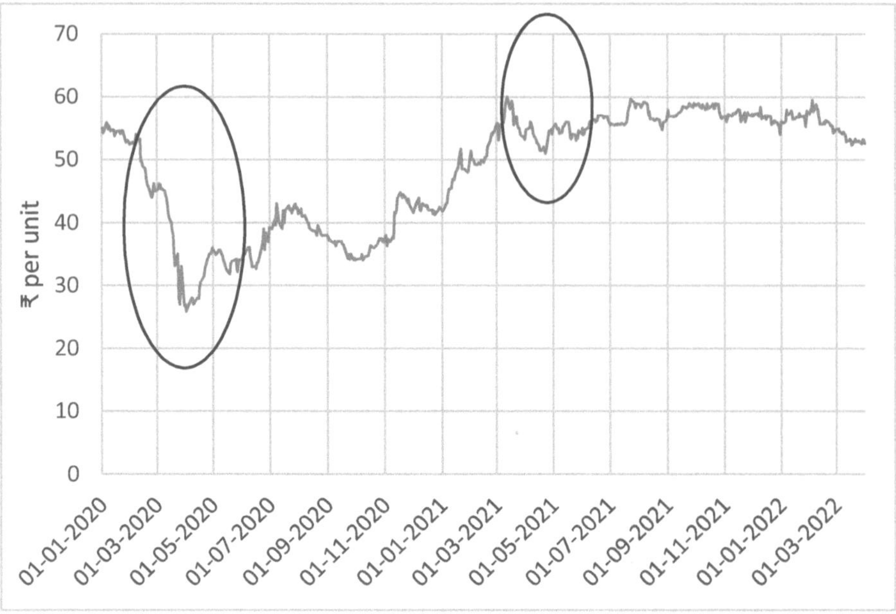

Fig. 6 IRB InvIT unit price traded on the NSE

Validation Through Macro-Data – Effect on the Roads Sector

We have seen the trends of Gross Revenue earned by a set of roads managed by IRB InVit. We have observed the effect of the pandemic as well as the recovery period for these roads. But are these representative of the entire sector? To validate this, we look at some macro data. We conjecture that consumption of Diesel may be a proxy for the level of traffic across our highways. Similarly consumption of Bitumen may be a proxy for new construction of highways. We therefore collected data on these two parameters from the website of "Petroleum Planning and Analysis Cell." (Petroleum Planning and Analysis Cell, Ministry of Petroleum and Natural Gas, n.d.) The temporal trends of these two parameters as plotted in Fig. 7 show that while both highway traffic and construction were affected adversely during the first wave of the pandemic in April–June 2020, only traffic was affected in the second wave. This was primarily because only localized lockdown was observed during the second wave. The trends in the traffic as indicated by diesel consumption does validate our findings with respect to the IRB InvIT roads.

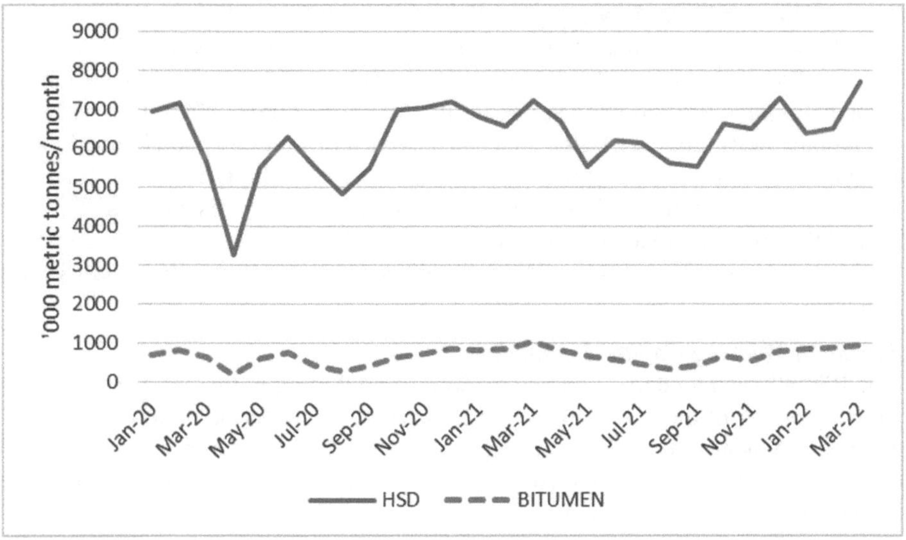

Fig. 7 Consumption of high speed diesel (HSD) and bitumen

Government Support

The concession agreements have a "Force Majeure" condition which includes non-political events which are described as under:

> A Non-Political Event shall mean one or more of the following acts or events: (a) act of God, *epidemic*, extremely adverse weather conditions, lightning, earthquake, landslide, cyclone, flood, volcanic eruption ..... (NHAI and IRB Surat Dahisar Tollway Private Limited, 2008)

As "epidemic" is covered under the force majeure condition and as the pandemic was a global phenomenon, government agencies had taken a decision to support PPP projects. For the Road sector, the following measures were taken to support the SPVs to face the disruptions in business due to the pandemic:

- Moratorium on loans
- Easing of working capital financing
- Reduction in interest rates
- Extension of concession period
- Deferment of premium payable to NHAI
- Proportionate release of retention money and performance guarantee

Moratorium on Term Loan Repayments

The Reserve Bank of India (RBI) had announced in March and May 2020 that borrowers of term loans from banks and lending institutions can avail moratorium on principal repayment and interest due during March to August 2020 for a period of six months (RBI, 2020a, b). IRB InvIT had availed this facility and obtained moratorium on repayment of principal amounting to ₹208 million ($ 2.77 million) and interest due amounting to ₹513 million ($ 6.84 million) for six months. This has helped the company to avoid defaulting on loan repayment. As we have seen previously, the business recovered in six months, and therefore, this facility was beneficial.

Easing of Working Capital Financing

The RBI allowed lenders to reduce working capital margin, thereby increasing the drawing power of the borrowers of working capital for a period up to March 2021. Interest payment due on Working Capital for the period March to August 2020 could also be deferred by converting it into a Funded Interest Term Loan, repayable by March 2021 (RBI, 2020a, b).

Reduction in Interest Rates

The RBI had gradually lowered the benchmark rates from 27 March 2020 to 22 May 2020 as follows: (Reserve Bank of India, n.d.)

- Bank Rate from 5.40 percent to 4.25 percent, a reduction of 115 basis points
- Repo Rate from 5.15 percent to 4.00 percent, a reduction of 115 basis points
- Reverse Repo Rate from 4.90 percent to 3.35 percent, a reduction of 155 basis points

The reduction in Bank Rate resulted in floating rate loans becoming cheaper, thus benefiting the SPVs. The difference between repo rate and reverse repo rate had increased, thereby increasing liquidity in the economy. This was a step to support the banking system which would have faced liquidity crunch due to the moratorium announced. For IRB InvIT, the reduction in rates had brought down the average cost of debt from 7.60 percent to 7.25 percent, a reduction of 35 basis points (IRB InVit Fund, 2022). The fund had term loans of ₹14,221 million ($190 million) as on 31 March 2021 (IRB InVit Fund Annual Report for 2020–21). Thus the reduction of 35 basis points in interest rates translated to a saving of ₹50 million ($0.66 million) annually. These rates continued till 4 May 2022, when they were increased to combat inflation.

Support from NHAI

NHAI announced and implemented a number of support measures (Ministry of Road Transport and Highways, 2020). These can be briefly stated as under:

- Extension of Concession Period
  Extension of concession period by three to six months was announced by NHAI to offset the adverse effects of the pandemic. IRB InVit has availed this and had got a three-month extension for all the SPVs.
- Deferment of premium payable
  The NHAI had offered and approved deferment of premium obligation (i.e. payment to be made to the NHAI by SPV for getting the rights to collect toll) for a period of six months (Ministry of Road Transport and Highways, 2020). The premium was to be paid later and attracted interest at the rate of 2 percent over the bank rate. At the prevailing bank rate of 4.25 percent that time, the deferment interest rate was cheaper than the average cost of debt. IRB InvIT had availed this deferment facility too. In order to assess the amount of benefit, we estimated the premium due for some of the SPVs whose concession agreements were available.

(i) Surat–Dahisar: Revenue share @ 38 percent in 2008–09 to be increased by 1 percent every year. Thus in 2020, the revenue share was 50 percent. For the two quarters (April–Sept 2020), revenue was ₹2484 million and 50 percent revenue share works out to ₹1242 million.
(ii) Tumkur–Chitradurga: Annual premium as on 2010 was ₹1404 million to be increased by 5 percent every year. This works out to ₹2287 million in 2020. Thus for six months, premium payable was ₹1144 million.
(iii) Bharuch–Surat: Upfront payment (also called Negative grant) of ₹5040 million paid to NHAI in 2007 itself. Hence premium is no longer payable.
(iv) Talegaon–Amravati: Project grant of ₹2160 million received from NHAI. Hence, no premium is payable.
The benefits due to the deferment on these roads can be calculated as (premium deferred x interest rate differential x period of deferment). As average cost of debt is 7.25 percent and deferment interest rate is 6.25 percent, the net saving is 1.0 percent per annum. The premium deferred for the four roads is ₹2386 million. The benefit due to lower interest rates works out to around ₹12 million for the deferment period of six months. For FY21Q1 and Q2, these four roads contributed about 80 percent of the toll revenues of the Trust. Hence, the total benefit from premium deferment may be around ₹15 million ($ 0.2 million).

- Proportionate release of retention money and nil deduction of retention money for a period of 3 to 6 months
- Release of performance guarantee on a pro-rata basis

The support provided by the governmental agencies as described above, coupled with the fact that traffic and gross toll revenues bounced back in less than a year, ensured that the Investment Trust Fund was able to meet its financial obligations to its lenders.

Effect of the Pandemic on Major PPP Sectors – Lenders' Feedback

Except for the complete lockdown period between 25 March 2020 and 7 June 2020, construction and industrial activities continued, though at a lower level due to supply chain constraints and delay in return of migrant labour. Focus interviews with three senior top managerial executives of two institutions – one a leading private sector bank and the other a leading NBFC, dealing with project finance, revealed that PPP project companies or Special Purpose Vehicles (SPVs) in various sectors were affected by the pandemic in the manner described below:

(a) *Airport PPPs*: Badly affected during the first three months and recovery slow thereafter as international flights were limited and optional travel was avoided by the populace
(b) *Renewable Energy PPP* (both solar and wind): Operating projects were not affected at all. In fact, due to the financial support given by the Union government for power sector, the PPA bills were paid well in time. However, new projects were affected due to supply chain disruptions. Respondents to our interviews said:

    - "Solar panel costs went up by 50% from 19 cents/watt to 27 cents/watt due to supply chain disruptions. Blanket extension of 4–5 months was given for solar power projects."
    - "State governments cleared their past dues to solar power PPP projects, nudged by stimulus package given by central government"
    - "No slack in demand in the renewable energy space"

- In effect, past dues of operating Solar projects were cleared; demand was robust and hence Covid-19 did not adversely affect these projects. For under construction projects, supply chain disruption and increase in costs affected the projects. However, extension of time was granted for completion of the projects.

(c) *Road transport sector PPP*: Badly affected during the first three months. But recovery was swift thereafter in operating assets. As far as new projects were concerned, there was minimal construction in the first three months (April–June, 2020) and recovery was gradual as migrant labour took time to return. Road construction picked-up thereafter. As one of the senior executives interviewed stated:

    - "Road PPP toll collection was impacted for 3 months but regained 90 percent of pre-Covid levels by August–September 2020."
    - "No defaults in loan repayment"

Thus, though there was financial impact during the peak Covid period, recovery was fast and the government support in terms of moratorium ensured that financial agreements were not breached.

Discussions, Learnings and Implications

In the previous sections, we have described the case taken up for study, analysed the effect of the pandemic on the road SPVs of the InvIT as well as how the governmental agencies helped the sector tide over the disruptions caused by the Covid-19 pandemic. In this section, we shall identify the implications of our findings that will help the authorities act in a beneficial way and make PPPs resilient in the wake of future pandemics.

Firstly, the SPV, and the private sector partner of a PPP, should be considered as a partner and not as an adversary. In the case of road SPVs, the NHAI followed this dictum during the pandemic and offered support in the form of deferment of premium payable and extension of concession period. The clauses in the concession agreements gave the provision for deferring premium as well as extending the concession period. NHAI was applying the same. The Concession Agreements also had "Force Majeure" conditions linked to epidemics. As the pandemic was a global epidemic, this clause was also used by NHAI to support the PPP projects.

Secondly, a pandemic should be considered as a national economic emergency (and not just a health emergency) and governments should help businesses overcome the problems. The Covid relief package announced by the Ministry of Finance had such an objective. The RBI also intervened to create more liquidity in the system as well as to reduce debt repayment difficulties for the PPP SPVs, by announcing moratorium period and reducing benchmark rates. Obviously, this cannot be incorporated in any concession agreement; however, it is hoped that the government acts in a similar way in future in case of any widespread distress in the economy. Perhaps, policies can be framed so that in the event of a future pandemic, or any similar national emergency, relief measures can be automatically triggered.

Implications

The response of the government and its agencies to deal with the unprecedented pandemic has implications for administration of PPP projects. The public sector partner should try to help the SPV to overcome hardships arising out of unexpected events. The pandemic was one such event and it might have resulted in the failure of the SPVs but for the timely support measures taken by the government and its various agencies. The SPVs might have, in such cases, been unable to meet their loan servicing commitments. This would have had a cascading effect on the economy, with Non-Performing Assets (NPA) piling up in the banking system. Thus, the timely countermeasures taken by the RBI and NHAI prevented such a catastrophe.

Conclusions

The Covid-19 pandemic, which had affected the global economy between 2020 and 2022, did not leave India unscathed. Of its 1.40 billion people representing a sixth of the world's population, over 44 million infections have been reported till 4 Sep

2022, which is around one-thirteenth of the total number of people globally infected. The pandemic was contained by an effective and stringent lockdown imposed in the early stages. However, this had an economic fallout in terms of loss in economic activity and GDP. It has also affected PPP Projects, though the effect was not uniform across sectors. India, being one of the leading PPP adopters in the world had to protect the PPP SPVs and alleviate the distress caused by the pandemic.

Through a case analysis, wherein we take seven road sector SPVs managed by a publicly listed Infrastructure Investment Trust, we show how the traffic in these roads reached pre-pandemic levels within a year. During the intervening period, i.e. from April 2020 to March 2021, the projects would have faced severe financial crunch but for the timely assistance provided by government agencies. Thus, a situation, where they may have reneged on their loan servicing commitments, was avoided due to interim relief measures of the government. Easing of interest rates, moratorium on interest and principal repayment as well as deferment of premium payable to the NHAI for the concessions were some of the measures that supported the SPVs during these difficult times.

"Force Majeure" clause in the concession agreement does include "epidemic" as one of the force majeure conditions. It is also seen that the relief measures taken by the RBI and NHAI were in response to the severe economic disruptions during the pandemic period; but they were discretionary. In our opinion, if any disruptive event such as this pandemic occurs in future, relief measures should be automatically set off.

References

Bloomberg. (2022). *UK slips behind India to become world ' s sixth biggest economy loss of status comes as ruling Tory party elects new premier.* https://www.bloomberg.com/news/articles/2022-09-02/uk-slips-behind-india-to-become-world-s-sixth-biggest-economy

Castelblanco, G., Guevara, J., & Salazar, J. (2022). Remedies to the PPP crisis in the Covid-19 pandemic: Lessons from the 2008 global financial crisis. *Journal of Management in Engineering, 38*(3), 1–18. https://doi.org/10.1061/(asce)me.1943-5479.0001036

Department of Economic Affairs, G. of I. (2019). *Design your Search.* https://www.pppinindia.gov.in/infrastructureindia/web/guest/search?p_p_id=advancedsearch_WAR_Projectportlet&p_p_lifecycle=0&p_p_state=normal&p_p_mode=view&p_p_col_id=column-1&p_p_col_count=1&_advancedsearch_WAR_Projectportlet_mvcPath=%2Fhtml%2Fadvancedsea

IRB InvIT Fund. (2020). *Quarterly results update.*

IRB InvIT Fund. (2021). *Heading ahead annual report 2020–21.*

IRB InVit Fund. (2022). *Transcript of Concal with investors* (Issue October 2020).

Jamieson, J., Chao, J., Sy, J., Dougherty, P., Paul, C., Baclagon, L., Kim, S., & Neves, P. (2021). Covid-19 and public-private partnerships practice note. *World Bank PPIAF*, 1–23.

Ministry of Road Transport and Highways, G. of I. (2020). *Covid relief Order.*

NHAI and IRB Surat Dahisar Tollway Private Limited. (2008). *Concession_Agreement.*

Petroleum Planning and Analysis Cell, Ministry of Petroleum and Natural Gas, G. of I. (n.d.). *PT_Consumption_Historical.* https://www.ppac.gov.in/content/147_1_ConsumptionPetroleum.aspx

RBI. (2020a). Covid-19 - regulatory package. *RBI Circular, 1* (March 2020), 1–16.
RBI. (2020b). Covid relief package RBI. *RBI Circular, 2*(May 2020), 1–3.
Reserve Bank of India. (n.d.). *Major monetary policy rates and reserve requirements - Bank Rate, Laf (Re* https://dbie.rbi.org.in/DBIE/dbie.rbi?site=home
Thaker, K., & Athar, M. (2022). Covid-19 pandemic, transport Ppps, and risk mitigations. *SSRN Electronic Journal*, 1–31. https://doi.org/10.2139/ssrn.4011694
World-Bank. (2020). Benchmarking infrastructure development 2020. In *Benchmarking infrastructure development 2020*. https://doi.org/10.1596/34608
Worldometers. (2022). *Coronavirus Cases Statistics*. https://www.worldometers.info/coronavirus/#countries

Contractual Governance in Public–Private Partnerships in the USA: Key Clauses and Impacts of COVID-19

Michael J. Garvin and Manik Ahmed

Introduction

Overview of the Infrastructure Environment in USA

Over roughly the last three decades, the methods for delivering infrastructure have evolved dramatically in the USA and worldwide. In the USA, the conventional approach of providing infrastructure through design-bid-build (DBB) has been complemented by an array of alternative delivery arrangements, including design-build (DB) and public–private partnership (PPP) models such as design-build-finance-operate-maintain (DBFOM). The transportation sector in the USA has seen the most PPP activity. However, infrastructure planning and delivery takes place within a relatively intricate landscape.

The USA has a federalist system with powers divided between the federal and state governments. Consequently, the environment for developing infrastructure in the USA is a complex one since projects are subject to federal, state, and local laws as well as prevailing regulations and procedures issued by executive agencies or particular jurisdictions. Not surprisingly, each project may face a varying set of conditions that influence its planning and implementation based on the entities involved.

At the federal level, the Federal Acquisition Regulation (FAR) that dictates requirements related to the purchase of goods and services and the statutory

M. J. Garvin (✉)
Virginia Tech, Blacksburg, VA, USA
e-mail: garvin@vt.edu

M. Ahmed
Kiewit Infrastructure Engineering, Fairfax, VA, USA
e-mail: manik@vt.edu

© The Author(s), under exclusive license to Springer Nature Switzerland AG 2023
T. Dolla et al. (eds.), *Revisiting Public-Private Partnerships*,
Contributions to Public Administration and Public Policy,
https://doi.org/10.1007/978-3-031-37015-1_8

requirements of the National Environmental Policy Act (NEPA) have the largest impacts on how major projects with federal funding in the USA proceed. Within infrastructure sectors, federal agencies can also influence projects. For example, the Federal Highway Administration (FHWA) oversees the national Interstate Highway System, so interstate highway projects are coordinated with FHWA oversight. FHWA also oversees the Transportation Infrastructure Finance & Investment Act (TIFIA) program, which has provided many subordinated TIFIA loans to PPP projects. Further, exceptions to the typical project delivery process for transportation projects are granted Special Experimental Projects (SEP) variances. Most PPPs with federal involvement are designated as SEP-15 projects. Beyond governing laws, regulations, and specific federal programs, the USA does not have any national infrastructure or PPP unit to coordinate activity within this market.

At the state level, each state enacts legislation that governs project delivery and procurement. Current legislation authorizing the use of PPPs is primarily focused in the transportation sector although legislation related to public buildings or education facilities is also in place. For example, Virginia's Public–Private Transportation Act (PPTA) of 1995 authorized private entities to construct, operate, and maintain transportation facilities when such an approach would result in making such facilities available in a more timely or cost-effective fashion. Currently, thirty-six states and one territory have legislation enabling PPP-type projects for transportation (FHWA, 2022). However, the legislative conditions differ considerably by state. Most states allow the private sector to submit unsolicited proposals, but quite a few states still limit PPPs to pilot projects. This has created a market where several states have been quite active in PPP implementation, some have experimented with them, and many have yet to move forward with a project even though they have the authority.

Hence, private sector participants have played an important role in establishing precedents and norms in the PPP market. Since major players are limited, PPP projects often have a common set of firms engaged that support public agencies or pursue PPP projects. Additionally, PPP agreements frequently rely on past agreements as the basis of risk allocation and contractual terms. Consequently, while the US PPP market is quite decentralized, normalization has occurred over time as successful practices have disseminated across jurisdictions.

Planning and Procurement of Transportation Projects

In general, each state's Department of Transportation (DOT) manages its state's transportation modes. In addition, state DOTs operate and manage the national Interstate Highway System (IHS) roadways within their state along with all other federal and state routes. With regard to PPPs, each DOT defines and executes the PPP program authorized by their state's legislation. Most state DOTs have divisions within them that handle PPPs. In some cases, special units are established to manage them. For example, the Colorado DOT has the Colorado Transportation

Investment Office (formerly the Colorado High Performance Transportation Enterprise), which is an independent, government-owned business charged with facilitating PPPs and innovative finance (for more information about this office, see https://www.codot.gov/programs/ctio).

As discussed, federal and state statutory environmental requirements have significant influence over project planning. Otherwise, PPPs in the transportation sector can have quite different development paths and structures. Quite a few well-known projects, such as the I-495 Express Lanes (Capital Beltway Express) in Virginia, are the consequence of unsolicited proposals. While the general requirements of the FAR (and complementary state procurement regulations) are followed, the procurement process for PPPs tends to vary by state. Competitive procurements have employed multistage processes where first the qualifications of bidders are evaluated, and bidders are shortlisted to participate in subsequent stages where best-value techniques are typically used to identify the preferred bidder.

Table 1 summarizes the characteristics of US highway and bridge PPP projects that reached commercial close between 2007 and 2019. The table illustrates the variability in PPP structures and procurements found in the highway market sector, which is a result of the overall environment for PPPs in the USA.

Context of the Inquiry

Overview of COVID-19 Impacts in the USA

At the start of 2020, few in the USA realized the impact that the novel coronavirus (COVID-19) would have. By mid-to-late spring, COVID-19 had forced lockdowns and widespread disruption of economic activity. New cases and deaths per day rose to nearly 25,000 and over 900, respectively, by the end of March; new case counts and deaths reached over 200,000 and 3000 per day by the end of December (New York Times, 2022). As of early summer 2022, the cumulative number of cases in the USA was over 82 million, while the death toll was nearing 1 million (New York Times, 2022).

With the onset of the pandemic, state and local governments faced revenue shortfalls, economic issues, and stressed healthcare systems (Deloitte, 2020). In the transportation sector, revenue sources started to experience declines as motor fuel taxes and user fees dropped as travel declined. Vehicle miles traveled (VMT) decreased by nearly 40% in April 2020 as lockdowns took effect. However, highway travel gradually rebounded throughout 2020. Figure 1 depicts the average daily vehicle-distance traveled (billions of miles) on urban highways in the USA in 2019, 2020, and 2021. The impact of the pandemic is clear throughout 2020. Yet, travel on urban highways had essentially recovered to pre-pandemic levels by the summer of 2021. Similar trends were observed on rural highways.

Table 1 US Highway and Bridge PPP projects from 2007 to 2019

Project	Route type	Mode	Jurisdiction	PPP model	Commercial close	Value ($millions)
I-95 Express Fredricksburg Extension	IHS	Highway	Virginia	DBFOM (RR)	2019	830
I-75 Modernization Segment 3	IHS	Highway	Michigan	DBFM (AP)	2018	1400
I-395 Express Lanes	IHS	Highway	Virginia	DBFOM (RR)	2017	554
Central 70	IHS	Highway	Colorado	DBFOM (AP)	2017	1271
Transform 66 – Outside the Beltway	IHS	Highway	Virginia	DBFOM (RR)	2016	3724
SH 288 Toll Lanes	State	Highway	Texas	DBFOM (RR)	2016	425
Southern Ohio Veterans Memorial Highway (Portsmouth Bypass)	State	Highway	Ohio	DBFOM (AP)	2015	819
Rapid Bridge Replacement	Various	Bridges	Pennsylvania	DBFOM (AP)	2015	1119
I-77 High Occupancy Toll (HOT)	IHS	Highway	North Carolina	DBFOM (RR)	2014	655
I-4 Ultimate Improvements	IHS	Highway	Florida	DBFOM (AP)	2014	2323
Goethals Bridge Replacement	IHS	Bridge	NY/NJ Port Authority	DBFM (AP)	2013	1350
US 36 Managed Lanes—Phase 2	Federal	Highway	Colorado	DBFOM (RR)	2013	175
North Tarrant Express (3A and 3B) (NTE 3A-3B)	IHS	Highway	Texas	DBFOM (RR)	2013	1350
East End Crossing	IHS	Highway	Indiana	DBFOM (AP)	2012	763
I-95 Express Lanes	IHS	Highway	Virginia	DBFOM (RR)	2012	923
Presidio Parkway (Phase II)	Federal	Highway	California	DBFOM (AP)	2011	362
Elizabeth River Tunnels	IHS & State	Tunnel & Highway	Virginia	DBFOM (RR)	2011	2100
I-635 LBJ Managed Lanes	IHS	Highway	Texas	DBFOM (RR)	2009	2600

(continued)

Table 1 (continued)

Project	Route type	Mode	Jurisdiction	PPP model	Commercial close	Value ($millions)
North Tarrant Express (1 and 2A) (NTE 1-2A)	IHS & State	Highway	Texas	DBFOM (RR)	2009	2000
Port of Miami Tunnel	State	Bridge	Florida	DBFOM (AP)	2009	651
I-595 Express Lanes	IHS	Highway	Florida	DBFOM (AP)	2009	1760
SH 130: Segments 5 and 6	State	Highway	Texas	DBFOM (RR)	2007	1380
I-495 Capital Beltway Express	IHS	Highway	Virginia	DBFOM (RR)	2007	2068

IHS part of national Interstate Highway System, *DBFOM* Design-Build-Finance-Operate-Maintain, *DBFM* Design-Build-Finance-Maintain, *RR* Revenue Risk (or Toll Concession), *AP* Availability Payment (or Annuity Type Payment)

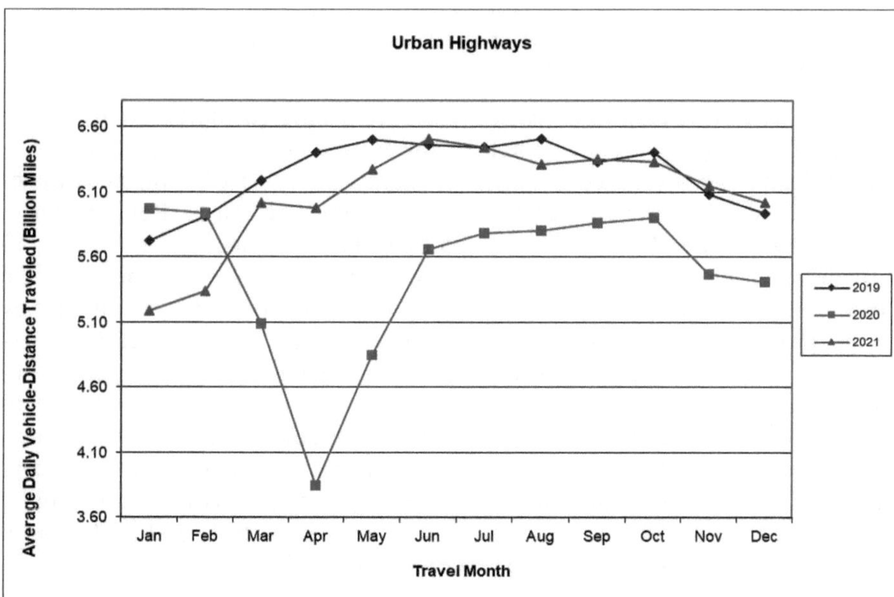

Fig. 1 Average daily vehicle-distance traveled on US urban highways, 2019–2021. (Source: https://www.fhwa.dot.gov/policyinformation/travel_monitoring/tvt.cfm)

COVID-19 Impacts on US PPP Highway Market

The US PPP market was not excluded from the pandemic's impacts. Revenue risk (toll concession) PPPs in the operations phase certainly felt the impact of traffic drops, while availability payment (annuity type) PPPs faced the threat of governments not fulfilling contractual obligations brought about by pandemic-related budgetary shortfalls (Casady & Baxter, 2020). Based on the decentralized nature of the US PPP highway market, however, impacts from COVID-19 were generally addressed on a project-by-project basis. In other words, the contractual framework and the project-specific circumstances dictated how COVID-19 was handled on each project. Nearly all PPP contracts in the USA have relief provisions that govern particular events or unforeseen circumstances. Within many US PPP contracts, "relief event" clauses stipulate requirements for concessionaires to request relief that may result in additional compensation or time extensions. For example, Provision 10.2 of the I-595 Express Lanes contract stipulated:

> Concessionaire shall be entitled to certain compensation and performance relief for Relief Events in accordance with this Section 10.2. Except as otherwise provided in this Agreement, the remedies provided under this Section 10.2 shall not preclude Concessionaire's other remedies provided under the Contract Documents and Concessionaire shall be entitled to Extra Work Costs, Delay Costs, time extensions and other relief for Relief Events in accordance with the Contract Documents.

The contract further defined a "Relief Event" by listing qualifying events, which included force majeure events, changes in law, Florida DOT changes, Florida DOT-caused delays and several other events. Similarly, the I-635 LBJ-Managed Lanes contract listed force majeure events (along with many others) as a "Relief Event."

The I-595 Express Lanes and the I-635 LBJ-Managed Lanes agreements exemplify the structure and characteristics for relief granted in most PPP contracts in the USA. Some contracts have comparable "Compensation Event" and/or "Delay Event" provisions that effectively offer the same opportunities for relief to concessionaires. Further, force majeure events within this broader "family" of event mechanisms are likely to more specifically address the circumstances of the COVID-19 pandemic, so they are the most likely contractual remedy for COVID-19 impacts. Every contract in Table 1 includes a force majeure provision or definition; if a contract only defines a force majeure event, then such an event is treated as a relief event, compensation event and/or delay event. For instance, the I-635 LBJ-Managed Lanes contract defines a "Force Majeure Event" in Exhibit 1, p. 30 as follows:

> Force Majeure Event means the occurrence of any of the following events that materially and adversely affects performance of Developer's obligations, provided that such events (or the effects of such events) could not have been avoided by the exercise of caution, due diligence, or reasonable efforts by Developer: (a) war (including civil war and revolution), invasion, armed conflict, violent act of foreign enemy, military or armed blockade, or military or armed takeover of the Project, in each case occurring within the State; (b) any act of terrorism or sabotage that causes direct physical damage to the Project; (c) nuclear explo-

sion or contamination, in each case occurring within the State; (d) riot and civil commotion on or in the immediate vicinity of the Project; and (e) flood, earthquake, hurricane and tornado, in each case that causes direct physical damage to the Project, to the extent any such event is no longer deemed a Relief Event under clause (b) of the definition of Relief Event because insurance for the risks of such events became commercially unavailable under Section 16.1.2.13 of the Agreement.

Notably, this definition does not include reference to a pandemic, endemic, or any comparable health crisis. Another possible avenue for relief from the COVID-19 pandemic is a "Change in Law" or possibly a legal injunction estopping a private concessionaire from the performance of its contractual obligations (World Bank, 2022).

Accordingly, two case studies of PPP highway projects in the Commonwealth of Virginia are explored to examine more deeply: (a) how they were impacted by COVID-19; (b) what remedies were available within each project's contract; and (c) what actions were taken by the public and private sectors.

Case Studies

The Virginia Department of Transportation (VDOT) is responsible for constructing, maintaining, and operating the network of roads, bridges, and tunnels in the Commonwealth of Virginia; this includes multiple corridors of the national IHS, federal and state highways, and other roadways. Virginia has the third largest state-maintained highway system in the USA. Historically, VDOT has used dedicated state and federal sources to provide the revenues or funds necessary for its mission. However, the Virginia legislature passed the Public–Private Transportation Action (PPTA) in 1995, which enabled VDOT to enter into agreements with private entities to construct, improve, maintain, and operate transportation facilities. The PPTA permitted both solicited and unsolicited proposals for selection and negotiation. Since its passage, the PPTA has been amended to modify certain conditions and requirements of the act.

Since enactment of the PPTA, VDOT has issued and amended implementation guidelines for PPTA projects that establish processes for the evaluation and selection of solicited and unsolicited projects. It has also considered and implemented a number of projects where the private sector has played a substantial role in design, construction, operations and/or financing. The first project was the Pocahontas Parkway, which opened for service in 2002. Table 1 identifies the more recent PPTA projects in Virginia. Among these are the Elizabeth River Tunnels (ERT) and the I-95 Express Lanes projects; the former reached commercial close in 2011 and the latter in 2012. Both of these projects are now in the operations phase of their agreements, and they were selected as case studies to examine the impacts of COVID-19. Basic characteristics of these projects are illustrated in Table 2.

Table 2 Characteristics of case study projects

Project	Mode(s)	Contract value ($US millions)	Financial close	Contract duration	Private concessionaire (at close)	Financial structure at close (millions)
Elizabeth River Tunnels	Tunnels & Highway	$2088	2012	58 years	Elizabeth River Crossings Skanska Infrastructure Development Macquarie Financial	Federal TIFIA Loan: $422 Private Activity Bonds: $675 Private Equity: $272 State Funds: $408 Toll Revenues: $268 TIFIA Capitalized Interest: $43
I-95 Express Lanes	Highway	$923	2012	76 years	95 Express Lanes LLC Fluor Transurban	Federal TIFIA Loan: $300 Private Activity Bonds: $252.6 State Grant: $82.6 Private Equity: $280.4 TIFIA Capitalized Interest: $6.5 Interest Earnings: $0.6

Elizabeth River Tunnels

Background

ERT is an approximately $2.1 billion project in the Hampton Roads region in Virginia. The project is located in the cities of Portsmouth and Norfolk and consists of five construction components involving three facilities: the Midtown Tunnel (MTT), the Downtown Tunnel (DTT), and the Martin Luther King Freeway Extension (MLK Freeway Extension). The existing Downtown and Midtown Tunnels were built in the 1960s and tolls were initially imposed to pay for the revenue bonds issued for building the facilities. In the late 1980s, however, tolls were removed when the bonds were paid off. In the late 1990s, the tunnels were operating well over their design capacity and daily congestion was routine. Operational safety was also another issue in the tunnels, which prompted the need for safety and mobility improvements. Additionally, truck traffic on the MLK Freeway and through DTT had created congestion issues. Consequently, an extension for the MLK Freeway was needed to connect the freeway to Route 58 to divert truck traffic away from downtown Portsmouth and through the Midtown Tunnel (Messina, 2010).

In 2008, VDOT solicited Conceptual Proposals for improvements to the tunnels (MTT and DTT). However, only a private consortium named Elizabeth River Crossings (ERC) responded. After a comprehensive review by the state's Independent Review Panel (IRP) in 2009, VDOT entered into an Interim Agreement with ERC to negotiate and develop a Comprehensive Agreement for the design, construction, finance, operation and maintenance of the ERT project in January 2010. Tolls were the project's principal source of revenue. To provide revenue sooner and reduce expected long-term toll rates, VDOT and ERC agreed to impose tolls on the two tunnels during construction. The Interim Agreement advanced to a Comprehensive Agreement between VDOT and ERC in December 2011 (VDOT, 2011). Subsequently, ERC became responsible for developing the project according to provisions of the comprehensive agreement. Financial close was achieved in April 2012, and construction commenced in June 2012 and was substantially complete in 2016.

Yet, the affordability of the toll rates remained a point of contention between state and local officials as well as citizens in the region. Both state and local public officials as well as local citizens were pushing to reduce the toll rates and to delay tolling of the tunnels until construction was complete (Ghadimi, 2017). Prior to the planned commencement of tolling on the existing tunnels in September 2012, Governor Bob McDonnell took action to mitigate concerns about the tunnel tolls; his administration delayed the tunnel tolls until January 2014 by allocating $100 million from state transportation funds to cover the lost revenue (Samuel, 2012; Walker, 2012). In addition, the McDonnell administration exempted local trips from tolls on the MLK Freeway Extension (Samuel, 2012). Despite these actions, a lawsuit was filed against VDOT and ERC in July 2012 to halt the tunnel tolls. In May 2013, the Portsmouth Circuit Court ruled in favor of the plaintiffs concluding that the tolls were unconstitutional. Subsequently, VDOT and ERC appealed the Portsmouth Circuit Court ruling to the Supreme Court of Virginia, and the Supreme Court reversed the Circuit Court's ruling finding that the tolls were constitutional in October 2013. Shortly thereafter, Terry McAuliffe was elected as the state's new governor. Once in office in January 2014, Governor McAuliffe received approval of the Commonwealth Transportation Board to spend $82.6 million over three years to reduce the initial toll rates from $1.84 and $1.59 to $1.00 and $0.75 during peak and off-peak hours, respectively.

Tolling of the existing tunnels finally commenced on February 1, 2014. In accordance with the Toll Rate Schedule of the comprehensive agreement, ERC may increase tolls at the start of each calendar year after review by VDOT for compliance with contractual obligations. Accordingly, ERC announced an increase of $0.25 for both peak and non-peak tolls to start on January 1, 2015. In July 2015, the state and ERC reached another agreement to alleviate the toll burden on area residents; the two parties decided to eliminate the tolls on the MLK Freeway Extension altogether in exchange for a state payment of $78 million to ERC. Further, ERC agreed to transfer $5 million over the course of ten years to a "toll relief fund" to help low-income users to pay for the tunnel tolls. In 2017, ERC began funding the 10-year Toll Relief Program at $500,000 per year; users of the tunnels living in Portsmouth and Norfolk who earned less than $30,000 per year became eligible to receive toll relief.

Clearly, the actions taken by VDOT and ERC as well as the executive decisions made by both Governor McDonnell and Governor McAuliffe illustrate the significance of the toll rates and their affordability for users in the region. In total, the state contributed $582 million to the project after the comprehensive agreement was signed to reduce the initial toll rates on DTT and MTT as well as to defer their commencement and to eliminate tolls on the MLK Freeway Extension. Further, a Toll Relief Program was implemented to reduce the burden of tolls on low-income users in the region.

Relevant Contractual Provisions

The ERT comprehensive agreement (i.e., contract) included compensation event and delay event provisions to give the concessionaire relief as specified in the contract. The contract's definition of a "Delay Event" includes a "Force Majeure Event." The agreement defined a "Force Majeure Event" as follows (VDOT, 2011, Exhibit A, p. A-24):

> Force Majeure Event means the occurrence of an event, act, omission, condition or circumstance beyond either parties' reasonable control and due to no fault of either party, or those for whom either party is responsible, that materially prevents or delays the Concessionaire from performing any of its obligations pursuant to the Agreement.

The agreement does exclude specific circumstances that disqualify an event from being a force majeure event to include: (1) the negligence or misconduct of the Concessionaire Party; (2) market conditions and economic conditions affecting the availability, supply, or cost of labor, equipment and materials, construction equipment and supplies, or commodities; or (3) market conditions and economic conditions affecting traffic volumes, traffic revenue or the Concessionaire's ability to meet its financial obligations for the project. As noted previously, any force majeure event is treated as a Delay Event, which entitles the concessionaire to extensions of time.

The ERT agreement does not specifically mention endemics or pandemics as qualifying events. However, the contractual language "…beyond either parties' reasonable control and due to no fault of either party, or those for whom either party is responsible…" likely affords the Concessionaire the opportunity to claim that the COVID-19 pandemic qualifies as a force majeure event. Yet, the exclusion of market and economic conditions affecting the availability of construction materials, equipment, etc., and traffic volumes and traffic revenue does potentially give VDOT the grounds to contest such a claim. Consequently, the contractual language appears to leave claiming the pandemic as a force majeure event open for interpretation.

Within the agreement, a "Compensation Event" can entitle the concessionaire to collect damages, and its definition lists qualifying events that include: "…(d) any Discriminatory Change in Law; (e) one or more injunctions or other legal proceedings enjoining or estopping the Concessionaire from the performance of its obligations pursuant to the Agreement, in any case for more than 30 days in the aggregate;…" (VDOT, 2011, Exhibit A, p. A-10). A "Discriminatory Change in Law" is defined in Exhibit A, p. A-20 as:

> Discriminatory Change in Law means the adoption of any State Law or any change in any State Law or in the interpretation or application thereof during the Term that has the effect of discriminating solely against the Project, the Concessionaire, or private operators of toll roads in the State, except where such State Law or change in State Law or in interpretation or application is (a) in response, in whole or in part, to any failure to perform or breach of the Agreement or other Project Agreement, violation of Law or Governmental Approval, culpable act, omission or negligence on the part of any Concessionaire Party, or (b) otherwise permitted under the Agreement.

Hence, pandemic-related responses such as executive orders to restrict activities or impose public health measures would need to target the ERT project, its concessionaire or private toll road operators specifically to meet the threshold of a discriminatory change and concomitantly qualify as a compensation event.

Onset of COVID-19

In spring 2020, COVID-19 began to impact Virginia and other regions of the USA. In April, traffic in the ERT tunnels fell by 39% compared to the same month in 2019. By the end of June, year to date traffic and revenue were down 16.3% and 10.2% compared to the same period in 2019; however, traffic counts began to improve in July with a drop of only 11% versus the July of 2019 (Fitch, 2020). By the end of June 2021, year to date traffic and revenue in the tunnels had nearly recovered to their pre-pandemic levels; in fact, traffic counts in the tunnels in June 2021 were up by 3.6% compared to June 2019 (Fitch, 2021). In general, the traffic in the tunnels is more stable since it is a well-established corridor, and users have to travel some distance to non-tolled fixed crossings, which are operating at capacity. Further, the pattern of traffic decline and recovery in the ERT project in 2020–2021 are comparable to daily travel on urban highways, as shown in Fig. 1.

Amidst the pandemic, VDOT and ERC amended the comprehensive agreement in October 2020 to incorporate three key changes (VDOT, 2020a). First, ERC would agree to keep its maximum toll rate on the Elizabeth River Tunnels flat during 2021 to mitigate the economic impacts of COVID-19 on the region; in January 2022, ERC could increase toll rates to the maximum level permitted by the agreement. Second, the original Toll Relief Program would be extended for ten years until 2037. Finally, previously implemented changes to the billing and customer service practices designed to lower costs of toll transactions for users were formally incorporated into the amendment (VDOT, 2020b). This amendment reinforced Virginia's commitment to reduce the effects of tolling on low-income citizens in the region. Further, it illustrated ERC's willingness to continue to work with the state on such matters.

Meanwhile, ERC's equity partners Macquarie Infrastructure Partners II and Skanska were finalizing a deal to sell their stakes in the concession company. In December 2020, Abertis Infrasestructuras, an international toll road management firm headquartered in Spain, in consortium with Manulife Investment Management, acquired ERC for a price of $2.3 billion with $1.3 billion in equity and $1.1 billion in debt; the sale was approved following a consent review by VDOT in accordance with the comprehensive agreement. Abertis became the new operator of the Elizabeth River Tunnels (DTT and MTT). Abertis CEO Jose Aljaro commented, "Abertis looks forward to working for the benefit of local communities and building on a constructive and mutually beneficial relationship with VDOT" (VDOT, 2020b).

By November 2021, VDOT and ERC's new owners had mutually negotiated another amendment to the comprehensive agreement, which modified the Toll Relief Program. Starting in 2022, ERC agreed to pay $3,227,200 into the program, which is more than six times prior annual contributions; in subsequent years, contributions will increase by 3.5% until the program ends in 2037. The program now provides its low-income participants a 50% discount on tolls for up to five round-trips per week, and it more than doubles those eligible for the program (VDOT, 2021a). ERC CEO David Sullivan stated, "This is our commitment to easing the financial burden that we know our tolls have on income-restrained residents…This $2.7 million increase in toll reduction funding is the most significant commitment our company has ever made to the community" (Schulte, 2021). "We deferred the increase last year mainly because of COVID. It was the right thing to do, and we'll resume increases in January," Sullivan said (13News Now, 2021). In addition, the toll rate increase scheduled for 2022 was spread over three years. For its part, VDOT agreed to pay ERC $1,727,220 in 2022 to support operating and maintenance expenses on untolled portions of the project such as the MLK Freeway Extension; this public contribution would also increase at 3.5% per year until the end of the program (VDOT, 2021a).

I-95 Express Lanes

Background

The I-95 Express Lanes project developed 29.4 miles of high occupancy vehicle (HOV)/high occupancy toll (HOT) lanes along I-95 and I-395 in Northern Virginia. The initial conception of this project began with an unsolicited conceptual proposal from Clark-Shirley in 2003; in accordance with VDOT Implementation Guidelines, the department posted a notice regarding its receipt and solicited competing proposals. In March 2004, Fluor submitted a competing conceptual proposal. Following review, both proposers were invited to submit detailed proposals. In June 2005, detailed proposals were submitted by Clark-Shirley and Fluor and Transurban (Transurban had been listed as a subcontractor in the Fluor conceptual proposal). The detailed proposals were reviewed by an appointed Advisory Panel, and it recommended that the detailed proposal from Fluor and Transurban be further developed in accordance with the PPTA and VDOT's Implementation Guidelines. In October 2006, VDOT and the Fluor-Transurban team entered into an Interim Agreement to pursue development of the project. After environmental clearances were obtained and project scope adjustments were made, VDOT reached a comprehensive agreement with 95 Express Lanes, a consortium of Fluor and Transurban, for the design, construction, finance, operation and maintenance of the HOV/HOT lanes in July 2012 (VDOT, 2012). Financial close was achieved shortly thereafter. Construction began in August 2012, and the lanes opened to traffic in December 2014. The Fluor-Transurban consortium also developed the I-495 Express Lanes project in Northern Virginia. The I-95 project's lanes connect with the I-495 lanes at the Springfield Interchange (where I-95, I-495, and I-395 intersect). Consequently, this project was a second arrangement between VDOT and the Fluor-Transurban consortium that expanded the network of managed lanes in the Northern Virginia/metropolitan Washington, DC area. In 2014, Transurban acquired Fluor's 10% share in both the 495 Express Lanes and the 95 Express Lanes (Transurban, 2014).

In 2016, VDOT and Transurban amended the I-95 Express Lanes Comprehensive Agreement to extend the HOT lanes approximately 2.2 miles south as a "Department Project Enhancement" in accordance with Section 12.02 of the comprehensive agreement that authorized VDOT to request such an enhancement and gave the concessionaire the right, but not the obligation, to undertake the enhancement upon mutually agreeable terms. Subsequently in June 2017, VDOT and Transurban negotiated and agreed to an Amended and Restated Comprehensive Agreement to extend the HOT lanes an additional eight miles north along I-395 to the Virginia border with Washington, DC (VDOT, 2017). Construction started in August 2017, and the lanes opened in late 2019. In November 2017, Transurban submitted a proposal to VDOT to further extend the I-95 Express Lanes. In April 2019, the parties negotiated a Second Amended and Restated Comprehensive Agreement, for the Fredericksburg Extension project (called FredEx) will expand the I-95 lanes 10 miles south to Fredericksburg, VA (Arcieri, 2019; VDOT, 2019). Construction started in July 2019, and the lanes are expected to open to traffic in 2023. Additionally, Transurban began working with VDOT on plans for the 495 Express Lanes Northern Extension project (called 495 NEXT), which will involve expanding the I-495 managed lanes north by 2.5 miles (Arcieri, 2019). In October 2021, VDOT and Transurban executed a comprehensive agreement for the 495 NEXT project, and Transurban announced it had selected Lane Construction as its design-build contractor (VDOT, 2021b). Construction is expected to start in the summer of 2022 with an opening date anticipated in 2025.

Relevant Contractual Provisions

The comprehensive agreement (i.e., contract) and the amendments for the I-95 Express Lanes project, which added the I-395 lanes to the north and the Fredricksburg Extension to the south, have the same provisions and structure as the ERT comprehensive agreement, which were described previously. A force majeure event is defined the same, and such an event will generally be treated as a Delay Event. Similarly, treatment of a pandemic as a force majeure event is subject to interpretation. In addition, the contractual language associated with compensation events, changes in law, and discriminatory changes in law are identical.

Onset of COVID-19

When lockdowns associated with the pandemic started in spring 2020, the I-95 Express Lanes were significantly impacted. In April, traffic fell by 80% compared to traffic counts in the previous year. Similarly, revenue dropped by 90%; these trends continued through May and June of 2020 (Moore, 2020). However, traffic and revenue started to recover in the last quarter of 2020. Still, the pandemic's impact was clear. In FY2021, Transurban reported a proportional toll revenue decrease for all of its toll roads in North America of 39.9%, while average workday toll revenue on the I-95 Express Lanes decreased by 21.4% (Transurban, 2021). By 2021, however, traffic and revenue had begun to rebound toward pre-pandemic levels (Transurban, 2022).

In December 2020, Transurban announced that Australian investors AustralianSuper and UniSuper and the Canada Pension Plan Investment Board would acquire half the interest in its 495 Express Lanes and I-95 Express Lanes assets in a $2.1 billion deal; Transurban would continue to operate and manage the express lanes. Transurban explained that selling its stakes would provide capital for other opportunities in Virginia and Maryland (Lazo, 2020).

Case Study Analysis and Discussion

No Claims

In both the ERT and I-95 case studies, claims for a force majeure event, a discriminatory change in law or, more broadly, relief due to the pandemic were not made. Sources familiar with these projects confirmed that no formal claims were filed. In addition, a search of all content published by Engineering News Record (ENR), which reports on the construction industry in the USA and worldwide, from January 2020 to August 2022 using keywords such as "claims," "disputes," "covid-19," "public-private partnerships" and "PPPs" did not identify any articles related to these two case studies or any articles about claims or disputes in PPP projects in the USA.

Each case study project had identical contractual structures for overall relief and provisions related to changes in law and force majeure. As noted, the change in law contractual language required that executive or legal actions related to COVID-19 be "discriminatory" in order to grant the concessionaire relief. In other words, only such actions exclusive to these projects or toll road operators/managers would have provided a basis for relief. In general, the workplace restrictions imposed by executive action in Virginia throughout 2020–2021 affected public and private employers alike (VOSH, 2021; Husch and Blackwell, 2022). Hence, the statewide imposition of such restrictions provided little to no basis for a claim for relief. Alternatively, the force majeure contractual language likely provided the counterparties a position to argue for and against such a claim. For the concessionaires, the definition of a force majeure event as being "beyond either parties' reasonable control and due to no fault of either party" could certainly open the door for a claim. Yet, the exclusion language regarding *market and economic conditions* affecting construction labor, equipment and materials, and traffic volumes and revenues provided the public agency with a basis for countering such a claim, particularly since the pandemic was not an event exclusive to these projects.

The contractual language in the case study agreements was compared with two more recent PPP agreements, SH-288 Toll Lanes in Texas and Central 70 in Colorado. In these agreements, relief related to changes in law was also limited to discriminatory changes. However, force majeure events were more strictly defined as being limited to events such as war or violence; terrorism; blockades or embargoes; labor disputes or strikes; or floods, hurricanes, and tornadoes. "Relief Event" mechanisms were delineated in both the SH-288 and Central 70 agreements, but these provisions did not extend to pandemics either. Hence, the agreements in the two case study projects in Virginia likely provided the stronger potential for a pandemic-related claim.

Certainly, traffic and revenue in both case studies were disrupted with the I-95 Express Lanes experiencing greater impacts likely because general purpose lanes were readily available for non-tolled use. While the drops in traffic and revenue were significant, they were relatively short-lived. Both case study projects had difficult second quarters in calendar year 2020, but traffic and revenue began to recover throughout the balance of 2020. By 2021, the traffic in both projects had nearly recovered to pre-pandemic levels. The impacts observed in both cases mirrored traffic declines and recovery at the national level. Hence, the short-term effect of the pandemic on traffic volumes may also help explain why no claims were filed. While the financial effect on these projects was substantial, it was brief.

Contextual Issues and Shadow of the Future

Contextual issues are another plausible rationale for the lack of pandemic-related claims in the case studies. In the ERT case, the affordability of the tolls was a key issue from the outset of the project. VDOT and ERC had worked through establishing and adjusting the toll rates, overcoming a legal challenge to the tolls, and creating and subsequently amending a toll relief program for lower income citizens using the project's tunnels. From ERC's perspective, sustaining the tolls at a financially acceptable level was certainly a priority for the viability of the project. Similarly, state officials and VDOT desired to mitigate the toll burden to the extent that they could. VDOT and ERC had a history of negotiating adjustments to tolling on the project – such as elimination of the tolls on the MLK Extension in exchange for a state contribution. Consequently, in lieu of any claim, ERC and VDOT enhanced the toll relief program already in place once the pandemic hit, with ERC increasing the funds available and extending the program in exchange for the state contributing toward the project's operating and maintenance expenses. Moreover, the agreed suspension of toll rate increases for a single year in 2021 is a relatively short impact for a project with a 58-year concession period.

In the I-95 case, when the pandemic struck, Transurban had just negotiated a second amendment of the I-95 comprehensive agreement with VDOT to develop the Fredericksburg Extension (FredEx) in 2019 and was negotiating the 495 Northern Extension (495 NEXT) agreement with VDOT. Completing both of these projects was strategically important to both VDOT and Transurban. Doing so would complete the network of express lanes in Northern Virginia in and around the metropolitan DC area. Hence, neither party would likely have risked this objective as well as their longstanding relationship over a pandemic-related claim.

In both cases, the shadow of the future likely furthered behavior for the good of each project over opportunistic behavior (Henisz et al., 2012). Maintaining a reasonable tolling program and providing toll relief to low-income citizens in the region likely helped secure long-term support from multiple stakeholders in the ERT case. Sustaining the strong relationship the public and private sectors had forged throughout the development and operation of the tolled express lanes in the region supported progress toward the planned expansions (FredEx and 495 NEXT) of the express lanes network in the I-95 case.

Market Transactions Not Deterred

Interestingly, both case study projects experienced changes in their ownership structure during the pandemic. Macquarie and Skanska sold their stakes in ERC entirely, while Transurban sold half of their shares in their Northern Virginia express lane assets. Clearly, such transactions remain plausible even in turbulent periods if the terms and conditions benefit buyers and sellers and comply with contractual consent requirements by public agencies. Further, the timing of these transactions in late

2020 is an additional explanation for why the concessionaires did not pursue any pandemic-related claims since such could have impacted these sales.

Implications for Theory

Evidence from the two case studies demonstrates different facets of governance in PPP projects. The express contractual provisions related to change in law provided clarity during the pandemic in both case projects; these provisions made it clear that only discriminatory changes would entitle the concessionaire to relief. Here, contractual or regulative governance mechanisms proved sufficient to direct counterparty behavior (Henisz et al., 2012; Roehrich & Lewis, 2010). Alternatively, the force majeure provisions arguably left open the possibility for a pandemic-related claim. Yet, no formal claims were made. As noted previously, the shadow of the future likely influenced the concessionaires' behavior since future business opportunities were at stake in each case; moreover, the concessionaires involved were likely concerned about their reputational capital (Chan 2010). Additionally, Henisz et al. (2012) argue that prior interactions among counterparties can introduce a "social shadow of the future" to mitigate opportunistic behavior. Further, they argue that the duration and intensity of counterparty interactions are positively associated with the normative and cognitive supports for relationships that can buttress contracts and promote cooperation. In both cases, VDOT and the concessionaires had longstanding and complex interactions to plan, implement and operate the case projects. Hence, the cases provide some evidence to support these arguments in the extant literature.

Implications for Practice

The cases examined support calls for complementing contractual governance practices with relational governance practices in construction projects generally (Ling et al., 2014) and PPP projects specifically (Warsen et al., 2019). Their combination is likely to minimize counterparty opportunism and improve cooperation. Practices such as frequent and transparent communication, co-location, and partnering warrant greater consideration in PPP project implementation and management.

Conclusion

This chapter has characterized the PPP market in the USA and explored the impacts of COVID-19 on US PPPs by examining two case studies in the Commonwealth of Virginia – the Elizabeth River Tunnels project and the I-95 Express Lanes project.

Contractual provisions focused on adverse events such as a pandemic were examined to determine how contractual designs may have offered relief. The ERT and I-95 Express Lanes cases are representative PPP highway projects in the USA market. Both are revenue risk arrangements with comparable contractual structures for relief, changes in law, and force majeure events. Each experienced significant drops in traffic and revenue as a consequence of the COVID-19 pandemic, particularly in the spring of 2020. Neither project experienced any pandemic-related claims. Why? Notably, the change in law provisions were clear that relief would only be granted if legal or regulatory actions were discriminatory, which was not the case. However, the force majeure contractual language likely gave the concessionaires and VDOT alike grounds for and against a claim, respectively; this may have deterred such claims. More importantly though, circumstances in each project likely precluded any claims. In both cases, VDOT and the concessionaires had longstanding relationships, pending business opportunities, and shared priorities such as reasonable but affordable toll rates in the ERT case and the build-out of the express lanes network in Northern Virginia in the I-95 Express Lanes case. These apparently outweighed the short-term problems posed by the pandemic. Future research can examine more deeply whether the coupling of contractual and relational governance mechanisms found in these two cases deters opportunism and advances mutual cooperation and benefits.

References

13News Now Staff. (2021, November 18). Tolls for Elizabeth River Tunnels will increase starting Jan. 1. Norfolk, VA.

Arcieri, K. (2019, January 29). Virginia, Transurban ink agreements for $1B in transportation projects. *Washington Business Journal.*

Casady, C. B., & Baxter, D. (2020). Pandemics, public-private partnerships (PPPs), and force majeure: COVID-19 expectations and implications. *Construction Management and Economics, 38*, 1077. https://doi.org/10.1080/01446193.2020.1817516

Deloitte. (2020). *Transportation infrastructure and COVID-19: A moment that matters.* Rosslyn, VA.

Federal Highway Administration (FHWA). (2022). State P3 Legislation. Retrieved August 19, 2022 from https://www.fhwa.dot.gov/ipd/p3/legislation/

Fitch Ratings. (2020, September 17). Fitch Affirms Elizabeth River Crossings, LLC PABs & TIFIA Loan at 'BBB'; Outlook Negative. Rating Action Commentary. Retrieved May 17, 2022 from https://www.fitchratings.com/research/us-public-finance/fitch-affirms-elizabeth-river-crossings-llc-pabs-tifia-loan-at-bbb-outlook-revised-to-stable-29-09-2021

Fitch Ratings. (2021, September 29). Fitch Affirms Elizabeth River Crossings, LLC PABs & TIFIA Loan at 'BBB'; Outlook Revised to Stable, Rating Action Commentary. Retrieved May 17, 2022 from https://www.fitchratings.com/research/us-public-finance/fitch-affirms-elizabeth-river-crossings-llc-pabs-tifia-loan-at-bbb-outlook-revised-to-stable-29-09-2021

Ghadimi, B. (2017). *Impact of project delivery method on stakeholder issues and involvement practices in megaprojects: Evidence from fixed crossing case studies.* PhD Dissertation, Virginia Tech, Blacksburg, VA.

Henisz, W. J., Levitt, R. E., & Scott, W. R. (2012). Toward a unified theory of project governance: economic, sociological and psychological supports for relational contracting. *Engineering Project Organization Journal, 2*(1–2), 37–55.

Husch and Blackwell. (2022). *Virginia: State-by-State COVID-19 Guidance*. Retrieved August 19, 2022 from https://www.huschblackwell.com/virginia-state-by-state-covid-19-guidance

Lazo, L. (2020, December 17). Northern Virginia toll road operator Transurban to sell half its stake in lanes. *The Washington Post*.

Ling, F., Ong, S., Ke, Y., Wang, S., & Zou, P. (2014). Drivers and barriers to adopting relational contracting practices in public projects: Comparative study of Beijing and Sydney. *International Journal of Project Management, 32*(2), 275–285.

Messina, D. (2010). *Report: Midtown Tunnel expansion a high priority*. Retrieved May 17, 2022 from http://hamptonroads.com/2010/04/reportmidtowntunnelexpansionhighpriority

Moore, J. (2020, August 12). DC-area toll revenue plunges 90% amid coronavirus pandemic. *WTOP News*.

New York Times. (2022). *Coronavirus in the U.S.: Latest Map and Case Count*. Retrieved May 16, 2022 from https://www.nytimes.com/interactive/2021/us/covid-cases.html

Roehrich, J. K., & Lewis, M. A. (2010). Towards a model of governance in complex (product–service) inter-organizational systems. *Construction Management & Economics, 28*(11), 1155–1164. https://doi.org/10.1080/01446191003762249

Samuel, P. (2012). Virginia gone to financial close on $2.1b Norfolk crossings P3, compromises on toll timing, coverage. *TollroadNews*. tollroadnews.com

Schulte, K. (2021, November 15). VA expands Elizabeth River Tunnels toll relief program. *Virginia Business*. Retrieved May 17, 2022 from https://www.virginiabusiness.com/article/va-expands-elizabeth-river-tunnels-toll-relief-program/

Transurban. (2014, August 5). Transurban Group Appendix 4E Year ended 30 June 2014. *ASX Release*. Victoria, Australia.

Transurban. (2021, August 9). Transurban FY21 Results, *ASX Release*. Victoria, Australia.

Transurban. (2022, February 17). Transurban 1H22 Results. *ASX Release*. Victoria, Australia.

Virginia Department of Transportation (VDOT). (2011, December 5). *Comprehensive Agreement Relating to the Downtown Tunnel/Midtown Tunnel/Martin Luther King Freeway Extension Project by and among Virginia Department of Transportation and Elizabeth River Crossings OpCo, LLC*. Richmond, VA.

Virginia Department of Transportation (VDOT). (2012, July 31). *Comprehensive Agreement Relating to the I-95 HOV/HOT Lanes Project by and between Virginia Department of Transportation and 95 Express Lanes LLC*. Richmond, VA.

Virginia Department of Transportation (VDOT). (2017, June 8). *Amended and Restated Comprehensive Agreement Relating to I-95/395 HOV/HOT Lanes Project by and between Virginia Department of Transportation and 95 Express Lanes LLC*. Richmond, VA.

Virginia Department of Transportation (VDOT). (2019, April 18). *Second Amended and Restated Comprehensive Agreement Relating to I-95/395 HOV/HOT Lanes Project by and between Virginia Department of Transportation and 95 Express Lanes LLC*. Richmond, VA.

Virginia Department of Transportation (VDOT). (2020a, October 26). *Amendment No. 8 to the Comprehensive Agreement Relating to the Downtown Tunnel/Midtown Tunnel/Martin Luther King Freeway Extension Project*. Richmond, VA.

Virginia Department of Transportation (VDOT). (2020b, December 30). Elizabeth River Crossings Sale to Abertis Infraestructuras Finalized. *Press Release*. Richmond, VA. Retrieved May 17, 2022 from https://www.virginiadot.org/newsroom/statewide/2020/elizabeth-river-crossings-sale-to-abertis-infraestructuras-finalized12-30-2020.asp

Virginia Department of Transportation (VDOT). (2021a, November 10). *Amendment No. 9 to the Comprehensive Agreement Relating to the Downtown Tunnel/Midtown Tunnel/Martin Luther King Freeway Extension Project*. Richmond, VA.

Virginia Department of Transportation (VDOT). (2021b, October 15). Virginia Department of Transportation and Transurban Execute Comprehensive Agreement to Build 495 Express

Lanes Northern Extension Project; Transurban Selects Lane Construction as Design-Build Contractor. *Press Release*. Richmond, VA. Retrieved May 17, 2022 from https://virginiadot.org/newsroom/northern-virginia/2021/virginia-department-of-transportation-and-transurban-execute-comprehensive-agreement-to-build-495-express-lanes-northern-extensi10-5-2021.asp

Virginia Occupational Safety and Health Program (VOSH). (2021, January 27). *16VAC25-220, Final Permanent Standard for Infectious Disease Prevention of the SARS-CoV-2 Virus That Causes COVID-19*. Virginia Department of Labor and Industry.

Walker, J. (2012, April 17). McDonnell backs postponing tunnel tolls until 2014. *The Virginia-Pilot*. Retrieved May 17, 2022 from pilotonline.com

Warsen, R., Klijn, E. H., & Koppenjan, J. (2019). Mix and match: How contractual and relational conditions are combined in successful public–private partnerships. *Journal of Public Administration Research and Theory, 29*(3), 375–393.

World Bank. (2022). *Covid-19 and PPP Contracts*. Retrieved August 19, 2022 from https://ppp.worldbank.org/public-private-partnership/covid-19-and-ppp-contracts

Part III
Risk Management

Governance for Sustained Success of PPPs During COVID-19: The Case of Ogal Shiwa Project

Yuji Nemoto

Introduction

Current State of Infrastructures

Infrastructure investment in Japan peaked during the high growth period of the 1970s. Now, 50 years later, the infrastructure is aging en masse, requiring enormous renewal investment (Nemoto, 2022). However, no budget has been allocated for this. Public capital formation (i.e., public fixed investment) accounted for 10% of nominal GDP in the 1970s, but is now only in the 5% range, meaning that the public fixed investment budget has shrunk significantly.

In addition, it is difficult to increase the issuance of government bond further since the government's debt dependency (government debt outstanding vs. nominal GDP) has risen from 50% in the 1970s to 250% today (Chart 1).[1]

Current State of PPP Methods

Japan's PPP system is as shown in Table 2. The roles are shifting from the top to the bottom, i.e., from the public to the private sector.

---

[1] Calculated by the author from SNA statistics <https://www.esri.cao.go.jp/jp/sna/menu.html> and IMF World Economic Outlook Database <https://www.imf.org/en/Publications/WEO/weo-database/2022/April>

Y. Nemoto (✉)
Toyo University, Tokyo, Japan
e-mail: nemoto@toyo.jp

© The Author(s), under exclusive license to Springer Nature Switzerland AG 2023

T. Dolla et al. (eds.), *Revisiting Public-Private Partnerships*,
Contributions to Public Administration and Public Policy,
https://doi.org/10.1007/978-3-031-37015-1_9

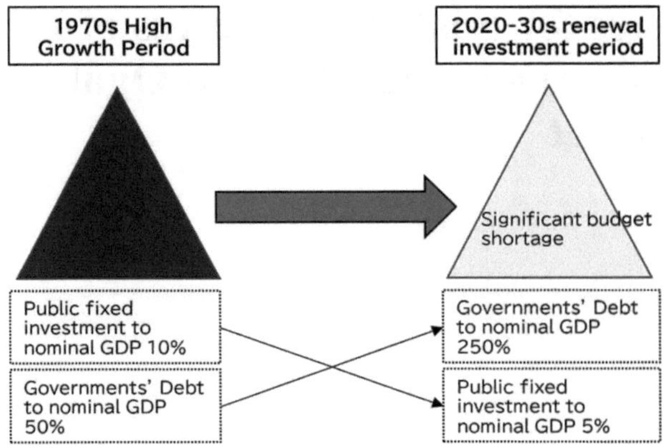

Figure 1 Japan's public fixed investment and renewal investment budget shortfalls. (Source: Prepared by the author)

type		basis law	regulatory agency	policy making	de-sign	bui-ld	Fina-nce	own	ope-rate	mainte-nance	repair	rene-wal
Pure public works				Public								
PPP	Comprehensive Outsourcing	Local Autonomy Law	Ministry of Internal Affairs and Communications (MIAC)									
	Designated Manager System	Revised Local Autonomy Law(2003)	MIAC									
	Market Testing	Public Service Reform Act(2006)	Cabinet Office									
	PFI(BTO)	PFI Act(1999)	Cabinet Office									
	PFI(BOT)	PFI Act(1999)										
	Concession	Revised PFI Act(2009)										
	Public Real Estate	National Property Law Local Autonomy Law	Ministry of Finance, MIAC									
Pure private business				Private								

Table 2 List of PPP schemes in Japan. (Source: Prepared by the author)

At the top is the pure public project (public services performed by the national and local governments), and at the bottom is the pure private project (private services performed by the private sector), and in between is PPP. Comprehensive outsourcing" refers to the outsourcing of multiple tasks to a single private company.

Simple outsourcing is not classified as PPP since there is virtually no risk transfer to the private sector, while comprehensive private outsourcing is classified as PPP due to the significant risk transfer to the private sector.

Under the designated manager system, ownership remains with the local government, but the authority for maintenance and operation is transferred to the private sector. This is often implemented in existing facilities as a system introduced under the Revised Local Autonomy Law of 2003. It has been introduced in many libraries and public sports facilities nationwide, with a total of 76,268 projects (survey by the Ministry of Internal Affairs and Communications, March 2018).

In market testing, the public and private sectors compete under the same conditions, and the superior proposal is selected through a "public-private competitive bidding" process. If the private sector wins the bidding, the work will be outsourced, and if the public sector wins, the work will be directly managed. The system was introduced in accordance with the 2006 Public Service Reform Act.

PFI is a pioneering approach in Japan's PPP, which was legislated in 1999. This is often used for newly built large public facilities. The number of projects is 875 (according to the Cabinet Office survey in March 2021). PFI is classified into BTO (Build Transfer Operate), BOT (Build Own Transfer), and BOO (Build Own Operate) methods, depending on when ownership is transferred. The concession method, in which the government retains ownership but transfers all authority for project implementation to the private sector, was introduced in accordance with the revision of the PFI Act in 2009.

Public real estate is a method under which the private sector implements projects using publicly owned land or buildings. Cases include the sale of public land to attract factories and the conversion of consolidated schools to hotels or offices.

The methods from comprehensive private outsourcing to concession are characterized by the fact that they target public services, whereas public real estate targets private projects and the private sector is responsible for them.

Among the above methods, PFI and concession are governed by the PFI Act. The Cabinet Office, which has jurisdiction over the PFI Act, has published many documents, including guidelines, contract templates, a collection of questions and answers, case studies, and statistical data.

After the national or local government announces its implementation policy, it publicly invites private businesses to take on the project, which are then screened based on previously disclosed criteria. During the project operation phase, the execution of the contract is to be monitored. All of these processes are set forth in laws and guidelines. Other systems are similarly defined in their respective basis laws and guidelines. Thus, Japan's PPP system is modeled on the system of the PFI Act. Each method is governed by the appropriate regulatory agencies, which have established approval processes and dispute resolution mechanisms based on the laws and guidelines.

Context of the Inquiry

Consequences of the COVID-19 Pandemic

Figure 3 shows the number of new COVID-19 cases and the number of severe cases in Japan. Japan has experienced six waves of infection, and as of March 2022, the country is in the midst of the sixth wave. Compared to the fifth wave, the number of new cases has increased dramatically, while the number of severe cases has been decreasing.

The number of severe cases and deaths is not as high as in other countries, and economic and social activities are gradually recovering. To date, there have been no cases of PPP projects failing as a consequence of the COVID-19 pandemic.

PPP Policies on the COVID-19 Pandemic

In July 2020, the Cabinet Office (2020) published a document on the impact of COVID-19 pandemic on PFI, advising the national and local governments to discuss in good faith with PFI-SPCs (special purpose companies) the sharing of additional costs for infection control measures and the review of required standards for services.

Local governments will help PFI-SPCs to take advantage of various grants for the COVID-19 pandemic control.

After that, the Cabinet Office conducted a questionnaire survey among local governments. According to the survey results, of the 138 "affected by COVID-19 pandemic" projects out of the 612 that responded, 54% had "conducted" consultations

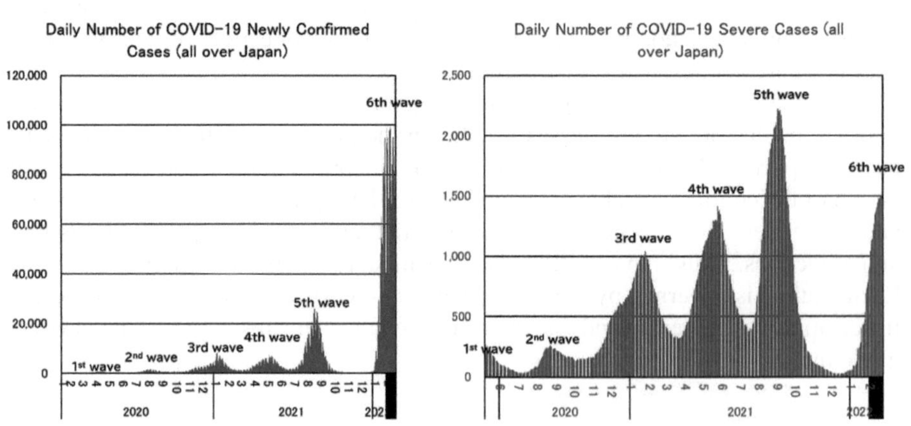

Figure 3 Number of newly confirmed and severe COVID-19 cases by day. (Source: Prepared by the author based on government data)

between the public and private sectors regarding the project and 40% are "currently conducting" consultations, which indicates that almost all projects have taken some action. On the other hand, it was pointed out that the definition of force majeure events is unclear, which makes consultations time-consuming, and that contract modifications require a resolution by the council, which makes it difficult to respond flexibly.

Based on these results, the Cabinet Office indicated that the criterion for determining whether an event constitutes force majeure is "whether business operations would be hindered even if all the precautions and preventive measures normally considered necessary are taken."

In addition, it was recommended that minor contract changes be designated in advance as matters for exclusive decision (Article 180, Paragraph 1 of the Local Autonomy Law) so that they can be made promptly. Although the results of consultation for individual projects have not been disclosed, it is assumed that consultations were concluded to enable the continuation of the project, since no cases of cancellation of PFI project contracts or project failure have been reported so far.

Although these sets of policies are formally intended for PFI, they can be also applied to other PPP methods.

Brief Description of the Case

Project Overview

The case study in Japan to be presented here is the Ogal Project in Shiwa Town, Iwate Prefecture UNECE (2018). The Shiwa town, located in the northeast region of Japan, has a population of 32,000 as of February 2022 (Figure 4).

Morioka City is located to the north and Hanamaki City to the south, with the JR Tohoku Main Line running through the center of the city. The Ogal Project is a mixed-use development project on approximately 10 hectares of town-owned land in front of Shiwa Chuo Station on the JR line.

The land was purchased from the prefectural government, which had owned it as a site for relocating an aging town hall in another location. Subsequently, the land was left unutilized due to Shiwa's deteriorating financial condition. The town then consulted Toyo University in 2006 in order to develop this land through PPP.

Subsequently, a representative from the town's private sector and a representative from the town hall enrolled in the PPP school to learn about it. Also, faculty members, including the author, and other graduate students collaborated to conduct a feasibility study on PPP implementation. Later, the Ogal Project was led by these two representatives (Table 5).

Project Timeline

- 2007 PPP feasibility study by Toyo University

2009 Shiwa Town PPP Basic Plan

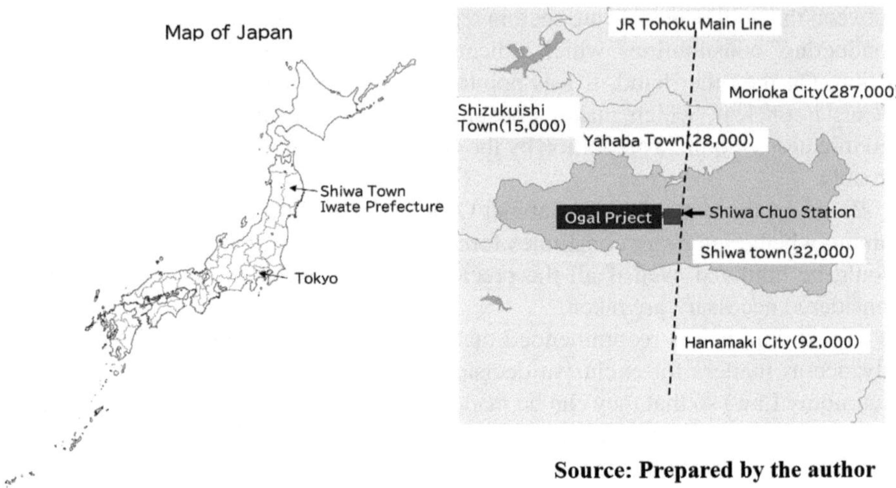

Figure 4 Locations where the Ogal Project was implemented. (Source: Prepared by the author)

2010 Establishment of Ogal Shiwa Co.
2011 Open of the Football Center
2012 Open of the Ogal Plaza
2013 Sales start of Ogal Town Residential land
2014 Opening of the Ogal Base
2015 Opening of the Shiwa Town Hall
2016 Opening of the Ogal Center.

The Ogal Project consists of the following nine sub-projects: (1) Football Center (Iwate Football Association), (2) Ogal Plaza (a complex of facilities including a public library, community center, farmer's market, restaurants, etc.), (3) Ogal Base (a complex of facilities including a gymnasium for indoor volleyball, a hotel, restaurants, etc.), (4) Energy Station (offices of a solar power generation company), (5) Town Hall (owned by Shiwa Town), (6) Ogal Center (a complex of facilities including a town-run children's center, pediatrics department, pharmacy, etc.), (7) Ogal Childcare (a private daycare center), (8) Ogal Square (green space and BBQ space), and (9) Ogal Town (56 units for private housing).

These projects are being developed using various PPP methods, including PFI (town hall building), public real estate (town-owned land lease), and the PPP agent.[2]

Although Shiwa town has a population of only 32,000, it is a region with remarkable economic impacts, including 1.04 million visitors per year, 250 jobs created, and land prices have risen for the last eight consecutive years. These facts make it one of the most famous PPP projects in Japan.

[2] In this chapter, "PPP agent" is used as a company established by the local government to reflect the will of the local government in the project.

	1.Football Center	2.Ogal Plaza	3.Ogal Base	4 Energy Station	5.Shiwa Town Hall	6.Ogal Center	7.Ogal Chirdcare	8.Ogal Square	9.Ogal Town
Project owner	Iwate Prefecture Football Association	SPV	SPV	Shiwa Green Energy	Shiwa town	SPV	Kyojokai Social Welfare Corp.	Shiwa Town	purchasers
methods	Land lease	PPP agent Land lease	PPP agent Land lease	Land lease	PFI(BTO)	PPP agent Land lease	Land lease	direct management	residential land sales
facility	Soccer ground(artificial turf)	Library, Community center, Childcare, Farmer's market, Restaurants, Retail shops, Clinic, Office	Hotel, Volleyball court, Restaurants, Convenience store	District heating	Public administration office	Public children's centre, Paediatrics, Nursery, Retail shops, Restaurants, Gym, Lodging	Childcare	Green space, Outdoor, BBQ spaces	56 private houses
Cost <Public financial burden>	$175M	$10.7M	$7.2M	$5m	$33.8M	$3.1M	$3.3M (Subsidy)	N.A.	N.A.
Financing	corporate finance	project finance	project finance	corporate finance	project finance	project finance	corporate finance		
Completed	April 2011	June 2012	July 2014	July 2014	May 2015	December 2016	April 2017		2014-
Land usage	Lease	Fixed-term lease	Fixed-term lease	Fixed-term lease		Fixed-term lease	Fixed-term lease	direct management	sale
Land owner	Shiwa town								purchasers

Table 5 Ogal Shiwa Project list. (Source: Prepared by the author based on materials provided by Shiwa town)

Consequences of the COVID-19 Pandemic

As of March 2022, Shiwa is included in the area covered by Iwate Prefecture's own state of emergency declaration. This declaration was issued at the sole discretion of Iwate Prefecture, in addition to the national-level state of emergency declaration designated by the central government. Iwate Prefecture refers to "the number of new cases per 100,000 people in the prefecture in the last week" as the standard for issuing a state of emergency declaration. Since the Omicron COVID-19 variant is highly contagious, the number of new cases exceeded this standard.

While a state of emergency is declared, people are asked to refrain from going out in crowded places or places with a high risk of infection, and to take basic infection control measures such as wearing non-woven masks with high droplet prevention effects, washing hands frequently, prohibiting conversations in close proximity, avoiding closed spaces, crowded places, as well as close-contact settings, shortening meal times, and so on.

In the Ogal Project, the town hall and library are open as usual after taking these basic measures. In addition, private tenants such as restaurants, commercial facilities, hospitals, and daycare centers are continuing to operate, albeit with reduced operating hours.

However, the decision was made to cancel some of the large-scale events. Accordingly, the volleyball tournament that was scheduled to be held at the Ogal Base gymnasium after January 2022 has been canceled. This gymnasium is the only one in the country dedicated to volleyball and is one of the most widely attended venues for the Ogal Project.

That is why the tournament had to be canceled to avoid crowding. Currently in Japan, on the condition that infection prevention measures are implemented, not only outdoor events such as baseball and soccer tournaments but also indoor events such as sumo tournaments and professional table tennis tournaments are permitted, and in light of these factors, relatively harsh measures were taken this time.

These adequate measures have been successful, and so far no clusters of COVID-19 cases have been reported. In addition, the nine sub-projects as a whole have been able to continue, although some private tenants have been replaced. Therefore, it can be evaluated that the impact of the COVID-19 pandemic has been minimized in this project.

Analysis

In this section, we present an analysis of the characteristics of the Ogal Project. This is based on interviews previously conducted with Mr. Senichi Kamata, Director of the Planning Division of Shiwa Town (graduate student of Toyo University), who was in charge of promoting the Ogal Project, and Mr. Sam Tabuchi, Professor Emeritus of Toyo University (then Professor), who conducted the survey at Toyo University, with the author's views added.

Compactization

The first characteristic is compactization. In Shiwa, as in the rest of Japan, the infrastructure is deteriorating. The town hall building is so old that it was at high risk of collapsing in the event of a major earthquake. As for libraries, there was only a small library set up in the old town hall building, which did not meet the needs of the residents.

There were no facilities to support parents raising children, including a daycare center, which is in high demand. If these facilities were to be built separately, a large investment would be required for each, including related infrastructure such as roads and parks. The town therefore decided to reduce the financial burden by consolidating these facilities in the Ogal area, where the site for the relocation of the town hall was once planned.

Market Potential

The second characteristic is market potential. The Ogal area is not only large in area, but is also located in front of a station on the East Japan Railway Company line. The population within a 30-km radius of this station totals 600,000. In other words, the Ogal district is not only the center of a town with a population of 32,000 but also the center of a metropolitan area with a population of 600,000. In short, this was an attractive location with market potential for the private sector.

Adoption of Various PPP Methods

The third characteristic is the adoption of various PPP methods. Generally, in PPP, the public and private sectors share roles within a single project. When a problem arises, the public and private sectors consult with each other in accordance with the procedures stipulated in the contract. However, when an unexpected circumstance such as the COVID-19 pandemic arises, it may take some time for the consultations to be concluded, which may prevent a quick response.

This is the reason why the Cabinet Office document [2020] referred "treating the issue as a force majeure event and holding consultations between the public and private sectors." In the individual Ogal projects, either the public or private sector is primarily responsible for the risk. For example, for town hall and Ogal Square, the town bears the risk, while the private sector bears very little risk.

In complexes such as Ogal Plaza, Ogal Base, and Ogal Center, the town and private tenants each assume full risk for the leased portions themselves. The private residences are completely financed by the sale of the land by each party, and there is no residual risk to the town after the sale. This clear division of roles between the public and private sectors for each individual sub-project enabled the town to respond quickly when risks arose.

PPP Agent

The fourth characteristic is the involvement of the PPP agent. In explaining the third characteristic, I mentioned that there is a clear division of risk between the public and private sectors in individual projects, but this creates the risk of inconsistency in the overall concept of the Ogal project. The PPP agent that managed the overall concept, Ogal Shiwa Corporation helped to address this risk.

The company was a joint venture funded by the town and private companies, and there were concerns that confusion would arise from operating the company with personnel from both the public and private sectors. However, from the beginning, the town took the stance of leaving the day-to-day management to the private citizen(s), as long as they adhered to the basic concept of the Ogal district. This avoided a situation in which conflicting interests between the public and private sectors would have led to a disunified concept.

Risk Management Experiences

A fifth characteristic is the experience in risk management. Specifically, this experience was gained through the Great East Japan Earthquake. On March 11, 2011, just before the opening of the Ogal Project, the Great East Japan Earthquake occurred. The earthquake was accompanied by a tsunami in addition to strong tremors, resulting in a total of 18,425 deaths and missing persons. The town was in the process of recovering from the disaster, and the opening of the Ogal Project was delayed for about a month.

A soccer tournament was held as part of the opening event, to which youth soccer teams from coastal areas who had lost the opportunity to practice were invited. While various events were canceled due to self-restraint in Tokyo, where the damage was less severe, the project was opened with a clear intention of the affected area to convey a message of recovery. A series of measures were quickly implemented in consultation with the town and the PPP agent.

Thus, the experience of responding well to unexpected situations was also reflected in the response to the COVID-19 pandemic.

Discussion

In this part, the results of the above analysis are verified. The tool used for verification is the Structure Sheet, which is also utilized in case studies at Toyo University's PPP School. The sheet is used to check the rationality of the flow of funds, the balance of risks and returns borne by the parties involved, the existence of governance to ensure contractual performance, and the ability to flexibly adjust in the event of unforeseen circumstances, by illustrating the names of the participating entities in the project and their relationships with each other.

As a result, the strengths and weaknesses of the target project can be identified for improvement. The structure sheet for the Ogal Project is shown in Chart 6.

The first strength we focused on is the implementation of compactization in areas with high market potential. This was one of the biggest success factors of the project, as it created attractive spaces not only for the nine projects, but also for the spaces between them, and created a sense of anticipation among the public as to what could be done next, thus attracting even more attention. In addition, the fact that visitors could enjoy the event even when they were outdoors also functioned effectively as a countermeasure against the COVID-19 pandemic.

The next strength we focused on is the various types of PPP. Basically, the land lease reduces the risk for the town because the lessee assumes responsibility for the project. In contrast, the town mainly bears the risk for the facilities it owns, such as city hall, etc. Through the land lease, the town receives land rent income (the flow

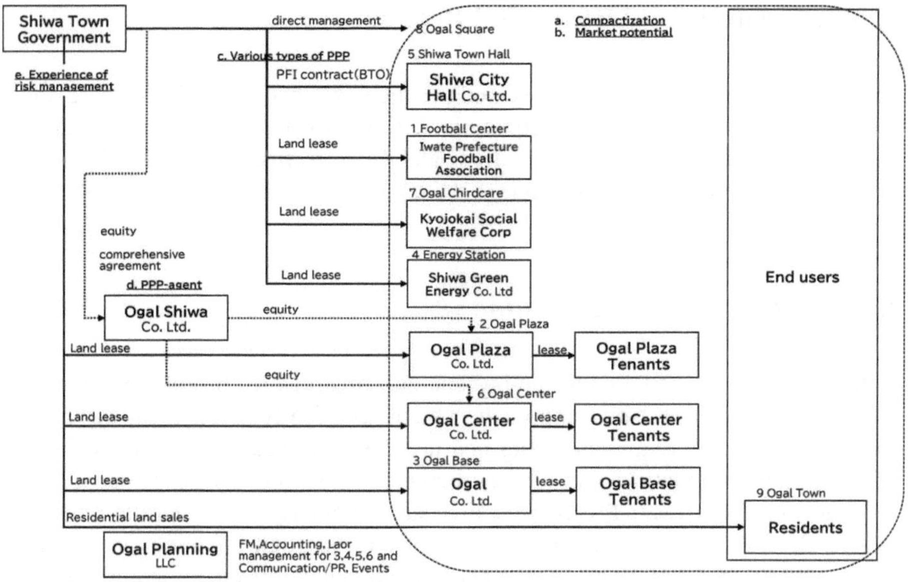

Figure 6 Ogal Project's structure sheet. (Source: Prepared by the author)

of funds is in the opposite direction of the arrow in the chart 6), which it can use to cover the costs of the project it implements. The town refers to this structure as "earning infrastructure." This is a groundbreaking recognition that infrastructure is not a cost center in which taxpayer money is invested, but a profit center that generates its own revenue to cover the costs incurred.

A final strength is the PPP agent, which is responsible for unifying the overall concept. Ogal Planning LLC has replaced Ogal Shiwa Corporation, which initially played the primary role of the PPP Agent. The company continues to be represented by a private citizen who played a key role in the Ogal Shiwa Corporation, thus ensuring the consistency of the concept. This person has extensive experience in risk response, having also played a key role in working with the town during the Great East Japan Earthquake and COVID-19 pandemic response.

These are the identified strengths of the Ogal Project. On the other hand, (1) the Ogal area has no room for further investment, so it is necessary to spread the effects of the revitalization of the area to the entire town, and (2) the know-how cultivated in the area is currently limited to the individuals, so it is necessary to devise ways to ensure that it is passed on throughout the organization. These are two issues that need to be addressed. However, these are not weaknesses but rather issues that need to be considered in preparation for the future.

Key Inferences for Theory and Practice

The three key inferences for theory and practice obtained through this case study are: (1) effectiveness of compactization, (2) effectiveness of clear risk sharing between the public and private sectors, and (3) effectiveness of the PPP agent involved in unifying the concept across the region.

Effectiveness of Compactization

Compactization was applied to the investment. This practice has proven the effectiveness of the compact city approach, which has been recommended throughout Japan as infrastructure aging countermeasures because it can minimize the amount of investment in updating aging infrastructure. Although many people continue to visit the area under Iwate Prefecture's own state of emergency declaration, no clusters of COVID-19 have occurred because of the thorough infection control measures in place. In other words, it was also shown that compactization and infection control are compatible.

Effectiveness of Clear Risk Sharing Between the Public and Private Sectors

This is a clear division of risk between the public and private sectors. Generally, in PPP, the public and private sectors share roles within a single project, but when a force majeure event such as the COVID-19 pandemic occurs, it takes time to discuss how to share the increased costs and compensate for the loss of revenue. In this respect, the Ogal Project was able to deal with the situation quickly without spending a lot of time in discussions, because a main responsible party was assigned to each of the nine projects.

Effectiveness of the PPP Agent Involved in Unifying the Concept Across the Region

Placing different responsible entities in charge of each project runs the risk of creating a disunified concept for the district as a whole. In the Ogal project, however, the Shiwa town, which owns most of the land, sets the policy for the unified concept for the entire district, and the PPP agent is responsible for implementing it. In addition, by having a private citizen with a good understanding of PPP take on the role of the

PPP agent, a close relationship with the town was established and uniformity of policy was ensured.

Conclusion

Japan and many other countries developed their infrastructure in a relatively short period of time during the twentieth century. Therefore, these infrastructures will all be aging at the same time, creating the need for renewal investment. As a countermeasure, "compactization," which improves investment efficiency by concentrating infrastructure investment in specific regions, and PPP to utilize private-sector capabilities and funds, or "compactization through PPP," will undoubtedly be effective.

Meanwhile, the spread of viral infections will continue to be a major risk in all countries. Even if the COVID-19 pandemic itself comes to an end, there is still the risk of another viral outbreak. In the future, we must design our economy and society based on the assumption that we do not know when and what kind of infectious diseases may occur and spread. In such a situation, of course, "compactization through PPP" carries the same risks.

I hope that the insights presented in this chapter will be of some help.

References

Cabinet Office. (2020, July 7). *Response to the impact of the spread of COVID-19 infection on PFI projects*. https://www8.cao.go.jp/pfi/corona/pdf/corona_tsuuchi.pdf

UNECE (2018), Case. 30: Japan, smart and sustainable cities sector. Ogal Shiwa. Database of Case Study Material, International PPP Centre of Excellence, United Nations Economic Commission for Europe. (2018, May). https://unece.org/fileadmin/DAM/ceci/documents/2018/PPP/Forum/Documents/Case_Study_Database_2018.pdf

Yuji, Nemoto. (2022). *Consideration on infrastructure aging countermeasures and renewal investment finance* (draft). Financial Review, Ministry of Finance. https://www.mof.go.jp/english/pri/index.htm

Revisiting Issues and Challenges in Indonesia's PPP Water Supply System: A Case Study

Andreas Wibowo

Introduction

Indonesia has emerged as one of the most active public-private partnership (PPP) markets in the Southeast Asian region in the last decade (2010–2020). According to World Bank (2021), the country's PPP investment reached USD 42.4 billion (Indonesian Rupiah (IDR) 635.5 trillion), with greenfield projects accounting for the largest share.[1] However, it is worth noting that Indonesia is not new to the PPP market for the procurement of public infrastructure services, with PPP usage dating as far back as the late nineteenth century, during Dutch colonialism (Wibowo & Permana, 2015).

Presently, PPP is widely accepted among public authorities in Indonesia, and its applications have spread across infrastructure sectors to varying degrees. The most common PPP contract is Build-Operate-Transfer (BOT), where the private sector is required to build an infrastructure facility, operate it for a certain concession period—usually between 20 and 30 years, and transfer the asset to the government at the expiry date of the concession. In 2021, for instance, the Government of Indonesia (GoI) offered 54 PPP investment projects worth about USD 21 billion across different sectors. Seven projects were ready to proceed to the bidding stage, and 47 were in preparation.[2] In that year alone, the GoI already tendered 21 PPP

[1] 1 USD is approximately equal to IDR 15,000.

[2] These seven projects consist of two transportation and five road projects. The 47 projects include four transportation projects, ten road projects, eight water supply projects, four waste treatment

A. Wibowo (✉)
Center of Excellence in Urban Infrastructure Development and Department of Civil Engineering, Parahyangan Catholic University, Bandung, Indonesia
e-mail: andreas_wibowo@unpar.ac.id

© The Author(s), under exclusive license to Springer Nature Switzerland AG 2023
T. Dolla et al. (eds.), *Revisiting Public-Private Partnerships*,
Contributions to Public Administration and Public Policy,
https://doi.org/10.1007/978-3-031-37015-1_10

projects, which are in the transaction phase (see details in Ministry of National Development Planning (2021)).

In the water supply sector, the GoI has also set high expectations on PPP to help it improve the country's drinking water service. In 2019, Indonesia only had 14.7 million water connections to serve 74 million people. In January 2020, the GoI issued the Presidential Regulation (PR) 18/2020 that sets out the 2020–2024 Medium Term Development Plan (The Government of Indonesia, 2020a). The plan addresses the GoI's commitment to adding ten million water connections to provide 50 million people with access to piped water, increasing the country's piped water coverage from 20% in 2019 to 30% in 2024. Furthermore, the program is estimated to cost about USD 6.1 billion, of which about USD 369.2 million (or 6%) is expected to take the form of PPP (Ministry of Public Works and Housing, 2019).

However, empirical evidence suggests that the water supply system is among the infrastructure sectors where PPP has not progressed as expected. For example, during 2015–2019, the GoI had investment opportunities in the sector for over USD 1.3 billion, but it could only attract private financing worth USD 255.2 million (19% of the total) in seven water supply projects.[3] There are some reasons for this failure, but poor feasibility studies and uncertain tariffs are often reported as the main problems. Despite these experiences, the GoI remains optimistic about private financing, especially PPP, as it finds it challenging to address infrastructure deficits when relying only on the public budget.

In March 2020, Indonesia, like all other countries, was shocked by the unprecedented coronavirus disease (Covid-19). At the time of writing this chapter, the pandemic has been ongoing for 2 years, taking a toll on the economy (and other aspects of life) in many ways. Indonesia fell into recession after experiencing two consecutive quarters of negative Gross Domestic Product in 2020. However, Indonesia was able to overcome the recession in August 2021, recording the first positive economic growth since the onset of the pandemic in 2020 (Statistics Indonesia, 2021). However, many experts predicted that the pandemic would have long-term economic consequences, and the GoI believes that the need for PPP is now inevitable and crucial to deal with the resulting fiscal austerity, at least during the recovery period.

Amidst the pandemic's disruption, some PPP projects (including water supply projects) continued, albeit at a slower pace, such as the Jatiluhur I Project and the Karian-Serpong Project. These two projects obtained their winning bidders in open biddings held by the Ministry of Public Works and Housing (PWH), and everything

projects, and some projects in telecommunication, urban facility, public lighting management, and industrial sectors.

[3]These seven projects are four PPP projects: the Umbulan Project with an installed capacity of 4000 liters per second (lps) worth USD 80 million, Bandar Lampung (750 lps; USD 32 million), West Semarang (1000; USD 31 million), and Dumai (450 lps; USD 33 million), and three business-to-business projects: Jatisari Bekasi (200 lps; USD four million), Angke in South Tangerang (200 lps; USD 20 million), and Gresik (1000 lps; USD 53 million). Please see Agency for Promoting Drinking Water Supply (2020).

seemed to be going smoothly, even during the difficult times. However, it has not been as straightforward as might be expected. Once the procurement was completed, other challenges emerged. In fact, the issues and challenges have existed for years, but the pandemic helped to highlight them further. Whether the pandemic provided new insight into the PPP business model in Indonesia can be subject to discussion, but, for sure, it exacerbated the already problematic situation in Indonesia's PPP water supply projects.

This chapter presents the issues and challenges in Indonesia's PPP water supply projects and offers possible directions for future discourses toward a sustainable water supply system. This chapter uses the Jatiluhur I Project as a case study because it is a large-scale, cross-provincial, unsolicited project, the epitome of Indonesia's most complex projects. Together with Karian-Serpong, the Jatiluhur I is also the first central government's PPP water supply project and is listed as one of the country's national strategic projects (Cabinet Secretariat of the Republic of Indonesia, 2021).

The rest of this chapter is organized as follows: The subsequent sections briefly describe Indonesia's PPP and water supply system to provide context. The case study section introduces the chronological development, description, and key stakeholders of the Jatiluhur I Project. The following section discusses the case study project's issues and challenges. This chapter provides lessons learned and implications for theory and practice and ends with some concluding remarks.

Public-Private Partnerships

In the 1990s, the GoI embarked on massive PPP projects, although most projects, if not all, had to be put on hold following the 1997/8 Asian economic crisis. The PPP program was later resumed in 2004 during the Yudhoyono administration—the year that also marked the beginning of the new PPP format, as is largely seen today.[4]

The PPP continued to gain momentum under the Joko Widodo administration, which focused on public infrastructure development as the main agenda. For 2014–2019, the total infrastructure investment had been estimated at USD 320 billion, but only 41% of the public budget's total requirement could be met, thereby leaving a prominent funding gap. About USD 117 billion or 37% of the required funding was hoped to be from the private sector, including PPP, with the rest from state-owned enterprises. For 2020–2024, the private sector contribution was expected to increase to USD 180 billion (41% of the total funding) in the economic and social infrastructure sectors.

[4] The existing format has different features from the previous ones in terms of, for instance, the coverage of infrastructure sectors to be implemented as PPP, the definition of the private sector, the determination of the minimum size of the PPP project to call for open bidding, the procurement evaluation, the provision of the government contingent and non-contingent supports, the value for money requirement, the policy for USP, foreign direct investment relaxation.

Central government support has also been made available to render infrastructure projects more attractive for private financing. Support is offered in such forms as the provision of the Viability Gap Fund (a capital grant via the Ministry of Finance), partial construction support through the responsible line ministry to reduce construction costs, and government guarantees through the Indonesian Infrastructure Guarantee Fund (IIGF) to protect private investors against government-driven risks. The GoI also provides line ministries with Project Development Facilities to deal with the lack of quality business cases (one of the classical issues faced for many years) to implement their projects under the PPP scheme.

The PPP initiatives can be based on proposals prepared by the public sector (solicited) and ones submitted by the private sector (unsolicited). An unsolicited proposal (USP) can be approved if the following conditions are met: (i) the proposed project is technically integrated with the masterplan of the corresponding sector, (ii) the proposed project is economically and financially feasible, hence not requiring any government support except the government guarantee, and (iii) the private sector can prove its ability to fund the project (The Government of Indonesia, 2015b).

In the case of solicited proposals, a public authority will be responsible for, among others, preparing a strategy, outline, and final business case. In contrast, in the case of USP, the private sector must already be ready with at least a pre-feasibility study when submitting their proposal to the responsible public authority. According to PR 38/2015 (The Government of Indonesia, 2015b), when the public agency accepts the proposal, the private sector as the original proponent will be given one of three possible incentives: a bid bonus of 10% of the final evaluation score, a Right-to-Match (RTM), or a developer's fee.

As for the cost recovery for the private sector, the available options are the user charge or Availability Payment (AP), but they cannot be mixed within a PPP project; only one method can be implemented. Under the user charge scheme, the private sector is renumerated via tariffs collected from the users and assumes demand risk, while under the AP scheme, the private sector is renumerated through fixed and scheduled performance-based payments irrespective of demand. Other options are conceivable, provided they do not violate applicable law and regulation. It is not completely clear whether USP can propose the AP scheme as the cost recovery method in existing PPP-related rules. However, conventional wisdom hitherto suggests it is not.

There is an alternative model to PPP for private sector participation in the water supply sector, known as Business-to-Business (B2B). Table 1 shows the key features of PPP and B2B models. The B2B model shares the same features as the PPP, but B2B projects cannot enjoy the specific advantages of PPP. However, the B2B arrangements are usually simpler than those of PPP due to the involvement of fewer project stakeholders.

Table 1 Key features of PPP and B2B models

	PPP model			B2B model		
Type of proposal	Availability payment	User charge	Support[a]	Availability payment	User charge	Support
Solicited	●	●	●	○	●	○
Unsolicited	○	●	○	○	●	○

Note: [a] = government guarantee is possible for USP if needed; ● = applicable; ○ = not applicable

Water Supply Systems

Indonesia's water supply legal framework is Government Regulation (GR) 122/2015 (The Government of Indonesia, 2015a). According to the regulation, the systems consist of piped and non-piped water supply systems, with the first comprising raw water, treatment or production, distribution, and service units. In practice, the raw water and production units are the upstream side of the piped system, while distribution and service units are the downstream side. Depending on the responsibility level, national or municipal water utilities, community groups, and business entities will operate a water supply system and ensure water supplies' quality, quantity, and continuity. The system can be single with one production unit for one off-taker and regional with one production unit for multiple off-takers.[5]

Based on GR 122/2015, the public water utilities are allowed to partner with the private sector if they do not have the financial capacity to fund required piped water supply systems within or beyond their service areas. Moreover, private investment can only take the form of (i) intake and production units, (ii) distribution units on the condition that the Operation and Maintenance (OM) must be under the control of the respective water utilities, and (iii) technology supplies for OM under the Performance-based Contract (PBC). Thus far, there are four appropriate contract types in the water supply projects under the GR 122/2015: BOT, BOT-Plus, lease contract, and PBC (see Table 2). These contracts apply to PPP as well as B2B projects.

As shown, private sector participation is allowed for the upstream side.[6] While this restriction is mainly intended to maintain the state's controlling power in the

[5] Private participation in the water sector was initially governed in Law 7/2004. However, the law was later deemed controversial; it faced fierce criticism for encouraging the privatization and commercialization of water resources at the expense of the people's rights to water (Ardhianie, 2015). In 2013, the Constitutional Court revoked Law 7/2004, stating that the private sector's scope of using water resources for commercial purposes was too broad (The Constitutional Court of the Republic of Indonesia, 2013). Following the annulment of Law 7/2004, the GoI issued GR 122/2015. In 2019, the GoI issued Law 17/2019 (The Government of Indonesia, 2019) to replace Law 7/2004. Nevertheless, the issuance does not necessarily end the debate concerning private and public interests (Wirayani, 2019). The GR 122/2015 should be revised accordingly to comply with Law 17/2019. When writing this chapter, the revision is still under preparation.

[6] Earlier PPP contracts feature different natures of investment; for instance, the two well-known BOT contracts between the PAM Jaya, a municipal water utility under the Jakarta Provincial

Table 2 Private participation in Indonesia's water supply systems

	Water supply system			
Type of contract	Intake	Production	Distribution	Services
BOT	●	●	○	○
BOT-plus	●	●	◐	○
Lease contract	○	○	◐	○
PBC	○	◑	◑	○

Note: ● = full provision by the private sector; ○ = full provision by public water utilities; ◐ = piped distribution by the private sector but OM by the public water utilities; ◑ = technology provided by the private sector but OM by the public water utilities

water supply sector, it also creates an interface problem between up- and downstream as the two sides are not always compatible. Experience suggests that public water utilities spearheading the delivery of drinking water services often struggle with insufficient capacity and resources, leading to poor performance. This fact will affect the likelihood of a PPP project being successfully sustained to a large extent, as any PPP contract must, by regulation, involve at least one water utility to act as an off-taker.

Case Study: Jatiluhur I Project

The Jatiluhur I Project has a long story. The original idea was proposed as early as 2015, although the formal process commenced in 2017. That year, a private consortium filed a letter of intent (LoI) to the Minister of PWH because the project is a cross-provincial and nationally strategic project. In the letter, the consortium, consisting of one large construction firm and two local government-owned enterprises, intended to be the proponent of the Jatiluhur Project (later referred to as Jatiluhur I to differentiate it from Jatiluhur II, which is under preparation).[7]

In response to the LoI, the Minister of PWH mandated that the Director of Perum Jasa Tirta II (PJT) acts as the Contracting Agency (CA) and begins preparations for the project. After approving the feasibility study submitted by the consortium, the PJT issued the approval letter in November 2017, declaring the Jatiluhur I Project as an unsolicited project and the consortium as the project's proponent. The consortium opted for the RTM, meaning that, if unsuccessful, it would retain the right to

Government, and two large international firms in 1998 covered the private sector's responsibility from upstream to downstream, known as concession. However, these two contracts were later renegotiated after drawing intensive controversies and criticism regarding their terms, which were considered strongly in favor of the private sector. In fact, these PPP water concessions were perceived as failing to deliver what the contracts specified.

[7] The members of the consortium are PT Jaya Konstruksi Manggala Pratama, a firm owned by the Jakarta Province; PT Tirta Gemah Ripah, a firm owned by the West Java Province; and PT Wijaya Karya, a state-owned construction firm.

match the best proposal to win the contract. The prequalification of bidders took place in March 2018, with four bidders, including the proponent, selected as qualifiers.

All went smoothly until PJT II reported to the Minister of PWH that they could not act as the CA as mandated due to its constrained financial capacity. As a result, the Jatiluhur I Project was left with uncertainty for months. Later, the Minister of PWH decided to revoke the mandate and take over the PJT's Government CA (GCA) role. Due to the GCA change, the completed prequalification process had to be canceled and redone. The original proponent had no option but to accept this change; otherwise, the procurement processes would violate the law. The new prequalification resulted in two qualified bidders, including the original proponent, in February 2020. In October 2020, the Minister of PWH announced that the consortium, as the original proponent, won the contract.

Brief Project Description

The estimated capital expenditure of the project is USD 111 million with a total duration of 30 years, including a two-year construction period. The project scope is to design, build, finance, operate, maintain, and transfer the water intake and treatment facilities with 5000 lps and 4750 lps, respectively, on a BOT basis. A financial-close agreement was reached between a project company, a Special Purpose Vehicle (SPV) established exclusively for the project by the winning consortium, and the lenders in November 2021. The first Commercial Operation Date (COD) is expected to be May 2024. The project received a guarantee scheme, with the same coverage as before, from the IIGF.

Of the total production, 4000 lps (84.2%) will be supplied to Jakarta; 300 lps (6.3%) to Bekasi City; 100 lps (2.1%) to Bekasi Regency; and 350 lps (7.4%) to Karawang Regency. The raw water will be collected from the Jatiluhur Dam, managed by PJT. The project will require a ramp-up of 5 years to absorb the total capacity.

Under the BOT contract, the SPV is responsible for supplying water following the specifications detailed in the agreement and transmitting it to off-take points specified in the long-term contract (upstream). The GCA will off-take the water on a take-or-pay basis and deliver it to other off-take points, as set forth in four purchase agreements, each signed between the GCA and the corresponding municipal water utility, also on a take-or-pay basis. The water utilities will distribute to their customers from this point (downstream) as mandated by PR 122/2015 (please see Table 2 again).

Key Project Stakeholders

The Jatiluhur I Project encompasses many stakeholders and entails complex interactions between them. First, the Minister of PWH as the GCA signed the agreement with PT Wika Tirta Jaya Jatiluhur as the SPV. Later, the Minister of PWH delegated his role to the General Director of PWH Financing to be responsible for preparation and procurement and the General Director of Human Settlements to serve as the acting GCA responsible for daily operations.

Four municipal water utilities will off-take the water from the Minister of PWH under purchase agreements. These utilities are PAM Jaya (Jakarta Province), Perumda Tirta Patriot (Bekasi City), *Perusahaan Daerah Air Minum* (PDAM) Tirta Bhagasasi (Bekasi Regency), and PDAM Tirta Tarum (Karawang Regency). The project required a Memorandum of Agreement (MoA) signed between the heads of the region (Governor, Mayor, or Regent) as the sole shareholders of municipal water utilities and the Minister of PWH to comply with Law 23/2014 as amended by Law 9/2015 regarding the Local Governments. The MoA can support the project in many ways as the utilities may seek approval from public authorities.

Another key stakeholder is IIGF, which signed a guarantee agreement with the SPV and a regress agreement with the Minister of PWH. A regress agreement is essentially a counter-guarantee, requiring the GCA to reimburse IIGF if the SPV calls the guarantee. Hence, this agreement also serves as a risk-mitigating instrument to prevent the GCA from moral hazards. The Ministry of Finance also has a share in the Jatiluhur I Project to provide the budget for government support. A dedicated escrow unit must also be created to act as the payment agent to the SPV and receive payments from off-takers. Fig. 1 illustrates the contractual relationships of the project's direct and indirect stakeholders.

Relevant Issues, Challenges, and Discussion

There are many issues and challenges to address, but this section will focus on those arising from the restricted scope of a PPP project.

The Capacity of Off-takers

While the project on the upstream side was in progress, the Jakarta Province Government, the shareholder of PAM Jaya, the largest off-taker on the downstream side, was reported to face acute financial problems induced by the Covid-19

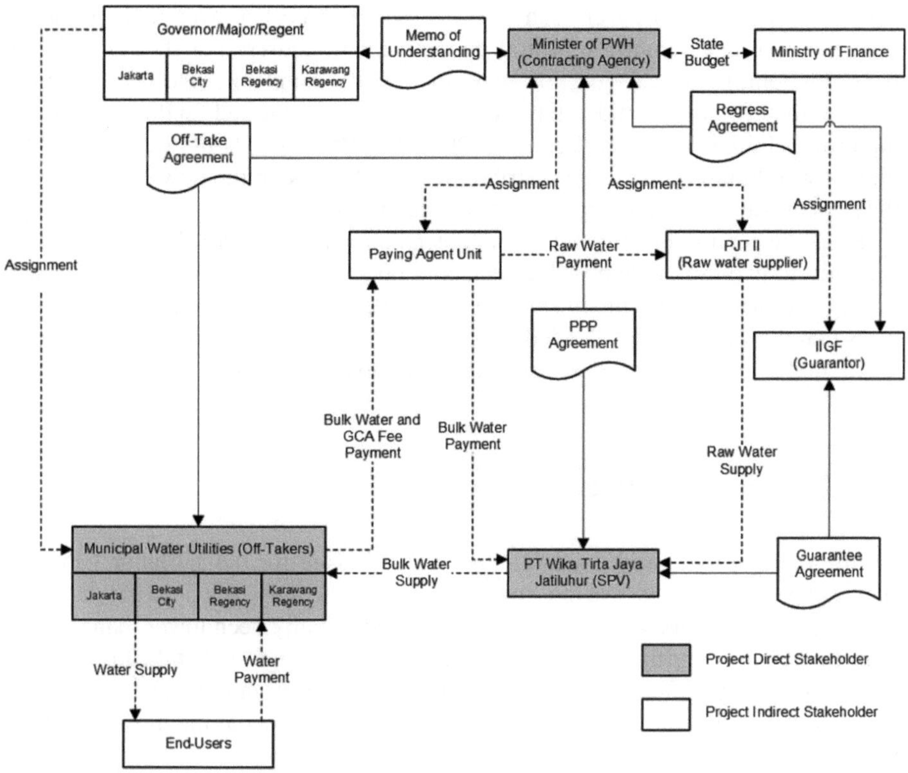

Fig. 1 Contractual relationships of key stakeholders

pandemic and be unable to fund the necessary water distribution systems.[8] In 2020, the Province's budget had to be revised from USD 5.9 billion to USD 4.2 billion, representing a contraction of 28%, even though the Province's fiscal capacity indexes were rated for years as very high.[9]

An early estimate indicates that the Province must provide between USD 600 million and USD 667 million, five times the project's total cost, to develop the distribution network to supply water to end-users.[10] As the Province's fiscal room was

[8] Until today, other off-takers, which will absorb about 16% of the Jatiluhur I Project's total capacity, were not reported to have the same problem as Jakarta. However, the progress on their side must be routinely monitored and evaluated to avoid unnecessary delay.

[9] A fiscal capacity index reflects a local government's fiscal capacity relative to the national average. The fiscal capacity is calculated as the difference between the collected revenue from multiple sources, including locally generated revenue and revenue transfer from the central government, and the sum of earmarked revenue and expenditure. A fiscal capacity is considered very high if the index is equal to or greater than 1.75 (Ministry of Finance, 2021). Jakarta had an index of 7.87, 9.25, and 11.47 in 2017, 2018, and 2019, respectively.

[10] PAM Jaya is also the off-taker for the Karian-Serpong PPP Project, which is expected to reach the COD in the third quarter of 2024, which is almost the same as the expected COD of the

deemed insufficient to cover such a high investment cost, it eventually asked for financial assistance from the central government to address the shortfall.[11] Apart from this, one rhetorical question may arise: if the pandemic had not happened, whether the Province would still be able to provide the required funding. Given that the project initiative was conceived in 2015, the Province should be aware of the high cost of building the water distribution to end-users on the downstream unless the project was not well coordinated from the outset.

Since the central government also adopted budgetary austerity, it encouraged the Province to explore every possible financing option, including solicited PPP using the AP contract. A preliminary study, which the central government prepared, indicates that the PPP AP and blended financing are feasible. However, the action plan is still under discussion, and the path forward remains unclear.

End-User Tariff Setting

Setting the end-user tariff poses another critical issue for the Jatiluhur I Project. Increasing water tariffs can be challenging, significantly when tariffs have not changed for years and worse when they have traditionally been lower than the economic cost of supplying it. However, experience also suggests that the tariff setting is also politically sensitive as it often requires approval from the legislation, which can urge the utilities to maintain the tariffs charged to users at the most affordable prices possible.

The Minister of Internal Affairs Regulation 21/2020 (The Ministry of Internal Affairs, 2020) requires the local government to provide a municipal water utility with a tariff subsidy to ensure it can operate at a total cost recovery and invest in infrastructure to improve delivery services.[12] However, the enforcement of this new regulation still needs to be tested in practice because the old regulation regarding the tariff subsidy had not been effectively implemented to a large extent, especially for those from a low-income background.

Under the PPP and long-term purchase contracts, the tariff is increased at a fixed rate of 10% every two years. An increase in tariff on the upstream must be reflected in an increase in end-user tariff on the downstream. If the tariff on the downstream cannot keep pace with the tariff on the upstream, the water utility will operate at an

---

Jatiluhur I Project in the second quarter of 2024. The total investment cost for the distribution systems for the two projects is about USD 814 million.

[11] The issue with the off-takers readiness is not exclusive to the Jatiluhur I Project. The Umbulan Project, a large, solicited, cross-municipal project, is often labeled best practice. However, it also had a similar problem where some water utilities were not fully ready to off-take the water from a PPP project. See details in (Zen, 2018).

[12] The Ministry of Internal Affairs also has an interest in the Jatiluhur I Project as local government-owned enterprises, including municipal water utilities, are under its supervision.

increasing loss for a period of time, which can affect the utility's performance (Tariq & Zhang, 2020).

Based on the Ministry of Public Works and Housing (2021), the ratio of the average tariff to the production cost in 2020 was 1.08, 1.05, 1.07, and 0.98 for Jakarta, Bekasi City, Bekasi Regency, and Karawang Regency, respectively, which shows that the end-user tariff can fully cover the total cost of water supply, expect for Karawang. There appears to be no problem with the initial tariff at the project's COD, but current evidence might suggest that increasing the end-user tariff by 10% every two years would be highly questionable.

Setting the end-user tariff to cover the operating cost must take into consideration water losses in terms of physical and apparent losses from the off-take point to end-users, as the GCA transfers the risk associated with the water supply to the corresponding off-taker at the off-take point. While the national target for the Non-Revenue Water (NRW) is around 20%, the NRW level of the project's off-takers is regarded to be still relatively high: 30.8% for Jakarta, 20.2% for Bekasi City, 30.8% for Bekasi Regency, and 30.8% for Karawang (Ministry of Public Works and Housing, 2021), meaning that about one-third of the total volume of water supplied cannot be converted into revenue.

Upstream-Downstream Interface

Being the interface of the up- and downstream sides, the GCA must bear any cost arising from a mismatch between the two. The GCA must compensate the SPV for differences between the volume of water supplied and the water off-taken and the tariff the GCA pays to the SPV and receives from the off-takers. Thus, the cost can be high and increase over time in the case of intensified mismatch.[13] This compels the GCA to ensure that contractual conditions in the PPP contract are more relaxed or, at least, mirrored in the purchase contracts to mitigate the mismatch risk.

The GCA is put at quasi-commercial risk due to the up- and downstream mismatch on the volume of water supply and the tariff when the GCA pays the SPV based on a single, volumetric tariff, while off-takers use different tariff setting formulas. Although the IIGF will compensate the SPV for any contractual default attributable to the GCA as specified in the guarantee contract, it does not imply that the GCA is risk-free as it must reimburse IIGF under the regress agreement.

The possible mismatch mentioned above requires the GCA to develop appropriate risk management strategies. A study indicated that the risk management capability of water utilities was still at the initial stage; the adopted risk management postures are primarily supported only by unstructured, ad-hoc, and non-formal processes (Pangeran et al., 2012). Enhancing the risk management capacity of the

[13] The cost can be roughly calculated as $\Delta C = T_1 V_1 - T_0 V_0$ where T_1 and T_0 are the tariffs the GCA pays to the SPV and receives from the off-takers, respectively, and V_1 and V_0 are the volume of water supplied by the GCA and water purchased by the off-takers, respectively.

public sector, especially for the GCA of a regional PPP water project, must be encouraged as it will bear quasi-commercial project risks arising from the default of multiple utilities, which are beyond its control. The cost of the risks can be huge and undermine the Value for Money (VfM) that the PPP water supply project can offer.

Value for Money

The GoI requires that PPP projects demonstrate VfM for the public. There is no universal definition of VfM. In Indonesia, it is defined as an indicator to evaluate a PPP project based on economic, efficiency, and effectiveness criteria of the public spending and the quality of service to meet the public need (Ministry of National Development Planning, 2020). The economic and efficiency criteria are two related constructs concerning optimizing inputs and outputs, and effectiveness criteria concern outcomes. If economy refers to the minimization of inputs for a given set of outputs, efficiency refers to the maximization of outputs for a given set of inputs, while effectiveness refers to whether the outputs can deliver the outcomes as desired (Burger & Hawkesworth, 2011).

The VfM in most, if not all, of Indonesia's PPP projects was evaluated by the public sector using the Public Sector Comparator (PSC) despite the fact that it often cannot fully understand the analysis. The PSC estimates the whole-life cost of delivering service under traditional procurement. Therefore, a PPP proposal can only be accepted if it offers a cost lower than the PSC. The PSC-based evaluation requires necessary resources, particularly robust knowledge and data, when quantifying project-related risks that the public sector must retain or transfer to the private sector in a PPP project. The absence of these resources can lead to poor decision-making. In some cases, pessimism bias can occur, which overestimates the risks, rendering the PSC expensive and the PPP project more favorable.

The Jatiluhur I Project's approved pre-feasibility study reported the VfM analysis result. While the ex-ante project's VfM contained in the study can be subject to debate, the ex-post VfM resulting from the open bidding is compelling. Based on the original proponent's proposal, the GCA had set and announced the ceiling water price at about 22.0 cents (IDR 3296) per m^3 for Jakarta in the bid documents. The winning bid offered 18.7 cents (IDR 2799) per m^3, representing a rough VfM of about 15%, which is regarded as appealing considering the project's nature.[14] Hence, the project provides VfM in terms of economy and efficiency. However, the VfM cannot be viewed as fully attained when the water supply cannot reach the end-users as intended (effectiveness). In other words, the project's VfM cannot be optimal when up- and downstream sides are not well connected.

[14] It is calculated based on the difference in the initial tariff only. However, a VfM of 15% can be substantial in the Project. A further rough estimate can suggest a cost saving of about USD 239 million in nominal terms or USD 40 million in present value terms, with revenues discounted at the Project's weighted average cost of capital.

Coordination Among Stakeholders

The Jatiluhur I Project will commence construction in 2022 and is expected to be completed on schedule. However, the journey to get to this stage has not been easy. As previously mentioned, the project includes many stakeholders with occasionally conflicting interests, which creates vertical and horizontal coordination problems. As the project proponent was required to have sufficiently addressed the interests of the stakeholders on up- and downstream sides and reflected them in the feasibility study, it was not straightforward to safeguard the interests of multiple stakeholders. For instance, the agreements on the volume of water allocated and the tariffs with off-takers were not easily reached and kept changing over time. Certainty on these matters was required to make financial assumptions for the project. The Agency for Promoting Water Supply Systems facilitated coordination with stakeholders during the preparation stage.[15] However, in July 2020, the GoI dissolved the Agency via PR 82/2020 (The Government of Indonesia, 2020b).[16] It remains unclear whether the institution that takes the Agency's role is similarly capable.

Lessons Learned

The issues and challenges discussed earlier can be relevant and provide valuable lessons for similar projects. First and foremost, key project stakeholders must understand the project's scope. While some may be familiar with PPP water supply projects, others may not and perceive them similarly to traditionally procured water projects, although these two types of projects can feature different characteristics and be governed by diverse regulatory frameworks. One common and longstanding problem with public authorities is the lack of knowledge transfer from senior to new government officials, causing a lack of institutional knowledge accumulation and leading to the wheel needing to be reinvented every time. A knowledge management system can help manage and distribute institutional knowledge.

A PPP water supply project is typically complex and involves several stakeholders on the up- and downstream sides. Therefore, close coordination among stakeholders at all levels must be established. Adopting a clear-cut standard and operation procedure can help streamline and expedite decision-making processes. It is particularly relevant in the case of USP, where the GCA has limited time to evaluate the proposal.[17] Insufficient technical skills and the capacity of local actors are some of

[15] Also the Karian-Serpong Project.

[16] The Agency was established based on PR 90/2016 (The Government of Indonesia, 2016) to implement the GR 122/2015, which mandates an establishment of a special agency to promote water supply systems and assist municipal water utilities.

[17] According to the Minister of National Development Planning/Head of National Development Agency Regulation 2/2020 (Ministry of National Development Planning, 2020), the GCA is only

the challenging issues faced (Purbo et al., 2019). Therefore, it is still essential for the public agencies to possess knowledge and skillsets concerning the PPP in order to evaluate the USP. These include legal, technical, financial engineering and modeling, risk management, procurement, negotiation, and contract design skills. The public sector capacity must be continuously improved to ensure that the unsolicited PPP water supply projects can effectively help the GoI improve water service delivery. The assistance of external experts is essential in many cases, but it is worth noting that the GCA must first understand what it really wants from the PPP project from the public interest perspective.

A strong political commitment is a key to ensuring the sustainability of PPP water supply projects, and the commitment can manifest in many forms. Although water utilities are not the PPP contracting parties, they are the direct off-takers of the water supplied by the projects. The local governments can allow and encourage their water utilities to adopt cost-recovery principles in a disciplined manner; otherwise, they must provide tariff subsidies for those from a low-income background. They can also make sufficient capital contributions for developing distribution networks. One worth noting here is that the cost of the downstream side can be more expensive than that of the upstream, as demonstrated in the case study project. Another commitment that can be undertaken, as done in Jakarta, is the prohibition of groundwater use.

A high-quality USP is also critical to making the project delivery process more manageable (Surachman et al., 2020). Evaluating poor-quality proposals will waste a significant amount of the public agencies' time and effort. For instance, a USP must be based on a clear and demonstrable need for water through a valid and reliable Real Demand Survey (RDS). The private sector must communicate the RDS results to the water utility to obtain its insight. Ideally, the identified need is aligned with the utility's business plan to avoid conflicting service areas.[18] This is useful to prevent the so-called pet project suspicion. Setting stringent minimum submission requirements can filter out incomplete, low-quality, and uncommitted proposals (World Bank, 2017).

Preparing a USP for a regional water supply project can be challenging from the private sector's standpoint. Obtaining agreements from direct stakeholders on up- and downstream is never easy due to the interconnections between the two sides and high levels of power dynamics. The reality is that the terms already discussed and agreed upon with one stakeholder can change over time, affecting the financial assumptions made for the overall project's feasibility and sustainability.

As previously discussed, the two most important problems that must be considered are the volume of water supplied to off-takers and the setting of tariffs. The discussion of these problems can be a circular and prolonged process. Thus, the

given 30 and 60 working days to evaluate the pre-feasibility and feasibility study of the PPP project initiated as an unsolicited proposal. However, the GCA can notify the proponent with reasons and a new deadline when the GCA intends to extend the evaluation period.

[18] According to the Ministry of Public Works and Housing (2021), 306 out of 388 (or 78.9%) water utilities have business plans.

private sector must anticipate the risk and have sufficient resources to deal with it. It is worth noting that reaching an agreement between up- and downstream sides often requires a solid financial commitment from the private sector and a great deal of time and effort, especially when PPP is new to off-taker candidates. Intensive coordination and communication with clear target milestones must be established. In most cases, the support from the central government to catalyze the agreements between the private sector and the concerned stakeholders, particularly local governments and water utilities, is inevitable.

Implications for Theory

Indonesia's PPP water supply projects feature specific nature, which differs from other infrastructure types. This distinctive characteristic creates unique problems, as the case study can suggest. These problems can offer directions for future research agendas.

One area that deserves to be further explored is the contingent liability of the contracting agency on the upstream side due to the mismatch risk between up- and downstream concerning tariffs and volume of water under the take-or-pay contract. A simulation-based option theory can be considered to address the problem when the risk parameters can be reasonably assumed.

Another problem relates to the tariff setting for different off-takers. It should optimally reconcile conflicting interests of the critical stakeholders, particularly the end-users, the off-takers, the contracting agency, and the private investor. Computing an optimal financial model needs to consider, among others, the affordability, the capital and operation expenditure allocation on up-and downstream sides, the project financial viability and bankability, and project uncertainties.

Exploring the VfM assessment can also be exciting for future research, especially to find an appropriate methodology that can eliminate bias in favor of a particular project delivery model. Other research areas can focus on the international benchmarking of USP practices and the selection of incentives for USP to achieve the best VfM, which both appear to be relatively understudied in the existing global PPP studies.

Implications for Practice

Several practical issues can be brought forth from the case study project. However, this chapter focuses on two implications for practice relating to the issues of the performance of municipal water utilities and the private investment restriction in the existing PPP business model.

The first issue requires urgent attention owing to the fact that water utilities are at the forefront in providing quality water services to the public. Based on the 2021

Municipal Water Utilities' Performance (Ministry of Public Works and Housing, 2021), out of 388 utilities, only 225 (58%) were evaluated as good, with an average performance score of 3.39 out of 5.00. The remaining were assessed as less than good (27%, 2.22) and poor (15%, 1.56). The NRW percentage remained high at 33.24%; only 143 utilities (36.86%) applied the full-cost recovery tariffs, and the percentage of coverage areas still accounted for 22.63% (in administrative terms).[19] The overall performance did not relatively improve from that of previous years. A benchmarking study by Wibowo and Alfen (2015) indicates that the efficiency of municipal water utilities was around 55% and 32% in terms of serviceability and profitability, respectively.

The PPP will not effectively solve water problems if the issue with the performance has not been resolved. A synergy between the Ministry of PWH, the Ministry of Internal Affairs, and local governments and, more importantly, a strong commitment and concrete actions are needed to upgrade the utilities' capacity.

The second issue creates challenges for the GoI to ensure that the quality water from a PPP project can be distributed to the targeted end-users at affordable prices. The complexity will considerably increase for regional water supply systems involving multiple off-takers. Innovative delivery systems are needed to address the issue without violating the laws.

When writing this chapter, one private consortium submitted a USP to the Minister of Public Works and Housing to build the Ir Djuanda/Jatiluhur II Project, a large-scale PPP water supply project worth about USD 1.1 billion. This project introduces a creative concept of "from source to tap," integrating up- and downstream sides. The project will bundle two PPP types: the BOT contract on the upstream and the lease and PBC contracts with multiple contract agencies on the downstream under the so-called omnibus contract. However, it is still a long way to reach the deals, especially between the private consortium and municipal water utilities. If realized, the project will be the first of its kind and can be a reference for future PPP water supply projects in Indonesia.

Concluding Remarks

Due to population growth and urbanization, Indonesia's water supply system sector is faced with rising demand. However, the public fiscal capacity cannot afford to fund the infrastructure needed to meet the demand. For this reason, the GoI has encouraged the private sector to participate in the water supply system development

[19] It may come as a surprise that around 58% of water utilities were rated as good, while only 37% adopted the full cost recovery principle. This is because the performance was measured through the balanced scorecard method, using 18 indicators in four aspects (financial, services, operational, and human resources), with tariffs not being part of the evaluation. It would be highly questionable for a water utility that cannot sufficiently cover capital and operation expenditures to be rated as good. Some experts have suggested a revision of the existing performance evaluation methodology.

under a PPP scheme. However, previous experience suggests that attracting private interest is not as simple as it appears, despite the presence of a huge investment opportunity. However, the GoI remains optimistic about the PPP to help close the funding gap.

This chapter discusses relevant issues and challenges in Indonesia's PPP water supply system sector from a case study, representing a complex PPP project as it is a large-scale, cross-provincial, and unsolicited project. The specific nature of PPP water supply projects restricts the scope of the private sector participation, thus creating some challenges that add to the project's complexity. The issues and challenges have simmered for years and have been exacerbated by the pandemic.

Indonesia's water supply sector is differentiated between up- and downstream, where only the upstream service is allowed for a PPP project while the downstream is exclusively reserved for municipal water utilities. This limitation can create mismatch and interface problems when the two inextricable sides do not cooperate harmoniously; one cannot operate without the other. The challenges increase for a regional water system, which supplies water to multiple off-takers. The capacity of municipal water utilities to off-take water, the setting of end-user tariffs, the interface between up-and downstream, the VfM, and the coordination among key stakeholders are among the key issues that cause concern and need to be resolved.

The case study provides valuable lessons for future PPP water supply projects of similar size and characteristics. Some efforts can be made to deal with the issues and challenges highlighted, such as improving the understanding of the PPP water supply project's nature, enhancing the public sector capacity, building solid political commitments, and ensuring high-quality proposals.

The issues and challenges discussed in this chapter are not exhaustive but can serve as an outline of the fundamental problems in Indonesia's PPP water supply projects. Some other cases also need to be settled, for example, the clarity of license provision for water extraction, the availability of raw water, the establishment of a payment agent, the determination of the GCA, and regulations that conflict and overlap, all of which were not covered in this chapter. However, this chapter can help the relevant stakeholders focus on the key issues and challenges facing Indonesia's PPP water supply projects.

References

Agency for Promoting Drinking Water Supply. (2020). *Alternative funding models for drinking water supply systems*.

Ardhianie, N. (2015, March 3). What next after the water law annulled. *Jakarta Post*. https://www.thejakartapost.com/news/2015/03/03/what-next-after-water-law-annulled.html.

Burger, P., & Hawkesworth, I. (2011). How to attain value for money: Comparing PPP and traditional infrastructure public procurement. *OECD Journal on Budgeting, 11*(1), 91–146. https://doi.org/10.1787/budget-11-5kg9zc0pvq6j

Cabinet Secretariat of the Republic of Indonesia. (2021). *Government to develop Jatiluhur drinking water system to improve people's quality of life.* https://setkab.go.id/en/govt-to-develop-jatiluhur-drinking-water-system-to-improve-peoples-quality-of-life/.

Ministry of Finance. (2021). *Minister of Finance Regulation 116/PMK.07/2021 on fiscal capacity mapping.*

Ministry of National Development Planning. (2020). *Minister of National Development Planning/Head of National Development Agency Regulation 2/2020 on the procedure of public-private partnership in infrastructure provision* (No. 2).

Ministry of National Development Planning. (2021). *Public private partnership infrastructure projects plan in Indonesia* (Issue July). Ministry of National Development Planning/National Development Planning Agency.

Ministry of Public Works and Housing. (2019). *The ten million new water connection program.*

Ministry of Public Works and Housing. (2021). *Municipal water utility performance 2021.* Ministry of Public Works and Housing.

Pangeran, M. H., Pribadi, K. S., Wirahadikusumah, R. D., & Notodarmojo, S. (2012). Assessing risk management capability of public sector organizations related to PPP scheme development for water supply in Indonesia. *Civil Engineering Dimension, 14*(1), 26–35. https://doi.org/10.9744/ced.14.1.26-35

Purbo, R. K., Smith, C., & Bianchi, R. (2019). Lessons learned from public–private partnerships in Indonesia's water sector. *Bulletin of Indonesian Economic Studies, 55*(2), 193–212. https://doi.org/10.1080/00074918.2018.1550250

Statistics Indonesia. (2021). Indonesia's economic growth in the second quarter of 2021. In *Berita Resmi Statistik* (Issue 60). https://www.bps.go.id/pressrelease/2020/02/05/1755/ekonomi-indonesia-2019-tumbuh-5-02-persen.html.

Surachman, E. N., Handayani, D., Suhendra, M., & Prabowo, S. (2020). Critical success factors on PPP water project in a developing country: Evidence from Indonesia. *Journal of Asian Finance, Economics and Business, 7*(10), 1071–1080. https://doi.org/10.13106/jafeb.2020.vol7.no10.1071

Tariq, S., & Zhang, X. (2020). Critical failure drivers in international water PPP projects. *Journal of Infrastructure Systems, 26*(4), 04020038. https://doi.org/10.1061/(asce)is.1943-555x.0000581

The Constitutional Court of the Republic of Indonesia. (2013). *Constitutional Court Decision 85/PUU-XI/2013 on the water resource case.* 85/PUU-IX/2013.

The Government of Indonesia. (2015a). *Government Regulation 122/2015 on the drinking water supply system* (No. 122).

The Government of Indonesia. (2015b). *Presidential Regulation 38/2015 on the public-private partnership in infrastructure provision* (No. 38).

The Government of Indonesia. (2016). *Presidential Regulation 90/2016 on Agency for Promoting Water Supply Systems* (No. 90).

The Government of Indonesia. (2019). *Law 17/2019 on the water resources* (No. 17).

The Government of Indonesia. (2020a). *Presidential Regulation 18/2020 on the national medium-term development plan for 2020–2024* (No. 18).

The Government of Indonesia. (2020b). *Presidential Regulation 82/2020 on the Covid-19 handling and the national economic recovery committee* (No. 82).

The Ministry of Internal Affairs. (2020). *Minister of Internal Affairs Regulation 21/2020 on water tariff setting* (No. 21).

Wibowo, A., & Alfen, H. W. (2015). Benchmarking the efficiencies of Indonesia's municipal water utilities using Stackelberg data envelopment analysis. *Benchmarking, 22*(4), 588–609. https://doi.org/10.1108/BIJ-01-2014-0009

Wibowo, A., & Permana, A. (2015). Defining public-private partnership in infrastructure within the Indonesian context. In A. Akintoye & M. Kumaraswamy (Eds.), *Public–private partnerships: A global review* (pp. 153–179). Routledge.

Wirayani, P. (2019, October 8). Water Law: Govt must examine its own capacity. *Jakarta Post*. https://www.thejakartapost.com/academia/2019/10/02/water-law-govt-must-examine-its-own-capacity.html.

World Bank. (2017). *Review of experiences with unsolicited proposals in infrastructure projects* (Issue March). World Bank.

World Bank. (2021). Private participation in infrastructure (PPI) database. https://ppi.worldbank.org/en/ppi.

Zen, F. (2018). *Public-private partnership development in Southeast Asia (Issue 553).*

Influence of PPP Transportation Projects on Socio-Economic Development in Thailand and Impact of COVID-19 on PPP Projects

Nakhon Kokkaew

Introduction

Thailand has a population of about 69.8 million people in 2020 (The World Bank, 2022). Bangkok is the capital of the country with the total population of about 10.7 million in 2021 (Statista Research Department, 2022). Some useful information about Thailand is shown in Table 1. As shown in Table 1, Thailand's GDP grew on average about 6% per year over the past 30 years (1990–2020). The country's tax revenue as a percentage of GDP is about 14% in which about 20% of this total is used to fund government spending on infrastructure projects. As for public borrowing, the current public debt level is on the rise since 2020 (i.e., about 60% in 2021, see Fig. 1) mainly due to an increase in government borrowing to tackle the economic impacts of the COVID-19 pandemic, coupled with the decrease in GDP in the first year of the spread of the COVID-19 in 2020, as shown in Fig. 2.

This chapter is to present the current status of PPP market in Thailand, the impacts of the development of PPP economic infrastructure on the socio-economy in Bangkok, and the financial impacts of the COVID-19 pandemic on existing PPP infrastructure using four case study projects (i.e., project-level), as well as the impacts of the pandemic on the financial performance of concessionaire firms (i.e., firm-level). In addition, the implications and lessons learned from the case studies will be provided so as to help policy makers, concession firms, and investors better understand the repercussions of the "low-probability, high-impact" risk that no one could have predicted such as the outbreak of the COVID-19 pandemic.

N. Kokkaew (✉)
Center of Excellence in Infrastructure Management, Department of Civil Engineering, Faculty of Engineering, Chulalongkorn University, Bangkok, Thailand
e-mail: Nakhon.k@chula.ac.th

© The Author(s), under exclusive license to Springer Nature Switzerland AG 2023

T. Dolla et al. (eds.), *Revisiting Public-Private Partnerships*, Contributions to Public Administration and Public Policy,
https://doi.org/10.1007/978-3-031-37015-1_11

Table 1 Useful information about Thailand

	1990	2000	2010	2020
Population, total (millions)	56.56	62.95	67.20	69.80
GDP (current US$) (billions)	85.34	126.39	341.1	501.79
Inflation, GDP deflator (annual %)	5.8	1.3	4.1	−1.1
Tax revenue (% of GDP)	16.9	13	14.9	14.6
Public debt to GDP (%)	–	57.80	43.80	50.50

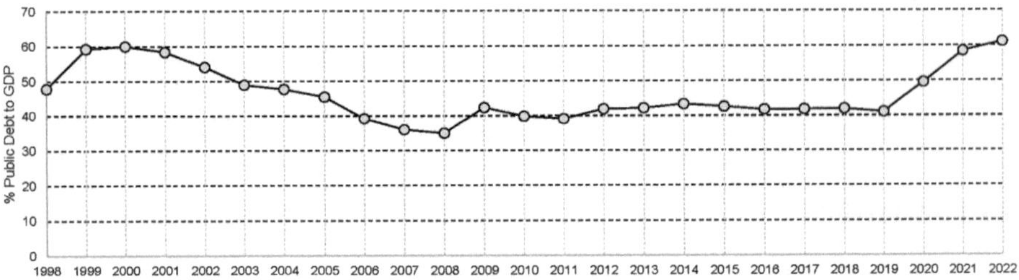

Fig. 1 The level of public debt to GDP. (Source of data: The Public Debt Management Office 2022)

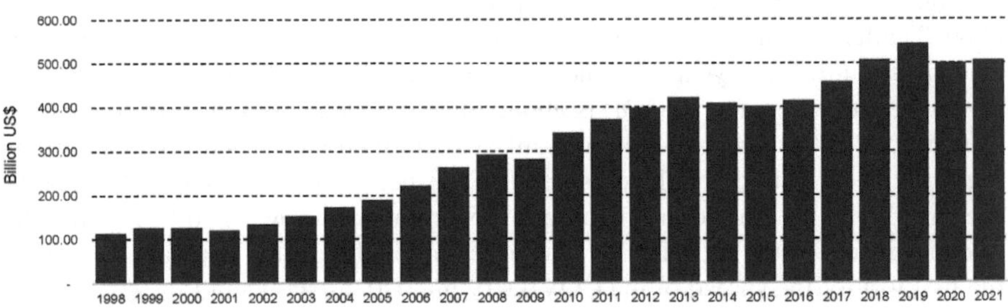

Fig. 2 The country's GDP from 1998 to 2021. (Source of data: https://data.worldbank.org/country/thailand)

PPP Infrastructure Procurement in Thailand

Economic infrastructure, which may be defined as those physical structures and systems that facilitate the use of land and the movement of people, goods, and information from one place to another (Shuldiner, 1994), plays an important role in the economic and social development (Miller, 2000). Thailand has a long history of employing Public-Private Partnerships (PPPs), as a way to finance its economic infrastructure projects such as roads, power plants, rapid mass transit, and water supply systems. Before the first Thai PPP law was enacted, the laws dealing with granting right for the private sector to participate in public projects relied upon the discretion of a responsible public agency (Kokkaew, 2015; Ashurst, 2009; Suwannoi, 2012). In 1992, the first PPP legislation called the Private Participation in State Undertaking Act (PPSU Act 1992) was enacted. The purpose of the legislation was to promote transparency about project. There are many successful PPP projects under the PPSU Act, such as mass rapid transit projects and elevated toll roads (Susangarn, 2007).

Despite the improved and transparent processes in implementing several PPP projects, private sector often criticized the PPSU Act 1992 for its lack of clarity on scope, definitions, project size valuation methodologies, and its absence of contract amendment procedures (Susangarn, 2007). These were the main concerns raised by the private sector about the PPSU Act 1992, and they urged the Thai government to reform the institutional framework and the PPP laws (World Trade Organization, 2012). Subsequently, in 2013, the Thai government revised its PPP laws and named it the Private Investment in State Undertaking Act 2013 (PISU Act 2013).

However, it seemed that several PPP projects, especially small- and medium-size projects, were also subject to the PISU Act 2013 because it required that projects with the value of 1000 million Thai baht or more be subject to the newly enacted PISU Act 2013. Moreover, several public agencies may require private investment in some projects that are not their main responsibility required by laws such as commercial building complex developments of the State Railway of Thailand. Accordingly, in 2019, the Thai government decided to amend its PPP law and named it "Public-Private Partnership Act 2019 or the PPP Act 2019." The PPP Act 2019 clearly specifies the types and values of PPP projects that must strictly follow the PPP law.

Over the three periods of Thai PPP laws (i.e., (1) the PPSU Act 1992, (2) the PISU Act 2013, and (3) the PPP Act 2019), the issues of government subsidies (e.g., minimum revenue guarantees) and flexible concession terms (e.g., flexible concession duration) were almost absent in the circle of Thai policy makers. The main reason for the lack of progress in addressing PPP contract designs to handle uncertainty prevalent in PPP projects could be legal issues. Therefore, it is not surprising that, in an attempt to deal with unforeseen events that could negatively impact the performance of PPP projects, concessionaires often seek renegotiation with contracting agency for compensations or for the extension of the concession period, as a result.

Current Environment of the Thai PPP Market

Thailand finances its infrastructure projects using several mechanisms such as fiscal budgets (about 20% of annual budget), state enterprises' retained incomes, government borrowing, state enterprises' initial public offering in the Stock Exchange of Thailand, PPP, and infrastructure fund (IFF).

Due to the nature of PPP economic infrastructure that requires a large amount of capital for constructing the project, *user fees* are often used as a mechanism to generate revenues to recoup the investment made in the construction, and to pay for the

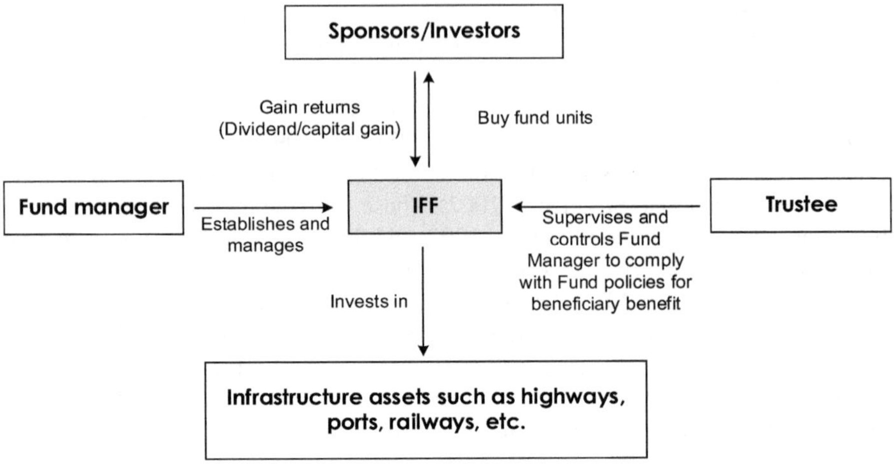

Fig. 3 Structure of infrastructure fund (IFF)

operation and maintenance of the projects. Most of the past PPP projects in Thailand are concentrated in the densely populated areas of Bangkok Metropolitan Region. Examples of past PPP projects in the Bangkok Metropolitan Region include Don Muang Tollway (DMT), Second Stage Expressway System (SES), and Bangkok Mass Transit System (BTS), and Mass Rapid Transit System (e.g., the MRT Blue Line and the MRT Purple Line).

Currently, PPP is a preferred alternative source for financing the country's expansion of large-scale infrastructure projects such as highways, expressways, railways, rail mass transit systems, and ports. For instance, according to the State Enterprise Policy Office, a public agency responsible for administering PPP projects, there are currently 92 projects worth about $US33 billion in the pipeline (Chunlakittiphan, 2022).

As for an infrastructure fund (IFF), it is an innovative financial instrument investing in a portfolio of *stable revenue-producing infrastructure projects* such as mass rail transits, toll roads, power plants, and telecommunications towers. A typical structure of IFF is presented in Fig. 3.

Public agencies and concessionaires may use IFF to raise needed capital for a new project by selling the right to future-flow receivables of an existing project to IFF. Therefore, IFF can be used as useful supplements by public agencies and concessionaires to help reduce the cost of raising finance since *revenues of infrastructure projects are believed to be stable and inflation-proof.* Over the past decade, private concessionaires and public agencies successfully raised the money using this financing technique. Examples of IFFs include BTS Rail Mass Transit Growth Infrastructure Fund (BTSGIF) and Thailand Future Fund Infrastructure Fund (TFFIF).

Table 2 Descriptions of PPP case projects

Case project	Types of concessions	COD	End of concession	Total operation years
1. BTS Core Green Line	BOT	1999	2029	30
2. MRT Blue Line	PPP Net Cost	2007	2050	43
3. Don Muang Tollway	BOT→BTO[a]	1994	2034	42
4. Second Stage Expressway System	BTO	1993	2035	40

[a]The Don Muang Tollway's concession contract was changed from BOT to BTO after the extension of the original contract period of 25 years with the rearrangement of benefits and risk to be shared between the contracting parties

Case Study Projects

Two types of PPP projects were chosen as the case study: (1) mass rail transit systems and (2) tollways. The case study projects include

1. The BTS Core Green Line
2. The MRT Blue Line
3. The Don Muang Tollway
4. the Second Stage Expressway

Descriptions about the four case projects are shown in Table 2.

Since the PPP contract is not standardized in Thailand, some PPP projects such as highways included construction years into the concession period while others such as rail mass transit projects do not. Accordingly, the author uses the total operation years starting from the commercial operation date (COD) to the end of concession to represent the duration of operation years. In addition, the concession contracts of the DMT and the SES were extended, making the total operation years of 40 and 42 for the DMT and the SES, respectively. The concession of the MRT Blue Line was also extended from 25 years to 42 years because the concession company won the PPP contract of the extension the MRT Blue Line, thereby making the operation and services of the existing and new projects seamless.

Positive Impacts of Transportation PPP on Socio-economic Development in Thailand

Bangkok, the capital of Thailand, is well known for its traffic congestion problems. Before the 1990s, to solve the congestion problems, the Thai government tended to focus the development of transportation infrastructure on increasing the supply of roads, i.e., widening existing roads and building new ones. One of the outputs of this transport policy favoring roads over other transportation systems such as public mass rail transit systems was the implementation of several concession roads in

Bangkok where most of them are elevated toll roads (e.g., the First and Second Stage Expressway and the Don Muang tollway). One of the consequences of the development of concession roads was an increase of low-density residential housing development in the outskirts of Bangkok and its neighboring provinces in the 1990s, a phenomenon known as *urban sprawl.*

Later in the 1990s, the local government of Bangkok (Bangkok Metropolitan Authority or BMA) began the development of the first heavy rail network consisting of dark and light green lines, which are later called the BTS system, to be funded and implemented by a private entity under a BOT arrangement with a concession period of 30 years. The private entity who won the bid was Bangkok Transit System Corporation Ltd. (BTSC). This move of the BMA was, perhaps, the tipping point of Bangkok's infrastructure development that significantly helps change the landscape of Bangkok's real estate development. Meanwhile, the central Thai government in 2000 decided to establish a public agency called the Mass Rapid Transit Authority of Thailand or MRTA to be responsible for developing the city's mass rail transit systems (Mass Rapid Transit Authority of Thailand, 2022). The MRTA was responsible for building the Blue Line with Bangkok Expressway and Metro (BEM), a private company, taking over under a service concession to operate the line. The MRT Blue Line, the second rail mass transit in Bangkok, began its operation in 2004.

After the opening of the BTS Green Line and the MRT Blue Line, the number of passengers gradually increased from about 55 million passengers in 2000 to almost 250 million passengers in 2019 for the BTS Green Line and from about 58 million passengers in 2005 to more than 114 million passengers in 2019 for the MRT Blue Line (see Figs. 4 and 5). As observed by Folch (2008), infrastructure developments, such as transportation improvements, can help increase the demand of residential properties in the improving area. This is the case for developing the BTS Green Line Skytrain and the MRT Blue Line in Bangkok, which essentially helped spur the development of high-rise condominiums along the rail lines because of the high

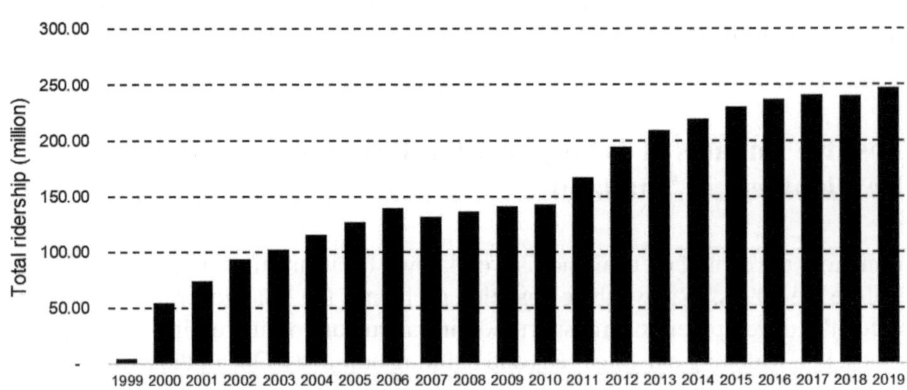

Fig. 4 Total ridership of the BTS Green Line from 1999 to 2019. (Source of data: The Office of Transport and Traffic Policy and Planning)

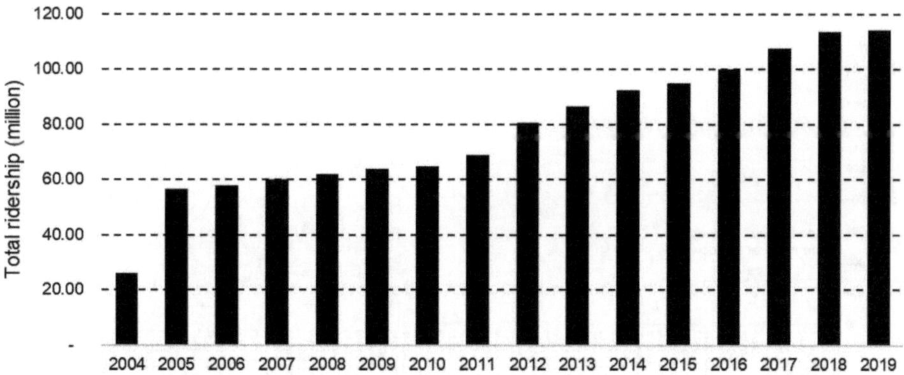

Fig. 5 Total ridership of the MRT Blue Line from 1999 to 2019. (Source of data: MRTA and BEM)

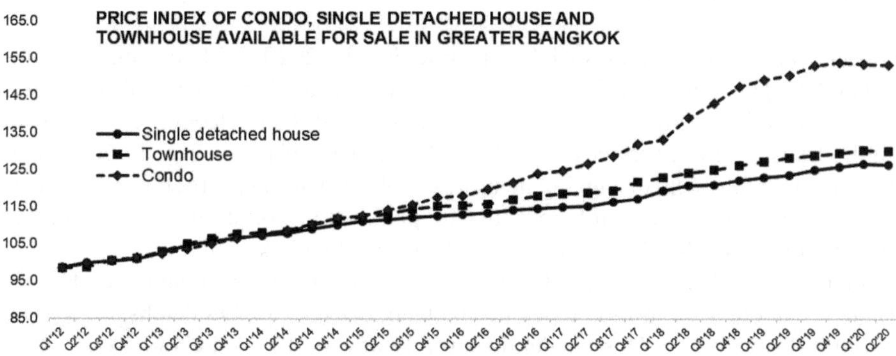

Fig. 6 Housing price index in Bangkok (Bangkok Post, 2020)

demand for residential properties in the area. As a result, the price index of Bangkok's condominiums, which are densely located along the developed rail lines, grew on average about 6% per year over the past decade during the pre-COVID years of 2012–2020, while single-detached houses grew on average at about 3.5% per year (see Fig. 6).

Impacts of the COVID-19 on PPP Transportation Infrastructure: A Project-Level Analysis

COVID-19 Situation in Thailand

The COVID-19 pandemic is perhaps one of the worst pandemics the world has experienced since the 1918 influenza pandemic. It certainly changes the ways of how people work, travel, and communicate, which ultimately can have several

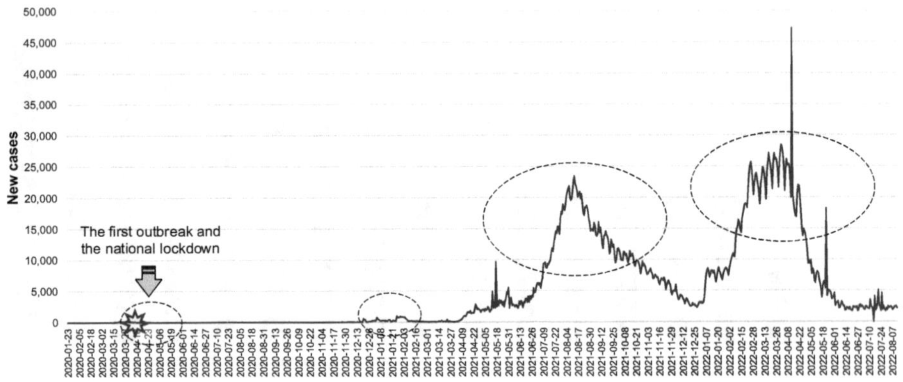

Fig. 7 Daily new confirmed cases of COVID-19 in Thailand. (Source of data: Our World in Data (https://ourworldindata.org/coronavirus))

impacts on economic and social infrastructure. In 2020, with the onset of the COVID-19 pandemic, the Thai government ordered a 75-day national lockdown, which created an immediate and deep economic recession (Komin et al., 2021). Public transportation services must limit the number of passengers to 50% of its capacity, with physical distancing measures in place. This measure severely affected the farebox revenues and toll revenues of public transportation services such as mass rapid transit (MRT) systems and tollways in Bangkok.

In Thailand, there are at least four waves of COVID-19 pandemic (see Fig. 7). There are about 4.62 million cases in Thailand, causing 31,798 deaths so far (Our World in Data, 2022). This pandemic severely affects the Thai economy in which tourism is a significant sector, generating about US$ 57 billion in 2019 and contributing to almost about 11% of the country's GDP (Surawattananon et al., 2021).

Impacts of COVID-19 on Traffic Volume and Ridership of the Case Projects

Existing PPP transportation projects such as the BTS's Dark and Light Green Lines, the MRT Blue and Purple Lines, the Second Stage Expressway System and the Don Muang Tollway are, to some degree, affected by government measures and responses to contain the spread of the COVID-19 such as the curfew and lockdown that began in early 2020. In this section, the analysis of the impacts of the COVID-19 pandemic on the four case study projects was divided into two parts: (1) mass rail transit systems and (2) tollways.

Impacts of COVID-19 on Ridership of Mass Rail Transit Systems

Mass rail transit, also known as heavy rail, metro, or subway, is a type of high-capacity public transportation generally found in urban areas. Unlike a system in cities such as New York City in which the Metropolitan Transportation Authority (MTA) is responsible for developing and implementing a unified mass transportation policy for the City of New York, Bangkok has a fragmented system of three different subsystems in operation, each with different operators and responsible public agencies.

The first mass rail transit system is the BTS, currently operated by a private company named Bangkok Mass Transit System PCL. The second system is the MRT operated by a listed company named Bangkok Expressway and Metro (BEM). As for the third one, the Airport Rail Link (ARL), the system is owned and operated by the State Railway of Thailand (SRT), a state-owned enterprise responsible for the country's development and operation of long-distance railways.

Before the spread of the COVID-19 in early 2020, the concessionaires of mass rail transit systems in Bangkok enjoyed a steady growth of passengers. This is mainly due to the new developments of residential and office buildings along the mass transit lines and the extension of mass transit lines. In 2020, during the lockdown and curfew, the total number of passengers per day of the three mass rail transit systems (i.e., BTS, MRT, and ARL) dropped significantly, as shown in Table 3, with the ARL being the hardest hit (e.g., a 74% drop of passengers per day) because of the temporary close of the airports during the travel restrictions.

As can be seen in Table 3, two privately built mass rail transit systems, i.e., the BTS and the MRT, were severely affected by the lockdown and the curfew imposed by the Thai government in an attempt to contain the spread of the COVID-19 pandemic. The impacts of the pandemic on the ridership of selected mass rail transit systems in the period of 2022–2022 are presented as follows.

1. *Impacts of COVID-19 on the Ridership of the BTS Green Line Core Network*

The revenues generated by BTS Green Line Core Network is now owned by BTS Rail Mass Transit Growth Infrastructure Fund (BTSGIF), an infrastructure fund listed in the Stock Exchange of Thailand. The Core Network comprises 2 lines totaling 23.5 km and 24 stations. Before the spread of the COVID-19, the ridership of the BTS Green Line Core Network reached 241.20 million trips for FY18/19 (April

Table 3 Number of passengers of rail transit systems before and during the lockdown and curfew in March–April of 2020

	Average passengers per day				
	SRT	ARL	MRT	BTS	Total
2019	85,443	71,953	337,015	734,411	1,228,822
March–April of 2020	15,023	19,061	137,019	246,590	417,693
Percent reduction	82%	74%	59%	66%	66%

Source of data: Impact of COVID-19 on rail passengers (2021)

Table 4 Ridership on the Green Line Core Network

	FY16/17	FY17/18	FY18/19	FY19/20	FY20/21	FY21/22
No. of ridership (million)	238	241	241	237	125	74
Growth rate (%)	2%	1%	0%	−2%	−47%	−47%

Source of data: Announcements of BTS Rail Mass Transit Growth Infrastructure Fund (https://www.btsgif.com/en/investor-relations/newsroom/set-announcements)

2018–March 2019), as shown in Table 4. Then, for FY19/20, the total passengers slightly dropped to 237 million trips, and for FY20/21 the total passengers substantially dropped to 125 million trips, which is about 47% decline from the previous fiscal year. During the lockdown and curfew in March and April of 2020, there was about 66% drop of passengers.

2. *Impacts of COVID-19 on the Ridership of the MRT Blue Line*

The MRT Blue Line is operated by BEM under a concession contract called "PPP net cost," equivalent to BTO, in which the public agency, MRTA, invests in all civil works and the private operator, BEM, is responsible for M&E works and the operation and maintenance (O&M) of the project. The MRT Blue Line consists of (1) the first phase or Section 1 opened in 2004 and (2) the second phase opened in 2017 and 2020 for Sections 2, and 3, respectively. The private operator is responsible for demand and O&M cost risks for 30 years after the completion of the entire route in 2020. Key information about the MRT Blue Line is shown in Table 5, and the ridership of the MRT Blue Line before and after the spread of the COVID-19 is shown in Table 6.

As shown in Table 6, the ridership of the MRT Blue Line reached 123 million trips in 2019 and dropped to 95 and 54 million trips in 2020 and 2021, respectively. During the first lockdown and curfew in March and April of 2020, the daily ridership dropped from about 337,000 passengers per day to about 137,000 passengers per day or about 59% reduction from the pre-COVID period.

Impacts of COVID-19 on Traffic Volume of Bangkok's Toll Roads

In Bangkok, there are several toll roads, owned and operated by either public agencies or private concessionaires. Publicly owned toll roads include Inter-City Motorway System, Chalong Rat Expressway (RAE), First Stage Expressway (FES), and Burapha Withi Expressway (BNBP). Privately built toll roads include Don Muang Tollway (DMT), Second Stage Expressway (SES), Si Rat–Outer Ring Road Expressway (SOE), and Udon Ratthaya Expressway (SES "C+"). The impact of the COVID-19 pandemic on the toll roads in Bangkok in terms of traffic volume is summarized in Table 7.

Table 5 Key information about the MRT Blue Line

MRT Blue Line	First phase (Section 1)	Second phase (Sections 2 and 3)
Concession type	PPP net cost	PPP net cost
Concession period	2004–2050	2017–2050
Distance (km)	20	28

Table 6 Yearly ridership on the MRT Blue Line

	2016	2017	2018	2019	2020	2021
No. of ridership (million)	100	108	114	123	95	54
Growth rate (%)	5%	8%	5%	8%	−23%	−44%

Table 7 Impact of COVID-19 on toll roads in Bangkok

Toll road	Length (km)	Average vehicles/day		Reduction (%)
		2019	2020	
Don Muang Tollway (DMT)	21	147,290	95,283	−35.31%
First Stage Expressway (FES)	27	373,498	313,434	−16.08%
Second Stage Expressway A&B (SES "A" and SES "B")	22	317,306	266,113	−16.13%
Second Stage Expressway C (SES "C")	8	187,579	154,647	−17.56%
Second Stage Expressway D (SES "D")	9	203,298	167,604	−17.56%
Chalong Rat Expressway (RAE)	28	230,181	205,779	−10.60%
Si Rat–Outer Ring Road Expressway (SOE)	17	64,241	58,702	−8.62%
Udon Ratthaya Expressway (SES "C+")	32	91,467	78,187	−14.52%
Burapha Withi Expressway (BNBP)	55	155,520	131,758	−15.28%
Total		*2,020,895*	*1,697,638*	*−16.00%*

Source of data: Expressway Authority of Thailand (2020) and Don Muang Tollway (2021)

1. *Impacts of COVID-19 on Traffic Volume of the DMT*

Don Muang Tollway (DMT) is an elevated toll road from the center of Bangkok to Don Muang Airport. Based on the traffic and toll revenue of the company operating the DMT, in 2020, traffic volume dropped about 35% from 53.8 million trips in 2019 to 34.9 million trips in 2020 (see Fig. 8). For toll revenues, the project generated annual revenues of THB 2816 million and THB 2047 million in 2019 and 2020, respectively, which is about 27% reduction.

2. *Impacts of COVID-19 on Traffic Volume of the SES*

The second PPP toll road in this study was the SES, which is financed and operated by BEM. Toll revenues of the SES will be shared between the private concessionaire (BEM) and the Expressway Authority of Thailand, a contracting agency. The annual average daily traffic volume (AADT) of the SES from the pre-COVID years to 2020 is shown in Fig. 9. As Fig. 9 shows, annual average daily traffic volume moderately decreased from about 708,000 vehicles per day in 2019 to about 588,000 vehicles per day in 2020 or about a decrease of 17%.

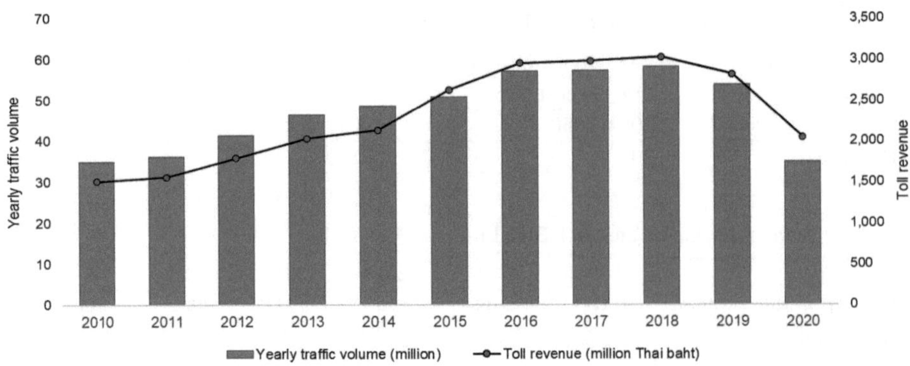

Fig. 8 Annual traffic volume and toll revenue of the DMT. (Source of data: Don Muang Tollway PCL 2021)

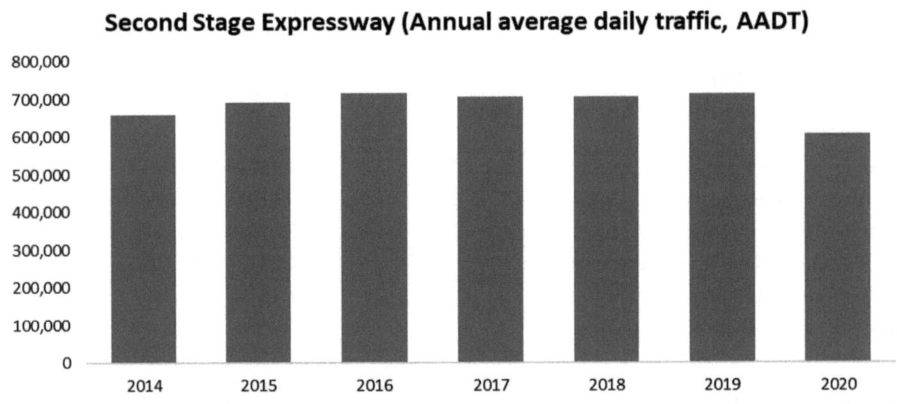

Fig. 9 Annual average daily traffic volume of the SES

Financial Impacts on the Case Projects

Due to the predetermined, fixed (i.e., inflexible and rigid) period of PPP concession contracts in Thailand, which usually has a concession period of 30 years before the extension or renewal of the contract, the levels of the impacts of the ongoing spread of the COVID-19 on each case study project will be affected by the remaining duration of the concession as well.

For instance, the BTS Green Line Core Network, which has only 9 years remaining during the first spread of the COVID-19 in the early 2020 (see Fig. 10), will certainly have less time to cure for the loss from this ongoing incident. As for the MRT Blue Line, the concession contract is to expire in 2050 or about 30 years from the first spread of the pandemic in 2020 (see Fig. 10). Therefore, it can be seen that, in the long term, this project is in a better position than the BTS Green Line Core Network to recover from the loss of operating revenue during 2020–2022.

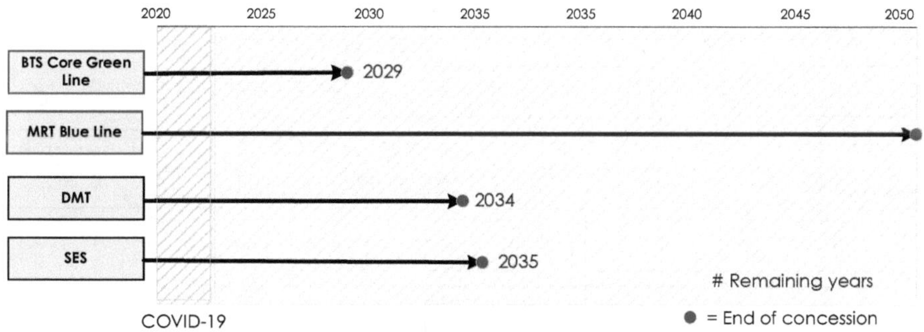

Fig. 10 The remaining concession years of the four case study projects

Table 8 Financial performance of the case study projects

Case projects	Operating revenues (THB million) 2019	2020	2021	Average reduction	Average reduction
1. BTS Green Line Core Network	4818	2113	1687	32%	30%
2. MRT Blue Line	3165	2606	1468	27%	
3. Don Muang Tollway	2816	2047	1209	29%	23%
4. Second Stage Expressway	5028	4177	–	17%	
Average				26%	

Source of data: the company websites and the Stock Exchange of Thailand

Operating revenues of the four case projects are shown in Table 8. In Table 8, operating revenues of the rail systems dropped, on average, by about 30% in 2021, whereas those of the tollways dropped by about 23% in 2021. For the DMT, the drop in traffic volume is quite significant because the project receives most toll revenues from people traveling to Don Muang Airport, and, with the air travel restrictions, it can be anticipated that the reduction of the traffic volume of the DMT would be significantly higher than that of the SES, which serves people in the center of Bangkok.

Financial Impacts of COVID-19 on PPP Infrastructure Firms

In this section, the focus is on the analysis of the financial impacts of the COVID-19 pandemic on the firm level. There are three firms owning the concession contracts of the case study projects, namely, BTSC, BEM, and DMT PCL, as shown in Fig. 11.

As can be seen in Fig. 11, the structure of BTSC, the company operating the BTS Green Line Core Network, is quite different from the other two, DMT PCL and BEM. BTSC focuses their investment mainly on the rail business, whereas DMT

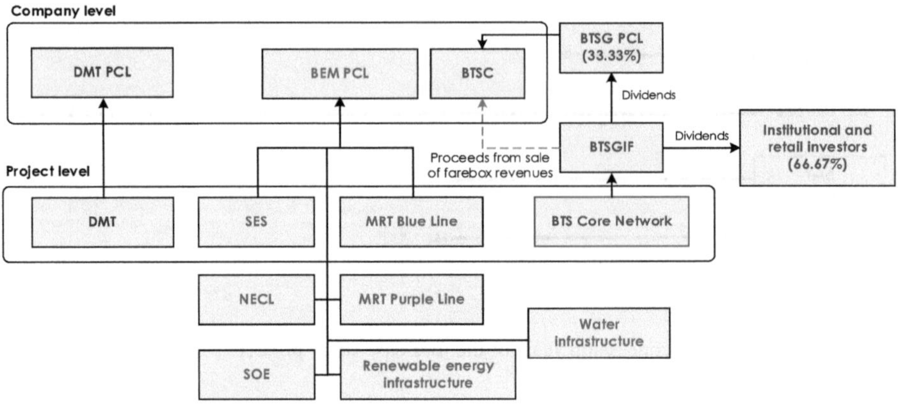

Fig. 11 Structure of the three PPP infrastructure firms operating the DMT, SES, MRT Blue Line, and BTS Green Line Core Network

PCL has its investment in only one tollway. BEM, on the other hand, allocates its investment not only in rail and expressway projects but also in water and renewable energy projects. In other words, BEM diversifies its investment risks in a portfolio of several infrastructure assets.

Bangkok Transit System Corporation Ltd. (BTSC)

In April 2013, BTSC decided to sell its rights to *future net farebox revenue* from the Green Line Core Network to an infrastructure fund named BTSGIF listed in the Stock Exchange of Thailand. In Thailand, infrastructure owners, both public and private, may raise new capital for a greenfield project and for the extension or upgrading of the existing systems using an investment unit (e.g., mutual fund) called an infrastructure fund (IFF) listed on the Stock of Exchange of Thailand. The purpose of the infrastructure fund is to alleviate the government budget allocation and the country's public debt. The fund will also become an alternative source of financing for the private sector involved in PPP infrastructure projects. Infrastructure funds will obtain the returns from investing in the infrastructure projects both directly and indirectly and will share the profits with investors.

With an initial public offering (IPO) of BTSGIF of THB 10.80 per investment unit (share) and the total investment units of 5788 million (BTSGIF, 2022), BTSC received sale proceeds of about THB 62,510 million in 2013. By forfeiting future farebox revenues, the BTSC remains only the operator of the core network, with BTSG (a parent company of BTSC) holding about 33.33% of stakes of total investment units in BTSGIF.

In other words, BTSC sold the operating revenue risks to investors through the Stock Exchange of Thailand, who at the time bought what was taught to be low-risk, inflation-proof assets in the hope of moderate return on the investment (e.g., 5%–7% yield), with the expectation of higher future dividends from (1) demand growth and (2) inflation-adjusted user fees.

After BTSC transferred most (i.e., 66.67%) of its operating revenue risks to investors, the company used the sale proceeds for constructing the extension of the light green line, which also helps increase the number of passengers of the Core Network owned by BTSGIF.

Bangkok Expressway and Metro (BEM)

Bangkok Expressway and Metro is a listed company in the Stock Exchange of Thailand. It has several infrastructure assets in its current portfolio. For example, based on its annual report (BEM 2020 Annual Report, 2021), the company (BEM) is also a major shareholder in CK Power PCL and TTW PCL, both are listed companies in the Thai stock market.

BEM itself has two major sources of revenue: expressway business and rail business. Revenues from the two businesses of BEM in 2019–2021 are shown in Fig. 12.

As shown in Fig. 12, operating revenue of BEM reduced from the year before the spread of the COVID-19. Operating revenue from the expressway business reduce by about 20% in 2020, and by about 20% in 2021. However, operating revenues from the rail business reduced by about 10% and 24% from the previous year in 2020 and 2021, respectively. Note that, despite a significant reduction in operating revenues of the MRT Blue Line as presented in the previous section, BEM has another rail line operating under a *PPP gross cost*, which is equivalent to an O&M management for fee contract. Therefore, operating revenues of the rail business of BEM are moderately affected by the reduction of passengers due to the COVID-19.

The investment strategy of BEM essentially helps the company navigate the hardships during the spread of the COVID-19. Despite the reduction in operating

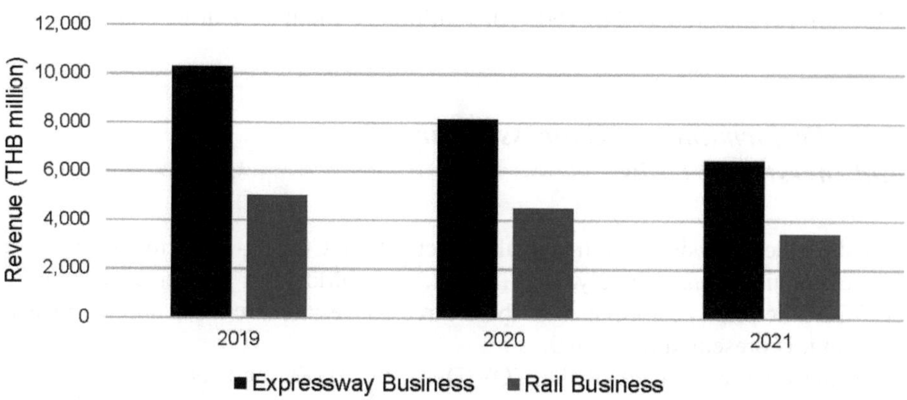

Fig. 12 Operating revenues of BEM. (Source of data: Bangkok Expressway and Metro PCL)

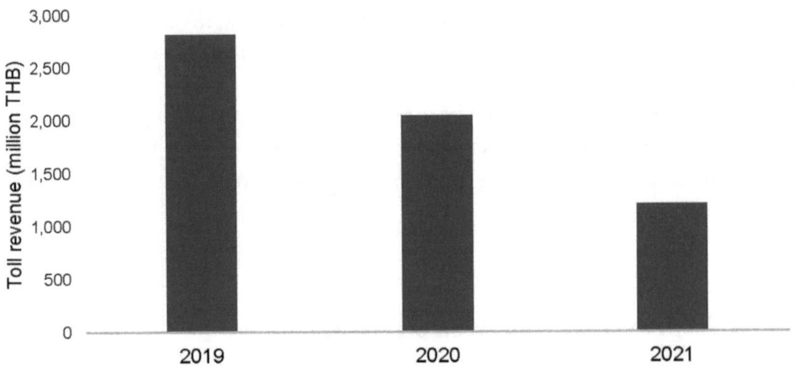

Fig. 13 Operating revenues of DMT PCL from 2019 to 2021

revenues, both from the expressway and rail business, the company still receives dividends from its investment in CKPower PCL and TTW PCL, whose operating revenues were not affected by the pandemic. In contrast, both CKPower and TTW recorded higher profit in 2021. Therefore, despite (1) the 23% and 44% reduction in total passengers of the MRT Blue Line in 2020 and 2021, respectively, and (2) about 16% reduction in traffic volume of the SES in 2020, the company still manages to perform well by reporting positive net income in year-end 2021.

Don Muang Tollway PCL (DMT PCL)

DMT PCL manages the DMT project, which is the only project owned by the company. Therefore, the company is fully exposed to demand and revenue risks. Toll revenues of the DMT project from 2019 to 2020 is shown in Fig. 13.

In Fig. 13, operating revenues of DMT PCL reduced from THB 2816 million in 2019 to THB 2047 million in 2020 or about 27% drop from the previous year. In 2021, toll revenue reduced to THB 1029 million or about 41% drop from 2020.

Price Performance of Concessionaire Firms and Investment Units

Based on the analysis of the financial impacts of the COVID-19 on the revenues of concessionaire firms, namely, BTS, BEM, and DMT, and one investment unit, BTSGIF, the price performance of these three concessionaire firms and the investment unit is presented in Table 9.

In the ongoing spread of the COVID-19, the BTSC and its parent company BTSG limits its exposure to operating revenue risks of the Green Line Core Network

Table 9 Price performance of firms and investment units

Firm and investment units	Price on December 30, 2019	Price on December 30, 2021	Price performance (% change)
BTS	THB 13.20	THB 9.30	−30%
BTSGIF	THB 9.95	THB 4.34	−56%
BEM	THB 10.90	THB 8.45	−22%
DMT	–	THB 11.50	–

to *a maximum of 33.33%*. Stock prices of the BTSG (Ticker as BTS in the Stock Exchange of Thailand) are indeed about 30% below its price movements before the start of COVID-19 pandemic (see Table 9). However, shareholders of the BTSGIF, who are fully exposed to demand risks, are still under water. Additionally, with only about 7 years remaining, the chance of the price recovery of the BTSGIF could be low. Therefore, in the future, the use of IFF as a risk transfer instrument could face a significant headwind due to risky events such as the spread of the COVID-19, which could jeopardize the future revenues of the project. As for the price performance, BEM's stock is valued at a discount of about 22% of the price at the end of 2019 (see Table 9). For the DMT PCL who floated its shares on the Thai stock market in April 2020, year after its IPO, its stock prices continue to drop from a high of about THB 16.00 in April 2020 to about THB 11.50.

Lessons Learned

This chapter has investigated the financial impacts of the COVID-19 pandemic on the project level and the firm level. Lessons learned can be drawn on the results of case study projects, and implications for the betterment and promotion of good PPP environment and policies are to be given. Lessons learned from this study are as follows.

Lesson Learned #1 Diversification of PPP infrastructure projects matters.

The diversification of investment by concessionaire firms helps mitigate not only unsystematic risks such as economy conditions but also extreme risks, i.e., risks of high consequences but of low probability.

As shown in the case analysis, BEM has a portfolio of diversified infrastructure projects such as expressways, rails, hydroelectric power plants, and water management providers. Despite the severe impacts of the COVID-19 pandemic on its rail business, the company has still performed quite well to date.

Lesson Learned #2 Assumptions about innovative financing tools such as IFF may need to be revised.

The infrastructure fund (IFF) is thought to be an innovative financing technique before the arrival of the COVID-19. However, the COVID-19 changed investors' perception of IFFs as low risk, stable yield, inflation-proof investment vehicles. These investment units were previously preferred by institutional investors such as insurance companies, pension funds, and university's fund managers. However, risks surrounding IFFs were revealed to be moderate to high. Investors are left fully exposed to the risks that were not present before. Therefore, the employment of this innovative financing instrument will certainly face more headwinds in the future, and the risk-adjusted discount rate of forecasted future cash flow generated from infrastructure projects will surely be higher.

For instance, the Thailand Future Fund Infrastructure Fund (TFFIF), a Thai IFF investing in two toll roads in Bangkok, is currently priced in the Thai stock market at about THB 8 per share with an expected dividend of about THB 0.40 in 2022 (almost the same as the dividend paid to unit holders before the COVID-19 pandemic), which is about 5% yield. The dividend is expected to grow over time because of increasing traffic volume (about 3% before the COVID-19) and toll price adjustment (about 3%), and in the end the fund will have no value to the unit holders. Thus, by using the discount cash flow (DCF) method, the market currently prices in present value the future stream of dividends with a risk-adjusted discount rate of about 8.5%. If the assumption about stable yield, inflation-proof investment vehicles still hold true, the discount rate would be lower and the price of the TFFIF would be higher (its price was used to be at about THB 11.00 before the COVID-19 pandemic).

Lesson Learned #3 Inflexible parameters of PPP contracts such as the concession period need to be rethought.

One of the most commonly used PPP arrangements in transportation infrastructure in Thailand is build-transfer-operate (BTO). Under this PPP arrangement, construction cost risk and operational risks are transferred to the private party. As recommended by the United Nations Economic and Social Commission for Asia and the Pacific (ESCAP, 2008), the concession period can range from 15 to 30 years, depending on the results of the project's financial analysis. Therefore, based on the *ex-ante* financial analysis, predetermined or fixed concession period is explicitly stated in the concession contract. Predetermined or fixed concession period works well when things go as expected or as forecasted.

However, as pointed by Neufville and Scholtes (2011), forecasts are always wrong. Certain researchers such as Vassallo (2006) recognized this issue and recommended using a method called Least Present Value of the Revenues (LPVR) instead of a fixed and predetermined concession period. Under this LPVR agreement, concession will expire when the required return rate of the investment of the concessionaire (i.e., project company) reaches an agreed level, such as 6.5%. Therefore, in the event of the COVID-19 that leads to lower operating revenues of the project over the short period, the concessionaires will still have time to recover the loss of operating revenues during the spread of the COVID-19. Governments, on the other hand, may need not worry about the seeking of the concession contract renegotiation by those concessionaires affected by the public safety measures imposed by the government.

Implications to Theory and Practice

Infrastructure is essential to today's economic and social development. As presented in this chapter, Thailand uses both public and private resources to finance its infrastructure. For PPP transportation infrastructure, the impact on the socio-economy is very evident since it facilitates the land use and spurs new development as a result. For instance, the BTS and the MRT rail systems in Bangkok help the traveling in Bangkok more efficient and pleasant. This in turn led to new residential and office buildings along the rail lines.

This study contributes to the body of PPP knowledge and risk management practices in the follow issues. First, in the past, market risks such as demand risks are modeled using historical data in which risky events such as the spread of contagious viruses are extremely unlikely events. However, some extremely low-risk events may turn out to have high impacts. This is in fact the case of the COVID-19 pandemic. PPP contracts in Thailand, like those of several other countries', are quite inflexible in terms such as remedy period in the case of unexpected events and the threshold level of government support or sharing of revenue to help mitigate unforeseen risks. Therefore, based on the results presented in this chapter, a greater level of contractual flexibility should be more welcomed by theorists and practitioners. In fact, there are several researchers who strongly advocate using flexible PPP arrangements (e.g., Dong and Chiara, 2010; Cruz and Marques, 2013; Domingues et al., 2014). For instance, Zhao et al. (2004) incorporated uncertainties such traffic demand into the financial model and model risks and opportunities as real options embedded in PPP highways. Similarly, Chiara and Kokkaew (2009) proposed an approach to quantitatively assess contractual risks and to mitigate risk that exceeds an acceptable level using government support, which can be modeled as real options. Second, the concession period should be adjustable, not by renegotiation, but by a trigger of certain parameters such as accumulated net revenues. Examples of researchers who urged the rethinking about inflexible concession period include Engel et al. (2019) and Vassallo (2006). The results of case study analysis support this approach to the determination of concession period to minimize the renegotiation of concession period extension.

Conclusion

Thailand has a long history of employing Public-Private Partnerships (PPPs) as a way to finance its key infrastructure projects such as highways, mass rapid transit systems, and high-speed rails. Most of the PPP transport projects in Thailand are still concentrated in Bangkok due to high demand for the services, thereby making them less exposed to market risks. This study investigated the impacts of PPP transportation projects on the socio-economy and impacts of the COVID-19 during 2020 and 2021 on existing PPP transportation projects in Thailand through four case study projects: (1) the BTS Core Green Line, (2) the MRT Blue Line, (3) the Don Muang Tollway, and (4) the Second Stage Expressway System.

Results of the study found that the impacts of PPP transportation infrastructure, in particular the BTS and the MRT rail systems, on the economy and quality of life were evidently confirmed, based on the observation of the demand growth of new residential and office buildings along the rail lines. The results of the financial impacts of the COVID-19 on the case projects indicated that, in terms of the reduction of operating revenues, mass rail systems were highly affected by the pandemic (i.e., about 30% reduction of operating revenues) while tollways were moderately affected (i.e., about 20% reduction of operating revenues). As for the results of the financial impacts of the COVID-19 pandemic on the concession firms operating the project(s), BTSG and BEM fared better than DMT PCL in terms of price performance. The reason is because both BTSG and BEM employ risk management tools, each with different strategy: revenue or demand risk transfer through IFF for BTSG and risk diversification of investment portfolio for BEM.

Considering the ongoing spread of the COVID-19, this chapter also exposes the vulnerability of PPP contracts and its *seemingly innovative risk management* in which market risks such as demand and revenue risks could be transferred to retail and institutional investors through an infrastructure fund (IFF). Three lessons learned provided by this study include: (1) diversification of PPP infrastructure projects matters; (2) assumptions about innovative financing and risk management tools may need to be revised; and (3) inflexible parameters of PPP contracts such as the concession period need to be rethought. The results of the case study analysis presented in this chapter could be of practical use to policy makers responsible for improving PPP environment in their country.

References

Ashurst. (2009). *Thailand's new PPP framework*. Ashurstinsight: infrastructure opportunities, March 2009.

Bangkok Post. (2020). *Back to earth*. https://www.bangkokpost.com/property/2011047/back-down-to-earth

BEM. (2021). *2020 Annual report*. https://bem.listedcompany.com/misc/ar/20210326-bem-ar2020-en.pdf

BTSGIF. (2022). *Company summary*. https://classic.set.or.th/set/factsheet.do?symbol=BTSGIF&ssoPageId=3&language=eng&country=TH

Chiara, N., & Kokkaew, N. (2009). Risk analysis of contractual flexibility in BOT negotiations: A quantitative approach using risk flexibility theory. *International Journal of Engineering and Management, 1*(1), 71–79.

Chunlakittiphan, E. (2022). *Public-private partnerships market in Thailand*. https://www.tradecommissioner.gc.ca/thailand-thailande/market-reports-etudes-de-marches/0006475.aspx?lang=eng

Cruz, C. O., & Marques, R. C. (2013). Flexible contracts to cope with uncertainty in public–private partnerships. *International Journal of Project Management, 31*(3), 473–483.

Domingues, S., Zlatkovic, D., & Roumboutsos, A. (2014, September). Contractual flexibility in transport infrastructure PPP. *In European transport conference* (Vol. 29).

Don Muang Tollway PCL (2021). *Analyst Meeting 1H2021 Presentation by the Don Muang Tollway Public Company Limited, August 2021.*

Dong, F., & Chiara, N. (2010). Improving economic efficiency of public-private partnerships for infrastructure development by contractual flexibility analysis in a highly uncertain context. *The Journal of Structured Finance, 16*(1), 87–99.

Engel, E., Fischer, R., Galetovic, A., & Soto, J. (2019). Financing PPP projects with PVR contracts: Theory and evidence from the UK and Chile.

ESCAP. (2008, June). *Public-private partnerships in infrastructure development: A primer.* https://www.unescap.org/sites/default/files/PPP-Primer-Final-Original-edited.pdf

Expressway Authority of Thailand. (2020). *Annual report.* https://www.exat.co.th/en/annual-report/

Folch, M. (2008). *Note on real estate investments.* Ivy Management Services, Richard Ivey School of Business, The University of Western Ontario.

Impact of COVID-19 on Rail Passengers. (2021, August 10). *Prachachart business.* https://www.prachachat.net/property/news-732583

Kokkaew, N. (2015). 19 PPP development in Thailand. *Public Private Partnerships: A Global Review,* 313.

Komin, W., Thepparp, R., Subsing, B., & Engstrom, D. (2021). COVID-19 and its impact on informal sector workers: A case study of Thailand. *Asia Pacific Journal of Social Work and Development, 31*(1–2), 80–88. https://doi.org/10.1080/02185385.2020.1832564

Mass Rapid Transit Authority of Thailand. (2022). *Background of the MRTA.* https://www.mrta.co.th/en/about_mrta/history/

Miller, J. B. (2000). *Principles of public and private infrastructure delivery.* Springer Science+Business Media.

Neufville, R., & Scholtes, S. (2011). *Flexibility in engineering design.* MIT Press.

Public Debt Management Office. (2022). *Public debt FY 1998 to the present.* https://www.pdmo.go.th/en/

Shuldiner, P. W. (1994). Investing in economic infrastructure. *New England. Journal of Public Policy, 10,* 6.

Statista Research Department. (2022). *Population of Bangkok in Thailand 2012–2021.* https://www.statista.com/statistics/910999/thailand-population-in-bangkok/

Surawattananon, N., Reancharoen, T., Prajongkarn W., Chuanantatham, S., Simakorn, Y., & Gultawatvichai, P. (2021). *Revitalising Thailand's tourism sector.* https://www.bot.or.th/Thai/MonetaryPolicy/EconomicConditions/AAA/27062021_RevitalisingThailandTourism.pdf

Susangarn, C (2007). Public private partnership in Thailand: Past experiences and future Prospect. *In The Asia-Pacific Ministerial Conference on PPPs in Infrastructure,* 4–6 October 2007, Republic of Korea.

Suwannoi, P. (2012). Thailand's newly proposed public-private partnership law. *Informed Counsel,* 17 August 2012, p 3.

Vassallo, J. (2006). Traffic risk mitigation in highway concession projects - the experience of Chile. *Journal of Transport Economics and Policy, 40*(3), 359–381.

World Bank. (2022). *Thailand – World Bank Data.* https://data.worldbank.org/indicator/SP.POP.TOTL?locations=TH

World Trade Organization. (2012). *Trade policy review body – Report by Thailand.* Geneva, Switzerland.

Zhao, T., Sundararajan, S. K., & Tseng, C. L. (2004). Highway development decision-making under uncertainty: A real option approach. *Journal of Infrastructure Systems, 10*(1), 23–32.

PPP State-of-the-Art in Turkey During COVID-19 Outbreak: Evidence from a Transportation Project

Asli Pelin Gurgun, Kerim Koc, Güzin Akyıldız Alçura, and Mustafa Gürsoy

Introduction

The COVID-19 pandemic has significantly affected all the stages of public-private partnership (PPP) projects around the globe (Asian Development Bank, 2021). Most common impacts were incapacity of workers due to infections or anxiety, additional expenses to maintain operation process (meeting health and safety regulations), requirements of isolation, and changes in contractual requirements. The World Bank (2020) addressed that disruption of material deliveries, delay in the execution of projects, and revenue losses compelled the operation and stability of the PPPs. A report by PricewaterhouseCoopers (PWC) (2020) highlighted that many governments were expected to be overwhelmed by a burden of long-term financial problems due to the COVID-19 pandemic. The same report also underpinned that the PPPs can be regarded as a valuable post-COVID recovery alternative for many governments.

Turkey is among the initial developers of PPP laws (Gurgun & Touran, 2014), which has become one of the leading countries in terms of PPP investments (World Bank Group, 2016). The first law regarding the PPP in Turkey was enacted in 1984, authorizing private companies to generate and distribute electricity under build-operate-transfer (BOT) or transfer of rights (TOR) models (Official Gazette, 1984). Other PPP models were subsequently considered and enacted in Turkey such as build-operate (BO) and build-lease-transfer (BLT). Figure 1 shows the distribution of PPP models (awarded contracts) regarding BOT, TOR, BO, and BLT between 1986 and 2018 (Presidency of the Republic of Turkey Strategy and Budget Authority,

A. P. Gurgun (✉) · K. Koc · G. A. Alçura · M. Gürsoy
Department of Civil Engineering, Yildiz Technical University, Istanbul, Turkey
e-mail: apelin@yildiz.edu.tr; kerimkoc@yildiz.edu.tr; akyildiz@yildiz.edu.tr; gursoy@yildiz.edu.tr

© The Author(s), under exclusive license to Springer Nature Switzerland AG 2023

T. Dolla et al. (eds.), *Revisiting Public-Private Partnerships*,
Contributions to Public Administration and Public Policy,
https://doi.org/10.1007/978-3-031-37015-1_12

Fig. 1 Distribution of PPP models awarded in Turkey

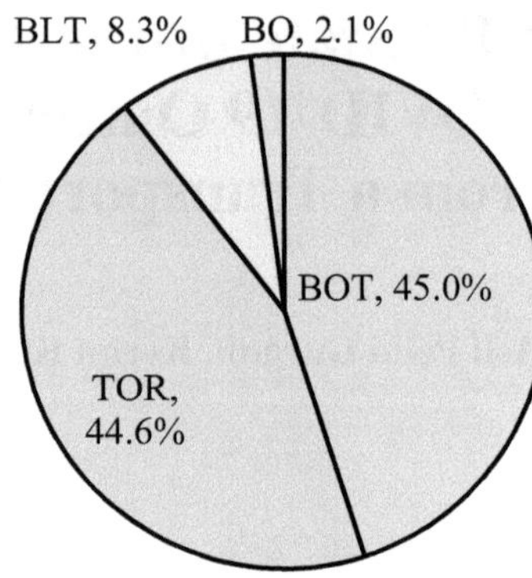

2019). Accordingly, the vast majority of the signed PPP projects are procured through BOT and TOR models. The report also underlined that the energy (37.6%), highway (17.4%), harbor (9.8%), hospital (9.3%), and airport (7.9%) projects encompassed most of the investments regarding all PPP models.

There have been controversial opinions regarding the advantages and disadvantages of PPPs in Turkey. Top and Sungur (2019) found that major stakeholders from several agencies (non-governmental organizations, social security institutions, Ministry of Finance, Ministry of Development, private sectors, etc.) expressed diverse opinions about the advantages and disadvantages of using PPP models. The researchers underpinned that the non-governmental organizations and residents had negative thoughts about PPPs, while professionals from both public and private sectors posed mainly positive views. Despite the volume of PPP projects, the successful achievement of PPP objectives has been a common concern in the Turkish PPP market. In this context, Budayan (2018) investigated the key performance indicators of PPP projects in Turkey and identified several factors including technical feasibility, effective tender process, reasonable public control, and applicability of the projects. In addition, several scholars addressed that limited number of PPP models applied in Turkey might also be an important burden affecting the success of projects during the implementation stage (Budayan, 2018; Gurgun & Touran, 2014).

Disputes are inevitable in construction projects, and PPP model is not an exception. Due to the complex nature of PPP projects and their implementation in new and unknown areas, numerous uncertainties and disputes are common in PPP projects (Top & Sungur, 2019). Time, cost, and quality pressures are usually at the highest level in PPP projects. It is important to note that whenever the public sector is a contracting party, then administrative justice can be considered as an appropriate dispute resolution mechanism (Boz, 2013). On the other hand, ordinary court (private law) is another alternative for dispute handling. For instance, in Turkey, Law No: 6428 (2013) states that public services of health performed under PPP models are based on private law. Under this law, arbitration is another applicable dispute resolution method, while disputes can also be handled with the corresponding agreement between public and private entities in the contracts (Aygül & Erdoğan,

2020). Besides, there are improvements in BOT law providing the possibility of arbitration as a dispute resolution mechanism to attract international investors and finance circles (Yılmaz, 2021). Still, there has not been any particular law with respect to PPP contracts addressing particular dispute resolution method in Turkey, which needs to be developed to ensure speed in decision-making during the execution phase, aiding to solve potential disputes in an effective manner (Boz, 2013).

With the provided brief background, the aim of this research is to provide an outlook about the response of the Turkish PPP market to the COVID-19 pandemic, with a particular focus on a mega bridge and highway connection project – "1915 Çanakkale Bridge and Highway." For this purpose, three semi-structured interviews were performed with professionals from different parties of the case project to probe into diverse response mechanisms to the pandemic. Then, crisis management, responses, and decision-making process during this period were addressed, and corresponding recommendations were proposed. With the significant PPP experience and a high number of cases, this study is expected to present the management experience of Turkey during the Covid outbreak through a BOT project as a case study.

Context of the Inquiry

The extent and unprecedented severity of the COVID-19 pandemic has generated destructive consequences since December 2019. Globally, nearly 269 million COVID-19 cases with 5.3 million deaths have been reported up to 12 December 2021 (World Health Organization, 2021). The pandemic has also forced the limits of many sectors around the world such as water sector (in relation to water scarcity) (Antwi et al., 2021), transportation sector (Cui et al., 2021), tourism sector (Jaipuria et al., 2021), food sector (Galanakis et al., 2021), banking sector (Demirgüç-Kunt et al., 2021), and construction sector (Stiles et al., 2021).

During the early spread of COVID-19, Turkey's response to COVID-19 was mostly regarded as successful, even praised by the World Health Organization (WHO), with one of the lowest case fatality ratios (2.57%), compared to other countries (World Health Organization, 2020). The progress of COVID-19 cases in Turkey has then showed a similar trend to the global scheme with nearly 8.7 million cases and 80.000 death tolls (as of 13 December 2021) (Ministry of Health, 2021). Figure 2 shows the death tolls in Turkey due to the COVID-19 pandemic.

Since its beginning, social distancing and wearing face masks have been regarded as the most efficient ways to minimize the spread of the pandemic. As most of the significant economic and social activities involve face-to-face human interactions, many sectors needed to adapt themselves to living with COVID-19 to minimize its spread. In this context, the typical and most commonly adopted mitigation measure was changing the operation from physical interaction to online interaction (Ozili, 2021), which has showed a good performance in some sectors such as shopping, education, and for white-collar employees in several sectors. However, some of the

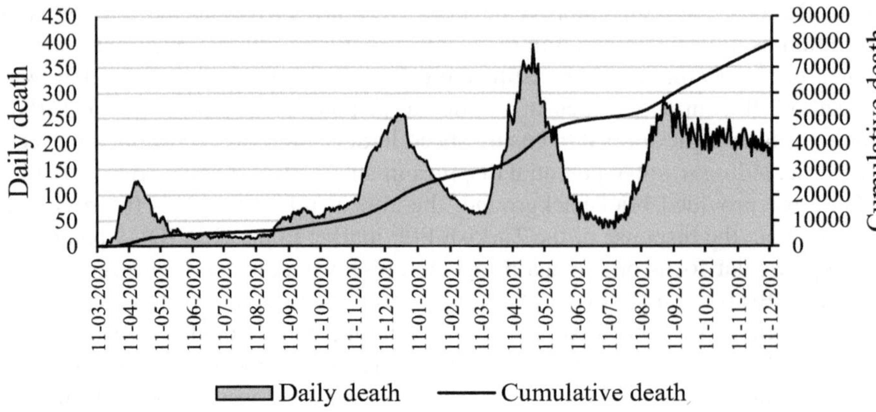

Fig. 2 Deaths due to COVID-19 in Turkey

fundamental works in human society can be performed neither online nor with complete protection from social distancing, such as construction (Araya, 2021). The construction industry is among the leading sectors in Turkey (Ceylan, 2012), and according to the Turkish Statistical Institution (TUIK) (2021), 6.4 million workers are employed in the construction industry (as of October 2021) accounting for 6.12% of the total employment. In addition, workers tend to spend more time at construction sites in Turkey compared to developing countries (Koc et al., 2022), which make them more vulnerable to COVID-19 due to the higher probability of physical human interaction. By considering the volume of PPP projects in the country (242 contracted and 210 completed PPP projects as of 2018) (Presidency of the Republic of Turkey Strategy and Budget Authority, 2019), Turkey can be considered as an example for investigating the impacts of COVID-19 on PPP projects.

COVID-19 brought significant issues to the PPP market. One of the most open-ended discussions on the pandemic-PPP relationship is probably about the term "force majeure" (i.e., whether COVID-19 is regarded as a force majeure event or not). Despite some requirements of force majeure have been addressed (such as occurrence without any control of parties, being unprecedented), there is no clear definition of the force majeure in Turkish law. However, in Law No: 3996 (Official Gazette, 1994), which is related to the implementation procedures of BOT projects, it is stated that the force majeures need to be defined and included in the contracts. Some experts also suggest that COVID-19 can be considered as a force majeure in projects under PPP contracts that included "pandemic" as a force majeure event.

Other major issues in the PPP market can be listed as: (i) preparing a proper bid document under extreme uncertainty in the feasibility phase, (ii) ensuring the health of the workers and performance of work packages (with decrease in productivity under strict time and cost constraints) in construction phase, and (iii) achieving required transition rate in the operation phase (particularly in BOT transportation projects). It should be noted that most of the responses to risks due to COVID-19 were related to construction phase of PPP projects in Turkey. Many PPP projects prepared their response plans when COVID-19 was first deemed as "pandemic" by WHO, while some companies prepared themselves even before the first COVID-19 case. Then, most of the PPP projects (similar to other construction projects) transformed their site and management plans to prevent the spread of the pandemic, mainly based on the notifications of the Ministry of Health. In this context, some of the most initially adopted mitigation measures can be listed as follows: (i) mandating the use of face masks, (ii) providing home-office opportunity for elderly and those with chronicle diseases, (iii) taking workers' temperatures on site, (iv) scanning the "life fits home (LFH)" code (HES code in Turkish; an application developed by Ministry of Health, addressing the COVID-19 condition of the citizens), and (v) placing disinfectants in the work environments.

In this study, "1915 Çanakkale Bridge and Highway" is presented as a case study to investigate the effects of COVID-19, which was in the construction phase at the time the pandemic broke out and will be in the operational phase with the existence of COVID-19 for an unforeseen future. The rationale and brief description of the case project are provided in the following two sections.

Rationale of the Project

Dardanelles Straight is located between European and Asian parts of Çanakkale (Dardanelles) as a seaways on the west of Marmara region in Turkey. Existing transportation services between two continents in the region have been mainly performed with ferries causing several transportation concerns. The major bottleneck for the feasibility of transportation is the average travel time, which is usually disrupted by adverse weather conditions. In addition, loading and unloading activities increase the time required significantly for the ferries to take off. Demographic and economic structures of the region as well as the current transportation networks reveal the following opportunities for the region:

- Despite the study area being closed to the most developed and densely populated cities in Turkey, the existing infrastructure still requires significant improvements. The project has the potential to close the gaps in the matter.
- By connecting the two sides of the Dardanelles, the project can promote a better interaction among the cities and towns in the region regarding agriculture, industry, tourism, and service sectors.
- The region will have a great potential for further growth, with increased accessibility and improved transportation alternatives.

Brief Description of the Case

This study focused on the "1915 Çanakkale Bridge and Highway Project," which is commonly known as "1915 Çanakkale." Governing body of the project is the Republic of Turkey, Ministry of Transport and Infrastructure (from now on will be referred to as the Ministry) and a joint venture was established as "Çanakkale Highway and Bridge Building, Investment and Operation IC" for the implementation. The project was awarded with a BOT contract and the tendering phase was managed in accordance with the BOT Law in Turkey (Law No. 3996). The contract was signed on March 21, 2017, between the government and the joint venture company. The duration of the contract was declared as 16 years, 2 months, and 12 days, which encompasses all project phases including both building and operation. Accordingly, the company has taken the responsibility of design, building, rebuilding (if necessary), and operation. The total estimated investment amount is around over 2.7 billion USD. Once the bridge is constructed, it will be the longest middle-span length suspension bridge in the world. The total length will be 4608.00 meters, of which 2023 meters will be the middle span, 770 meters of side spans (both), and 365 and 680 meters of access viaducts at each side. The height at the top point of the bridge will be 334 meters, which makes the bridge the tallest suspension bridge.

The project is a part of the 2023 national development goals, which include improving the highway infrastructure across Turkey. The project is a proper alternative to the Northern Marmara Motorway passes through Istanbul city on the way from Western Anatolia to Europe. The project is expected to facilitate long-distance journeys and road freight transport from Western Anatolia to Europe by ensuring that the vehicles do not have to get into the congested metropolitan traffic of Istanbul city.

Figure 3 shows the highway network around the project (Fig. 3a) as well as the major sections of the project (Fig. 3b) and representation of the bridge (Fig. 3c) (Ministry of Transportation and Infrastructure, 2022). The project is subdivided into three sections (Fig. 3b):

- A: Malkara Connection – Gallipoli South Connection (length 72,529 km; access road length 9595 km).
- B: Gallipoli South Connection – Çanakkale 1 Connection (1915 Çanakkale Bridge).
- C: Çanakkale 1 Connection – Çanakkale 2 Connection (7885 km of length, 3.11 km of access road lengths; 568.8 m of a viaduct).

Regarding the important dates, early-stage studies have been performed between the second half of 2017 and first quarter of 2018. Seabed dredging activities for the foundations of bridge towers began at the beginning of 2018. On the other hand, the completion of the bridge is planned for March 18, 2023, which is also an official grand opening of the project, commemorating the Battle of Gallipoli during World War 1. In addition, the road construction works are planned to be finalized in August

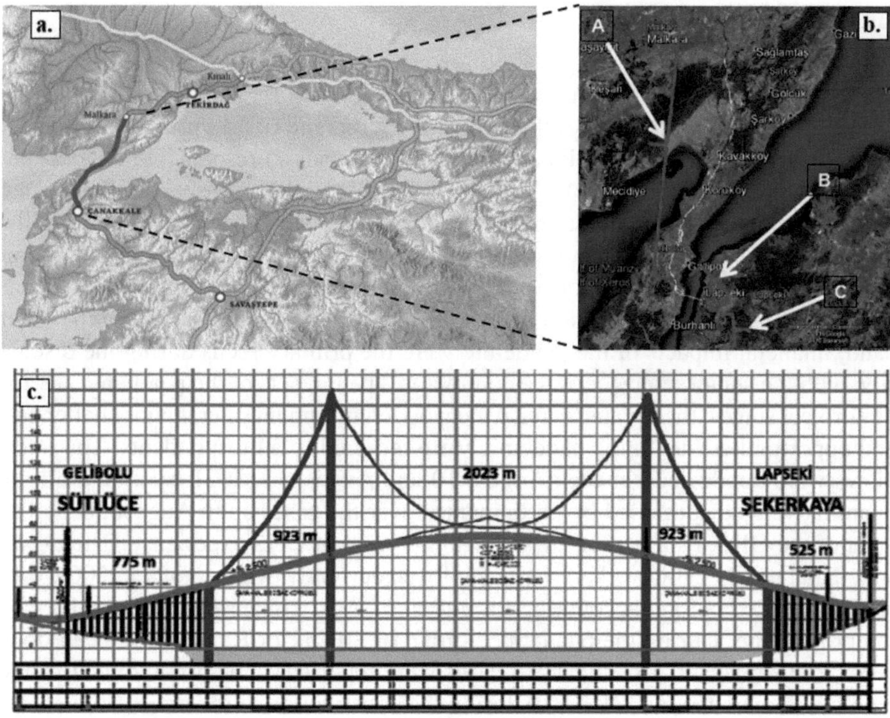

Fig. 3 The project location. (Modified from Ministry of Transportation and Infrastructure, 2022). (**a**) Highway network around the Marmara Sea and Çanakkale 1915 Bridge Section. (**b**) Major sections in the project. (**c**) Representation of the bridge

2023. The construction of the bridge includes six major stages: (i) tower foundation, (ii) tension support/tower, (iii) catwalk construction, (iv) installation of cables and suspension rope, (v) installation of decks, and (vi) completion of the bridge as a whole. The project consists of a total of 88 km of highway, 13 km of connector roads, and a part of the Kınalı–Tekirdağ–Savaştepe Highway Project with a length of 324 km. A total of 16.4 million m^2 surface area is expected to be subjected to expropriation, including 12 million m^2 of private property.

A contract has been signed by the ministry and 25 financial institutions from 10 countries around the world for the project financing. Around 2.265 billion EUR of credit, 70% of them from foreign institutions, was catered for a 15-year period and the initial payment will be made 5 years later. The project is expected to contribute to the Gross Added Value of as much as the 11.2 billion Euro, as well as creating a total economic activity accounting for nearly 14.5 billion Euro with direct, indirect, and incentivized effects. The project is anticipated to generate 2.5 billion Euro tax revenues by the end of the concession period, as well as creating an employment for 285,000 people.

Case Analysis

Three semi-structured interviews were performed with (i) a subcontractor of the project, (ii) a senior manager of the main contractor, and (iii) a group of officials of the consortium (three professionals in a single interview) responsible for occupational health and safety (OHS). The measures taken with the onset of the epidemic and the difficulties encountered in the implementation were the primary focus of the discussion with the OHS team. Most of the discussion with the sub-contractor included the challenges that took place during the initial period of the pandemic as well as corresponding mitigation measures to prevent the spread of it. On the other hand, financial impacts of the pandemic were the primary focus during the discussion with the senior manager of the contractor. The impacts of the pandemic at various project stages, their plans to make the work environment safer, major challenges, and opportunities due to the pandemic were inquired to all respondents. The interviews were conducted between August 10 and August 13, 2021, such that all the quantitative data addressed by participants cover the cases up to August 2021. The head of the OHS team was an expert with 20 years of OHS experience. The expert stated that nearly 2800 workers were employed currently, while another 7200 workers had worked before, accounting for a total of approximately 10,000 workers on the project site. During the pandemic, a total of 30,452 PCR tests have been done and 396 positive and 457 contacted cases were reported. In addition, only 1 of the employees died due to COVID-19 during the construction of the project.

The responses were quite adequate for the project environment, such that first measures were immediately addressed just after the declaration of the first case (in China) in January 2020 to prevent the spread of the pandemic. These measures include providing hand sanitizers, increasing the frequency of cleaning up risky places, recruiting additional health and safety personnel, etc. The response strategies adopted by the project team soared during the upcoming days due to the uncertain nature of the pandemic. The information related to COVID-19 was added to the OHS brochures and included in the OHS training programs to raise the awareness of the employees. With the first declaration and rapid spread of the pandemic in Turkey in March 2020, international travels were ceased, and a 14-day quarantine practice was initiated for those coming from other countries. The company established a professional health committee in March and April 2020 to manage the effects of the pandemic more systematically. White-collar employees with chronic diseases were sent away to work from home, while paid leave was provided to the blue-collar workers with chronic diseases. Measures were taken to encourage employees for vaccinations and only vaccinated employees were allowed to the offices.

During the 15-day full lockdown period at the beginning of May, all employees were placed in the contracted hotels nearby. In some of those hotels, additional administrative and health personnel were employed, and virus-infected or contacted employees were also isolated effectively. Entry to and exit from the construction sites were provided only by shuttle services and private vehicles were not allowed in the construction site. In the cafeterias, dormitories, and other social service facilities, people were ensured to keep the appropriate social distance. Several other measures were also taken such as not allowing face-to-face meetings and extending the mealtime in shifts to control the density in the dining hall. Visual reminders of the precautions regarding masks and 2-meter social distance were exhibited at various places at the construction site. Booklets published by the Ministry of Health were distributed to personnel, and no one were allowed outside the site other than for emergencies. On-site vaccination was performed four times with special permission, and corresponding legal arrangements were set to include international employees in the national vaccination system. Private ambulances of the company were used in cases where the public emergency helpline service was insufficient to treat the infected and sick employees. An agreement was signed with a private health institution to get the PCR test results as early as possible and this approach provided significant improvement in the management of COVID-19 cases. During the first days of the outbreak, workers who were recruited to work in construction sites were required to provide a PCR test and wait in quarantine until the negative results were guaranteed. Employees had to repeat the process if they left the construction site for more than 3 days. One of the major difficulties was that the period of full lockdown was declared coincided with the period when the number of employees was at its peak. Therefore, the productivity and efficiency in the construction site were observed to decrease especially due to the quarantine conditions, measures, and psychological stressors among employees.

The interviewed subcontractor was responsible for the Gallipoli leg, which employed approximately 300 workers. The interviewee stated that the impact of the pandemic was greater in the PPP project compared to their other conventional projects. It was addressed that only in this project, several stricter measures were taken such as restriction of the site entry and exit to the site. In other projects, common preventive actions such as temperature measurement, wearing mask, and distance restriction warnings with posters were applied. The interviewee stated that the major reason for stringent measures in PPP projects was the presence of public sector organizations and international private stakeholders. Due to the decrease in productivity and efficiency, the subcontractor experienced more than 30% of delay such that the work scheduled for 6 months was completed in about 8 months. During this period, the profit of was decreased to almost 5% from 25% expectation, particularly due to the stringent time pressure of the project forcing the subcontractor (as well as other subcontractors) to increase the number of employees. Extra wages and expenses for special needs (grocery expenditures, private vehicles, etc.) that were provided to employees to persuade them to continue to work in quarantine conditions were other major reasons for cost overrun. The subcontractor also stated that if they were to bid for the project again, they would have included additional costs for the backup team in the bid document.

The manager (similar to the subcontractor representative) stated that human resource management was one of the major managerial and operational challenges due to the pandemic. This included the inability to find required personnel on site as well as providing the logistics of the special teams and materials from abroad, which caused delays in particular construction activities. To overcome this barrier, Turkish employees (if they exist) among the special teams were encouraged to come to Turkey instead of other international employees. The senior manager of the contractor also highlighted the major financial difficulties that emerged due to the pandemic. Other than these challenges, a significant decrease in the motivation of the workers was also observed, which required particular attention to the psychological aspect of human resource management. Necessary actions were taken, and continuous monitoring and improvement approach has been considered. Similar to the subcontractor, time pressure and strict project completion requirement of the project were also emphasized by the senior manager of the contractor company. Being the major responsible project party, the contractor was expected to complete the construction phase on time, despite the challenges due to the pandemic, to enable the transition to operation phase based on the original time plan. This would also enable payments to the contractor to start according to the BOT contract conditions, which was one of the major drivers for the contractor company to finish the activities on time. Despite the significant pressure due to contractual requirements, the contractor also followed the decisions made by the National Scientific Committee, most of which were not mostly in favor of a construction site. Still, some of the decisions made based on the recommendation of this committee, such as remote working whenever possible, have proven to have advantages. It was possible to perform some critical activities by staying in touch online with the foreign partners who prefer to return to their countries, participate in online tenders, and make online procurement decisions. All these also came with a certain reduction in travel costs.

In this context, the critical role of information technology (IT) and the quality of employees in related departments were visible significantly. The companies with strong information technology infrastructure adapted to the disrupted working environments that have changed due to the outbreak of the pandemic.

Discussion

This study examined the effects of the COVID-19 pandemic on a BOT project in Turkey, which was in the construction phase when the pandemic first outbroke in 2020. It is a common fact that time, cost, and quality are the primary performance criteria for the evaluation of project success (Negash & Hassan, 2020; Parker et al., 2015), and are essential elements of project management (Eydi et al., 2016) along with other indicators such as safety (Wanberg et al., 2013) and dispute (Besaiso et al., 2018). There are a myriad of studies underlying the importance of these criteria in this respect. However, the emergence of the COVID-19 pandemic brought the evaluation of these criteria to another level with its unprecedented impact in the global working environments. Investigations presented in this study showed that adverse impacts of the COVID-19 pandemic on project performance criteria were inevitable in construction projects, including mega projects procured through PPP procedures. Opinions of the contractor, a subcontractor, and OHS managers were sought to pinpoint the extent of the adverse impacts and present the adopted strategies to overcome the challenges imposed by the pandemic in a major BOT project, "1915 Çanakkale Bridge and Highway Project."

The subcontractor company stated that approximately 30% delay occurred in their activities, which resulted in a significant decrease in the estimated profit. The major reason for the delay can be related to the isolation rule of the infected and/or contacted workers, which caused the recruitment and employment of additional employees, resulting in cost overruns. OHS managers stated that the original OHS budget increased by approximately four times with the existence of COVID-19. Psychological implications were not easy to manage and keeping the work motivation was difficult with the increasing number of infected workers, bringing the necessity of health care due to side effects of the virus or staying in self-isolation which triggered psychological issues.

PPP projects have unique characteristics compared to the projects delivered with conventional methods, which can be summarized as follows: (i) involvement from public and private entities, and several international stakeholders with diverging interests that make it difficult to perform proper risk and stakeholder management (Le et al., 2019), (ii) long concession periods with risks due to the uncertainty longer than conventional projects (Zhang et al., 2019), in which changes are inevitable throughout the project lifecycle (Lam & Javed, 2015), (iii) additional financial risks with high investment amounts (Li & Zou, 2011), and (iv) receiving significant public and media attention as public projects, which requires more transparent implementation of strategic decisions (Derakhshan et al., 2019). Therefore, the impacts of COVID-19 on PPP projects can be different from projects procured through traditional delivery systems due to inherent risks and their unique natures. The experts participated in this study particularly mentioned the stricter measures addressed in the project due to the involvement of both public and international parties. Since the operation phase would start under the effects of the pandemic, potential operational uncertainties need to be considered prior to the completion of the project.

Although the interviewed stakeholders shared their opinions, all participants expressed the difficulties brought about by the measures taken due to the pandemic for the employees in common. The challenges in the procurement processes were the second highlighted issue during the interviews. The uncertainty in the early stages of the pandemic and the adverse impacts of the addressed measures on productivity significantly caused a loss of motivation among the employees during the implementation of the activities. All these unexpected and undesired factors resulted in additional costs due to the necessity of backup teams or extension of the deadlines. The subcontractor also stated that these additional costs will be considered as normal cost items in the future projects.

In general, this study showed that the impacts of the pandemic were mostly adverse, causing problems related to project performance criteria. On the other hand, it also revealed that the construction sector acted immediately to minimize these adverse impacts, particularly in PPP projects with international stakeholders and high budgets.

Implications to Theory and Practice

This study examined the impacts of COVID-19 on a mega PPP project in Turkey. The results of three semi-structured interviews have some theoretical and practical implications. First, contractors who are to bid for future PPP projects are advised to consider additional costs, particularly regarding the backup teams and improvement in their IT departments. In this respect, human resource management has become one of the key project management elements in PPP projects, not only for recruiting adequate employees but also for providing employees with necessary physical and psychological support when necessary. Hence, construction companies should invest more on human resource management and develop strategies to perform continuous improvement in human resource management activities.

During the lockdowns and the following periods, some of the employees other than the workers, who were required to be on site, had to work from home. This experience showed that a hybrid working environment is possible for construction projects up to a certain extent and the existence of central offices would be seriously evaluated in the future. Hybrid working environment might be an opportunity for construction companies to reduce office rent costs, overhead costs, and required office area. As a result of the unexpected difficulties due to "the pandemic," companies started including the additional contingencies and costs in the contracts and insurance articles as force majeure. With experience and insights gained during the pandemic, future PPP contracts can be prepared diligently due to the difficulties related to potential pandemic, lockdowns, or other challenges as a result of such extreme environments. The OHS department of construction companies should also improve their strategies and trainings related to pandemic measures in their usual training packages given the lessons learned.

Besides these, the project parties implied that the ongoing pandemic would result in the implementation of "negotiated tendering" with respect to 21(b) clause of the public procurement law (Law No: 4734) (Official Gazette, 2002), which allows the "negotiated tendering" in case of an epidemic. The interviewees suggested that a period or the extent of the pandemic should be stated in the law to ensure the quality of the projects, in which the most competitive bidders can award the contract with "open tendering" or "tendering with prequalified bidders" procedures. Hence, considering the extent and the period of the pandemic in the law can be a regulative implication of this study.

Conclusion

PPP projects have been commonly practiced in the Turkish construction industry since the 1980s with a significant acceleration in the last decade, making Turkey an experienced implementer of projects procured through several PPP models. In this study, "1915 Çanakkale Bridge and Highway Project" was selected as a case study, due its budget, context, and strict completion date of the project. The groundbreaking of the project was before the outbreak of the pandemic, the construction phase continued in this extraordinary environment and is expected to be operated under the ongoing effects of the pandemic. The project is financed by several financial institutions from 10 countries, with an investment amount of 2.7 billion USD. A number of 10,000 workers worked at the project and 396 positive cases were detected through 30,452 tests. Data regarding the impacts of COVID-19 on the project and corresponding measures related to the case study was collected through three semi-structured interviews with professionals from one subcontractor, main contractor, and the OHS department. With this approach, the impacts of COVID-19 could be examined from different perspectives such as subcontractor, contractor, and OHS sides, which supported to address a diverse range of outlooks for the same challenging environment.

The findings illustrate the measures to minimize the spread of the COVID-19 primarily included wearing face masks, maintaining social distance and limiting face-to-face meetings, providing disinfectants at the work site, and controlling entrance to work site. OHS expenditures significantly increased based on preventive actions. Some of the most outstanding lessons learned were about working from home, reducing office areas, specifying pandemic as one of the force majeure, and considering possible pandemics and their effects in future bid offers. With the pandemic, the critical roles of proper human resource management, stakeholder management, risk management, and IT infrastructure have become visible. The construction companies are advised to develop their IT departments based on the requirements of remote working such as providing software support and integrated requirements. PPP projects might impose significant and unique risks, particularly to contractors and corresponding subcontractors. Hence, these parties should work on the risk premium, particularly when bidding works in PPP projects.

References

Antwi, S. H., Getty, D., Linnane, S., & Rolston, A. (2021). COVID-19 water sector responses in Europe: A scoping review of preliminary governmental interventions. *Science of the Total Environment, 762*, 143068. https://doi.org/10.1016/j.scitotenv.2020.143068

Araya, F. (2021). Modeling the spread of COVID-19 on construction workers: An agent-based approach. *Safety Science, 133*(September 2020), 105022. https://doi.org/10.1016/j.ssci.2020.105022

Asian Development Bank. (2021). *COVID-19 and public-private partnerships in Asia and the Pacific: Guidance note*. https://creativecommons.org/licenses/by/3.0/igo/

Aygül, M., & Erdoğan, E. (2020). Arbitration on the resolution of disputes arising from public-private-partnership agreements in healthcare industry. *Ankara Hacı Bayram Veli Üniversitesi Hukuk Fakültesi Dergisi, 14*(4), 61–100.

Besaiso, H., Fenn, P., Emsley, M., & Wright, D. (2018). A comparison of the suitability of FIDIC and NEC conditions of contract in Palestine: A perspective from the industry. *Engineering, Construction and Architectural Management, 25*(2), 241–256. https://doi.org/10.1108/ECAM-10-2016-0235

Boz, S. S. (2013). Kamu özel işbirliği (ppp) modeli. *İnönü Üniversitesi Hukuk Fakültesi Dergisi, 4*(2), 277–332.

Budayan, C. (2018). Analysis of critical success factors in public private partnership projects by triangulation method: Turkey perspective. *Journal of the Faculty of Engineering and Architecture of Gazi University, 33*(3), 1029–1044. https://doi.org/10.17341/gazimmfd.416404

Ceylan, H. (2012). Analysis of occupational accidents according to the sectors in Turkey. *Gazi University Journal of Science, 25*(4), 909–918.

Cui, Q., He, L., Liu, Y., Zheng, Y., Wei, W., Yang, B., & Zhou, M. (2021, February). The impacts of COVID-19 pandemic on China's transport sectors based on the CGE model coupled with a decomposition analysis approach. *Transport Policy, 103*, 103–115. https://doi.org/10.1016/j.tranpol.2021.01.017

Demirgüç-Kunt, A., Pedraza, A., & Ruiz-Ortega, C. (2021). Banking sector performance during the COVID-19 crisis. *Journal of Banking and Finance, 133*. https://doi.org/10.1016/j.jbankfin.2021.106305

Derakhshan, R., Turner, R., & Mancini, M. (2019). Project governance and stakeholders: A literature review. *International Journal of Project Management, 37*(1), 98–116. https://doi.org/10.1016/j.ijproman.2018.10.007

Eydi, A., Farughi, H., & Abdi, F. (2016). A hybrid method based on fuzzy AHP and VIKOR for the discrete time-cost-quality trade-off problem. *Journal of Optimization in Industrial Engineering, 19*(2), 105–116.

Galanakis, C. M., Rizou, M., Aldawoud, T. M. S., Ucak, I., & Rowan, N. J. (2021). Innovations and technology disruptions in the food sector within the COVID-19 pandemic and post-lockdown era. *Trends in Food Science and Technology, 110*(July 2020), 193–200. https://doi.org/10.1016/j.tifs.2021.02.002

Gurgun, A. P., & Touran, A. (2014). Public-private partnership experience in the international arena: Case of Turkey. *Journal of Management in Engineering, 30*(6), 04014029. https://doi.org/10.1061/(asce)me.1943-5479.0000213

Jaipuria, S., Parida, R., & Ray, P. (2021). The impact of COVID-19 on tourism sector in India. *Tourism Recreation Research, 46*(2), 245–260. https://doi.org/10.1080/02508281.2020.1846971

Koc, K., Gurgun, A. P., Ozbek, M. E., Kalan, D., Clevenger, C., & Omur-Ozbek, P. (2022). Comparative analysis of work–life balance perceptions of civil engineering students. *Journal of Civil Engineering Education, 148*(2), 04021016. https://doi.org/10.1061/(ASCE)EI.2643-9115.0000057

Lam, P. T. I., & Javed, A. A. (2015). Comparative study on the use of output specifications for Australian and U.K. PPP/PFI projects. *Journal of Performance of Constructed Facilities, 29*(2), 04014061. https://doi.org/10.1061/(ASCE)CF.1943-5509.0000554

Le, P. T., Kirytopoulos, K., Chileshe, N., & Rameezdeen, R. (2019). Taxonomy of risks in PPP transportation projects: A systematic literature review. *International Journal of Construction Management, 22*(4), 1–16. https://doi.org/10.1080/15623599.2019.1615756

Li, J., & Zou, P. X. W. (2011). Fuzzy AHP-based risk assessment methodology for PPP projects. *Journal of Construction Engineering and Management, 137*(12), 1205–1209. https://doi.org/10.1061/(ASCE)CO.1943-7862.0000362

Ministry of Health. (2021). *COVID-19 information platform*. https://covid19.saglik.gov.tr/

Ministry of Transportation and Infrastructure. (2022). *1915 Çanakkale*. https://www.1915canakkale.com/

Negash, Y. T., & Hassan, A. M. (2020). Construction project success under uncertainty: Interrelations among the external environment, intellectual capital, and project attributes. *Journal of Construction Engineering and Management, 146*(10), 1–13. https://doi.org/10.1061/(ASCE)CO.1943-7862.0001912

Official Gazette. (1984). *Law No: 3096. In Law on the Authorization of Enterprises other than the Turkish Electricity Institution to Produce, Transmit, Distribute and Trade Electricity (Issue 1)*. https://www.mevzuat.gov.tr/MevzuatMetin/1.5.3096.pdf

Official Gazette. (1994). *Law No: 3996. In Law Regarding Some Investments and Services Performed within the Framework of Build-Operate-Transfer Model*. https://www.mevzuat.gov.tr/mevzuatmetin/1.5.3996.pdf

Official Gazette. (2002). *Law No: 4734. In public procurement law*. https://www.mevzuat.gov.tr/MevzuatMetin/1.5.4734.pdf

Official Gazette. (2013). *Law No 6428: In Sağlık Bakanlığınca Kamu Özel İş Birliği Modeli ile Tesis Yaptırılması, Yenilenmesi ve Hizmet Alınması ile Bazı Kanun ve Kanun Hükmünde Kararnamelerde Değişiklik Yapılması Hakkında Kanun*. https://www.mevzuat.gov.tr/MevzuatMetin/1.5.6428.pdf

Ozili, P. K. (2021). COVID-19 pandemic and economic crisis: The Nigerian experience and structural causes. *Journal of Economic and Administrative Sciences, 37*(4), 401–418. https://doi.org/10.1108/jeas-05-2020-0074

Parker, D. W., Parsons, N., & Isharyanto, F. (2015). Inclusion of strategic management theories to project management. *International Journal of Managing Projects in Business, 8*(3), 552–573. https://doi.org/10.1108/IJMPB-11-2014-0079

Presidency of the Republic of Turkey Strategy and Budget Authority. (2019). *Public-private-partnership report 2018*.

PricewaterhouseCoopers. (2020). *Leveraging public private partnerships in the GCC post COVID-19*.

Stiles, S., Golightly, D., & Ryan, B. (2021). Impact of COVID-19 on health and safety in the construction sector. *Human Factors and Ergonomics in Manufacturing, 31*(4), 425–437. https://doi.org/10.1002/hfm.20882

The World Bank. (2020). *PPPs and COVID-19 resources*. https://www.worldbank.org/en/news/factsheet/2020/04/09/ppps-and-covid-19

Top, M., & Sungur, C. (2019). Opinions and evaluations of stakeholders in the implementation of the public-private partnership (PPP) model in integrated health campuses (city hospitals) in Turkey. *International Journal of Health Planning and Management, 34*(1), e241–e263. https://doi.org/10.1002/hpm.2644

Turkish Statistical Institute (TSI). (2021). *Employment statistics by sector*. https://data.tuik.gov.tr/Bulten/Index?p=Isgucu-Istatistikleri-Ekim-2021-37491

Wanberg, J., Harper, C., Hallowell, M. R., & Rajendran, S. (2013). Relationship between construction safety and quality performance. *Journal of Construction Engineering and Management, 139*(10), 04013003. https://doi.org/10.1061/(ASCE)CO.1943-7862.0000732

World Bank Group. (2016). *Infrastructure public-private partnerships in emerging markets & developing economies 1991–2015. In World Bank Group (Issue June)*. http://booksandjournals.brillonline.com/content/journals/10.1163/156853010x510807

World Health Organization. (2020). *Turkey's response to Covid-19: First impressions (Issue July)*. https://www.euro.who.int/en/countries/turkey/publications/turkeys-response-to-covid-19-first-impressions-ankara,-turkey,-11-july-2020

World Health Organization. (2021). *Weekly epidemiological update on COVID-19*. https://www.who.int/publications/m/item/weekly-epidemiological-update-on-covid-19%2D%2D-14-december-2021

Yılmaz, İ. (2021). The improvement of Public Private Partnership in the Turkish Health Law. *İstanbul Ticaret Üniversitesi Sosyal Bilimler Dergisi, 20*(41), 807–852. https://doi.org/10.46928/iticusbe.766600

Zhang, L., Sun, X., & Xue, H. (2019). Identifying critical risks in Sponge City PPP projects using DEMATEL method: A case study of China. *Journal of Cleaner Production, 226*, 949–958. https://doi.org/10.1016/j.jclepro.2019.04.067

Part IV
PPP Stakeholder Management

Stakeholder Management for Public-Private Partnership (PPP) Hospital Projects in Australia During the COVID-19 Pandemic

Sajani Jayasuriya, Pauline Teo, Roshani Palliyaguru, and Rebecca Yang

Introduction

The COVID-19 pandemic impacted multiple sectors around the world where the World Bank estimated a 5.2% drop in the global economy (World Bank, 2020). In this setting, the pandemic has negatively impacted the performance of various global and national sectors, including the construction sector in Australia. Among all, the construction projects procured through public-private partnerships (PPP) have been under considerable stress due to the fluctuations risk and uncertainties in the market for toll roads and airports during COVID-19 (Casady & Baxter, 2020), as well as facing challenges such as construction delays and supply chain disruptions (Monteiro & Sakrak, 2020). In hospitals, there are additional operational costs in association with COVID-19, for example, disinfection of equipment and facilities, and workforce shortages (Monteiro & Sakrak, 2020). Therefore, it is worth exploring how PPP projects have been impacted by the COVID-19 pandemic.

Among the five actions proposed by PWC (2020) to mitigate the negative effects of the risks associated with long-term economic impacts from COVID-19, clear communication with all stakeholders is a key aspect. To maintain proper communication channels, it is essential to have a robust Stakeholder Management (SM) framework. The popularity of SM strategies as means of managing the post-COVID

S. Jayasuriya · P. Teo · R. Yang
School of Property, Construction and Project Management at RMIT University, Melbourne, VIC, Australia
e-mail: sajani.jayasuriya@rmit.edu.au; pauline.teo@rmit.edu.au; rebecca.yang@rmit.edu.au

R. Palliyaguru (✉)
Oxford Brookes University, Oxford, UK
e-mail: rpalliyaguru@brookes.ac.uk

© The Author(s), under exclusive license to Springer Nature Switzerland AG 2023

T. Dolla et al. (eds.), *Revisiting Public-Private Partnerships*, Contributions to Public Administration and Public Policy,
https://doi.org/10.1007/978-3-031-37015-1_13

world can be further gauged with studies conducted by Akomea-Frimpong et al. (2022) in the construction sector and in general management literature by Hill et al. (2021) and Nicolescu and Nicolescu (2022). With the involvement of multiple stakeholders whose interests are inherently contradicting in a PPP structure, it is essential to maintain a robust SM. These multiple stakeholders are affected by the pandemic in many ways due to measures related to social distancing, restrictions on projects, lockdowns, and mandatory vaccination rules. Further, it has influenced the country's law to make effective the new rules imposed by the government.

Considering the dramatic environmental changes because of COVID-19, the study presented in this chapter aims to explore how innovative SM practices in PPP projects have emerged in the Australian context. This chapter begins with a cursory review of existing knowledge on the topic of SM in the context of PPP projects, and subsequently, it elucidates the development of PPP projects in Australia and how the COVID-19 pandemic has impacted the Australian PPP market. Thirdly, a detailed analysis of innovative SM strategies adopted in a PPP project undertaken during the COVID period in Australia has been presented as a contemporary evidence-based case study, which is followed by a discussion of the findings of the case study. Finally, conclusions have been drawn, together with further research directions.

Literature Review

Stakeholder Management in Construction

According to Cleland (1994), SM is an important part of the strategic management of organisations. SM can be generally defined as the process of identifying, analysing, negotiating, and engaging stakeholders and developing relationships among stakeholders to minimise project risks, facilitate effective and timely delivery of projects, and ultimately achieve successful and acceptable outcomes for the stakeholders. Engaging with stakeholders also includes communicating and sharing information about stakeholders; developing strategies; and following up (Karlsen, 2002). SM requires a formal, structured approach for the success of a project because projects are subject to many changes and thus informal methods are inadequate (Cleland, 1994). For a successful project, SM should provide project teams with decision-making judgement. Several SM frameworks for construction projects have been proposed for project success by many authors such as Karlsen (2002) and Yang and Shen (2015).

As a result, SM has attracted the interest of many authors in the construction management field. SM is one of the most important branches of project management as well, as a project involves many temporary conflicts between stakeholders when working as a team to complete it to the client's satisfaction (Jepsen & Eskerod, 2009). Furthermore, as project stakeholders may influence projects either positively or negatively, the assessment of stakeholder influence is an important task for project managers to enhance the likelihood of project success (Cleland, 1994).

Stakeholder Management for PPP Projects

The PPP concept offers a variety of services to the general public by combining the efforts of the private and public sectors to deliver capabilities that are usually delivered by the public sector. Therefore, PPPs can be defined as "a contracting arrangement where a private party acquires the responsibility of finance and long-term maintenance or operation of a facility to provide long-term service outcomes" (Duffield et al., 2008). To meet such a delivery, private parties usually form a special-purpose vehicle to cooperatively work with public-sector organisations to achieve common goals. PPP projects bring two institutionally different organisations to operate under a single project organisation (Matinheikki et al., 2021). The differences in legal, normative, and cognitive elements of institutions (Scott, 2014) inevitably arise in these organisations when a PPP project gets underway. Furthermore, the general consensus is that the government is the most trusted sector in the community for delivering infrastructure facilities. Therefore, the risks that have embedded unquantifiable social and public values tend to be best left with the government (Chung et al., 2010). In contrast, the private sector is driven by profits, value exchange, and market competitiveness. Therefore, it is important to find ways to reconcile the interest gaps between the private and public sectors.

Furthermore, the general community is a key stakeholder in PPP projects, and it is important to keep them informed and engaged (Jayasuriya et al., 2019). Otherwise, they would feel that they are marginalised to an extent where they feel like they are outsiders to the PPP development and are only regarded as customers of the finished public liability of paying tariffs (El-Gohary et al., 2006). Chinyio and Akintoye (2008) and Kwak et al. (2009) also endorse this point for PPP projects, given the high stakeholder complexity expected due to the involvement of multiple stakeholder relationships in a PPP procurement structure. Thus, managing multi-stakeholders in a PPP structure is a complex and prolonged process that needs honest communication and trust (Henjewele et al., 2013). In their work, Jayasuriya et al. (2019) have highlighted the impacts that the poor management of stakeholder relationships has been a contributory cause of the failure of PPP projects in the global context. Jayasuriya (2017) developed an SM framework for PPP projects considering the whole life cycle of the project due to the complex nature of managing multiple stakeholder relationships in PPP projects.

SM is an essential element of the overall risk management strategy of any construction work, which has undoubtedly been very significant for PPP projects too. Generally, a PPP project consists of stakeholders such as the government; the PPP consortium, which includes the equity provider, financier, design, and construction contractor, and facilities management company; user groups; independent reviewers; and the community. Based on this setting, it is imperative that the State coordinates the participation of all relevant stakeholders, especially those with an interest in the project from a social and public standpoint, given its essentiality in SM. Given the complexity in SM of PPP projects, it is very important to get all stakeholders involved and engaged where Jayasuriya et al. (2020) have established empirically that stakeholder engagement (SE) is a key to successful PPP projects.

Stakeholder Engagement in PPP as a Key Strategy

SE attempts to minimise the conflicts between project stakeholders and to explore the project priorities clearly throughout the project life cycle through the effective involvement of project stakeholders. SE is defined as "communicate, involve, and develop relationships with stakeholders" (Chinyio & Akintoye, 2008). SE is used as a generic, inclusive term to describe the broad range of interactions between decision-makers and other stakeholders in very large projects. It can include a variety of approaches, such as one-way communication or information delivery, consultation, involvement, collaboration in decision-making, and empowered action in informal groups or formal partnerships (Department of Sustainability and Environment, 2005).

SE can be used to improve cooperation among group members, promote social learning platforms, and improve the ethical needs to maintain fairness and equity (Mathur et al., 2008). Deegan and Parkin (2011) identified two key benefits of engagement as involving information giving and consultation to improve knowledge sharing among stakeholders and to minimise stakeholder resistance by improving stakeholder participation. SE in the PPP project context has also attracted the interest of many researchers in the construction management field to develop frameworks for SE implementation for effective public involvement (e.g., El-gohary et al., 2006). However, all the above studies were undertaken pre-COVID. COVID-19 has triggered the world into new normal measures, resulting in digitalisation having a significant influence on the SE strategies as they still enable face-to-face communication, but in a different environment than the usual physical environment. Therefore, it is worth exploring how new SE strategies have emerged to respond to pandemic measures.

Context of the Inquiry

The first wave of COVID-19 infections grew in Australia in March 2020, and protective health and travel measures were imposed by the federal and state governments. To manage the pandemic in Australia, like many other countries, it tightly controlled its international borders. The state government of Victoria implemented lockdown restrictions in March and July 2020. The Australian construction sector continued to operate as it contributes to a huge proportion of Gross Domestic

Product (GDP) and workforce in the Australian economy. According to the Reserve Bank of Australia (2022), the construction industry has generated approximately 7.6% of the Australian GDP in 2020 and 7.4% in 2021. To stabilise the economy during the pandemic, the government relied on infrastructure investment as a stimulus package (Grimsey & Cotter, 2020). In response to COVID-19, the Australian Government announced in June 2020 that it is providing a stimulus package of AUD 1 billion (in total) to any new projects that can commence within the next 6 months and in addition AUD 500 million only for Targeted Road Safety Works delivered by states and territories that can be completed within the next 12 months (Department of Infrastructure, Transport, Regional Development, Communications and the Arts, 2022). PPP is a popular procurement strategy to deliver major infrastructure in Australia, and the PPP projects reached a total amount of USD 69 billion between 2000 to 2019 in Australia (IMC Europe, 2022). Figure 1 shows the number of PPP projects and project values from 2000 to 2021 in Australia (Infrastructure Partnerships Australia, 2022).

According to Fig. 1, there is no evidence that COVID-19 has affected the trend of Australian PPP projects. This point was confirmed by the Asian Development Bank (2021), as there were not many PPP projects cancelled due to COVID-19, although there is a notable slowdown of government projects globally. Furthermore, with the onset of COVID-19, bidders had to price tender bids amidst a lot of uncertainties. It was very challenging for construction companies to forecast the risks of increasing supply costs associated with lump sum contracts with many unknowns at the time. In fact, several large to small construction companies had gone into insolvency and were put under the management of Licensed Insolvency Practitioners after the major lockdowns were lifted.

In this study, a PPP hospital case study project in its request for proposal phase during the pandemic was to be selected because the health sector was one of the most heavily impacted sectors with pandemic measures to cater to the high demand. Thus, the complexities of managing a higher volume of stakeholders involved in hospital projects than in normal times due to the massive influx of COVID-19

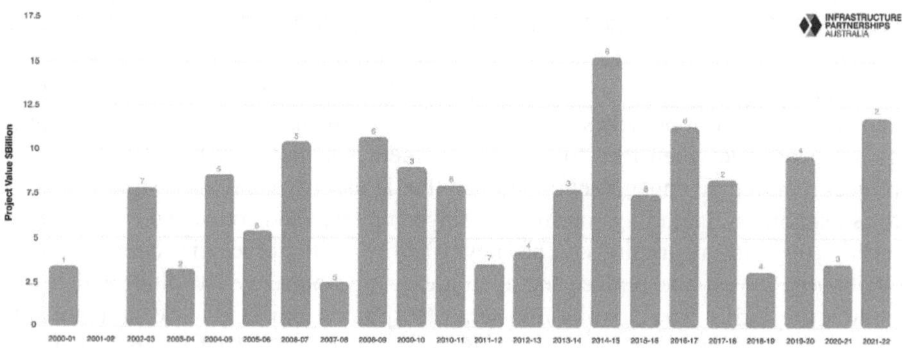

Fig. 1 Trend of PPP projects in Australia. (Source obtained from: Infrastructure Partnerships Australia, 2022)

patients to the hospitals and the interest developed among the general public themselves for new and renovation work of hospital projects were instrumental in selecting a PPP hospital project as a case study. The case study demonstrates how it addresses the SM challenges it faced during the pandemic.

Research Methods

In this study, the case study method is adopted, as it enables an in-depth understanding of the contemporary phenomena within its real-life context (Yin, 2009). This major strength is beneficial in studying the complex nature of both the construction industry and major infrastructure procurement in the public sector. The case study involves data gathered from three semi-structured interviews undertaken with senior personnel in Victorian Health Building Authority (VHBA) within the project who have been involved in the project since inception. Further, secondary data were gathered from publicly available information about the project. The case study predominantly involved collating data about the background and special features of the project, that is, how the project was impacted by COVID-19, and the SE strategies adopted by the project, with a special reference to the process of the project's transformation into the new normal with the pandemic. Thematic analysis was then adopted to evaluate the collected information where different themes were recognised to understand and interpret the views of the interviewees and the publicly available data on multiple websites. The themes were driven based on theory generated from the empirical data (inductive) or based on prior research-driven approaches (deductive) (Boyatzis, 1998), which are discussed below under four themes.

Case Study Description

A hospital in Melbourne was selected as the case study, which is known as the New Footscray Hospital. The total estimated investment of the New Footscray Hospital is AUD 1.5 billion which is the largest PPP health infrastructure being delivered in Victoria. The project is an exemplary case study to examine the impact of the pandemic on its SM approaches, as SE was carried out in the midst of the ongoing global pandemic when face-to-face engagement was not possible. The landmark project required an engagement approach that is inclusive and accessible to ensure the stakeholders, including community, stayed updated and connected to the project during ongoing restrictions. The new facility will serve the community in Melbourne's west and replace the ageing existing Footscray Hospital, which was built in the 1950s. The existing Footscray Hospital is expected to be shut and sold for housing when the replacement facility opens in about 2025 (Pallisco, 2019). The new hospital is designed to provide 500 inpatient beds, acute facilities, specialist facilities, clinical support spaces, car parking, teaching, training, and research spaces. It will be a world-class hospital providing complementary facilities such as childcare, a medical clinic, consulting suites, a retail pharmacy, a gymnasium, food and beverage outlets, small retail, and central open space together with the ordinary services delivered by a typical hospital. The project is being procured as an "availability-based" PPP under the Partnerships Victoria policy. Based on Partnerships Victoria (2018), in an availability-based PPP model, the private finance used to build the asset is recovered by the payment from the government over the operational phase of the project, ensuring continuing availability of the facility. The State government of Victoria undertook extensive market sounding to explore the suitability of the PPP model with the relevant industry participants, including sponsors and third-party equity investors, debt financiers, design and construction contractors, and facilities management contractors. With the feedback from the above parties, the State confirmed that a PPP model would provide the best value for money for all parties concerned. Figure 2 shows the project timeline.

Accordingly, the project was started in 2019, which is when the community consultative committee was formed. The committee was established to provide a forum for local community members to participate in the development of the new hospital through open dialogue and consultation. The project was at the Expressions of Interest (EoI) stage in June 2019 and, following the evaluation of EOIs, three consortia were shortlisted in October 2019. With COVID-19 restrictions being imposed in March 2020, the tender process was temporarily paused for approximately two months to allow for the redeployment of the project's public and private resources to the State's response to the COVID-19 pandemic. Once the state of COVID-19 stabilised in Victoria and restrictions started to ease, the tender process recommenced in June 2020. As such, this project was heavily impacted by COVID-19 as by the time the shortlisted bidders were pricing the bids, it was in the midst of uncertainty given the many prevailing unknowns at that time. With the social distancing measures, almost all the face-to-face engagement activities were also hibernated. Figure 3 shows the stakeholder map for the project following the contract award in March 2021.

The State is the lead stakeholder for the project and is responsible for signing the project deed and ancillary project documents. The Minister for Health is given the authority to execute the contract on behalf of the State. Therefore, the Minister for

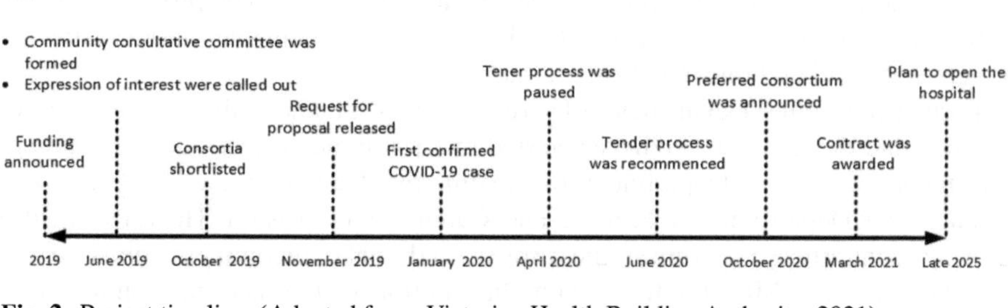

Fig. 2 Project timeline. (Adapted from: Victorian Health Building Authority, 2021)

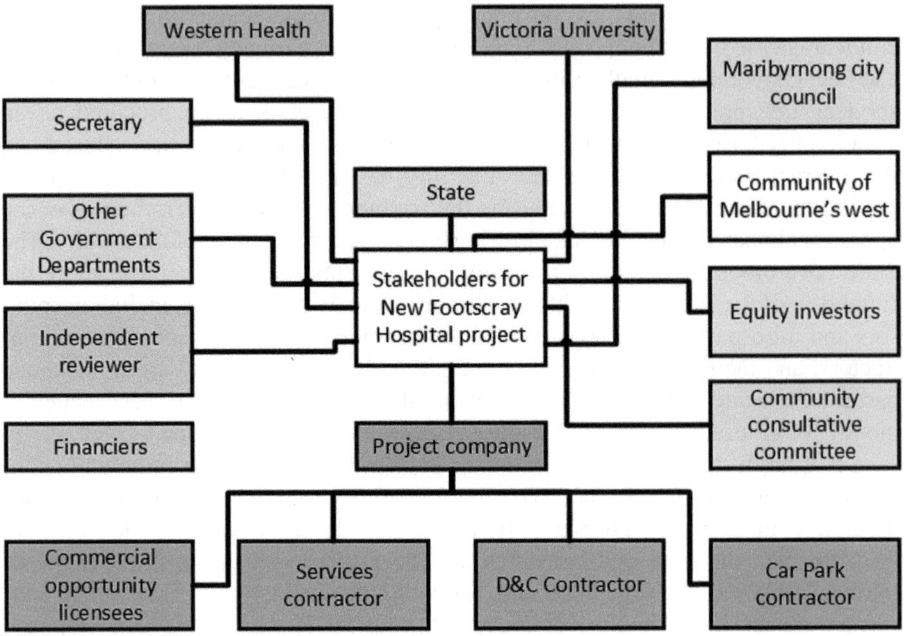

Fig. 3 Stakeholder map. (Adapted from: Victorian Health Building Authority, 2021)

Health is accountable to ensure the State's project objectives are met. The Secretary has signatory power for specific project documents. The Minister for Health has transferred the responsibility for management of the project, including management of risks associated with the project, to the VHBA which is within the Department of Health. These aspects include SE; the conduct of the tender process; securing relevant planning approvals; oversight of project delivery; and ongoing contract management during the operational phase. Western Health is also a key stakeholder in the project as it is they that are going to be operating and provide all clinical services at the new hospital. Upon completion of the project, Western Health will be a lessee of the hospital and deliver the clinical services at the new hospital. The PPP consortium includes the project company, finance company, D&C contractor, services contractors, car park contractor, equity investors, and financiers. The project company is the counterparty to the project deed and therefore is responsible for delivering the project as agreed and thus must enter a range of contracts.

Furthermore, the Department of Treasury and Finance, the Department of Premier, and the Cabinet also have a vested interest in the project. As such, the representatives from the Department of Health, the Department of Treasury and Finance, the Department of Premier and Cabinet, and Western Health formed a steering committee to oversee the project and make recommendations to the Secretary and the Minister for Health. In addition to the steering committee, a Project Planning Team was established with representatives from VHBA, Western Health, and the Department of Treasury and Finance to report directly to the Steering

Committee via the New Footscray Hospital Project Director. Victoria University has committed to funding part of the project, where the project company will develop some additional research and educational space and a pedestrian footbridge. Finally, the community of Melbourne's West is considered a major stakeholder in the project. The next section presents the SE strategies that have emerged from the project case study in response to the pandemic measures.

Results

Online Tools in Engaging with Bidders and User Groups

Based on the Partnerships Victoria policy, any PPP project must adopt an interactive tender process where a series of workshops are held involving the state, representatives of the state, and the individual private sector tenderers. Usually, between three and ten workshops are recommended by the Partnerships Victoria policy, consisting of technical, service specification, and commercial clarifications. Upon resumption of the tender process in June 2020, the project team was required to shift swiftly to utilise online modes of communication and online tools, including "Microsoft Teams", for the remainder of the interactive tender workshops although the majority of them were held in person before the temporary suspension. It was a huge learning curve, especially given the potential probity and confidentiality risks presented by online modes of communication with the shortlisted bidders. Furthermore, probity risk in an online setting had been carefully managed. According to the Partnerships Victoria policy, maintaining independence and impartiality in any transaction, establishing an equitable and respectful dialogue between parties, managing all project documents/information in an equitable and respectful manner, and managing confidentiality need to be always considered.

For the user groups, there was an initial challenge to transition from face-to-face sessions into an online environment within a very short amount of time. However, the project team was able to manage this challenge and adopt online tools to facilitate the inputs from the various user groups. One of the key users in the case study is Western Health. The hospital is designed to have more than 500 inpatient beds, as well as a range of acute and sub-acute services. Therefore, it was critical for the project to engage with Western Health and their staff especially during both the tender and development phase. Although the clinicians were focused on responding to the service demands presented by COVID-19, it was necessary to get input from the clinicians on the design and the functional planning aspects of the project, and online methods were utilised. Online meetings were mostly carried out as they provided flexibility in engaging with clinicians who are often time poor. Further, the functional design of the hospital has been adopted to respond to lessons learned by Western Health during the COVID-19 pandemic in areas such as air ventilation, waste management, cleaning regime, access, and the ability to isolate the wards to pandemic wards when needed. The following design changes were incorporated to respond to future pandemics.

- Designating expansion areas for the intensive care unit.
- Designing some inpatient unit wards to operate in pandemic mode and allowing for increased capacity to treat critically ill or infectious patients.
- Designing the emergency department to ensure it can continue to operate safely and efficiently during a pandemic by including a clear expansion zone and a pre-triage streaming area.
- Provision of an ambulatory clinic area that can operate as a pandemic clinic.

Therefore, the project team has made a commendable effort to engage with the bidders and user groups during the pandemic with quick adoption of online tools. The flexibility in the online tools was a greater advantage for the project team when engaging with the user groups.

Virtual Engagement Room for Stakeholder Engagement

The vision for the new Footscray Hospital is to be an exemplary and enduring tertiary hospital that enables delivery of world-class health care to the community of Melbourne's west. While a hospital first and foremost, it will also be a catalyst for change, supporting the development of a broader health, education, research, and community precinct, and as such it is important to understand what the neighbourhood community expects. VHBA had carried out extensive community consultation, such as "pop-up" information sessions at popular shopping centres, online surveys, community engagement sessions, and community information sessions. The feedback from the sessions helped to formulate the meaning of a new hospital to the community based on their culture, expectations, and issues. It had helped the VHBA and the project company to prioritise the main ideas and the vision for the hospital's important spaces.

Community consultations had commenced prior to COVID-19, and a community consultation committee was established in June 2019 to gather the local community's input into the project planning and development. They had met face-to-face as well as several online sessions, including an induction session and two working sessions to generate and prioritise ideas for the hospital. All the above consultation activities with the community helped to attract valuable information which was circulated among the shortlisted bidders to consider in the design, construction finance, and maintenance of the new hospital.

However, COVID-19 began shortly after, and the implementation of the hard lockdown in Melbourne had created significant challenges for the project communications team to enable effective communications with various stakeholders. Once the contract had been awarded, the project team was not able to undertake planned "meet the builder" sessions in a physical location due to the COVID-19 restrictions.

Nevertheless, it is vital to arrange such an engagement to showcase the project to the community. In this context, the project team had to create an innovative tool to promote the project and the final design to the community.

To support the engagement events with COVID-19 restrictions, VHBA engaged a digital and creative firm to create a dynamic and bespoke virtual consultation approach to achieve its aim of providing information to and enabling engagement with the public. Through ongoing consultations with VHBA, the digital firm designed an innovative and adaptive digital virtual engagement room, which consists of a digital replica of the in-person engagement space. The user experience is highly prioritised, and the user interface is made easy to use for all age groups. The users can experience extraordinary functionality and visual content, and a realistic environment with shadows and lighting. For example, the users can navigate through all the zones in the room easily. A dynamic zoom feature is incorporated to allow the 3D model to rotate on a 360-degree axis to view all the areas in large space. Static and dynamic assets were also featured in the digital space.

The key zones in the virtual engagement room are described in the following and are snapshotted in Fig. 4.

- A "Welcome area" with videos providing a project overview, welcome messages from the project directors, and introductions to the construction timeline and renders of the design.
- A "Meet the Builder" video which introduces some of the key personnel from the main construction company.
- Learn about the design, which provides an opportunity for the public to learn about the hospital design and construction and engage in three-dimensional interactions via a 3D tour of the hospital.
- A community corner which summarises the current community engagement; including the involvement of the Community Consultative Committee, a "colour in your community" activity for children, and a snapshot of the Footscray community and their involvement in the project. This section showcased how the community played a key role in the development of the hospital.

Figure 4 illustrates the snapshots of the engagement room.

Diversity and inclusion were featured through avatars and to reflect the demographics of the community. Translations and duplications of the room were available in Simplified Chinese and Vietnamese to cater to the two largest culturally and linguistically diverse communities in Footscray. Accessibility is a key feature of the digital engagement space, and especially for the health sector. The project communications team utilised a variety of channels to promote the virtual engagement room to the community. Initially, the engagement room was promoted via targeted social media campaigns on VHBA channels (Facebook, Twitter, and LinkedIn) in English, Simplified Chinese, and Vietnamese. In addition, the project communications team used a combination of communication tools such as project webpages, enterprise data management systems to project databases, and project newsletters. To ensure an extensive outreach to the community, communication packs were sent

Fig. 4 Engagement room. (Source: Victorian Health Building Authority, 2022)

out, which included key messages, images, videos, and posters to assist the community members to spread the message to their networks. The website is also mobile responsive and accessible from all devices. An accessible version of the virtual room information was also created to ensure inclusivity of engagement, such as the visually impaired community and translated to other culturally and linguistically diverse communities. The virtual engagement room had offered interactive and innovative tools for engaging and informing the community about the design and construction of the new hospital at different project milestones. The New Footscray hospital's virtual engagement room is one of the winners of the GOV Design Awards 2022 as part of the Melbourne Design Awards Elevate campaign for its innovative digital engagement platform.

Online Feedback Platforms for Continuous Engagement

The time capsule in the virtual engagement room provided an opportunity for the community to submit their ideas for a time capsule to be buried on the site of the new hospital. Figure 5 gives a snapshot of the time capsule. Time capsule ideas and suggestions were captured through a direct link to a dedicated Engage Victoria page. The capsule had the capacity to collect both qualitative and quantitative data. Throughout the 6 months that it was active for response, over 4000 people had utilised the time capsule to submit their feedback. According to the engagement team, they will meet only around 200 people in a regular face-to-face arrangement. The community was also able to submit questions and feedback directly to the project team via direct links embedded within the online feedback platform. The use of the innovative online tool has benefited the team with a tremendous improvement in the levels of engagement. It had an intelligent dashboard for VHBA to report the key findings from the feedback provided by the users. The feedback received via the

Fig. 5 Time capsule. (Source from: Victorian Health Building Authority, 2022)

virtual engagement room from the community and stakeholders was very positive as per the interviewees. This feedback and responses from the community were shared with the Project Company. After 6 months, the community was not able to submit the questions and feedback where the time capsule was disabled. However, the community can access the engagement room via the VHBA website if any community member needs to know about the project.

Risk Mitigating Strategies in the PPP Contract

In addition to the strategies implemented, there was a need to ensure that the potential economic risks were adequately considered and incorporated to ensure a robust relationship between the public and private sector. In this case study, the shortlisted bidders were in the process of finalising bids when COVID-19 hit Australia in early 2020. There were significant uncertainties in the market related to financial risks, supply chain issues, resource constraints, and pandemic directions leading to reduction in the risk appetite in the market at the time.

On resumption of the tender process in June 2020, the State incorporated a relief regime in respect of pandemic directions during the concession term, in relation to COVID-19 and future pandemics. This was agreed and negotiated by the parties and constitutes as a key departure from a standard Partnerships Victoria PPP Project Deed. The following specific risk-sharing regime was incorporated to mitigate the risks associated with COVID-19 and future pandemics (Victorian Health Building Authority, 2021):

- Occurrence of the pandemic – Risk of additional cost or delay resulting from a pandemic direction in *existence* at contract close during the *development* phase to be shared between the State and the project company.
- Risk of additional cost or delay resulting from a *new* pandemic direction after contract close during the *development* phase was assigned to the State.
- Risk of additional cost or delay resulting from a pandemic direction during the *operational* phase was assigned to the State.

The selected bidder was able to meet all the state's requirements for the project and its proposal includes several additional benefits for the State, hospital users, and the broader community. Its project value is AUD 582 million less than the State's public sector comparator.

Discussion

From the case study there were many lessons learnt for the better implementation of major infrastructure PPP projects during COVID-19 for SM practices. A project's success is dependent on how well the stakeholder concerns are taken into consideration during the project planning, designing, construction, operation, and maintenance, and the effectiveness of the adoption of online platforms and tools for SM could be dependent on the phase of the project life cycle. Due to the complex nature of stakeholder relationships in PPP projects, it is important to have continuous information sharing with the stakeholders to build strong relationships, throughout the whole project life cycle.

Engagement with stakeholders in the future could evolve into a hybrid mode where digital means will play a major role in SE. The study found the importance of having face-to-face information sessions at the beginning of the project. The public has the view that infrastructure projects should be delivered by the government (Matinheikki et al., 2021), and when the private sector is involved, protests may arise if effective community engagement is not carried out (De Schepper et al., 2014). Okdie et al. (2011) confirmed that face-to-face communication is critical in understanding social indicators, leading to reduced ambiguity. Therefore, face-to-face meetings are essential, especially during the initial stages of the project to build trust among stakeholders. The initial face-to-face meetings were helpful in preventing disengagement during the subsequent online sessions. During the online sessions, there could be a tendency for participants to stay in the background unless being called out. To avoid such disengagement, it is essential to facilitate online meetings for effective two-way communications with clearly set priorities.

The usage of Virtual Reality (VR) representation of the built asset provides an immersive environment for the stakeholders and enables active SE to occur (Grudzewski et al., 2018). According to Viglia et al. (2018), conventional practices of photos and videos may not provide an effective understanding of the project. Although VR has been extensively used for SE in other sectors such as real estate (Juan et al., 2018; Ozacar et al., 2017), its use in construction was limited prior to the pandemic (Delgado et al., 2020). Virtual means of engagement will stimulate the experience by providing ease of access for people that are traditionally hard to engage in a face-to-face setting, such as vulnerable groups, culturally and linguistically diverse community groups, the young and old, and full-time and shift workers. Furthermore, engagement spaces provide the community and stakeholders the opportunity to engage independently at their own pace to understand the impact of the project. The virtual environment provides insights and evaluation of communication through real-time data insights. Hence, the usage of VR has transformed the means of community engagement by enhancing visualisation and allowing them to contribute towards the project in a more convenient and relaxed manner.

Finally, the risk-sharing regime was a significant strategy undertaken to keep the relationship between both public and private parties robust. Effective risk-sharing helps protecting the project company in dealing with the risks arising from uncertainty and price fluctuations. Otherwise, the potential collapse of the project due to the pandemic could likely trigger force majeure contractual provisions (Casady & Baxter, 2020). Xia et al. (2018) propose to manage risks and stakeholders in a holistic and integrated way to enhance project performance. Therefore, effective risk management strategies can lead to a more robust SM framework.

Conclusion

The COVID-19 pandemic had a profoundly negative influence on many sectors around the world where the construction sector is one of the hardest hit sectors. There was no exception in the Australian construction industry, where PPP projects in various stages of project life cycles were experiencing difficulties due to fluctuating risk profiles and uncertainties caused by COVID-19 restrictions imposed by the government. PPP projects have complex stakeholder relationships which necessitates the use of effective and efficient SM techniques, without which it is impossible to handle the diverse demands and desires of stakeholders. The case study addressed within this book chapter demonstrates the possibility of enhancing SM and SE through online platforms and tools. The case study demonstrates the successful implementation of a virtual engagement room for community engagement in a context where face-to-face physical sessions with the public and other stakeholders such as clinicians were not possible. From the case study, it was found that face-to-face meetings during the initial stages of the project were essential in building trust among stakeholders. It is recommended that future projects are recommended with a hybrid mode of SE where an engagement strategy that promotes innovation at its best is essential so that projects can move forward irrespective of any unanticipated environmental changes.

Implications to Practice

The pandemic was an eye-opener for many practitioners with the huge uptake in the usage of online methods of SM. As such, SM has become more agile where the capabilities are all set, and the staff have been trained to meet online in future. The digital meetings gave more flexibility for some stakeholders, with reduced travel time. However, online methods of engagement may lead to diminished relationships among stakeholders. Therefore, face-to-face communication is recommended during initial stages of project life cycle, while online means of engagement provided better results in later stages. It is recommended to have a hybrid SM for projects moving out of the pandemic. Further, the proposed risk-sharing regime would avoid any possible collapse of relationships in PPP projects in case of future pandemics.

Implications to Theory

The current SM theories discussed in section "Literature Review" are not sophisticated in catering to a pandemic environment. The study found that hybrid means of engagement provide better results in the future. As such, future SM frameworks should consider embedding online components into the system. It is timely to develop a hybrid SM framework together with the implementation strategies for construction projects. Thus, the use of innovative online platforms and virtual reality tools could benefit PPP project teams with tremendous improvements in all levels of engagement. The success of the adoption of online platforms and tools for SE is something left to be assessed in the future by establishing appropriate key performance indicators. Finally, further research is required to explore technological solutions dealing with probity issues that may occur in the online mode.

Acknowledgements The authors would like to acknowledge VHBA for the support provided in participating in the study's interview to share their valuable experience of the New Footscray Hospital Project. However, all the analysis and comments are those of the authors alone and do not necessarily reflect the considered views of VHBA or the Department of Health.

References

Akomea-Frimpong, I., Jin, X., Osei-Kyei, R., & Tumpa, R. J. (2022). A critical review of public–private partnerships in the COVID-19 pandemic: Key themes and future research agenda. *Smart and Sustainable Built Environment*. (ahead-of-print).

Asian Development Bank. (2021). *COVID-19 and Public–Private Partnerships in Asia and the Pacific: Guidance Note*. https://www.adb.org/publications/covid-19-public-private-partnerships-asia-pacific-guidance-note. Accessed 10 July 2022.

Boyatzis, R. E. (1998). *Transforming qualitative information: Thematic analysis and code development*. Sage Publications, Inc.

Casady, C. B., & Baxter, D. (2020). Pandemics, public-private partnerships (PPPs), and force majeure| COVID-19 expectations and implications. *Construction Management and Economics, 38*(12), 1077–1085.

Chinyio, E. A., & Akintoye, A. (2008). Practical approaches for engaging stakeholders: Findings from the UK. *Construction Management and Economics, 26*(6), 591–599.

Chung, D., Hensher, D. A., & Rose, J. M. (2010). Toward the betterment of risk allocation: Investigating risk perceptions of Australian stakeholder groups to public–private-partnership toll-road projects. *Research in Transportation Economics, 30*(1), 43–58.

Cleland, D. I. (1994). *Project management: Strategic design and implementation* (2nd ed.). McGraw-hill.

De Schepper, S., Dooms, M. & Haezendonck, E. (2014). Stakeholder dynamics and responsibilities in Public–Private Partnerships: A mixed experience. International Journal of Project Management, 32 (7), 1210–1222.

Deegan, B., & Parkin, J. (2011). Planning cycling networks: Human factors and design processes. *Proceedings of the ICE-Engineering Sustainability, 164*(1), 85–93.

Delgado, J. M. D., Oyedele, L., Demian, P., & Beach, T. (2020). A research agenda for augmented and virtual reality in architecture, engineering and construction. *Advanced Engineering Informatics, 45*, 101122.

Department of Infrastructure, Transport, Regional Development, Communications and the Arts. (2022). *Infrastructure investment response to COVID-19*. https://investment.infrastructure.gov.au/about/national-initiatives/response-to-covid-19.aspx. Accessed 18 August 2022.

Department of Sustainability and Environment. (2005). *Effective engagement: Building relationships with community and other stakeholders*. The Community Engagement Network, Resource and Regional Services Division.

Duffield, C., Raisbeck, P., & Xu, M. (2008). Report on the performance of PPP projects in Australia when compared with a representative sample of traditionally procured infrastructure projects. In: *National PPP forum—Benchmarking study, Phase II*.

El-Gohary, N. M., Osman, H., & El-Diraby, T. E. (2006). Stakeholder management for public private partnerships. *International Journal of Project Management, 24*(7), 595–604.

Grimsey, D., & Cotter, S. (2020). *Where to now for the PPP model*? https://www.ey.com/en_au/strategy-transactions/where-to-now-for-the-ppp-model. Accessed 10 July 2022.

Grudzewski, F., Awdziej, M., Mazurek, G., & Piotrowska, K. (2018). Virtual reality in marketing communication–the impact on the message, technology and offer perception–empirical study. *Economics and Business Review, 4*(3), 36–50.

Henjewele, C., Fewings, P., & Rwelamila, P. D. (2013). De-marginalising the public in PPP projects through multi-stakeholders management. *Journal of Financial Management of Property and Construction, 18*(3), 210–231.

Hill, R., Sarkani, S., & Mazzuchi, T. A. (2021). Managing in a post-COVID-19 world: A stakeholder network perspective. *IEEE Engineering Management Review, 49*(1), 63–71.

IMC Europe. (2022). *Australia PPP market 2020*. https://www.infrapppworld.com/report/australia-ppp-market-2019. Accessed 10 July 2022.

Infrastructure Partnerships Australia. (2022). *Public Private Partnerships: Chart Centre*. https://infrastructure.org.au/chart-group/public-private-partnerships/. Accessed 10 July 2022.

Jayasuriya, S. (2017). A systematic stakeholder management framework for managing public private partnership projects in Australia (Doctoral dissertation, RMIT University).

Jayasuriya, S., Zhang, K., & Yang, R. (2019). Challenges in public private partnerships in construction industry: A review and further research directions. *Built Environment Project and Asset Management, 9*, 172–185.

Jayasuriya, S., Zhang, K., & Yang, R. (2020). Exploring the impact of stakeholder management strategies on managing issues in PPP projects. *International Journal of Construction Management, 20*, 666–678.

Jepsen, A. L., & Eskerod, P. (2009). Stakeholder analysis in projects: Challenges in using current guidelines in the real world. *International Journal of Project Management, 27*(4), 335–343.

Juan, Y. K., Chen, H. H., & Chi, H. Y. (2018). Developing and evaluating a virtual reality-based navigation system for pre-sale housing sales. *Applied Sciences, 8*(6), 952.

Karlsen, J. T. (2002). Project Stakeholder Management. *Engineering Management Journal, 14*(4), 19–24.

Kwak, Y. H., Chih, Y., & Ibbs, C. W. (2009). Towards a comprehensive understanding of public private partnerships for infrastructure development. *California Management Review, 51*(2), 51–78.

Mathur, V. N., Price, A. D., & Austin, S. (2008). Conceptualizing stakeholder engagement in the context of sustainability and its assessment. *Construction Management and Economics, 26*(6), 601–609.

Matinheikki, J., Naderpajouh, N., Aranda-Mena, G., Jayasuriya, S., & Teo, P. (2021). Befriending aliens: Institutional complexity and organizational responses in infrastructure public–private partnerships. *Project Management Journal, 52*(5), 453–470.

Monteiro, R. & Sakrak, O. A. (2020). *What is the COVID-19 crisis impact on Public-Private Partnerships*. https://blog-pfm.imf.org/pfmblog/2020/04/-what-is-the-covid-19-crisis-impact-on-public-private-partnerships-.html#_ftn1. Accessed 10 July 2022.

Nicolescu, O., & Nicolescu, C. (2022). *Stakeholder management and social responsibility: Concepts, approaches and tools in the covid context*. Taylor & Francis.

Okdie, B. M., Guadagno, R. E., Bernieri, F. J., Geers, A. L., & Mclarney-Vesotski, A. R. (2011). Getting to know you: Face-to-face versus online interactions. *Computers in Human Behavior, 27*(1), 153–159.

Ozacar, K., Ortakci, Y., Kahraman, I., Durgut, R., & Karas, I. R. (2017). A low-cost and lightweight 3D interactive real estate-purposed indoor virtual reality application. *ISPRS Annals of the Photogrammetry, Remote Sensing and Spatial Information Sciences, 4*, 307.

Pallisco, M. (2019). *Victorian government shortlists three groups to develop $1.5 billion Footscray Hospital*. https://www.realestatesource.com.au/government-shortlists-three-groups-to-develop-1-5-billion-footscray-hospital/#:~:text=The%20existing%20Footscray%20Hospital%2C%20built,to%20be%20announced%20next%20year. Accessed 10 July 2022.

Partnerships Victoria. (2018). *Partnerships Victoria. Availability PPP PV standard project deed – Guidance notes*. https://www.dtf.vic.gov.au/sites/default/files/2018-03/Availability%20PPP%20PV%20Standard%20Project%20Deed%20-%20Guidance%20Notes.DOCX#:~:text=An%20availability%20model%20is%20a,continuing%20availability%20of%20the%20asset%20. Accessed 10 July 2022.

PWC. (2020). *Five actions can help mitigate risks to infrastructure projects amid COVID-19*. https://www.pwc.com/gx/en/industries/capital-projects-infrastructure/publications/infrastructure-covid-19.html. Accessed 10 July 2022.

Reserve Bank of Australia. (2022). Reserve Bank of Australia, https://www.rba.gov.au/. Accessed 10 July 2022.

Scott, W. R. (2014). *Institutions and organizations: Ideas, interests and identities* (4th ed.). Sage Publications.

Victorian Health Building Authority. (2021). *New Footscray Hospital Project Summary*. https://www.dtf.vic.gov.au/sites/default/files/document/New%20Footscray%20Hospital%20-%20Project%20Summary.pdf. Accessed 10 July 2022.

Victorian Health Building Authority. (2022). *New Footscray Hospital Virtual tour*. https://consultationspace.com/VHBA/NewFootscrayHospital/. Accessed 10 July 2022.

Viglia, G., Pera, R., & Bigné, E. (2018). The determinants of stakeholder engagement in digital platforms. *Journal of Business Research, 89*, 404–410.

World Bank. (2020). *COVID-19 to Plunge Global Economy into Worst Recession since World War II*. https://www.worldbank.org/en/news/press-release/2020/06/08/covid-19-to-plunge-global-economy-into-worst-recession-since-world-war-ii. Accessed 10 July 2022.

Xia, N., Zou, P. X., Griffin, M. A., Wang, X., & Zhong, R. (2018). Towards integrating construction risk management and stakeholder management: A systematic literature review and future research agendas. *International Journal of Project Management, 36*(5), 701–715.

Yang, R. J., & Shen, G. Q. P. (2015). Framework for stakeholder management in construction projects. Journal of Management in Engineering, 31(4), 4014064. https://doi.org/https://doi.org/10.1061/(ASCE)ME.1943-5479.0000285.

Yin, R. K. (2009). *Case study research: Design and methods* (4th ed.). Sage Publications.

Part V
Renegotiation

Effects of Disruption Circumstances on Contract Renegotiation of Australian PPPs

Shijing Liu, Anthony Mills, and Chunlu Liu

Introduction

Australia is a world leader in constructing large-scale infrastructure projects by public–private partnership (PPPs). The development of PPPs in Australia can be divided into two generations (Jefferies et al., 2006). In the 1980s, the operations of Australian PPP projects achieved satisfactory results. Starting from the 1990s, the government began to introduce large amounts of private capital and, at the same time, the construction and operation risks were transferred to the private sector. Since 2000, Australia has learned from experience and formulated a special legal framework and utilised the advantages of both the public and private sectors to achieve a win–win situation. The establishment of Partnership Victoria in 2001 is generally regarded as the watershed. Another milestone was the publication of the National PPP Guidelines in 2008. The Guidelines identified the access principle of 'value for money' for PPP projects and established a whole-process performance assessment and supervision system, along with standard risk allocations. As a unified national framework, the Guidelines enabled the public and private sectors to work together to improve public service delivery (Infrastructure Australia, 2008). Across the country, state governments have formulated detailed local jurisdictional requirements which apply in conjunction with the national ones.

S. Liu
School of Management Science and Engineering, Shandong University of Finance and Economics, Jinan, China
e-mail: lsj2020@sdufe.edu.cn

A. Mills (✉) · C. Liu
School of Architecture and Built Environment, Deakin University, Geelong, Australia
e-mail: anthony.mills@deakin.edu.au; chunlu.liu@deakin.edu.au

© The Author(s), under exclusive license to Springer Nature Switzerland AG 2023

T. Dolla et al. (eds.), *Revisiting Public-Private Partnerships*,
Contributions to Public Administration and Public Policy,
https://doi.org/10.1007/978-3-031-37015-1_14

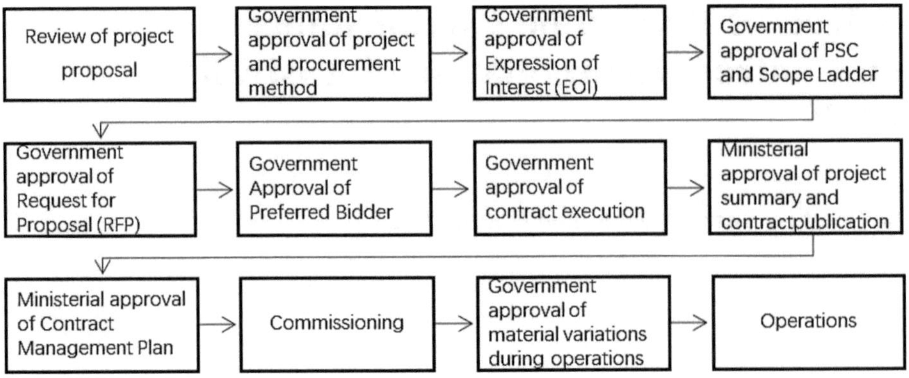

Fig. 1 Approval process for PPP projects

In the National Guidelines, a PPP is considered a potential procurement method for infrastructure or asset projects with capital investment over $50 million. In some cases, projects below the $50 million threshold may also be suitable for PPP if they provide sufficient value for money. The characteristics of specific types of PPP contracts are different and thus the payment mechanisms are also different. For example, most BOT projects are user-pays while DBFO projects are generally government-pays. PPP contracts usually have modification regimes to deal with variations throughout the concession period which contain a methodology calculating the potential financial change and impact on the performance of the project (Donnelly et al., 2015). There are a range of non-litigious dispute resolution methods, including negotiation through a dispute resolution panel, determination by an independent expert and arbitration. The approval process for a PPP project is shown in Fig. 1.

The PPP market in Australia presents differences in terms of geographical location. The three major states along the east coast – New South Wales, Queensland and Victoria – occupy the top three places in the implementation of Australian PPP projects. PPP projects implemented in these three states comprise over two-thirds of the total number and over 80% of the overall project value, which implies that the implementation of PPP projects is closely associated with the social and economic development of the states. At present, PPP has been applied to multiple infrastructure areas in Australia, such as road, rail, social facilities and water and waste.

COVID-19 in Australia

In the early days of the pandemic, most countries adopted isolation measures, there were a large number of shutdowns and the global economy experienced a recession. At the end of 2020, vaccines began to be used. Over 95% people aged 16 and over are fully vaccinated in Australia (Department of Health of Australia, 2022b). It is noted in the Australian Government budget review for the year 2020–21 that commitments in response to COVID-19 now total more than $16 billion, while new commitments will be around $4.9 billion. There will be $1.9 billion spent over two years to secure access to two dedicated COVID-19 vaccines and to facilitate access to alternative vaccines which are being developed worldwide. An additional $1.1 billion in funding is being provided to support public and private hospital activities during the pandemic. States and territories are being supported by the federal government to deliver public health activities associated with the pandemic which include the costs of care outside hospitals, paramedic services, personal protective equipment, community health services, staffing support in aged care and transport costs. A further 6-month extension to Medicare Benefits Schedule pathology items for freight workers and aged care staff is also being provided with an investment of $711.7 million and $42.0 million is being provided for dedicated pathology and collection centres in aged care facilities. Since the commencement of the pandemic, more than 7.6 million COVID-19 tests have been conducted. The budget also provides $42.5 million to continue support for emergency measures including the National Incident Room, national communication activities and a central patient triage hotline (Biggs & Grove, 2020).

Market environments continue changing throughout the life cycle of PPP projects. The project company may bear various risks that affect the operating revenue, which can lead to renegotiation or even project failure (Ng et al., 2010; Takashima et al., 2010). From the above description, the impact of COVID-19 on economic development has been enormous. Since PPP projects usually have long periods, ranging from a few years to 20 years or even 30 years, the impacts of COVID-19 occur in the context of PPP projects at various stages. PPP projects and key project participants may be affected by changes in supply chains, human resources and work arrangements. Smaller participants may find it harder to compete in a rapidly changing and uncertain environment. The Department of Health and Human Services of the Victorian State Government issued a guideline entitled *Best practice for managing construction sites in the COVID-19 environment* in March 2020. It is not a mandatory guideline, but the procuring agencies have directed contractors to comply with it within the powers given to them in the context of PPP contracts. Not all uncertain risks and changes in circumstances can be subject to contract adjustment and renegotiation. The circumstances for initiating contract adjustment must be specified within the framework of the contract system. According to PPP contract guidance from the World Bank (2019) and the spirit of PPP legislation in various countries, "force majeure" and "change of law" lead to a "change of circumstances" of a contract, as the main trigger factors for the adjustment and renegotiation of PPP contracts. Therefore, seeking claims due to a change in law or other change orders is the most probable approaches for PPP contractors to ensure the execution of contracts in Australia (Asian Development Bank, 2021; Casady & Baxter, 2020).

The closing of borders and reduction in immigrations due to the COVID-19 pandemic have exacerbated the effects of Australia's ageing population and significantly affected the Australian aged care industry (Andrikopoulos & Johnson, 2020).

The majority of deaths have been reported in people aged 70 years and over. The occupancy rate of aged care facilities has declined to varying degrees (Department of Health of Australia, 2022a). The operators are required to comply with the requirements in their state or territory to protect the residents and staff. These requirements include adjusting visits to common areas, introducing takeaway meal services or delivery services, closing or limiting use of shared facilities, hosting video meetings and ensuring residents and staff wear face masks (Department of Health of Australia, 2020). Therefore, when considering the effect of the pandemic on PPP projects, projects that involve aged care should be used for the analysis. For this chapter, a proposed PPP rental retirement village has been selected.

Various risk factors need to be considered during the implementation of PPP projects. The impact of unexpected and continuous risk events such as the COVID-19 pandemic is bound to trigger renegotiation between the government and the private sector, especially in terms of how to ensure the smooth operation of projects. Since the investment of PPP projects is long term with many uncertainties, the government guarantee plays a crucial role in reducing the risk of the private sector in some extreme circumstances (Liu et al., 2019). Governments commonly grant some guarantees to the private sector in concession agreements, especially when concessions last for a fixed term (Engel et al., 2014). As one of the most popular incentive mechanisms, a government guarantee can protect the private sector's interest around demand and revenue uncertainties. The private sector will be entitled to renegotiation for relief due to possible key risk events that in themselves have a material adverse effect on the private sector's capability during the contract term (Infrastructure Australia, 2011). The crisis will certainly have influences on the returns of PPP projects. For the private sector, it is a right to ask for renegotiation with the government for compensation when its interests are damaged under special circumstances and the exercise of this right relies on the extent to which the effect of the pandemic has weakened the profitability level (Liu et al., 2018). The government will then fulfil its guarantee responsibility and an option value will be generated.

Government Guarantee of PPP Projects under Special Circumstances

In the year j, there occurs the COVID-19 pandemic, which makes the actual benefit of the PPP project drop from B_t to $B_t^?$. When $j \leq t \leq T_c$, V_t, the option value of the PPP rental retirement village of year t can be represented as:

$$V_t = \begin{cases} 0, B_t^? \, ? \, G_t \\ G_t \, ? \, B_t^?, B_t^? < G_t \end{cases} \tag{1}$$

G_t here is the level of guarantee. The total option value of the PPP rental retirement village project V is:

$$V = \sum_{T_c}^{t=j} V_t = \sum_{T_c}^{t=j} \max\left(0, G_t ? B_t^?\right) \tag{2}$$

The adoption of changing the benefit distribution to guarantee the project will shorten the guarantee process, reduce the second tier of capital consumption and prevent additional social costs.

The benefit in year t of project B_t can be expressed as:

$$B_t = \frac{\left(\frac{P?i}{?} ??CO_t\right)?N_t?(1??)}{(1+r)^{T_0+t}} \tag{3}$$

where P is the weekly rent, i is the number of weeks per year, N_t is the number of units occupied in year t and αCO_t is the average operation cost per unit in year t, which includes the maintenance cost. α is a growth coefficient and $\alpha = 1$ when the project normally operates. μ is the percentage of rental income in total income, β represents the income tax rate, usually 30%, and r represents the discount rate. The government does not participate in the project benefit distribution until the private sector recovers its investment. All benefits of the project will be obtained by the private sector before the payback year T_p. From year $T_p + 1$, the government has the right to request the distribution of the project benefits in accordance with the agreed ratio to control the excess profits of the private sector. The total amount of benefits that the private sector can obtain during the operation of the PPP project in the concession period needs to meet the requirement of the expected return rate to the private sector R and then the government will collect the remaining benefits for welfare purposes. Therefore, from year $T_p + 1$ until the year that the concession period ends, the annual benefit obtained by the government $B_{gt} = X_g B_t$ and the annual benefit received by the private sector $B_{pt} = X_p B_t$, where X_g is the benefit distribution ratio of the government, X_p is the ratio of the private sector and obviously $X_g + X_p = 1$. The benefit distribution ratios can be expressed as:

$$\frac{X_g}{X_p} = \frac{\sum_{T_c}^{t=1} B_t ?(1+R) I_0}{R I_0} \tag{4}$$

Only by determining a certain level for the guarantee can the government grant the corresponding compensation when fulfilling its guarantee responsibility. Since the setting of the government guarantee is to ensure the smooth operation of the private sector for the expected benefits, the guarantee level of the project in year t, G_t, can be defined as:

$$G_t = \frac{1}{1+R} B_t \tag{5}$$

From year $T_p + 1$ to year T_c, the private sector can receive part of the G_t which equals $G_{pt} = X_p G_t$.

It is proposed that in year e, there occurs the COVID-19 pandemic, which may lead to changes in two aspects. One is a drop in the occupancy rate, which reflects that the number of occupied units declines from N_e to $N_e^?$. The other is an increase in the operating costs of the project due to rises in labour costs, management costs and prices of materials and equipment, which means $\alpha > 1$. The actual benefit of the project will change to $B_e^?$ from B_e. When $e \geq T_p$, the government can make a guarantee compensation through changing the benefit distribution ratio of the PPP project to reduce the secondary consumption of capital and to prevent additional social costs. The change in project benefit distribution can be regarded as a transfer of part of the option value held by the government to the private sector. Therefore, when the actual benefit of the project in year e satisfies $G_{pe} ? B_e^? ? \mathrm{G}_e$, the private sector's ratio of the benefit distribution is increased to $X_p^?$ to make sure that the private sector gains the government guarantee level, which means $X_p^? B_e^? = G_{pe}$. The new ben-efit distribution ratio in year e will change to $X_p^? = \frac{G_{pe}}{B_e^?}$, $X_g^? = 1 ? X_p^?$. If $B_e^? < G_{pe}$,the private sector will obtain all the project benefits and the government will have to fill the gap with extra capital support, that is, $G_{pe} ? B_e^?$. Therefore, when $e \leq t \leq T_p$, the extra support equals $G_{pt} ? B_t^?$ and the adjusted benefit distribution of the project can be written as:

$$X_p^? = \frac{G_{pt}}{B_t^?} \tag{6}$$

$$X_g^? = 1 ? X_p^? \tag{7}$$

The government will inevitably suffer losses when fulfilling its guarantee responsibility. The losses are defined as the government guarantee cost GC. When $B_t^? ? G_{pt}$ the costs are the benefit reduction due to the adjustment of the project benefit distribution and when $B_t^? < G_{pt}$ in addition to the benefits lost the costs also include the extra payment. In summary, the government GC can be represented as:

$$GC = \begin{cases} \overset{t=j}{\underset{T_p}{?}} \mathrm{V}_t + \overset{T_p+1}{\underset{T_c}{?}} \left[\left(X_g ? X_g^? \right) B_t^? \right], B_t^? ? G_{pt} \\ \overset{t=j}{\underset{T_p}{?}} \mathrm{V}_t . + \overset{T_p+1}{\underset{T_c}{?}} \left(G_{pt} ? B_t^? + X_g B_t^? \right), B_t^? < G_{pt} \end{cases} \tag{8}$$

Capital grants can be one form of government support to facilitate the participation of the private sector in the implementation of PPP projects (Queiroz et al., 2013). In the concession agreement, the government and the private sector agree on sharing the total investment I_0 to cover part of the construction cost of the project with K_g as the investment ratio of the government and K_p as the investment ratio of the private sector, where $K_g + K_p = 1$. The capital will be invested once in the construction period. Then the agreed benefit distribution ratios can be expressed as:

$$\frac{X_g}{X_p} = \frac{?_{T_c}^{t=1} B_t ? K_p I_0 ? RK_p I_0}{RK_p I_0} \quad (9)$$

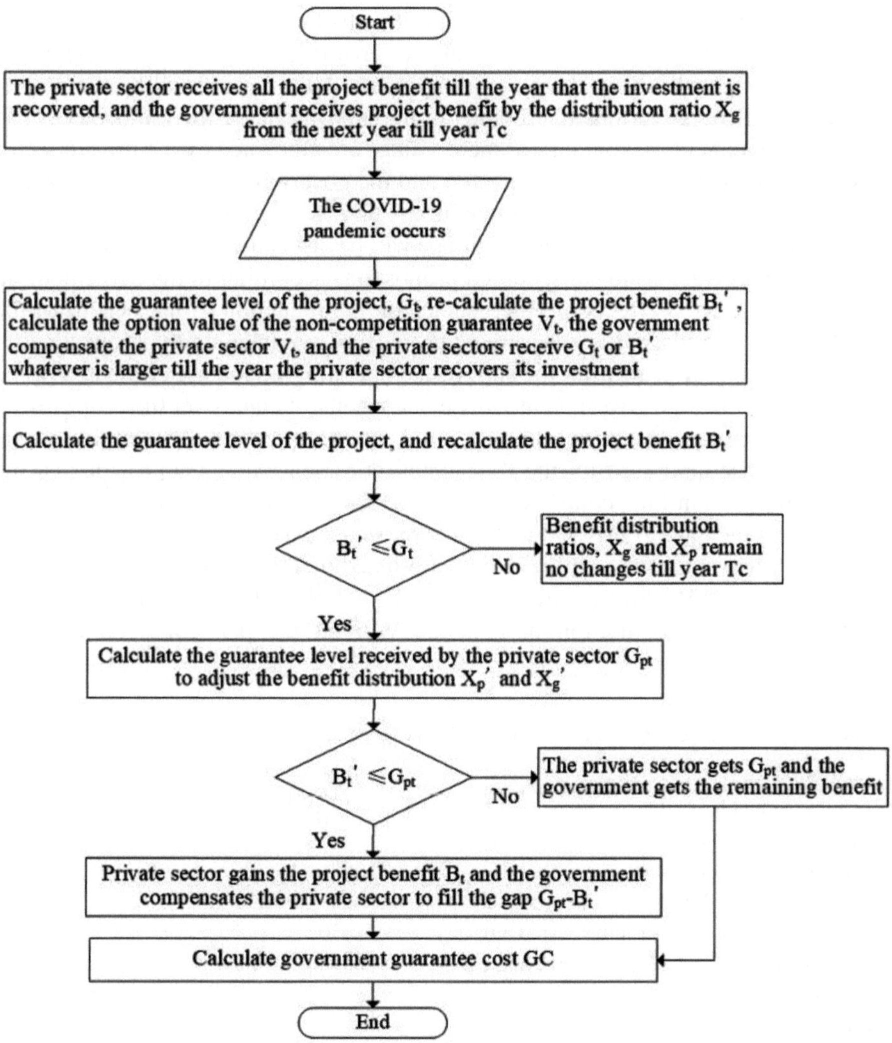

Fig. 2 Negotiation process for the government guarantee during the pandemic

The evaluation process for the government guarantee is summarised in Fig. 2. Changes in the government investment ratio will affect the value of the government GC under special circumstances and then influence the guarantee decisions of the government.

Application Example and Analysis Results

The case is a rental retirement village with 96 units located in the Geelong area in Victoria. The private sector completes all the investment and financing. After the completion of construction, the rental retirement village is operated by the project company and the government provides preferential policies for the project. The operating benefits of the rental retirement village are all owned by the private sector before the investment costs are recovered and the government will not seek project benefit distribution. After the investment of the private sector is paid back, the operating benefits of the rental retirement village will be distributed between the government and the private sector in specified proportions according to the agreement. In order to mitigate the effects of emergencies on the reduction of the benefit of the rental retirement village, the government provides a guarantee for the project within a certain number of years after the start of the operating period. After the end of the concession period, the government will decide whether to take over the project from the private sector or give permission for it to keep the operation. For simplicity, it is deemed that the land used for the PPP rental retirement village is provided by the government as an in-kind contribution with no charge. Details are shown in Table 1.

Applying the data to Eqs. (3) to (5), the expected cash flows and benefits of the project can be calculated and the results are listed in Table 2. It can be concluded that the project NPV turns positive in the 15th year, then the government begins to participate in the distribution of benefits. Without the pandemic, the ratio of

Table 1 Input variables of the PPP rental retirement village

Fixed variables	Value
Total investment I_0 (AUD)	11,219,160
Construction period T_0 (year)	2
Concession period T_c (year)	30
Weekly rent P (AUD)	330
Average operating cost per unit CO_i (AUD)	8630
Proportion of rental income in total revenue μ	0.6
Income tax rate β (%)	30
Discount rate r (%)	5.5
Expected return rate for private sector R (%)	12

Table 2 Expected operation of the project under normal circumstances

Year	Unit	Net cash flow	B_t	Project NPV	Government's NPV	Private sector's NPV	G_t
1	76	1,062,404	904,758	−10,314,402	0	−10,314,402	807,819
2	79	1,104,341	891,443	−9,422,960	0	−9,422,960	795,931
3	82	1,146,278	877,057	−8,545,903	0	−8,545,903	783,086
4	85	1,188,215	861,748	−7,684,155	0	−7,684,155	769,418
5	88	1,230,152	845,652	−6,838,503	0	−6,838,503	755,046
6	91	1,272,089	828,892	−6,009,612	0	−6,009,612	740,082
7	94	1,314,026	811,581	−5,198,031	0	−5,198,031	724,626
8	96	1,341,984	785,638	−4,412,392	0	−4,412,392	701,463
9	96	1,341,984	744,681	−3,667,711	0	−3,667,711	664,894
10	96	1,341,984	705,859	−2,961,852	0	−2,961,852	630,231
11	96	1,341,984	669,060	−2,292,792	0	−2,292,792	597,375
12	96	1,341,984	634,181	−1,658,611	0	−1,658,611	566,233
13	96	1,341,984	601,119	−1,057,492	0	−1,057,492	536,713
14	96	1,341,984	569,781	−487,711	0	−487,711	508,733
15	96	1,341,984	540,077	52,365	39,274	13,091	482,211
16	96	1,341,984	511,921	564,287	423,215	141,072	457,072
17	96	1,341,984	485,233	1,049,520	787,140	262,380	433,244
18	96	1,341,984	459,937	1,509,457	1,132,093	377,364	410,658
19	96	1,341,984	435,959	1,945,416	1,459,062	486,354	389,249
20	96	1,341,984	413,231	2,358,647	1,768,985	589,662	368,957
21	96	1,341,984	391,688	2,750,335	2,062,752	687,584	349,722
22	96	1,341,984	371,269	3,121,604	2,341,203	780,401	331,490
23	96	1,341,984	351,913	3,473,518	2,605,138	868,379	314,208
24	96	1,341,984	333,567	3,807,085	2,855,314	951,771	297,828
25	96	1,341,984	316,177	4,123,262	3,092,447	1,030,816	282,301
26	96	1,341,984	299,694	4,422,957	3,317,217	1,105,739	267,584
27	96	1,341,984	284,070	4,707,027	3,530,270	1,176,757	253,634
28	96	1,341,984	269,261	4,976,288	3,732,216	1,244,072	240,412
29	96	1,341,984	255,224	5,231,512	3,923,634	1,307,878	227,878
30	96	1,341,984	241,918	5,473,430	4,105,073	1,368,358	215,998

distribution of benefits between the government and the private sector can be calculated by Eq. (4), that is, $X_p = 0.25$ and $X_g = 0.75$. Assuming the COVID-19 pandemic occurs in the 18th year, this leads to two scenarios. In scenario 1, which is a guarantee under lower demand, the occupancy rate will reduce to 60% due to the withdrawal or death of residents, which means that the number of annual occupied units in the village with 96 units falls to 58 units. In scenario 2, which is a guarantee under higher operating costs, the average operation cost per unit increases by 50%, that is, $\alpha = 1.5$. Changing the data according to Eqs. (1) and (2), the option value of the project can be calculated and the government GC can be calculated by Eq. (8).

Tables 3 and 4 provide the results for the changing benefits of the rental retirement village under the two scenarios. The option values of the two scenarios are

Table 3 Changes in project benefits with the guarantee of scenario 1

Year	$B_t^?$	G_t	G_{pt}	$X_g B_t^?$	$X_g^? B_t^?$	V_t	GC_t
18	277,878	410,658	102,664	208,409	175,214	132,779	33,195
19	263,392	389,249	97,312	197,544	166,080	125,857	31,464
20	249,661	368,957	92,239	187,245	157,421	119,296	29,824
21	236,645	349,722	87,430	177,484	149,215	113,077	28,269
22	224,308	331,490	82,872	168,231	141,436	107,182	26,795
23	212,614	314,208	78,552	159,461	134,062	101,594	25,399
24	201,530	297,828	74,457	151,148	127,073	96,298	24,074
25	191,024	282,301	70,575	143,268	120,449	91,277	22,819
26	181,065	267,584	66,896	135,799	114,169	86,519	21,630
27	171,626	253,634	63,409	128,719	108,217	82,008	20,502
28	162,679	240,412	60,103	122,009	102,576	77,733	19,433
29	154,198	227,878	56,970	115,648	97,228	73,681	18,420
30	146,159	215,998	54,000	109,619	92,159	69,839	17,460

Table 4 Changes in project benefits with the guarantee of scenario 2

Year	$B_t^?$	G_t	G_{pt}	$X_g B_t^?$	$X_g^? B_t^?$	V_t	GC_t
18	360,556	410,658	102,664	270,417	257,892	50,101	12,525
19	341,760	389,249	97,312	256,320	244,447	47,490	11,872
20	323,943	368,957	92,239	242,957	231,704	45,014	11,253
21	307,055	349,722	87,430	230,291	219,624	42,667	10,667
22	291,047	331,490	82,872	218,285	208,175	40,443	10,111
23	275,874	314,208	78,552	206,906	197,322	38,334	9584
24	261,492	297,828	74,457	196,119	187,035	36,336	9084
25	247,860	282,301	70,575	185,895	177,284	34,442	8610
26	234,938	267,584	66,896	176,204	168,042	32,646	8162
27	222,690	253,634	63,409	167,018	159,282	30,944	7736
28	211,081	240,412	60,103	158,311	150,978	29,331	7333
29	200,077	227,878	56,970	150,057	143,107	27,802	6950
30	189,646	215,998	54,000	142,234	135,646	26,352	6588

$1,277,141 and $481,902, respectively. Taking year 20 of scenario 1 as an example, the actual benefit is $249,661, while the guarantee level is $368,957 and the level received by the private sector is $92,239. It can be seen that $B_{20}^{'} < G_{20}$ and $B_{20}^{'} > G_{p21} B_{21}^{?} > G_{p21}$. Therefore, in year 20, the private sector can obtain $92,239 from the yearly benefit and the rest belongs to the government. Applying the changed data to Eqs. (6) and (7), the adjusted ratios for the two scenarios $X_p^{'} : X_g^{'}$ equal 0.37:0.63 and 0.28:0.72, respectively. The occupancy rate declines by 40% while the benefits the private sector receives increase by 12%. The operating cost rises by 50% while the benefits the private sector receives increase by only 3%. It can be concluded that the change in occupancy rate has greater impact on the benefit distribution and government GC than the change in operating cost.

Whether the private sector will ask for renegotiation with the government depends on the impact of changes in the cash flow on the project benefits after the outbreak of the pandemic. It can be concluded from the calculation that when the occupancy rate is fully maintained, the operating cost must increase by more than 25% before the government needs to consider the guarantee, but when the operating cost remains unchanged and the number of occupied units drops by more than 10, the government needs to fulfil the guarantee liability. When the occupancy rate remains unchanged and the original cost is unchanged, the government GC increases by 0.1% for every 1% increase in the operating cost. When the original cost remains stable, the government GC increases by 0.2% for each unit of occupancy decrease. Changes in occupancy rate or revenue have greater impacts on the government GC than changes in operating cost, which is consistent with the findings of the previous calculations. When the two factors change at the same time, the impact on the government GC needs to be analysed according to the specific problems, as shown in Fig. 3.

The detailed results for the combined effects of changes in the occupancy rate and operating cost on the government GC are listed in Table 5. When the occupancy rate and operating cost change by 30% at the same time, the ratio of government GC to NPV increases by 6.9%. The government GC generally shows a relatively gentle change trend of equal proportions.

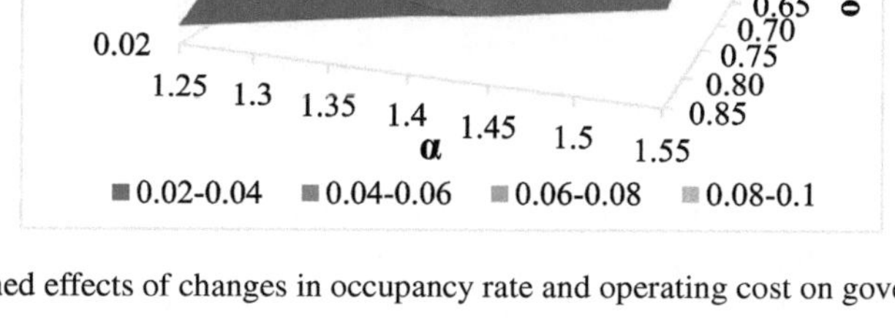

Fig. 3 Combined effects of changes in occupancy rate and operating cost on government guarantee cost

Table 5 Ratio of government guarantee cost to project NPV with different levels of occupancy rate and operating cost

		Occupancy rate						
		85%	80%	75%	70%	65%	60%	55%
Operation cost coefficient α	1.25	0.026	0.036	0.045	0.055	0.064	0.072	0.081
	1.3	0.03	0.039	0.049	0.058	0.067	0.074	0.083
	1.35	0.034	0.043	0.052	0.061	0.07	0.077	0.086
	1.4	0.038	0.046	0.055	0.064	0.072	0.079	0.088
	1.45	0.041	0.05	0.059	0.067	0.075	0.082	0.091
	1.5	0.045	0.053	0.062	0.07	0.078	0.085	0.093
	1.55	0.049	0.057	0.065	0.073	0.081	0.087	0.095

Effect of Government Investment on the Guarantee Cost

The behaviour of the government investment will affect the original benefit distribution ratio between the public and private sectors. In order to control the excess benefits of the private sector, whether or not the government participates in the project investment, the government has the right to seek the majority of the excess benefits. Applying different ratios to Eq. (9) and the other equations, the impact of the government investment ratio on the proportion of government benefit in the distribution under scenario 1 is shown in Fig. 4. The original benefit distribution ratio of the government increases by 0.11 with the growth of the investment ratio. The government guarantee is a process of option transfer. The less the government invests in the early stage, the longer the private sector has to gain recovery of its investment, which leads to greater transfer of the option value held by the government to the private sector and fewer benefits left for the government after fulfilling its guarantee obligations. With an increase in the government investment ratio, the gap between the original and adjusted benefit distribution ratios will become narrower, which means that the government's investment in the early stage can moderately reduce the impact of emergencies.

Key Inferences

Unforeseen changes are usually more difficult to reach consensus on than foreseeable changes, so the renegotiation procedure is mainly designed for unforeseen changes. When entering a PPP contract, the government and the private sector must consider the possibility of unforeseen changes and the function of renegotiation procedures to resolve any disputes in relation to such changes to ensure the sustainability of the PPP project. The renegotiation terms of PPP contracts should be sufficiently flexible to cover various changes that cannot be foreseen at the beginning of a contract. Also, the renegotiation terms should not include the risks that are clearly specified in the contract. The solution should be clearly specified in rigid

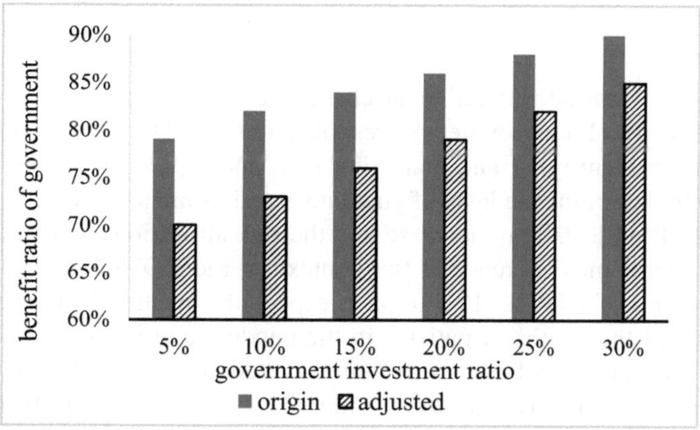

Fig. 4 Effects of government investment on proportion of government benefit in benefit distribution under scenario 1

terms in the contract for foreseeable changes, while unforeseen changes should be settled by a renegotiation flexibility clause.

The benefits of all stakeholders will be affected, sometimes even seriously, due to the occurrence of the COVID-19 pandemic. The government should evaluate the impacts of the pandemic on the construction and operation of PPP projects in a timely way, especially the consequences for the benefits to the private sector, and make corresponding remedies according to the degree of impact to promote the steady development of PPP projects. The bottom line of costs and benefits needs to be set in the contract. When approaching this elastic red line, it is necessary to start adjustment and renegotiation of the project contract. The private sector will have expectations and a minimum guarantee of the project benefits. Therefore, the ideal result of the renegotiation of PPP contracts caused by the pandemic is that the government makes a certain compromise by losing part of its own benefit or extending the concession period. In this case, the PPP project experienced a reduction in occupancy rate, a decline in service fee income and an increase in operating cost, which significantly reduced the income and increased the operating risk. Under the condition that the government guarantee level remains unchanged, the renegotiation result of the project is reflected in the government's redistribution of the benefit.

PPP projects are mostly public infrastructure construction, among which there are many public welfare projects, such as a PPP rental retirement village in this case. Stakeholders should fully consider the affordability of users when renegotiating a contract. In this case, considering that the retirees living in the village have a single source of income and are sensitive to the weekly expenditure of service fees, the original rent level has been maintained since the outbreak of the pandemic. It is important to pay close attention to the impact of the fee level on users in user-pays PPP projects and to keep users' expenditure at a stable level. In future PPP contracts, the adaptability of users' expenditure should be fully considered and the service fee under special circumstances such as COVID-19 agreed in advance, which not only allows users to prepare for change, but also has little impact on project operation.

Conclusion

COVID-19 has resulted in significant changes to human interactions worldwide. The uncertain overall environment in response to COVID-19 poses challenges for governments in identifying and managing risks more precisely, which influences their ability to determine the level of guarantees and estimate the GC. The value and volume of PPP projects may decrease and the risk allocations and assumptions of the private sector may increase in the context of the COVID-19 pandemic. The scope and depth of COVID-19's impact, especially on the elderly, are unprecedented. Most of the deaths of patients in the pandemic are among the elderly and many aged care facilities have accumulated infections, resulting in a reduction in the number of residents in aged care facilities. Therefore, PPP projects in retirement communities such as rental retirement villages should be paid more attention. The pandemic has caused changes for PPP rental retirement villages in two aspects, which are an increase in the operating cost and a decrease in the occupancy rate. It can be concluded from the calculation of the government GC that changes in occupancy rate have greater impact than changes in operating cost and so the former changes are more likely to trigger renegotiation. To reduce the GC, the government can inject one-time investment at the project financing stage. Also, flexible constraints on pandemic prevention and control of the project should be added during contract negotiation of PPP projects. In order to ensure the smooth renegotiation of PPP projects, when signing contracts it is necessary to clearly state what kind of special conditions the renegotiation will be started under, what the elastic areas of the renegotiation result are, the agreement on the responsibilities and obligations of stakeholders, and the possibility of PPP project failure.

References

Andrikopoulos, S., & Johnson, G. (2020). The Australian response to the COVID-19 pandemic and diabetes – Lessons learned. *Diabetes Research and Clinical Practice, 165*, 108246. https://doi.org/10.1016/j.diabres.2020.108246

Asian Development Bank. (2021). *COVID-19 and Public–Private Partnerships in Asia and the Pacific: Guidance Note*. Retrieved from Manila, Philippines.

Biggs, A., & Grove, A. (2020). Public health response to COVID-19. Retrieved from https://bit.ly/3bY7brk

Casady, C. B., & Baxter, D. (2020). Pandemics, public-private partnerships (PPPs), and force majeure | COVID-19 expectations and implications. *Construction Management and Economics, 38*(12), 1077–1085. https://doi.org/10.1080/01446193.2020.1817516

Department of Health of Australia. (2020). *Fact sheet: Advice for retirement villages*. Retrieved from https://bit.ly/3uVGdY3

Department of Health of Australia. (2022a). *COVID-19 outbreaks in Australian residential aged care facilities*. Retrieved from https://bit.ly/3c7e9dy

Department of Health of Australia. (2022b). *Vaccination numbers and statistics*. Retrieved from https://bit.ly/3O1bDCG

Donnelly, D., Ng, N., & Donaldson, B. (2015). Australia. In B. Werneck & M. Saadi (Eds.), *The public-private partnership law review*. Gideon Roberton.

Engel, E., Fischer, R., & Galetovic, A. (2014). *Finance and public-private partnerships*. Paper presented at the Financial Flows Infrastructure Financing, Sydney.

Infrastructure Australia. (2008). *National public private partnership guidelines overview*. Retrieved from Sydney, Australia: https://bit.ly/3OdQlSN

Infrastructure Australia. (2011). Volume 7: Commercial principles for economic infrastructure. In *National public private partnership guidelines*. Sydney.

Jefferies, M., McGeorge, D., Chen, S. E., & Cadman, K. (2006). *Sustainable procurement: A contemporary view on Australian Public Private Partnerships (PPP)*. Paper presented at the international conference on Construction Culture, Innovation and Management, British University in Dubai.

Liu, S., Jin, H., Xie, B., Liu, C., & Mills, A. (2018). Concession period determination for PPP retirement village. *International Journal of Strategic Property Management, 22*(5), 424–435.

Liu, S., Jin, H., Liu, C., Xie, B., & Mills, A. (2019). Government compensation and costs of non-competition guarantee for PPP rental retirement villages. *Engineering, Construction and Architectural Management, 27*(1), 128–149.

Ng, S. T., Xie, J., & Kumaraswamy, M. M. (2010). Simulating the effect of risks on equity return for concession-based public-private partnership projects. *Engineering, Construction and Architectural Management, 17*(4), 352–368.

Queiroz, C., Vajdic, N., & Mladenovic, G. (2013). Public–private partnerships in roads and government support: Trends in transition and developing economies. *Transportation Planning and Technology, 36*(3), 231–243.

Takashima, R., Yagi, K., & Takamori, H. (2010). Government guarantees and risk sharing in public–private partnerships. *Review of Financial Economics, 19*(2), 78–83.

World Bank. (2019). *Guidance on PPP contractual provisions*. Retrieved from Washington, DC: https://bit.ly/3nSbkjh

Implications and Feasibility of Contract Renegotiations of PPP in France

Pascale Accaoui Lorfing

Introduction

France is a country of civil law tradition which distinguishes between civil law, a branch of private law governing relations between private individuals, and administrative law, a body of specific rules, different from civil law rules, governing the activity of the Administration. These rules govern the organisation, functioning, and activity of public administrations. This means that concessions and public service delegations are governed by the principles of administrative law first, supplemented by the legal provisions specific to the matter, when they exist.

Therefore, the public-private partnership (PPP) may be defined as an administrative contract, of long-term duration, between the French State or a public authority and a private party (an operator), for the design, the build, the finance, and the management of equipment, works, or the construction to ensure a public service. PPPs range from the construction of buildings for the army, to the construction of the high-speed railway, to the courthouse, hospitals, highways, and schools (Vie publique, 2020).

The PPP was governed by an ordinance 2004-559 on partnership contracts (Ordinance No. 2004-559 of 17 June 2004 on partnership contracts). This ordinance established the legal and institutional framework for PPPs in France. This ordinance was supplemented by ordinance 2008-735 (Law n° 2008-735 of 28 July 2008 on Partnership Contracts), which incorporated the amendments made to ordinance 2004-559, with a view to improving the PPP framework in France. These improvements include local and regional government, urban planning, general taxation, and

P. A. Lorfing (✉)
CREDIMI, University of Burgundy, Dijon, Bourgogne-Franche-Comté, France

ESCP Business School, Paris, France

© The Author(s), under exclusive license to Springer Nature Switzerland AG 2023

T. Dolla et al. (eds.), *Revisiting Public-Private Partnerships*,
Contributions to Public Administration and Public Policy,
https://doi.org/10.1007/978-3-031-37015-1_15

monetary and financial policy. These laws established guiding principles, procurement procedures, and dispute resolution mechanisms. PPPs are known as partnership contracts. An author cited the difference to be aware of between partnership contracts and PPP contracts stating that.

> While the philosophy is unchanged, the three notable differences with the partnership contract are that (i) the partnership contract is not necessarily global (for example, a public entity may entrust the design, construction and financing of a work to the private partner, without entrusting it with its operation), that (ii) recourse to this type of partnership contract is only possible for projects whose value exceeds a threshold to be defined by decree, and (iii) that the criteria which made the contract eligible for a derogation from the ordinary law of public procurement are substantially modified. The criteria of urgency and complexity, which were used to justify the use of partnership contracts, have been removed. Only the criterion of economic efficiency remains. The purchaser must therefore demonstrate that the use of a partnership contract offers a more favourable cost-benefit ratio than the other public procurement methods available (Article 75 of the Order of 23 July 2015). (De Brux & Marty, 2016, 223–238)

In 2018, the French legal framework for PPPs was modernised, leading to a PPP Code, which came into force on 1 April 2018 (Ordinance No. 2018-1074, 2018, Decree n° 2018-1075 of 2 December 2018 (a) and (b). Article L6 of the Public Procurement Code (Ordinance No. 2018-1074, 2018) provides for the classification of contracts concluded by legal persons governed by public law as administrative contracts, as well as the power of control of the execution of the contract by the contracting authority, in accordance with the procedures laid down by the Code and by the contract. It also recalls the principle of the continuity of the public service, which imposes the continuation of the contract in the event of an unforeseeable event external to the parties, temporarily upsetting the balance of the contract, in return for a right to compensation for the co-contractor. It also provides for the power of unilateral modification of the contract by the contracting authority, provided that the balance of the contract is not disrupted, and compensation is paid. Finally, the power of unilateral termination of the contract by the contracting authority is provided for, for reasons of general interest, in return for compensation to the other party and subject to the provisions of the contract (Llorens, 2018; Llorens & Soler-Couteaux 2018).

The main risks associated with this contractual partnership lie in the impossibility or great difficulty of anticipating all the costs of the project. This constitutes both a potential source of contractual imbalance and perhaps a major financial risk (for the State) a posteriori, which has already been noted by the *Cour des Comptes* in France whose task is

> to ensure the proper use of public money and to inform the citizens. As an independent Court, it is at an equal distance from the Parliament and the Government, both of which it assists, in accordance with Article 47-2 of the Constitution. (*Cour des comptes France, 2022*)

Indeed, according to this partnership, the State will pay in return a rent to the private partner who will manage the operation. Therefore, the long-term costs may exceed the initial investments. To this must be added the lack of control by the State over the project, which is nevertheless of general interest.

The Structural Disadvantage Between the Parties

It is the very structure of this partnership that is the source of possible or even certain renegotiations. Indeed, the PPP contract is a long-term contract which aims to provide services which are both complex and have evolving costs, and as such will be subject to contingencies that are not always predictable. If this type of contract were not renegotiated to cope with the changes in the environment and thus adapt to them, it would not correspond to the provision of an adequate service in the general interest. It means that the performance of such a contract implies the inevitable renegotiation of its conditions throughout its generally long duration. This is more so because the contractual position of the public partner is unfavourable, since the latter will owe royalties to the private partner in return, whereas the latter will be in a favourable position during the renegotiation, having the necessary informational advantage to carry out the contract (de Brux & Marty, 2016, 224). Renegotiation of PPP contracts (Guasch et al., 2006, 55–73) is multiple and justified by various reasons (Guasch, 2004, 33–90).

Variety of Renegotiation

Early renegotiation, i.e., renegotiation that takes place in the year following the renegotiation, is when the private operator, the State's partner in the PPP, is likely, once the contract has been awarded to it, to renegotiate it in its favour, sometimes in the year following the signing of the contract, and consequently to the detriment of the State and the user, the ultimate beneficiary.

Far from being a theoretical approach, these opportunistic renegotiations have been very frequent in the world, although less frequent in France (Beuve et al., 2013, 117–148). Indeed, these renegotiations take place after the signature of the contract, on average 2.2 years after the signature. Their negative effect on users is reflected in the increase in tariffs and the delay in the commissioning of infrastructure. They also reflect the lack of commitment of the parties to respect the terms of the contract between them. Late renegotiations are those that take place in the year before the contract expires: they are also frequent.

Purpose of the Renegotiation

The purpose of the renegotiation (Beuve et al., 2013) may be a change in the tariffs charged to the users of the service (Beuve et al., 2013, para 38), or additional investments not foreseen in the initial contract (Beuve et al., 2013, para 39), either because of the requirements of the public party or because of a lack of anticipation on the part of the private operator Beuve et al., 2013, para 39), or to improve the service (Beuve et al., 2013, para 40) or concerning the conditions relating to the financial equilibrium of the contract (Beuve et al., 2013, para 41), or to agree on a short extension of the duration of the contract Beuve et al., 2013, para 42) or concerning the conditions relating to the financial equilibrium of the contract (Beuve et al., 2013, para 41), or to agree on a short extension of the duration of the contract (Beuve et al., 2013, para 42), the most common renegotiations being those related to the duration and the least frequent to the conditions of the financial equilibrium of the contract (Beuve et al., 2013, para 41).

Renegotiation of the terms of the contract may be provided for by clauses inserted in the contract, such as the indexation clause, which provides for the implementation of certain indices if the existing ones disappear. It can be also clauses related to service requirements, change to tariff or payment rules or formulae, etc. All these clauses have in common the financial equilibrium of the contract to be maintained during its execution (Beuve et al., 2013, para 41). These clauses also provide that in the event of the disappearance of certain indices, the parties will meet to renegotiate the contract (World Bank 2021).

Scope of Renegotiation

Renegotiating the terms of the contract allows the sometimes-divergent objectives of the public authority and the private operator to be reconciled and a win-win situation to be achieved. It also allows for better cooperation to achieve the project. Thus, from the point of view of the contracting authority, renegotiation of the contract will enable it to achieve the completion of a project of common interest. From the point of view of the private operator, renegotiation of the contract will enable it to recoup its investments through the implementation of the project. Renegotiation of the contract also enables the parties to maintain greater mutual trust, and therefore, the contracting authority, which has discretionary power in the choice of its co-contractor, to maintain its trust in the private partner for future projects, and for the private partner to have the prospect of potential future contracts. On the other hand, lack of cooperation between the parties may lead the public authority not to renew the contract with its private co-contractor. Similarly, lack of cooperation may damage the reputation of the private co-contractor and lead the public authority to sanction it in the future, notably by excluding it from possible future projects.

Unless it is implemented at an early stage, i.e., quickly after the signing of the contract, in which case the renegotiation of the contract appears to be opportunistic on the part of the private operator and hardly conducive to a contractual agreement, it appears that the renegotiation of the contract, far from appearing to be a weakness of the contract, is a strength, since the parties share their sometimes divergent points of view, are likely to reach an agreement (Guasch & Straub, 2006, 479–493), which will allow the contract to continue to be executed under conditions that have been renegotiated in the meantime, and thereby favour the completion of the project.

The Impact of the COVID-19 Pandemic on the French PPP and Tools to Address It

The COVID-19 pandemic had a considerable impact on French society and led to the adoption of containment measures by the French government which had an impact on the execution of contracts. On 16 March 2020, the French authorities took the first containment measures to contain the COVID-19 epidemic caused by the coronavirus (Rẻpublique Française Vie publique, 2020) involving very severe restrictions on the movement of persons required to complete an extremely restrictive move certificate and undermining the execution of contracts.

The major issue that has emerged considering COVID-19 is the potential rise of disputes and claims in relation to the impact of government measures on the performance of the contract. The French responses to the COVID-19 pandemic are illustrated by the financial help by the French Government to the companies that put in place a partial unemployment where the French State sets up a system to support the economic activity of companies facing a lasting reduction in their activity (reduction in employees' working hours) by paying for the hours not worked under certain (Decree n° 2020-325 of 25 March 2020). Measures concerning the PPPs have also been adopted that adapt its procedural and substantive rules (ordinance n° 2020-319 of 25 March 2020).

Brief Description Context

The chapter describes the specificities of the French PPP contract and the impact of the COVID-19 pandemic on its execution conditions, which modifies the contractual balance, as well as the legal concepts implemented and the decision of the French authorities to limit the effects and allow the PPPs to continue under the best conditions to pursue their objective.

Analysis

The analysis will consider the following issues: (a) the impact of COVID-19 on contracts, (b) the key issues, (c) the challenges faced in contract renegotiations, and (d) the steps needed to improve contract renegotiations.

The Impact of COVID-19 on Contracts

The impact of the pandemic on PPP has been to alter the performance of the contract either by making the performance excessively onerous or by making the performance of the contract temporarily or definitely impossible. *To each of these impacts, a specific legal concept is to be applied with its specific legal regime.* Indeed, the impact of the event on the performance of the contract will determine the concept to be applied. In French law, *imprévision* and FM are two different concepts of a specific legal regime.

The Key Issues

PPP is a contract the execution of which is important because it concerns a public service whose execution must not be interrupted, either by an external event or by an administrative decision, because the completion of the works and the realisation of the project as well as the amortisation of the investments inherent to the project are important.

The continued execution of the contract involves determining the impact of the pandemic on the conditions of execution of the contract, the legal concept and/or contractual clauses and the related conditions to be implemented, and the inclusion of the exceptional legislation adopted in times of pandemic in the criteria, conditions, and fate of the PPP.

Challenges Faced in Contract Renegotiations

Many challenges are faced in contract renegotiations. First, the determination of whether the renegotiation results from the law or from the contractual provision, as parties in the PPP may have chosen different conditions to be applied in case of change in circumstances that alter the equilibrium of the PPP. Second, to be aware of the legal concept to be applied, as two different concepts may play an important role depending on the impact of the pandemic on the performance of the contract: *imprévision* and FM. Lastly, having in mind that PPP is a contract submitted to the

French Administrative law that recognise specific and different conditions than those of the French civil law to both imprévision in Art. 1195 of the French Civil Code since 2016 and FM in Article 1218 of the French Civil Code since 2016.

The Steps Needed to Improve Contract Renegotiations

The steps needed to improve contract renegotiations lie in the conditions stated for either in the legal concept to be implemented as applicable law to the PPP or in the contractual provisions inserted in the PPP. The pandemic has had an impact on PPPs as it has fundamentally altered the conditions of their implementation. The challenges facing contract renegotiation are twofold: on the one hand, to determine (1) whether renegotiation results from the law or (2) whether it results from the contractual terms.

Renegotiation Results from the Law

PPP is a contract submitted to the French Administrative law. The change of circumstances is provided for in French law according to the impact of the pandemic on the PPP that will determine the implementation of the legal concept with its own legal regime. The change in circumstances that fundamentally altered the performance of the PPP may make it excessively difficult to perform; therefore, (i) the theory of *imprévision* will be applied, or the performance of the PPP is rendered temporarily or definitively impossible, and (ii) the theory of *Force majeure* in administrative law will be applied. In addition, (iii) crisis legislation has also been adopted to deal with the consequences of the pandemic on contract performance.

Theory of *Imprévision* in Administrative Contract

The theory of *imprévision* in French administrative law (Gaudemet, 2001) provides that if the performance of an administrative contract binding one of the parties to the administration is made more onerous because of an unforeseeable and temporary event, the private co-contractor must continue the performance of the contract because of the continuity of the public service inherent to the administrative contract in return of receiving compensation for the damage caused to the private operator (Marché Public, circular of 20 November 1974).

Previous well-known decisions were dedicated to the issue such as *Compagnie générale d'éclairage de Bordeaux (30 March*1916*)*, and *Compagnie de tramways de Cherbourg* (9 Decembre 1932). A recent decision, *Société Alliance*, (21 October 2019; Rassafi Guibal 2019) shows the Court (Conseil d'Etat) clarifying the conditions for the payment of an indemnity for unforeseen circumstances by recalling the constant position that

> An allowance for unforeseen circumstances presupposes an operating deficit which is the direct consequence of an unforeseeable event, independent of the action of the administration's co-contractor, and having led to a disruption of the economy of the contract

specifying as to the calculation of the indemnity that

> The concessionaire is then entitled to claim from the grantor an indemnity representing the share of the extra-contractual burden that the reasonable interpretation of the contract allows him to bear. This compensation shall be calculated considering, where appropriate, other factors which have contributed to the disruption of the economy of the contract, the unforeseeable circumstances compensation only being able to compensate for the part of the deficit linked to the unforeseeable circumstances.

Several conditions must therefore be cumulatively met. The event at the origin of the contractual situation must be unforeseeable, it must be independent of the Administration's contractual action, and it must have led to a disruption of the economy of the contract.

In other words, it is first necessary to define the event that caused this contractual disruption. In the context of the pandemic, it may be the pandemic itself, which it is easy to understand was unforeseeable, not so much in its existence, since it was not the first epidemic of its kind, such recalled by decisions *CA Saint Denis de la Réunion* (29 December 2009), on Chikungunya epidemic, started in January 2006, while the contract in question had been signed at a later date, and CA Nancy (22 November 2010) on Dengue epidemic considered as 'a phenomenon which is a recurrent feature, particularly in the French West Indies', and CA Besançon (8 January 2014) on H1N1 event that has been considered as a 'widely announced and planned', but in its scope and impact on the contract. It may also include containment measures adopted because of the pandemic, the effect of which was undoubtedly either to terminate the performance of the contract or to make such performance excessively onerous. In any event, it is necessary to establish the link between the event and the consequence of that link, i.e., the person claiming such a situation must establish the causal link between the event and its consequence on the contract.

The impact of the event on the contract, to be taken into account, must be the equivalent of an operating deficit, which excludes both a reduction in profit as reminded by a case law *Commune de la Courtine* (CE, 15 June 1928) or the usual risk taken by any contractor as recalled by a case law *Gaz de Brive* (CE, 8 August 1924). Once these conditions have been met, the judge may conclude that the burdened party should be awarded compensation. The injured party must recover the losses he has suffered, the extra-contractual burden that the parties did not foresee when they concluded the contract. The compensation then covers part of the charges paid by the contractor, or depending on the nature of the contract, an extension of the contract period, an increase in rates, etc. The compensation paid may be higher if the parties have taken care to insert clauses that are more favourable to the other party (Public-Private Partnerships, Reference Guide, 2017). The interpretation of these clauses will be based on the applicable legislation. This highlights the importance of the interpretation of the contract and consequently of the clauses contained therein, in particular, regarding the unforeseeability indemnity that the parties may have provided for in the contract.

Theory of *Force Majeure* (FM) in Administrative Contract

Force majeure in administrative French law (*Compagnie des tramways de Cherbourg,* CE, 9 December 1932) will apply if the conditions for its implementation are met, i.e., the existence of unforeseeable circumstances that disrupt the contract to such an extent that the new final situation does not allow the concessionaire to balance its expenses. It has been stated that

> (...) in the event that unforeseeable circumstances have had the effect of upsetting the contract and that the new economic conditions have moreover created a definitive situation which no longer allows the concessionaire to balance his expenses with the resources at his disposal, the new situation thus created constitutes a case of force majeure and authorises the concessionaire, as well as the grantor, in the absence of an amicable agreement on a new direction to be given to the operation, to ask the judge to terminate the concession, with compensation if necessary, and taking into account the stipulations of the contract as well as all the circumstances of the case. (*Commune de Staffelden,* CE, 14 June 2000)

The result is that both parties – the licensor and the licensee – have the possibility to try to reach an amicable agreement on the fate of the contract, or, failing that, to ask the judge to terminate the contract, possibly with compensation to the licensee, considering the contract and the circumstances of the case. The particularity of force majeure in administrative law is that it considers a performance that has not become impossible, as is the case for force majeure in private law, but a performance of the contract that has been totally disrupted but is still possible, requiring, however, that to continue, the concessionaire must incur expenses more than its resources. However, a publication by the Directorate of Legal Affairs (DLA) (Direction des affaires Juridiques, 2020) of the Ministry of Economy and Finance on 'The award and execution of public contracts in a health crisis situation' recalls the three conditions of the FM, i.e., an unforeseeable event, external to the parties (recognising that the pandemic fulfilled these two criteria) rendering the performance of all or part of the public contract (deadlines, quantities, compliance with certain specifications of the services to be carried out) absolutely impossible, temporarily or definitively, bringing this definition closer to that recognised in civil law.

The unforeseeability criterion must also be analysed according to the date of conclusion of the contract, it being understood that the pandemic cannot have been caused by one of the parties to the contract. In addition, the difficulties encountered by the parties must have a causal link with the pandemic. Finally, it will be necessary to determine the impact of the pandemic on the financial conditions of the concessionaire and more particularly its unbearable character before concluding that a situation of force majeure exists. It is understood that in the presence of clauses in the contract providing for force majeure, they shall have effect in accordance with their formulation by the parties.

In other words, when it comes to assessing both the conditions and the consequences of the pandemic on the performance of the PPP, it is both the emergency legislation adopted and the case law decisions that must be considered. The difficulty will lie in the sometimes-significant difference between the conditions and/or the effects of the event on the contract. Thus, the difference between *Force majeure* in the case law and the DAJ publication, as regards the impact of the event on the contract. The jurisprudential FM providing that the execution of the contract has become always possible but requiring the concessionaire to incur expenses exceeding its resources, when, according to the DLA publication, 'the service provider or the public purchaser finds it absolutely impossible to continue, temporarily or definitively, the performance of all or part of the public contract (deadlines, quantities, compliance with certain specifications of the services to be provided, etc.)' (Direction des affaires Juridiques, 2020). This assessment will also be carried out in the light of the emergency legislation adopted during the pandemic.

Specific Legislation in Times of Crisis

Due to the COVID-19 pandemic, specific legislation for PPP contracts has been adopted, providing for the adjustment of these contracts to the circumstances for a limited period as set out in the ordinance. PPP stabilization mechanisms were put in place by the French authorities during the pandemic. In response to the health crisis resulting from the pandemic of COVID-19, France has adopted an ordinance n° 2020-319 of 25 March 2020 (ordinance n° 2020-319 of 25 March 2020, Rassafi-Guibal (2020)) providing for measures to adapt the procedural and substantive rules relating to contracts subject to the code of public procurement.

This legislation applies to contracts in progress or concluded between 12 March 2020 and 23 July 2020 included as specified:

> Unless otherwise stated, the provisions of this Order shall apply to contracts subject to the Public Procurement Code and to public contracts not covered by it, in progress or concluded during the period from 12 March 2020 to 23 July 2020 inclusive.
>
> They shall be implemented only insofar as they are necessary to deal with the consequences, in the award and performance of such contracts, of the spread of the covid-19 epidemic and the measures taken to limit that spread.

This crisis legislation provides for an adjustment of these contracts to the circumstances from the time they are awarded until they expire. Thus, for example, *additional deadlines* are provided for, both for the receipt of applications and tenders, set by the contracting authority (Art. 2), and an *extension of the validity of expired contracts* when the organisation of a competitive tendering procedure is not possible (Art. 4). *Changes to the conditions for the payment* of the advance by purchasers are also provided for in the Ordinance.

Finally, and more particularly, Article 6 on performance difficulties is interesting. Thus, concerning non-compliance with the time limit for performance and if performance under the terms of the contract would involve a manifestly excessive burden, a *time limit is extended* 'by a period at least equivalent to that mentioned in

Article 1, at the request of the contractor before the expiry of the contractual time limit' (para. 1). Likewise, *the impossibility of performance by the concessionaire does not entail any contractual sanction or penalty, nor does it imply any liability on the part of the concessionaire*. A substitution contract with a third party is then envisaged, notwithstanding the exclusivity clause if it exists, thus protecting the buyer from any contractual liability (para. 2 a and b). If a measure taken by the administrative authorities in the context of a state of health emergency cancels a purchase order or terminates a contract, *compensation* is provided for (para. 3). The suspension of a fixed-price contract and an amendment determining the changes to the contract are provided for (para. 4). Suspension of a concession by decision of the grantor or due to an administrative police decision entails suspension of payment to the grantor, and an amendment determining the necessary changes will then be provided for (para. 5).

This legislation in times of crisis provides for *all situations* that may arise and have an impact on the performance of the contract, whether these situations result from an external event or from the public authority having adopted specific measures under conditions of health crisis. This *applies to the impossibility of performance, the suspension of the contract, or performance that has become excessively onerous*. This specific legislation, in advance, exonerates the party or parties whose responsibility could have been engaged because of the non-fulfilment of contractual obligations and provides for the addition of a rider determining the necessary changes. These contractual situations resulting directly from the pandemic and/or the administrative measures adopted will pave the way for the renegotiation of the contract between the parties so that they can genuinely agree on the content of the rider that will record the necessary changes made or that need to be transcribed if they have taken place (Pugeault, 2020).

The Key Implications of the Findings

From the above developments, we can draw the following valuable lessons:

Firstly, the nature of the PPP contract results in an imbalance between the parties which implies divergent interests between on the one hand, the Administration concerned with the general interest underlying the realisation of the object of the contract and its continued execution and, on the other hand, the private operator and the need to take into account the maintenance of the financial equilibrium of the PPP in order to ensure its continuation.

Secondly, in times of crisis such as the COVID-19 pandemic, particular attention must be paid not only to the contractual clauses that define the obligations of the parties and the mechanisms for resolving potential disputes, but also to the legal concepts and their own legal regime, which are called upon to provide the answers to maintaining the contract on renegotiated terms.

The French PPP is an interesting case because, as a civil law country, France has not only civil law rules governing civil law contracts but also administrative law rules governing contractual relations involving the administration and private operators. In addition, there are legal concepts specific to administrative law, bearing the same name as those existing in civil law, but which are significantly different because of the specificity of the contractual relationship requiring, for the maintenance of the public service, that it be adapted to the circumstances to allow the pursuit of its general interest objective. This explains and justifies the fact that during the pandemic, the French authorities adapted, through specific legislation, the maintenance of the PPP to the surrounding circumstances.

Conclusion

Renegotiation of the contract in ordinary times and in times of crisis is inherent to the PPP contract. On the one hand, by their very nature, these contracts are exposed to the risk of sovereignty because of the possible intervention of the conceding authority in the adjustment of the contract to the requirements of the public service for which it is the guarantor. On the other hand, the renegotiation of the PPP contract is made even more necessary because of the challenges caused by the pandemic to adapt PPP contracts to the circumstances. Indeed, the impact of the pandemic on the contract requires determining whether the performance of the contract has become excessively onerous but still possible and under what conditions, or temporarily or definitively impossible in order to determine the applicable concept according to both the ordinary legislation governing such contracts and the legislation adopted in times of crisis which makes adjustments to the usual solutions in order to limit the dramatic effects of the pandemic on the contracts and the contractors.

References

Beuve, J., de Brux, J., & Saussier, S. (2013). Renégocier pour durer: une analyse empirique des contrats de concession, Partenariats public privé et performances des services. *Revue d'économie industrielle, 141*(1), 117–148.

de Brux, J., & Marty, F. (2016). Les partenariats public-privé institutionnalisés : intérêts, limites et risques d'une structure hybride public-privé. *Revue française d'administration publique, 157*(1), 223–238. https://www.cairn.info/revue-francaise-d-administration-publique-2016-1-page-223.htm. Last accessed 21 April 2022

CA Besançon, 8 janvier 2014, N° RG 12/02291.

CA Nancy, 22 novembre 2010, N° RG 09/00003.

CA Saint Denis de la Réunion, 29 décembre 2009, N° RG 08/02114.

CE, 30 mars 1916, Compagnie générale d'éclairage de Bordeaux, Recueil Lebon, p. 125.

CE, 8 août 1924, Gaz de Brive, Rec. 817.

CE, 15 juin 1928, Commune de la Courtine, Rec. 757.

CE, 9 décembre 1932, Compagnie de tramways de Cherbourg, n° 89655, Rec. 1050, conclusion Josse, http://www.marche-public.fr/Marches-publics/Definitions/Entrees/Theorie-imprevision.htm. Last accessed 21 April 2022.

CE, Commune de Staffelden, 14 juin 2000, req n° 184722, Conclusions of Mr Gilles Pellissier, Public rapporteur in the same case https://www.conseil-etat.fr/fr/arianeweb/CRP/conclusion/2019-10-21/419155?download_pdf. Last accessed 21 April 2022.

CE, Société Alliance, 21 octobre 2019, Rec. N° 419155.

Cour des Comptes. https://www.ccomptes.fr/fr/cour-des-comptes/role-et-activites. Last accessed 21 April 2022.

Decree No. 2018-1075 (3 December 2018a). https://www.legifrance.gouv.fr/jorf/id/JORFTEXT000037696277.

Decree No. 2018-1225 (24 December 2018b). https://www.legifrance.gouv.fr/jorf/id/JORFTEXT000037852355. Last accessed 18 April 2022.

Décret n°2020-325 du 25 mars 2020, Ministère du Travail, du plein emploi et de l'insertion, Activité partielle – chômage partiel, https://travail-emploi.gouv.fr/emploi-et-insertion/accompagnement-des-mutations-economiques/activite-partielle-chomage-partiel/?TSPD_101_R0=087dc22938ab2000b2f697283835d93038b27fc1588fdb43819c5b4d74f63fc99df44f39197f30a308c09c33d4143000e83482e8e3ea75c7da29590b7218171bf392686a5a09ac4575489ace91d57e47bb48335ea01dda8e0157acd694ea58e9.

Gaudemet, Y. (2001). *Traité de Droit administratif*, 16ème édition, L.G.D.J.

Guasch, J.-L., & Straub, S. (2006). Renegotiation of infrastructures concessions: An overview. *Annals of Public and Cooperative Economics, 4*(77), 479–493. https://doi.org/10.1111/j.1467-8292.2006.00316. Last accessed 21 April 2022.

Guasch, J.-L., Laffont, J.-J., & Straub, S. (2006). Renegotiation of concession contracts: A theoretical approach. *Review of Industrial Organization, 1*(29), 55–73. https://link.springer.com/article/10.1007/s11151-006-9109-5. Last accessed 21 April 2022.

Guasch, J.-L. (2004). *Granting and renegotiating infrastructure concession: Doing it right.* The World Bank. https://openknowledge.worldbank.org/handle/10986/15024. License: CC BY 3.0 IGO. Last accessed 21 April 2022.

"La passation et l'exécution des marches publics en situation de crise sanitaire", Direction des affaires Juridiques (DAJ), Publication du Ministère de l'Économie et des Finances, 18 mars 2020., https://www.economie.gouv.fr/files/files/directions_services/daj/marches_publics/conseil_acheteurs/fiches-techniques/crise%20sanitaire/Passation_et_exécution_des_marchés_publics_en_situation_de_crise_sanitaire.pdf?v=1585566655. Last accessed 21 April 2022.

Law n° 2008-735 of 28 July 2008 on Partnership Contracts, JORF n°0175 du 29 July 2008, https://www.legifrance.gouv.fr/loda/id/JORFTEXT000019261845/. Last accessed 21 April 2022.

Llorens, F. (2018). Le projet de Code de la commande publique enfin dévoilé. *Contrats et marchés publics*, n° 8/9, (01/08/2018) https://documentation.departement06.fr/index.php?lvl=author_see&id=12932. Last accessed 21 April 2022.

Llorens, F. & Soler-Couteaux, P. (2018). La théorie administrative de l'imprévision est- elle dépassée?. Contrats et Marchés publics, n° 3, mars, repère 3.

Marché Public, The circular of 20 November 1974., http://www.marche-public.fr/Marches-publics/Definitions/Entrees/Theorie-imprevision.htm. Last accessed 21 April 2022.

Ordinance n° 2020-319 of 25 March 2020. https://www.legifrance.gouv.fr/loda/id/JORFTEXT000041755875/. Last accessed 21 April 2022.

Ordinance No. 2004-559 of 17 June 2004 on partnership contracts, https://www.legifrance.gouv.fr/loda/id/JORFTEXT000000438720/. Last accessed 21 April 2022.

Public Procurement Code, version in force since 1 April 2019, Ordinance No. 2018-1074 (26 November 2018). https://www.legifrance.gouv.fr/loda/id/JORFTEXT000037695219/.

Public-Private partnerships, Reference Guide, Version 3, 2017, The World Bank.

Pugeault, S. (2020). L'adaptation du cadre juridique de l'exécution des contrats de la commande publique aux conséquences de la crise sanitaire », *La commande publique en période de*

crise sanitaire, Dossier Hors-série, June, 5–10. https://www.parme-avocats.com/resources/files/2020/06/Complement_Commande_Publique_Juin_2020_PARME.pdf.
Que sont les partenariats public-privé? République Française, 1st July 2020., https://www.vie-publique.fr/fiches/20261-que-sont-les-partenariats-public-prive-ppp-marches-de-partenariat.
Rassafi – Guibal, H. (2019). L'imprévision n'est pas morte, mais elle est moribonde. Note sous CE, 21 octobre 2019, *Société Alliance*, req. n° 419155, *Revue générale du droit*, 2019, numéro 49745 https://www.revuegeneraledudroit.eu/blog/2019/11/03/limprevision-nest-pas-morte-mais-elle-est-moribonde/. Last accessed 21 April 2022.
Rassafi – Guibal, H. (2020). Crise sanitaire et contrats administratifs : quand l'urgence fragilise le droit – À propos de l'ordonnance n° 2020-319. *Revue générale du droit*, numéro 51955. https://www.revuegeneraledudroit.eu/blog/2020/04/23/crise-sanitaire-et-contrats-administratifs-quand-lurgence-fragilise-le-droit-a-propos-de-lordonnance-n-2020-319/. Last accessed 21 April 2022.
See also, Legislative dossier: Ordinance n° 2004–559 of 17 June 2004 on partnership contracts / Implementation schedule, https://www.legifrance.gouv.fr/dossierlegislatif/JORFDOLE000017761075/. Last accessed 21 April 2022.
World Bank Public – Private Partnership Legal resource Center. (2021). *Advantages et risks of PPP*. World Bank. https://ppp.worldbank.org/public-private-partnership/avantages-et-risques-des-ppp. Last accessed 21 April 2022

Conclusion

Tharun Dolla, Ganesh Devkar, and Boeing Laishram

Covid-19 and Infrastructure Delivery

In December 2019, the Covid-19 pandemic has thrown life out of gear across the world. While writing this chapter, the world has experienced waves of Covid-19 infections, and threats of new virus mutations and deadlier infections still loom at large. As the infrastructure is an underlying fabric, like veins and blood in a human body, on which society and nation prospers, like human body, it too got disrupted owing to Covid-19. This disruption has forced the policy makers and stakeholders associated with the infrastructure delivery process to rethink the entire value chain of right from planning, design, construction to operation of created facility. The extent of "disruption" became a point of debate owing to perception about the "infrastructure" that it is created by keeping in mind the long horizon (of time) and it is expected to have resilience, adaptability, agility, and responsiveness built it in. Few stakeholders termed it as a "black swan event" and tried to discuss it under the cloud of "uncertainty" and "one of off" phenomena. However, many stakeholders kept themselves away from coining Covid-19 as "Unknown" event because human civilization has experienced pandemics in the past and opened healthy debates on how the infrastructure delivery process responded in the times of Covid-19 and

T. Dolla (✉)
Department of Civil Engineering, Indian Institute of Technology Bombay, Mumbai, Maharashtra, India
e-mail: tharun@iitb.ac.in

G. Devkar
Faculty of Technology, CEPT University, Ahmedabad, Gujarat, India

B. Laishram
Department of Civil Engineering, Indian Institute of Technology Guwahati, Guwahati, Assam, India

© The Author(s), under exclusive license to Springer Nature Switzerland AG 2023

T. Dolla et al. (eds.), *Revisiting Public-Private Partnerships*,
Contributions to Public Administration and Public Policy,
https://doi.org/10.1007/978-3-031-37015-1_16

what are the areas of improvements to be made in the process to deal with disruptions of similar nature. The infrastructure is shaped and delivered to the customers under the influence of and interaction with varied elements like infrastructure policies, laws and regulations, contractual agreement, design drivers, financing mechanisms, and community consultation process. As each country has a different set of elements in force, the quality and quantity of emergent infrastructure and the service delivered are different. The Covid-19 pandemic unearthed these facets of infrastructure, especially in the delivery of healthcare services. Even it may be apt to say that the Covid-19 pandemic opened the can of worms, and debates raged over the process followed for financial allocation of different infrastructure sectors, policy measures undertaken by the governments to address the infrastructure backlog, accessibility of infrastructure to poor and marginalized communities, measures to reduce carbon footprint of existing, and planned infrastructure. Among these issues, the policy makers and news media were keenly observing and scrutinizing the infrastructure which is created and delivered with Public-Private Partnership (PPP) model.

Something Special About PPPs and This Book

This book covered a wide variety of projects, institutional setups, socio-economic conditions, funding mechanisms, and diverse end-user needs. A deeper look into these chapters reveals and opens a wide variety of insights and debates which are otherwise not clear to a casual reader. We intend to do that job in this conclusion.

The PPP model continues to attract attention across the world for a variety of reasons like orientation to the role played by the government in the infrastructure delivery process, complex financial web used for mobilizing debt and equity spanning national and international boundaries, conflicting intrinsic drivers of stakeholders (with often mentioned logic that the private sector is driven by profit motive while the public sector focuses on protection of poor and disadvantaged), risk allocation among a set of actors, and so on. Many economies use the PPP model extensively for infrastructure delivery, and the resilience of this model along with financial obligations, in the testing time of Covid-19 pandemic, also became a cause of concern for the governments. The reason for this concern was that the government is responsible for the delivery of uninterrupted infrastructure within the ambit of predecided norms and costs of services, and any disruption may create havoc in an economy and hardships to its citizens. Further to this, there is a prevailing sense that the use of PPP model in infrastructure delivery makes the water much muddier and attracting attention as mentioned earlier. The academic and research community working in the area of PPPs as well was eager to know the "evidence" on if PPP model succeeded or failed to deliver the promise. The evidence has so far been sparse because of reasons like availability of data in the form of interviews, government documents and so on, and also the overall drive toward containment of the pandemic when it was at its peak. Often, first-hand information about the performance of PPPs started to emanate in many economies with press coverage and announcement by governments to ensure smooth delivery of infrastructure, which is delivered with PPP mode. This book has brought together this early evidence on PPPs in the times of Covid-19 pandemic and analyzed it from varied perspectives like contracts, legislation, stakeholder consultation, and so on. The immense knowledge and experience from the countries brought together in this book serve as a treat to policy makers and researchers working keenly in PPPs. The richness and variety of evidence provide an impetus toward a fresh look, rather than creating a priori hypothesis to slice and dice this knowledge.

Unpacking the Evidence and Making Sense of It

There are varied perspectives that can be drawn for making sense of the evidence contained in the book chapters such as developing and developed country context, thematic analysis focusing on aspects like renegotiation, law, and so forth, and effect on planning and development phase vis-à-vis operation phase. After looking at the evidence from these perspectives, it became clear that there was a differentiation in the discourse, as it is reported in each chapter, based on the maturity of PPP marketplace in each country.

The evidence produced in this volume by various contributors is consistent with the understanding offered on maturity level of PPP marketplace. For example, the Infrascope Index Report[1] published by *The Economist* is quite popular, which evaluates the capacity of countries to implement sustainable and efficient public-private partnerships (PPPs). The index evaluates readiness and capacity by dividing the PPP-enabling environment into five components: Regulations and Institutions, Project Preparation and Sustainability, Financing, Risk Management and Contract Monitoring, Performance Evaluation and Impact (Ex-post).

The evidence indicates that the discourse in the economies having matured PPP marketplaces; for example, the USA shows that the actors involved in the delivery of PPP projects have taken a long-term perspective and decided not to behave opportunistically. This deterrent to the opportunistic behavior is also owing to the creation of level-playing field, which is enshrined in the legal and regulatory framework created for PPP projects in a specific country. Further to this, it is observed that the actors decided to maximize value for the project, within the boundaries created by earlier mentioned frameworks, with the collaborative spirit. For example, the evidence from Australia and Japan indicates that despite the uncertainty posed by the Covid-19 pandemic, the efforts were to enhance stakeholder value and infection control respectively. This evidence from the matured PPP marketplaces creates an impression that the water is less "muddy" or rather "clearer" owing to well-crafted and functional PPP ecosystem, and it is enabling the PPP projects to deal with the Covid-19 pandemic in more coordinal and less opportunistic manner. It is

[1] https://infrascope.eiu.com/country-reports/

interesting to see the efforts toward further refinement in the enablers of the PPP project. For example, the evidence from France indicates discourse in the direction of clarity and refinement of legal framework surrounding the PPP projects. There is one more underlying thread – the PPP stakeholders realized that the PPP project would "bounce back" in coming years and it may be pertinent to stick together in the difficult phase. Also, there is a sense that the PPP project may fail, similar to any business entity, and the public sector need not rush to alleviate this failure by going out of way, which is decided by overall legal, contractual, and regulatory framework.

The unearthed discourse from the nascent and maturing PPP marketplaces shows a relatively different picture. Firstly, the discussion centered on contractual interpretation of "Covid-19" event in terms non-political force majeure event and relief measures to be provided to the PPP project. The reliefs expected by the private sector were sometimes beyond the ambit of concession agreements in the form of financial support, lower interest rates, and so on. This necessitates the discussion among the PPP stakeholders about crafting the level-playing field and sticking to the "rules of game" decided by the contractual, legal, and regulatory framework. The evidence also indicated that gaps in financing arrangements and project structuring made the PPP projects more vulnerable to disruption caused by the Covid-19 pandemic. For example, the evidence from Indonesia indicates that often the public sector chooses to select a component in network infrastructure which is more amenable or rather doable with ease with PPP model without realizing the interconnected nature of infrastructure and the basic principle of cost recovery and network effect in infrastructure delivery. This stresses the importance of capacities required in both public and private sector to craft PPP concession and financing agreements which are more equitable, sustainable, and resilient.

In totality, the evidence corroborates the premise that the performance of PPP projects, in the amidst of Covid-19 pandemic, is influenced by enabling environment prevailing in a country. There are cultural nuances of PPP marketplace which are established by the overall evidence. The greater sense of cooperation between the public and private sector, and appreciation of events that unfold during the course of PPP project lifecycle, results into sustenance and resilience of PPP project. Hence, softer factors such as cooperation and collaborative spirit are required like an icing on the cake, made by robust legal and regulatory framework, for making the PPP arrangement truly fruitful (or tasty) for the end users. Finally, to answer a million-dollar question from the skeptics of PPP model about if the PPP model failed to deliver or is still a way ahead in this uncertain future. The answer is PPP model does not fail in reality rather the recipe adopted to make the model failed in varied instances. The evidence from varied economies in this book indicate the PPP model worked, wherein recipe was correct with vital ingredients of cooperation, legal and regulatory framework in right/equitable proportion while the imbalance in these vital elements would be a recipe for tensions or disaster in PPP projects. Alas, PPP model will continue to play a vital part of infrastructure cycle for years to come despite the apparent fury throwed on it by both researchers and practitioners.

MIX
Papier aus verantwortungsvollen Quellen
Paper from responsible sources
FSC® C105338

If you have any concerns about our products, you can contact us on
ProductSafety@springernature.com

In case Publisher is established outside the EU, the EU authorized representative is:
Springer Nature Customer Service Center GmbH
Europaplatz 3, 69115 Heidelberg, Germany

Printed by Libri Plureos GmbH
in Hamburg, Germany